Measuring National Well-being 2014
Contents 2014

CD containing supplementary articles, Infographics and reference tables relating to:

Chapter 1 - Commuting and Personal Well-being, 2014 - Tables
Chapter 3 - Children's Well-being, 2014 - Tables
Chapter 4 - Young People's Well-being, 2014 - Tables
Chapter 5 - National Well-being Measures, March 2014 - Tables
Chapter 6 - Life in the UK, 2014 - Infographic
Chapter 8 - Income, Expenditure and Personal Well-being, 2011/12 - Tables
Chapter 9 - Exploring Personal Well-being and Place - Tables
Chapter 10 - European Comparisons, 2014 - Infographic
Chapter 12 - Insights across Society, the Economy and the Environment, 2014 - Infographic
Chapter 13 - Personal Well-being in the UK, 2013/14 - Tables and Infographic
Chapter 14 - National Well-being Measures, September 2014 - Tables
Chapter 15 - Exploring the Well-being of Children in the UK, 2014 - Infographic

Supplementary article 1 - UK Natural Capital – Initial and Partial Monetary Estimates
Supplementary article 2 and tables - UK Environmental Accounts, 2014
Supplementary article 3 and tables - Sustainable Development Indicators, July 2014

Measuring National Well-being 2014

In replacement of 'Social Trends'

The data displayed in this document was correct at the time of downloading 13/01/15

Office for
National Statistics

Commuting and Personal Well-being, 2014

Abstract

This article examines the relationship between commuting to work and personal well-being using regression analysis. It identifies how time spent commuting and method of travel affect life satisfaction, a sense that our daily activities are worthwhile, and levels of happiness and anxiety.

1. Introduction

This article examines the relationship between commuting to work and personal well-being, and builds on earlier work published by ONS (ONS 2013a) which identified some of the personal characteristics and circumstances that matter most to personal well-being. Although that analysis included a wide range of factors thought to be related to personal well-being such as age, ethnicity, sex, self-reported health, relationship status, and economic activity, it did not look in detail at people's experiences of commuting.

Previous studies have found commuting to be negatively related to aspects of personal well-being such as life satisfaction (Stutzer and Frey 2008) or to wider measures of mental health and well-being (Robert, Hodgson and Dolan 2009). However, there are also benefits associated with commuting. In theory, a person chooses to commute (and thereby accepts the burden of doing so) when he/she is compensated, for example in the labour market by higher earnings or better career prospects or in the housing market by cheaper rents/mortgages or a nicer home further away from the job.

Using the relative size and strength of the relationship between commuting and personal well-being when other possible influences on well-being are held constant, this article specifically examines:

- Commuting compared with non-commuting
- Usual time spent commuting
- Method of travel.

2. Key Points

- Holding all else equal, commuters have lower life satisfaction, a lower sense that their daily activities are worthwhile, lower levels of happiness and higher anxiety on average than non-commuters.
- The worst effects of commuting on personal well-being were associated with journey times lasting between 61 and 90 minutes. On average, all four aspects of personal well-being were

negatively affected by commutes of this duration when compared to those travelling only 15 minutes or less to work.

- When commuting time reaches three hours or more, the negative effects on personal well-being disappear, suggesting that the small minority of people with this commuting pattern have quite different experiences to most other commuters.
- Combining both travel method used and the length of time spent commuting showed that taking the bus or coach to work on a journey lasting more than 30 minutes was the most negative commuting option in personal well-being terms.
- The effects of more active forms of commuting such as cycling and walking on personal well-being varied with the amount of time spent travelling in these ways.

3. Research Methods

This article presents the results of regression analysis, a statistical technique which analyses how responses to personal well-being questions vary by specific characteristics and circumstances of individuals while holding all other characteristics equal. The key benefit of regression analysis is that it provides a better method of identifying those factors which matter most to personal well-being than an analysis looking at the relationship between only two characteristics at a time.

3.1 Key definitions

The analysis is based on data from a subgroup of the Annual Population Survey (APS) comprised of people in employment collected from April 2012 to March 2013. It includes both employees and self-employed people. To identify those who did **not** commute, people were asked if they 'work from home in [their] main job?' Those who said they work in their own home or in the same grounds or buildings as home were considered to be non-commuters and were included in the analysis. Those who said they worked in different places using home as a base or that they worked somewhere quite different from home were excluded from the analysis as they may still spend an undetermined amount of time travelling for work-related activities.

Another question asking about travel time from home to work one-way was used to identify commuters. Anyone who said they spent one minute or more travelling to work was defined as a commuter.

The final sample included approximately 60,200 respondents of whom 91.5% were classified as commuters and 8.5% were classified as non-commuters. Full details of sample sizes for all variables included in the analysis are available in Reference Table 5 (62.5 Kb Excel sheet).

It is important to note that these questions may not perfectly capture the situation of people who regularly work from home part of the week and travel only on specific days or who live and work away for periods and only travel at the beginning and end of their working period. The data available do not allow us to look in detail at these types of commuting patterns.

In order to look at how personal well-being varies in relation to individual commuting patterns, we used the following four questions on personal well-being which are asked each year in the APS:

- Overall, how satisfied are you with your life nowadays?

- Overall, to what extent do you feel the things you do in your life are worthwhile?
- Overall, how happy did you feel yesterday?
- Overall, how anxious did you feel yesterday?

Respondents are asked to give their answers on a scale of 0 to 10 where 0 is 'not at all' and 10 is 'completely'.

3.2 The regression models

The analysis included the development of several alternative models to investigate the relationship between commuting and personal well-being. Different models were used to capture the different aspects of commuting, for example:

- Commuters versus non-commuters (does not include actual travel time or travel mode)
- Commuting time in minutes (from 1 to 179 minutes)
- Commuting time in banded time periods
- Travel mode only (without travel time)
- Travel mode and travel time (defined as 1-15 minutes, 16-30 minutes or more than 30 minutes) included together to explore interaction effects between travel method and time spent commuting.

All the models included:

- Age (defined both as age and age squared)
- Sex
- Ethnicity
- Migration (length of time since migrating to the UK)
- Relationship status
- Presence of dependent and non-dependent children in the household
- Self-reported disability
- Self-reported health
- Interview mode (telephone or face-to-face interview)
- Economic activity status (permanent employee, non-permanent or self-employed)
- Religious affiliation
- UK region

Reference tables with the coefficients from each of the models are available via links in the Technical Annex.

3.3 Interpreting what the numbers mean

The numbers included throughout the text and tables are the unstandardised coefficients for each variable included in the Ordinary Least Squares regression models. This shows the size of the effect that the characteristic being explored has on the specific aspect of personal well-being under consideration.

In interpreting the findings, it is important to remember that these numbers represent the difference between two groups, for example those who do not commute compared to a reference group of those who do, when all other variables in the model have been held constant. The comparisons are therefore between two people who are otherwise the same in every respect apart from the particular characteristic or circumstance being considered. This helps to isolate the effects of the characteristic or experience being considered, in this case commuting, on personal well-being.

In order to give a sense of the size of the relationship between each characteristic included in the model and personal well-being, we have used the following size classification:

- **Large** - a difference of 1.0 points or more between the average rating of the reference group and the group being studied after controlling for other factors
- **Moderate** - 0.5 points < 1.0 points difference between the groups
- **Small** - 0.1 points < 0.5 points difference between the groups
- **Very small** - a difference of less than 0.10 points but which is still statistically significant.

The classifications summarise the size of the difference between how an individual with the characteristic or experience being considered, for example a specific commuting time, would rate their well-being compared to someone from a specified reference group, all else being equal.

When results are referred to as 'significant at the 5% level', this means there is a probability of less than 0.05 (or less than one in twenty) that the result could have occurred by chance.

4. Does commuting matter to personal well-being?

Commuting can be regarded as a burden. However, individuals may choose to commute if compensated for doing so (for example by higher income or a larger house). This analysis explores whether all the burdens of commuting are indeed fully compensated by such factors[1]. If they are, then we would not expect to see any statistically significant associations between commuting and personal well-being in the tables and figures that follow.

The analysis clearly indicates an association between commuting and personal well-being after controlling for a range of individual characteristics[2]. The remaining sections of the report compare the experiences of those who commute to work with those who do not and the relationship of commuting with personal well-being. They also look at the personal well-being of those who commute for different periods of time. Results are then interpreted along with suggestions as to why individuals may choose to commute to work even though they may not be fully compensated for the burden of doing so.

4.1 Commuting versus non-commuting

Comparing the personal well-being of those who regularly travel to work (commuters) versus those who work from home in their main job (non-commuters), **Figure 1** shows that commuters were on average:

- less satisfied with their lives,
- rated their daily activities as less worthwhile, and
- reported less happiness and higher anxiety than non-commuters.

The reference group in Figure 1 are commuters and they are represented as the baseline of zero. The bars show how much higher or lower non-commuters rated each aspect of their personal well-being on average compared to commuters, after holding all else equal.

Figure 1: How the personal well-being of commuters and non-commuters differs after controlling for individual characteristics

United Kingdom

Source: Annual Population Survey (APS) - Office for National Statistics

Notes:
1. Commuters are the reference group represented as the baseline of zero. The bars show how much higher or lower non-commuters rated each aspect of their personal well-being on average compared to commuters, after holding all else equal.
2. All of the findings in Figure 1 are statistically significant at the 5% level.

Download chart

 XLS format
(27.5 Kb)

The effects of commuting on personal well-being were greatest for anxiety and happiness, suggesting that commuting affects day to day emotions more than overall evaluations of satisfaction with life or the sense that daily activities are worthwhile.

The scale of the differences between commuters and those who do not commute would be considered small according to the classification in section 3.3 but they are nonetheless statistically significant. Holding all else equal, non-commuters:

- rated their life satisfaction 0.14 points higher on average on the 0 to 10 point scale than commuters;
- rated the sense that their daily activities are worthwhile 0.10 points higher than commuters;
- rated their anxiety levels 0.18 points lower than commuters; and
- rated their happiness 0.19 points higher than commuters.

It is also important to consider that there may be systematic differences (both observed and unobserved) between those who regularly work from home and other people who do not. Our models were only able to control for observed demographic characteristics which would be expected to capture some but not all of these differences.

Notes

1. To be able to test for compensation effects, earnings (or income) related variables are not included in the regression specifications. Not controlling for variables through which people are compensated for commuting allows the commuting variable used in the analysis to adjust for compensation effects.

2. Different people may have different preferences for commuting as well, therefore controlling for personal characteristics can also be seen as capturing different preferences for commuting.

5. How important is actual commuting time?

For this analysis, commuting time is based on one-way travel time from home to work. The relationship between commuting time and personal well-being has been examined in two ways:

- Travel time from 1 minute to a maximum of 179 minutes[1] or more. This analysis shows how each additional minute of travel time affects personal well-being; and
- Travel time in seven banded time periods – to see how and whether personal well-being is affected by different lengths of time spent commuting. The following categories of usual home to work travel time were used: 1-15 minutes; 16-30 minutes, 31-45 minutes, 46-60 minutes; 61-90 minutes; 91-179 minutes; 180 minutes or more.

5.1 The commute: minute by minute

Looking first at how each additional minute of commuting time affects personal well-being, the results show that after holding other factors constant, life satisfaction, the sense that one's activities are worthwhile and happiness all decreased with each successive minute of travel. Meanwhile, average anxiety levels increased with each additional minute of the commute (**Table 1**). The results are statistically significant for each of the four aspects of personal well-being measured.

The numbers in the table show the size and direction of the change in each aspect of personal well-being associated with each additional minute of commuting time. For example, each minute of commuting time is associated an average reduction of 0.002 points in how people rate their life satisfaction on a scale from 0 to 10.

Holding all else equal, this means that a 10 minute increase in commuting time (one way) is associated with approximately 0.02 points decrease on average in life satisfaction, happiness and the sense that one's activities are worthwhile. It is also associated with 0.05 point increase in anxiety.

Table 1: Effects of each additional minute of commuting time on personal well-being after controlling for individual characteristics

United Kingdom

Coefficients

	Life satisfaction	Worthwhile	Happy yesterday	Anxious yesterday
Commuting time (in minutes)	-0.002*	-0.002*	-0.002*	0.005*

Table source: Office for National Statistics

Table notes:
1.   * shows that the relationship is statistically significant at the 5% level.

Download table

XLS XLS format
(27 Kb)

The commute: in different time periods

The second approach to the analysis involved comparison of those travelling 15 minutes or less each way to work (the reference group for this analysis) with those travelling either for longer periods, or not at all (non-commuters).

The findings indicate that all things being equal, average happiness levels begin to fall and anxiety begins to rise after the first 15 minutes of travel time, suggesting again that daily emotions are particularly affected by commuting (**Table 2**). Life satisfaction and the sense that one's daily activities are worthwhile appear to be more resilient to the strain of the daily commute. These aspects of personal well-being are not significantly negatively affected until the commuting time reaches more than half an hour in the case of daily activities being seen as worthwhile, or more than 45 minutes for life satisfaction.

Table 2: Effects of commuting for different lengths of time on personal well-being after controlling for individual characteristics

United Kingdom

Coefficients

	Life satisfaction	Worthwhile	Happy yesterday	Anxious yesterday
Reference group: Travel to work time of 1–15 minutes[1]				
Travel to work time of 16-30 minutes	-0.03	-0.037	-0.077*	0.181*
Travel to work time of 31-45 minutes	-0.014	-0.066*	-0.096*	0.214*
Travel to work time of 46-60 minutes	-0.071*	-0.08*	-0.079	0.318*
Travel to work time of 61-90 minutes	-0.166*	-0.11*	-0.188*	0.315*
Travel to work time of 91-179 minutes	-0.159	-0.187*	-0.207	0.285
Travel to work time of 180 minutes or more	0.068	0.003	-0.131	-0.005
non-commuter (working from home)	0.115*	0.071*	0.14*	-0.062

Table source: Office for National Statistics

Table notes:
1. The reference group are those with a travel to work time of 1–15 minutes.
2. * shows that the relationship is statistically significant at the 5% level.

Download table

 XLS format
(29 Kb)

In most cases, the worst effects of commuting on personal well-being are experienced during journeys lasting between 61 and 90 minutes (**Figure 2**). For example, holding all else equal, people travelling this length of time to work rated:

- their life satisfaction 0.17 points lower on a scale from 0-10 compared with those travelling only up to 15 minutes to work;

- the sense that their daily activities are worthwhile 0.11 points lower on average than those travelling up to 15 minutes to work;
- their happiness levels 0.19 points lower than those travelling up to 15 minutes to work; and
- their anxiety levels 0.32 points higher on average than those travelling up to 15 minutes to work.

Figure 2: How the personal well-being of those commuting 61-90 minutes differs from those commuting up to 15 minutes after controlling for individual characteristics

United Kingdom

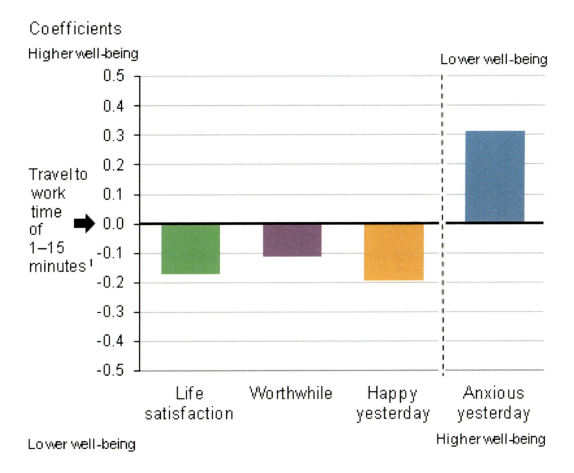

Source: Annual Population Survey (APS) - Office for National Statistics

Notes:

1. The reference group are those with a travel to work time of 1 to 15 minutes. They are represented as the baseline of zero. The bars show how much higher or lower people who travelled between 61 and 90 minutes to work rated each aspect of their personal well-being on average compared to those travelling only up to 15 minutes to work.
2. All of the findings in Figure 2 are statistically significantly at the 0.05 level.

Download chart

 XLS format

(28 Kb)

When the commute time reaches three hours or more, the negative effects on personal well-being disappear, suggesting that those with very long commutes have quite different experiences than those travelling less time. For example, people may be able to use their travel time more productively on a longer journey.

Further analysis showed that people with this commuting pattern are predominantly male (79%) and they have a higher net weekly mean wage on average than those spending less time on their commute. The data available do not allow any more detailed analysis of whether these people commute three hours or more (one way) on a daily basis or whether this is their usual commute, but undertaken less frequently.

Non-commuters who worked from home had higher personal well-being across all three positive measures of well-being not only compared to people with long commutes but also compared to those with commutes of less than 15 minutes.

Notes

1. The APS only collects detailed travel time in minutes up to 179 minutes. All travel time beyond this point is categorised as 180 minutes or more.

6. Does travel mode make a difference?

This section focuses on **how** we travel to work and whether different travel modes have different effects on personal well-being.

The APS includes data on the main mode of travel to work used by respondents. Where more than one travel mode is used (for example train and walking) only the main mode is recorded. The analysis in this section compares people whose main travel to work mode is a private vehicle such as a car, minibus or works van with those whose main travel to work mode is an alternative such as train, bus, walking or cycling (**Table 3**).

Holding other factors constant, the findings show that:

*   those who travel to work by bus or coach had lower levels of life satisfaction and a lower sense that their daily activities are worthwhile on average than those who travelled to work in a private vehicle;
*   people who take the train to work had higher anxiety levels on average than those who travelled in a private vehicle;
*   people who walk to work had lower life satisfaction and a lower sense that their activities are worthwhile on average than those who commute to work in a private vehicle;
*   those who reported travelling to work in 'some other way' had higher life satisfaction and lower anxiety levels than those travelling in a private vehicle.

Table 3: Effects of travel mode on personal well-being after controlling for individual characteristics

United Kingdom

Coefficients

Reference group: car, minibus, works van[1]	Life satisfaction	Worthwhile	Happy yesterday	Anxious yesterday
motorbike, moped, scooter	0.004	-0.121	-0.083	-0.114
bicycle	-0.065	-0.047	0.011	0.05
bus,coach, private bus	-0.119*	-0.119*	-0.029	0.123
taxi	-0.209	-0.192	-0.356	-0.145
railway train	0.055	-0.055	0.005	0.194*
underground train/ light railway/tram (GB only)	0.034	-0.076	0.067	0.209
walk	-0.076*	-0.096*	-0.024	0.029
other way of travelling	0.388*	0.168	0.351	-0.555*

Table source: Office for National Statistics

Table notes:
1. The reference group are those who travel to work by car, minibus or works van.
2. * shows that the relationship is statistically significant at the 5% level.

Download table

XLS format
(28.5 Kb)

7. Combining travel time and travel mode

The daily commute to work is likely to be experienced as a total package comprised of the time spent travelling as well as the qualitative experience of the journey itself. The final approach to the analysis looks at the interaction between travel time and travel mode and how these may affect personal well-being in combination.

Here, travel time (one way) was broken down into two categories (for the sake of simplicity and to maximise sample sizes in each category): 16 to 30 minutes and longer than 30 minutes. Each mode of travel was included in combination with a travel time of either 16-30 minutes or over 30 minutes. In each case, the comparison is with people who commute between 1 and 15 minutes to work (one way) via any travel method (**Table 4**).

Holding other factors constant, some of the key findings show that compared to people travelling between 1 and 15 minutes to work via any method:

- Those travelling to work in a private vehicle had lower levels of happiness and higher anxiety levels on average for all journey times (that is, both 16-30 minutes and over 30 minutes);
- People spending between 16 and 30 minutes cycling to work had lower happiness levels and higher anxiety on average;
- Those making long bus journeys to work of more than 30 minutes had lower life satisfaction, a lower sense that daily activities are worthwhile, lower happiness levels and higher anxiety;
- People commuting more than 30 minutes by train had higher anxiety levels on average; and
- Those walking between 16 and 30 minutes to work had lower life satisfaction, a lower sense that daily activities are worthwhile and lower happiness levels on average. People walking more than 30 minutes to work had higher anxiety levels on average.

Table 4: Effects of interaction between commuting time and travel mode on personal well-being after controlling for individual characteristics

United Kingdom

Coefficients

	Life satisfaction	Worthwhile	Happy yesterday	Anxious yesterday
Reference group: commute time 1–15 minutes - all types of methods[1]				
between 16–30 min and car, minibus,works van	-0.003	-0.005	-0.064*	0.164*
more than 30 min and car, minibus, works van	-0.029	-0.025	-0.111*	0.227*
between 16–30 min and motorbike, moped, scooter	-0.169	-0.204	-0.098	0.139
more than 30 min and motorbike, moped, scooter	-0.149	-0.307	-0.598*	0.425
between 16–30 min and bicycle	-0.094	-0.128	-0.232*	0.395*
more than 30 min and bicycle	-0.217	-0.105	-0.204	0.193
between 16–30 min and bus, coach, private bus	-0.042	0.006	-0.017	0.263*
more than 30 min and bus, coach, private bus	-0.254*	-0.272*	-0.155*	0.222*
travelled by taxi	-0.211	-0.192	-0.398	-0.063
between 16–30 min and train	0.018	-0.125	-0.084	0.181
more than 30 min and train	0.044	-0.059	-0.054	0.347*

between 16–30 min and underground, light railway, tram	0.146	0.015	0.138	0.233
more than 30 min and underground, light railway, tram	-0.015	-0.125*	-0.044	0.303*
between 16–30 min and walk	-0.201*	-0.249*	-0.21*	0.137
more than 30 min and walk	-0.213	-0.212	-0.095	0.519*
travelled by another method	0.381*	0.162	0.299	-0.454

Table source: Office for National Statistics

Table notes:
1. The reference group are those who spend between 1 and 15 minutes travelling to work using any travel method.
2. * shows that the relationship is statistically significant at the 5% level.

Download table

 XLS format
(30.5 Kb)

In terms of how travel time and method of travel combine to affect personal well-being, several types of commute were associated with a significant increase in anxiety compared to those travelling up to 15 minutes to work (by any method). These included:

- Travelling by car, minibus or works van; or by bus or coach for more than 15 minutes;
- Cycling between 16 and 30 minutes to work;
- Travelling by train, underground, light railway or tram for more than 30 minutes; and
- Walking for more than 30 minutes to work.

Long bus or coach journeys to work lasting more than 30 minutes were associated with a loss of personal well-being across all four measures.

Recent census results for England and Wales show that driving to work was the most common form of commuting used by 59.5% of the working population in England and Wales in 2011 (ONS, 2013b). The APS data analysed here suggest that commuting via car, minibus or works van is associated with lower levels of happiness on average and higher levels of anxiety after the first fifteen minutes of the journey and these negative effects increase as the journey time increases. By comparison, those travelling by public transport such as the train or underground do not on average experience a loss of personal well-being until the journey time increases to 30 minutes or more.

Only one form of commuting beyond 15 minutes was associated with increased personal well-being and that was 'travelling by another method'. Given that information about the specific form of travel was not collected, it is unclear what this entails. It could, for example, include people travelling to work by plane, helicopter or boat. People who said that they 'travelled by another method' had significantly higher life satisfaction than those travelling only 15 minutes or less to work and none of the other measures of personal well-being were affected by their commute, either positively or negatively. About half (51%) of those who responded in this way also said that their journey to work took three hours or more.

It is also important to note that there were several forms of commuting that were no worse for personal well-being on average than a short commute of up to 15 minutes, holding all else equal. These included:

- Riding a motorbike, moped or scooter for up to 30 minutes (though beyond this point happiness was negatively affected);
- Cycling for more than 30 minutes (cycling **less** than 30 minutes was associated with lower happiness and higher anxiety);
- Travelling by taxi (regardless of journey time); and
- Taking the train, underground, light railway or tram for up to 30 minutes (beyond this, the sense that activities are worthwhile was significantly lower and anxiety significantly higher).

8. Interpreting the results

The findings suggest that commuting is negatively related to personal well-being and that in general (for journeys of up to three hours) longer commutes are worse for personal well-being than shorter commutes. The size of the associations between commuting and personal well-being would generally be considered small according to the size classification suggested in section 3.3 and previous regression results (ONS 2013a) show that self-reported health, relationship status and employment status affect personal well-being more than commuting. However, the results are nevertheless significant and show that commuting is clearly and negatively associated with personal well-being.

8.1 Travel time and personal well-being

Given the loss of personal well-being generally associated with commuting, the results suggest that other factors such as higher income or better housing may not fully compensate the individual commuter for the negative effects associated with travelling to work and that people may be making sub-optimal choices. This result is consistent with the findings of previous studies such as Stutzer and Frey (2008). This is potentially important information both for those who commute, particularly for an hour or more, and for their employers.

Possible reasons for this may include short term constraints, or changes in circumstance, leading to a less than ideal commute journey for someone until they have a chance to adjust. Other individuals may wish to change their commuting pattern but not do so due to either inertia, or to ongoing constraints (e.g. financial or limited job opportunities). Another potential reason is that people may simply not recognise the potential benefits (to personal well-being) of changing their commute and therefore not seek to make any change even over the longer term. Finally, some individuals may choose to bear the short-term burden of commuting to bring about better future prospects. Longitudinal data would be required to examine these issues directly so it is not possible to take this further using a cross-sectional dataset like the APS.

Another possibility is that compensation may occur at the household level. In other words, while commuting is a burden for the individual, other members of their household may benefit from it, for example through the additional income, improved housing and neighbourhood or a better choice of schools. These other factors may be associated with higher well-being among other household members and this may be viewed as off-setting the loss of personal well-being associated with commuting. Therefore, the negative effects of commuting may disappear if we were to replicate this analysis at the household level rather than the individual level, but this is beyond the scope of this article.

8.2 Public transport and personal well-being

The 2011 Census results found that 7.2% of people in employment in England and Wales travelled to work by bus, minibus or coach, while 5.0% took the train and 3.8% travelled by underground, metro or light railway (ONS 2013b).

The results here indicate that taking the bus or coach to work on a journey lasting more than 15 minutes is associated with increased anxiety. As the journey time increases beyond 30 minutes, the negative effects of this form of commuting affect all aspects of personal well-being. Of the various public transport options, commuting to work by bus is most negatively associated with personal well-being.

By comparison, taking the train to work has no significantly negative effect on any aspect of personal well-being for journeys of up to 30 minutes. Beyond this journey time, the only aspect of personal well-being which is negatively affected is anxiety which is higher among those travelling more than 30 minutes by train compared to those spending only up to 15 minutes on their commute.

A similar picture emerges for those commuting via underground, light railway or tram. The results show no significantly adverse effects on personal well-being associated with commuting via these methods for up to 30 minutes. However, commuting in this way for more than 30 minutes is associated with increased anxiety and a reduced sense that one's daily activities are worthwhile compared to those commuting only 15 minutes or less to work.

8.3 Active versus non-active commuting

The most recent census results for England and Wales found that 12.6% of people walk or cycle to work (ONS 2013b). The results here show that those who walk between 16 and 30 minutes to work have lower life satisfaction, a lower sense that their daily activities are worthwhile and lower happiness than those who spend up to 15 minutes travelling to work (by any method). These effects disappear for those walking longer than 30 minutes to work, but anxiety levels among this group are significantly higher on average than among those who spend only 15 minutes commuting to work.

The results for cycling show a similar pattern: cycling for 16-30 minutes is associated with lower happiness and higher anxiety while cycling for longer periods of over 30 minutes does not have a negative effect on personal well-being. These results may suggest those cycling longer distances may be different in terms of motivation, fitness or other factors compared to those cycling shorter distances.

The results are consistent with a recent study (Humphreys, Goodman and Ogilvie 2013) that found greater time spent actively commuting (particularly 45 minutes or more) was associated with higher physical well-being, but not with mental well-being. These findings contrast with other research which shows a positive relationship between recreational physical activity and mental well-being. It is suggested that the more social context often associated with recreational physical activity may contribute positively to mental well-being in a way that active commuting to work does not.

It is also important to note that people may walk or cycle due to a lack of choice – either because of the costs of other forms of transport or limited local transport options. Other studies have found that the context and environment in which people walk or cycle affects the quality of their experience as well as their anxiety levels (Bostock 2001). For example, cycling between 16-30 minutes in heavy traffic might be a much more stressful experience than cycling more than half an hour on a quieter route.

Overall, the results suggest that although physical well-being may be enhanced by cycling and walking, getting exercise in this way on the daily commute may not necessarily have the stress-relieving qualities we would expect. However, more detailed research would be required to fully confirm this result, in particular on the extent to which it might be the lack of choice that is impacting well-being rather than the travel mode itself.

9. Technical annex

9.1 Why undertake a regression analysis?

In analysis which looks at the relationship between two variables, it can be tempting to infer that one variable is directly related to the other. For example, non-commuters may have lower anxiety levels than commuters, but can we assume that the differences observed in relation to anxiety ratings are primarily about differences in commuting? This conclusion would only be justified if we could show there were no other important differences between commuters and non-commuters which might affect the findings such as differences in health or relationship status or whether they have dependent children.

Regression analysis allows us to do this by holding all the variables in the model equal while measuring the size and strength of the relationship between two specific variables. If the regression results show a significant relationship between commuting and anxiety, then this means that two people who are identical in every way apart from their commuting behaviour would indeed rate their anxiety levels differently. This implies a direct relationship between commuting and anxiety even when the other variables included in the analysis are taken into account. Therefore, the key benefit of regression analysis is that it provides a better method than analysis looking at the relationship between only two variables at a time of indentifying those factors which matter most to personal well-being.

However, every analytical method has its limitations and regression analysis is no exception. The following sections summarise some key considerations which should be borne in mind in terms of the statistical assumptions underlying the techniques used here and the types of inference which can be drawn from the findings.

9.1.1 Using OLS for ordered responses and the robustness of the OLS estimates

A key implicit assumption in ordinary least squares (OLS) regression is that the dependent variable (the outcome we are trying to explain, such as the personal well-being rating) is continuous. Continuous data can take any value (usually within a range). For example, a person's height could be any value within the range of human heights or time in a race which could even be measured to fractions of a second. The personal well-being survey responses, however, are discrete, that is, they can only take on a relatively small number of whole integer values, between 0 and 10 with no other values possible such as halves in between.

OLS regression also assumes that the values of the dependent variable (e.g., personal well-being ratings) are cardinal. This means that the interval between any pair of categories such as between 2 and 3 is assumed to be of the same magnitude as the interval between any other similar pair such as between 6 and 7. As the personal well-being responses are based on subjective ratings, it is not possible to say with certainty that the distance between 2 and 3 is the same as the distance between 6 and 7 on the 0 to 10 response scale. For example, it may be that people move easily from 2 to 3 in their rating of life satisfaction, but it may take a lot more for them to jump from 6 to 7. This suggests that the OLS regression approach may not be ideally suited to modelling this kind of dependent variable.

There are a number of alternatives to OLS for modelling discrete response variables, such as logit or probit regression. In these models the categories of the responses are treated separately which means there is no implied order of the categories, for example 4 is not higher than 3. An important disadvantage of these methods is that the information contained in the ordering of the personal well-being ratings is lost. A way of overcoming this issue is to create two categories, for example ratings of life satisfaction above or below 7 on the 0 to 10 scale, but the resulting categories are artificial and do not capture people's actual ratings of their well-being.

An alternative method is to treat the response variable as ordinal and use regression techniques, such as ordered logit or ordered probit that are developed to deal with ordinal data. Ordinal data values can be ranked or ordered on a scale such as from 0 to 10 with each higher category representing a higher degree of personal well-being (or lower personal well-being in the case of anxiety) and unlike the OLS method, ordered probit or ordered logit regression does not assume that the differences between the ordinal categories in the personal well-being rankings are equal. They capture the qualitative differences between different scores. It is important to note that ordinal probit/logistic performs several probit/logistic regressions simultaneously, assuming that the models are identical for all scores. The latter assumption can be relaxed but the interpretation of the results becomes more difficult.

In common with much of the existing literature modelling subjective well-being, this analysis has used ordered probit models to explore the factors contributing to a person's personal well-being. As Greene (2000) points out, the reasons for favouring one method over the other (such as ordered probit or ordered logit) is practical and in most applications it seems not to make much difference to the results.

The major advantage of such models is that it takes the ordinal nature of the personal well-being ratings into account without assuming equality of distance between the scores. Similarly to OLS, it identifies statistically significant relationships between the explanatory variables, for example age, health, and relationship status, and the dependent variable which in this case is the rating of personal well-being. A difficulty that remains is that the estimated coefficients are difficult to explain clearly to a wide audience.

The existing literature also suggests that OLS may still be reasonably implemented when there are more than five levels of the ordered categorical responses, particularly when there is a clear ordering of the categories as is the case for the personal well-being questions which have response scales from 0 to 10 (Larrabee 2009). Several studies applied both methods to personal well-being data and found that the results are very similar between the OLS models and the theoretically preferable methods such as ordered probit. For example, see Ferrer-i-Carbonell and Fritjers (2004) for a detailed discussion of this issue.

The main advantage of OLS is that the interpretation of the regression results is more simple and straightforward than in alternative methods.

So for the sake of completeness, the analysis was conducted in both OLS and probit regression methods. This also acts as a sensitivity check for the robustness of the OLS results as the key assumptions for the OLS regression may not hold for the ordered personal well-being data.

It should be noted that this does not imply that the OLS regression estimates were completely 'robust'. Post regression diagnostics identified some violations of the OLS regression assumptions such as model specification and the normality of residuals. However, as some studies (for example see Osborne and Waters, 2002), suggest that several assumptions of OLS regression are 'robust' to violation such as normal distribution of residuals and others are fulfilled in the proper design of the study such as the independence of observations. In this analysis, using the survey design controlled for the potential dependence of the individual observations with each other (see section 5.2) and applying the survey weights provided some protection against model misspecification.

As there is no formal statistical test that can be used to identify multi-collinearity when the covariates in the model are dummy variables, an informal method of cross-tabulating each pair of dummy variables can be used. When cross-tabulations showed very high correlation between the variables they were not used in the regression.

Stata automatically computes standards errors that are robust to heteroskedasticity when the regressions are estimated incorporating survey design.

Additionally, estimating the models using different specifications as well as two methods (OLS and ordered probit) confirmed that the magnitude and the statistical significance of the parameter estimates did not significantly change and the general inferences from the analysis remained the same.

9.1.2 The explanatory power of the models

It is important to note that the explanatory power of the main regression model used here is relatively low. Indeed, the amount of variance that has been explained by the model is similar to that of other reported regression analyses undertaken on personal well-being. For the 'happy yesterday', 'anxious yesterday' and 'worthwhile' questions, around 4% to 7% of the variation between individuals is explained by the variables included in the model. By contrast, a much higher proportion (11%) of the individual variation in ratings for life satisfaction was explained by the model.

The lower explanatory power of the model could be due to leaving out important factors which contribute to personal well-being. For example, genetic and personality factors are thought to account for about half of the variation in personal well-being. It has not been possible to include variables relating to personality or genes in the models as the APS does not include data of this type.

The subjective nature of the outcome variable also means that it is probably measured with some imperfect reliability. The lower the reliability of the outcome variable, the more unclear its correlations with other variables will tend to be.

9.1.3 Omitted variable bias

In an ideal world, a regression model should include all the relevant variables that are associated with the outcome (i.e. variable being analysed such as personal well-being). In reality, however, we either cannot observe all the potential factors affecting well-being (such as personality) or are limited by whatever information is collected in the survey data used in the regression analysis.

If a relevant factor is not included in the model, this may result in the effects of the variables that have been included being mis-estimated. When the omitted variables are correlated with the included variables in the model, the coefficient estimates of those variables will be biased and inconsistent. However, the estimated coefficients are less affected by omitted variables when these are not correlated with the included variables (i.e. the estimates will be unbiased and consistent). In the latter case, the only problem will be an increase in the estimated standard deviations of the coefficients which are likely to give misleading conclusions about the statistical significance of the estimated parameters.

9.1.4 Causality

Regression analysis based on cross-sectional observational data cannot establish with certainty whether relationships found between the independent and dependent variables are causal. This is particularly the case in psychological contexts where there may be a reciprocal relationship between the independent and the dependent variables. For example, the usual assumption is that individual characteristics or circumstances like health or employment status are independent variables which may affect personal well-being (viewed here as a dependent variable). However, some of the association between health and well-being may be caused by the impact of personal well-being on health.

Furthermore, as the data used in the regression analysis here are collected at one point in time (i.e. cross-sectional), they are not able to capture the effect of changes over time and which event preceded another. For example, it is not possible to tell from this data whether the perception of being in bad health precedes a drop in well-being or whether a drop in well-being precedes the perception that one is in bad health. We can only definitely say that the perception of being in bad health is significantly related to lower levels of well-being compared to people who say they are in good health. Therefore, while the regression analysis here can demonstrate that a relationship between two variables exists even after holding other variables in the model constant, these findings should not be taken to infer causality.

9.1.5 Multi-collinearity-dependence (or correlations) among the variables

If two or more independent variables in the regression model are highly correlated with each other, the reliability of the model as a whole is not reduced but the individual regression coefficients cannot be estimated precisely. This means that the analysis may not give valid results either about individual independent variables, or about which independent variables are redundant with respect to others. This problem becomes increasingly important as the size of correlations between the independent variables (i.e. multi-collinearity) increases.

9.2 Taking the design of the APS sample into account in the analysis

The primary sampling unit in the Annual Population Survey is the household. That is, individuals are grouped into households and the households become units in sample selection.

Regression analysis normally assumes that each observation is independent of all the other observations in the dataset. However, members of the same household are likely to be more similar to each other on some or all of the measures of personal well-being than they are to members of different households. If the analysis ignores this within-household correlation, then the standard errors of the coefficient estimates will be biased, which in turn will make significance tests invalid.

Therefore, to correctly analyse the data and to make valid statistical inferences, the regressions are estimated in Stata with the specification of the survey design features. The survey weights were also used in the estimation of the model as these allow for more consistent estimation of the model coefficients and provide some protection against model misspecification.

9.3 Development of the regression models

- Overall, 5 regression models were constructed during this project, which were:
- Commuters vs. non-commuters
- Commuting for different lengths of time
- Commuting time in minutes
- Travel method
- Commuting for different lengths of time combined with travel method.

Each of these was analysed first using OLS and then using Ordered probit. All of these results are available in the Reference Tables, as follows:

Reference Table 1 (172.5 Kb Excel sheet) contains the results for each of the 5 regression models for the Life Satisfaction question.

Reference Table 2 (174 Kb Excel sheet) contains the results for each of the 5 regression models for the Worthwhile question.

Reference Table 3 (196 Kb Excel sheet) contains the results for each of the 5 regression models for the Happiness question.

Reference Table 4 (174.5 Kb Excel sheet) contains the results for each of the 5 regression models for the Anxiety question.

Reference Table 5 (62.5 Kb Excel sheet) contains details of the sample sizes for each of the variables used in the regression models.

Commuting is generally regarded as a burden, but individuals may choose to commute if they are compensated in some way for doing so (for example by higher income, a larger house, etc). This analysis starts from this premise and tests to see if all the burdens of commuting are indeed fully compensated by such factors.

The hypothesis is that if people are fully compensated for commuting, the following factors would be expected to be captured by the commuting coefficients:

- The negative effect of spending more time commuting
- The positive effect of earning a higher salary
- The positive effect of living in a nicer house or paying less rent.

The commuting coefficient gives an indication of how commuting is associated with well-being after both costs and benefits of commuting are taken into account.

The following variables in the APS are considered to capture the potential positive effects of commuting best:

- Wages (for employees only)
- Occupation - there is a very high correlation between earnings and a person's occupation
- Qualifications - similarly there is a high correlation between earnings and qualifications
- Housing tenure - although it is not a very good proxy for 'nicer' housing, it can still reflect a person's choice for housing, e.g., owning a house away from work place rather than renting a place near work place.

As these variables are considered to compensate people for the negative effects of commuting, they are excluded from the models in order to test the hypothesis above. Not controlling for variables though which people are compensated for commuting allows the commuting variable used in the analysis to adjust for compensation effects.

9.4 Methodological findings on mode of interview

The Annual Population Survey data is collected either by telephone interview or face to face in the respondent's home. The possibility of people giving different responses in these different interview contexts was the subject of a working paper for the National Statistician's Technical Advisory Group on Measuring National Well-being (December 2011). The paper explored the impact of these methods on the answers to the personal well-being questions and concluded that:

"There is a trade-off between the likelihood of errors caused by the telephone method and the fact that the telephone allows more privacy and confidentiality when answering. However studies have shown substantial differences in responses to scalar questions when asked by telephone versus visual modes, in that more positive responses are given in the telephone mode (Dillman et al., 2009). In addition the evidence gathered from the present study suggests the telephone is associated with misunderstanding and decreased rapport with the interviewer along with a decreased desire to take part". (Ralph, K., Palmer, K., Olney, J., 2011)

In order to hold constant the possible impacts of different interview modes when exploring the relationship of other variables to well-being as well as examining the possible impacts of interview mode on responses to the personal well-being questions, the regression models included method of the interview.

About the ONS Measuring National Well-being Programme

NWB logo 2

This article is published as part of the ONS Measuring National Well-being Programme.

The programme aims to produce accepted and trusted measures of the well-being of the nation - how the UK as a whole is doing.

Measuring National Well-being is about looking at 'GDP and beyond'. It includes headline indicators in areas such as health, relationships, job satisfaction, economic security, education, environmental conditions and measures of 'personal well-being' (individuals' assessment of their own well-being).

Find out more on the Measuring National Well-being website pages.

Background notes

1. These statistics are experimental in nature and published at an early stage to gain feedback from users. Should users have comments on the ONS approach to the measurement of personal well-being and or the presentation of the personal well-being questions they can email ONS at national.well-being@ons.gov.uk. It is the role of the UK Statistics Authority to

designate these statistics as National Statistics and this is one of the aspirations of the National Well-being programme is to see these statistics gain National Statistics status.

2. The data analysed in this report are derived from a customised weighted 12 month APS microdataset. This dataset is not part of the regularly produced APS datasets and was produced specifically for the analysis of personal well-being data. ONS is making the experimental APS microdata available to approved researchers to allow them to undertake further analysis of these experimental questions at an early stage and to provide further feedback to ONS.

3. A list of the job titles of those given pre-release access to the contents of this article is available on the website.

4. Details of the policy governing the release of new data are available by visiting the UK Statistics Authority or from the Media Relations Office.

5. © Crown copyright 2014

    You may use or re-use this information (not including logos) free of charge in any format or medium, under the terms of the Open Government Licence, write to the Information Policy Team, The National Archives, Kew, London TW9 4DU, or email: psi@nationalarchives.gsi.gov.uk.

6. Details of the policy governing the release of new data are available by visiting www.statisticsauthority.gov.uk/assessment/code-of-practice/index.html or from the Media Relations Office email: media.relations@ons.gsi.gov.uk

References

1. Bostock, L. (January 2001), 'Pathways of disadvantage?: walking as a mode of transport among low income mothers'. Health and Social Care in the Community, 9 (1), 11-18.

2. Dillman, D. A., Smyth, J. D., & Christian, L. M. (2009). 'Internet, mail, and mixed-mode surveys: The tailored design method'. Hoboken, NJ: Wiley.

3. Ferrer-i-Carbonell, A. and Frijters, P. (2004). 'How important is methodology for the estimates of the determinants of happiness'. The Economic Journal, 114, 641-659.

4. Greene, W. H. (2000) Econometric Analysis, Upper Saddle River, NJ: Prentice-Hall, fourth edition.

5. Humphres, D., Goodman, A., Ogilvie, D. (August 2013), 'Associations between active commuting and physical and mental wellbeing'. Preventative Medicine, 57(2), 135-139.

6. Larrabee, B. (2009), 'Ordinary Least Squares Regression of Ordered Categorical Data: Inferential Implications for Practice' Kansas State University.

7. Office for National Statistics (2011) Initial investigation into Subjective Well-being data from the ONS Opinions Survey.

8. Office for National Statistics (2013a) What matters most to personal well-being?

9. Office for National Statistics (2013b) Method of travel to work in England and Wales report, Table CT0015EW.

10. Osborne, J.W. and Waters, E. (2002). 'Four assumptions of multiple regression that researchers should always test'. Practical Assessment, Research, and Evaluation, 8(2).

11. Ralph, K., Palmer, K. and Olney, J. (2011), 'Subjective well-being: a qualitative investigation of subjective well-being questions' (344.6 Kb Pdf), Working Paper for the Technical Advisory Group on 29 March 2012.

12. Roberts, J,. Hodgson, R., and Dolan, P. (2009). 'It's driving her mad: gender differences in the effects of commuting on psychological well-being'. Journal of Health Economics 30 (5), 1064-76.

13. Stutzer, A., Frey, B. (2008). 'Stress that doesn't pay: the commuting paradox'. Scandinavian Journal of Economics 110(2), 339-366.

Office for National Statistics

Measuring National Well-being - Governance, 2014

Author Name(s): **Chris Randall, Office for National Statistics**

Abstract

This article is published as part of the Office for National Statistics (ONS) Measuring National Well-being Programme. The programme aims to produce accepted and trusted measures of the well-being of the nation – how the UK as a whole is doing. This article explores in more detail aspects of governance considered important for understanding National Well-being. It considers information on forms of civic engagement, notably satisfaction with government and democracy, interest in politics and participation in politics.

Introduction

A fundamental part of the work of government is to support a better life for its citizens and help build strong and resilient communities which in turn may improve the wellbeing of individuals. This was highlighted in the Office for National Statistics (ONS) National Debate on Measuring National Well-being. When people were asked what mattered most for the measurement of National Well-being, 'Governance' was one aspect that people considered as most important.

The ONS national well-being measures are organised into ten domains with a total of 41 headline measures. More information about all the measures can be found on the national well-being pages of the ONS website - Measuring National Well-being

This article explores the two measures under the 'Governance' domain:

- Those who have trust in national government.
- Voter turnout (in UK General Elections).

It also looks at associated data such as satisfaction with democracy, interest in politics, political activities undertaken and Freedom of Information requests.

Most of the data used in this article are from Understanding Society, the UK Household Longitudinal Study (UKHLS) 2011–12. The UKHLS collects information each year about the social and economic circumstances and attitudes of people. For more information see the section 'About Understanding Society, the UK Household Longitudinal Study'.

Key points

- Nearly a quarter (24%) of people aged 15 and over reported that they 'tended to trust' the government in the UK in autumn 2013.
- Those aged 16 to 24 were more likely to state no interest at all in politics (42%) than those aged 65 and over (21%) in the UK in 2011–12.
- Over 6 in 10 (64%) of adults aged 18 and over in the UK in 2011–12, agreed or strongly agreed that they would seriously be neglecting their duty as a citizen if they didn't vote.
- Voter turnout in UK General Elections peaked in 1950 with over 8 in 10 (82%) of the electorate voting, in 2010 the turnout was 61%.
- A lower proportion (57%) agreed they found politics too complicated to understand in 2012 compared with 69% in 1986 in Great Britain.
- A lower proportion (60%) agreed that 'voting is the only way to have any say' in 2012, compared with 73% in 1994 in Great Britain.

Satisfaction with government and democracy

Democracy can be defined as government by the people or their elected representatives. One of the measures of the National Well-being Governance domain is the percentage of those who have trust in national Government.

'If the people cannot trust their government to do the job for which it exists - to protect them and to promote their common welfare - all else is lost.' Barack Obama, 2006.

Figure 1: Percentage of those who have trust in national Government (1)

United Kingdom

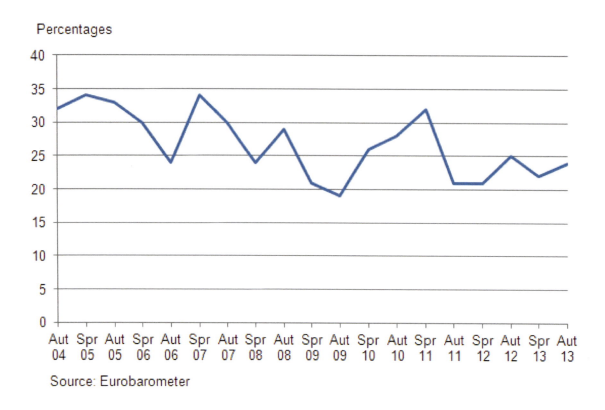

Source: Eurobarometer

Notes:

1. Respondents aged 15 and over were asked if they 'tend to trust' or 'tend to not trust' the UK Government. Percentages are for those who answered 'tend to trust'. Fieldwork was carried out in Spring and Autumn of each year.

Download chart

 XLS format
(28.5 Kb)

According to the Standard Eurobarometer survey published in December 2013, nearly a quarter of people (24%) aged 15 and over in the UK reported that they 'tended to trust' the government in the autumn of 2013. This was a rise of 2 percentage points since spring 2013 **(Figure 1)**. In the spring of 2007 the proportion of people that 'tended to trust' the government, stood at over a third (34%) but fell to just under a fifth (19%) in the autumn of 2009. These proportional declines occurred around the time of the UK parliamentary expenses scandal and the start of the financial crisis. From spring 2010, people's trust in government began to rise again to peak at 32% in spring 2011 (EB,2013).

In the autumn quarter of 2013, an estimated 23% of residents of the EU-28 aged 15 and over reported that they tended to trust their own governments. The highest proportions were in Sweden (57%) and Luxembourg (51%). The lowest proportions were in Spain (9%) and Greece, Italy and

Slovenia (10%). The low proportions in these countries may have been due to the recent Eurozone crisis. (EB,2013)

Just under a half (48%) of adults aged 16 and over in the UK who expressed an opinion were fairly or very satisfied with the way democracy works in the UK according to the UK Household Longitudinal Study in 2011–12. Similar proportions of men and women were fairly or very satisfied at 49% and 47% respectively. The proportion of those who were very or fairly satisfied with the way democracy works varied by age in 2011–12 from 52% of those aged 16 to 24 to 45% of those aged 45 to 54.

Table 1: Life satisfaction and satisfaction in the way democracy works in the UK (1), 2011–12

United Kingdom (Percentages)

	Satisfied with life[2]	Dissatisfied with life[2]
Very satisfied or fairly satisfied with the way democracy works	51	40
Very dissatisfied or a little dissatisfied with the way democracy works	49	60

Table source: Understanding Society, the UK Household Longitudinal Study

Table notes:
1. Respondents were asked 'On the whole, are you very satisfied, fairly satisfied, a little dissatisfied or very dissatisfied with the way democracy works in this country'.
2. Respondents were asked how satisfied they were with their lives overall and responded on a seven point scale from completely satisfied to completed dissatisfied. Satisfied with life includes those who reported a scale of 1 to 3 and dissatisfied with life those who reported 5 to 7. This table does not include those who reported a scale of 4.

Download table

 XLS format
(26.5 Kb)

Table 1 shows that 51% of those who reported being fairly or very satisfied with life and 40% who reported dissatisfaction with life also reported that they were fairly or very satisfied with the way democracy works in the UK. However, it must be noted that 49% of those who reported satisfaction with life and 60% who reported dissatisfaction with life also reported that they were a little or very dissatisfied in the way democracy works in the UK. This indicates that there are many other factors that impact on life satisfaction and in turn overall well-being.

Political interest and efficacy

'Political interest is one of the most powerful and persistent predictors of political participation, ... and is widely considered a vital component for a democratic citizenry'. Matthew Holleque, 2011

Adults aged 16 and over were asked on the 2011–12 UK Household Longitudinal Study (UKHLS) how interested they were in politics. Under half (44%) who expressed an opinion reported that they were very or fairly interested, 27% were not very interested and 28% were not at all interested. Interest in politics varied between men and women, with men more likely than women to be interested. Over half of men (52%) were very or fairly interested compared to 37% of women. Just under a quarter (23%) of men reported that they were not at all interested in politics compared to just under a third (33%) of women.

Figure 2: No interest in politics (1): by age, 2011–12

United Kingdom

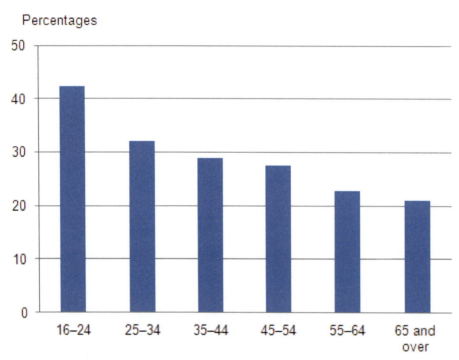

Source: Understanding Society, the UK Household Longitudinal Study

Notes:
1. Respondents were asked 'How interested would you say you are in politics?' This chart shows the percentage of those who answered 'Not at all interested'.

Download chart

 XLS format
(26 Kb)

The level of interest in politics varied by age with younger people being less interested than older people. In 2011–12 over 4 in 10 (42%) of those aged 16 to 24 who expressed an opinion had no interest at all in politics compared to around 2 in 10 (21%) of those aged 65 and over **(Figure**

2). Under a third (31%) of adults aged 16 to 24 in the UK were very or fairly interested in politics, compared to a half of those aged 55 to 64 and 65 and over (51% and 50% respectively).

The UKHLS also asked respondents whether they agreed or not that it took too much time and effort to be active in politics and public affairs. In 2011–12, over a third of adults aged 16 and over (36%) who expressed an opinion agreed or strongly agreed that it took too much time. Around the same proportion of men and women agreed or strongly agreed with this statement (37% and 35% respectively). However, proportions who agreed or strongly agreed with the statement varied by age, from a quarter (25%) of people aged 16 to 24 to 44% of those aged 65 and over.

Whether people are more or less likely to feel they have any say over how governments run the country may be an important factor to their continued political interest. The British Social Attitudes Survey asked people aged 18 and over in Great Britain whether they agreed or disagreed that:

- People like me have no say in what the government does.
- Sometimes politics and government seem so complicated that a person like me cannot really understand what is going on.
- Voting is the only way people like me can have any say about how the government runs things.

Table 2: Personal political efficacy (1)

Great Britain (Percentages)

	1986	1994	2003	2012
People like me have no say in what government does	71	64	64	59
Politics and government is too complicated to understand	69	70	60	57
Voting is the only way to have any say[2]	..	73	64	60

Table source: British Social Attitudes Survey, NatCen Social Research

Table notes:
1. Respondents were asked if they agreed or disagreed with the statements in the table. The table shows the proportion that agreed.
2. Question not asked in 1986.

Download table

XLS XLS format
(25.5 Kb)

The proportion of people agreeing with the statements fell over the four separate years as shown in **Table 2**. In 1986, around 7 in 10 people (71%) agreed that they had no say in what government does, by 2012 this proportion had fallen to just under 6 in 10 (59%). The proportion of those who agreed that they find politics too complicated to understand decreased by 12 percentage points between 1986 and 2012 (69% and 57% respectively). The proportion who agreed that voting is the only way to have a say fell by 13 percentage points between 1994 (73%) and 2013 (60%) (BSAS,2013).

Political participation

The second measure of the National Well-being Governance domain is the percentage of parliamentary election voters as a percentage of the voting age population.

'Voting can be seen as a resource that is transformed into well-being by citizens: they vote in order to affect the actions of government in ways that are meaningful to them.' How's Life? Measuring Well-being - Civic engagement and governance - Organisation for Economic Co-operation and Development (OECD).

In 1950 voter turnout in UK General Elections peaked with over 8 in 10 (82%) of the electorate voting according to the International Institute for Democracy and Electoral Assistance. By 1983, turnout was down to 72% - and despite an improvement in participation in both 1987 and 1992, the General Elections in 2001 and 2005 had relatively low turnouts (both 58%). In 2010 the turnout rose to 61% (IIDEA,2010).

Young people are less likely to vote than older citizens. Exact figures about the age of voters are not available in the UK because information about the identity of voters is kept secret. However IPSOS MORI estimated that 39% of registered young people aged 18 to 24 voted at the 2001 UK general election with 37% in 2005 and 44% in 2010 (MORI,2010).

Figure 3: Proportion of young people voting at a political election (1), 2013 (2)

EU Comparison

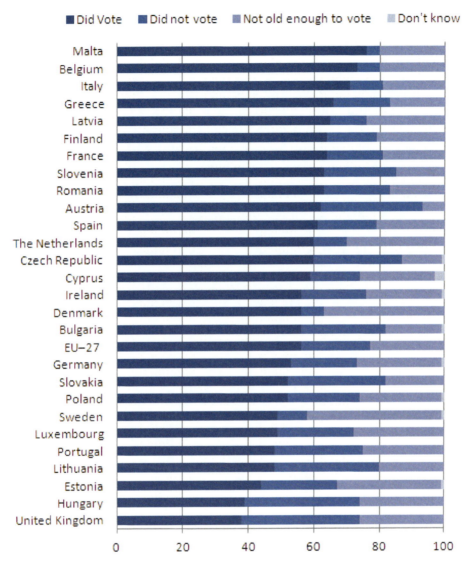

Source: Eurobarometer

Notes:

1. Respondents aged 15 to 30 were asked 'During the last 3 years, did you vote in any political election at the local, regional or national level? If you were, at that time, not eligible to vote, please say so'. In all member states of the EU the eligible voting age is 18 and over apart from Austria where it is 16 and over.

2. April 2013.

Download chart

 XLS format

(29.5 Kb)

Young people aged 15 to 30 were asked on a Flash Eurobarometer Survey in April 2013 whether or not they had voted in a political election in the three years prior to interview (including local, regional and national elections). It must be noted that a certain proportion of these young people were not eligible to vote because of their age[1]. In 20 of the EU Member States over half of young people had voted in a political election, with the highest proportion in Malta (76%), Belgium (73%) and Italy (71%) **(Figure 3)**. This compares with the EU average of 56%. The UK had the lowest proportion of young people voting in a political election at 38%, with 26% reporting they were not old enough (EB,2013).

According to the 2011–12 UK Household Longitudinal Study (UKHLS), 48% of people aged 18 and over who expressed an opinion and could vote, agreed or strongly agreed that they feel a sense of satisfaction when they vote. This compares to a quarter (25%) that disagreed or strongly disagreed. Feeling a sense of satisfaction when voting varies by age. Just under 3 in 10 (29%) of those aged 18 to 24 agreed or strongly agreed that they felt a sense of satisfaction when they voted. This increased to over 4 in 10 (42%) for those aged 35 to 44 and just over 6 in 10 (63%) for those aged 65 and over.

Figure 4: Voting as a civic duty (1): by age, 2011–12

United Kingdom

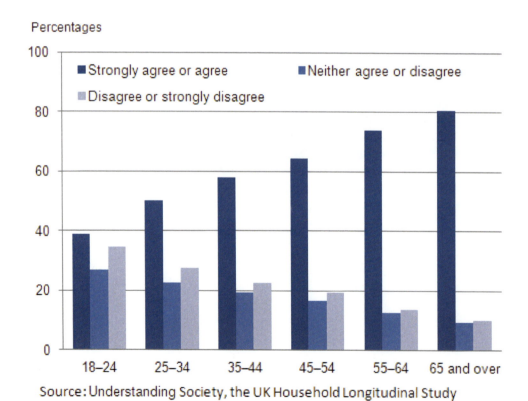

Source: Understanding Society, the UK Household Longitudinal Study

Notes:

1. Respondents were asked if they strongly agree, agree, neither agree nor disagree, disagree or strongly disagree with the statement, I would be seriously neglecting my duty as a citizen if I didn't vote.

Download chart

The UKHLS also shows that over 6 in 10 (64%) of people aged 18 and over who expressed an opinion in 2011–12, agreed or strongly agreed that they would seriously be neglecting their duty as a citizen if they didn't vote. There was also a variance among age groups. For example, just under 4 in 10 (39%) of those aged 18 to 24 agreed or strongly agreed that they would seriously be neglecting their duty as a citizen if they didn't vote compared with over 8 in 10 (80%) of those aged 65 and over **(Figure 4)**. Conversely, 34% of young people aged 18 to 24 disagreed or strongly disagreed that they would seriously be neglecting their duty as a citizen if they didn't vote compared to 1 in 10 (10%) of those aged 65 and over.

Table 3: Political activities undertaken (1)

Great Britain (Percentages)

	1983	1991	2002	2011
Signed a petition	29	53	43	37
Contacted your MP	10	17	17	16
Gone on a protest or demonstration	6	9	12	8
Contacted a government department	2	4	5	6
Spoken to an influential person	4	5	6	6
Raised an issue in an organisation you belong to	7	5	6	5
Contacted radio, TV or newspaper	2	4	6	5
Formed a group of like-minded people	2	2	2	2
None of these	62	37	46	55

Table source: British Social Attitudes Survey, NatCen Social Research

Table notes:

1. Respondents were shown a card and asked 'Have you ever done any of the things on this card about a government action which you thought was unjust and harmful?' Respondents could choose more than one answer and so columns do not add to 100%.

Download table

 XLS format
(26 Kb)

Table 3 shows that non-electoral participation has largely increased from 30 years ago. The British Social Attitudes Survey asked people aged 16 and over in Great Britain whether they had participated in a political activity about a government action which they thought unjust and harmful. People were more likely in 2011 to report signing a petition (37%) and contacting their MP (16%) than they were in 1983 (when the figures were 29% and 10% respectively). However the proportion doing these things in 2011 is smaller than was reported in 1991 and 2002. The proportion of those participating in other kinds of political activity were small but show increases since the 1980s in reporting activities such as going on a protest or contacting the media (BSAS,2013).

Another form of non-electoral participation is making a freedom of information request. The Freedom of Information Act 2000[2] (which came fully into force on 1 January 2005) provides public access to information held by public authorities. It does this in two ways:

- Public authorities are obliged to publish certain information about their activities; and
- Members of the public are entitled to request information from public authorities.

Figure 5: Number of Freedom of Information requests received (1)

United Kingdom

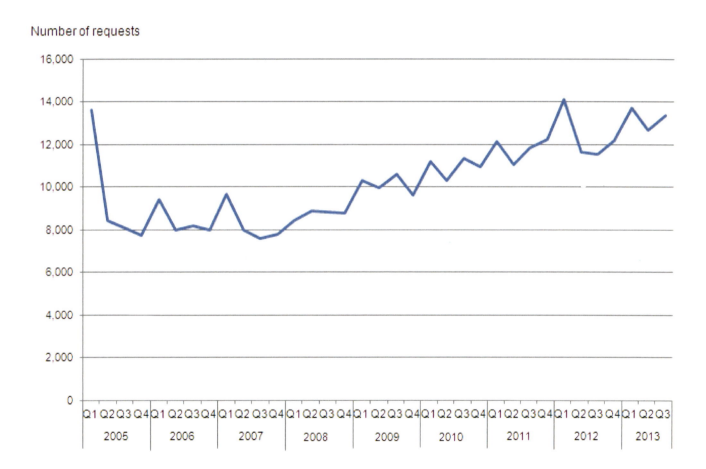

Source: Ministry of Justice

Notes:

1. Monitored central government bodies (Departments of State and other monitored bodies).

Download chart

XLS XLS format
(28 Kb)

In July to September (Q3) 2013 the monitored central government bodies[3] received a total of 13,370 non-routine FOI requests, 16% more than in Q3 of 2012 and 6% more than Q2 2013 **(Figure 5)**.

Departments of State accounted for nearly 7 in 10 (68%) of all requests received by monitored bodies in Q3 of 2013. This is an increase of 2 percentage points since Q3 2012 (66%) and 21 percentage points since Q3 2005 (48%).

Of the Departments of State, the Department for Work and Pensions reported having received 1,513 requests during Q3 2013, the highest departmental total followed by the Department for Transport (1,074 requests) and the Ministry of Justice (1,038 requests).

Notes

1. Voting is compulsory for at least some elections in Belgium, Cyprus, Luxembourg and Greece. The voting age is 18 for most of the elections in the EU Member States and in Croatia, with the exception of Austria where the voting age is 16.

2. The Act covers any recorded information that is held by a public authority in England, Wales and Northern Ireland, and by UK-wide public authorities based in Scotland. Information held by Scottish public authorities is covered by Scotland's own Freedom of Information (Scotland) Act 2002.

3. For more information on monitored central government bodies and more information on FOI requests see https://www.gov.uk/government/collections/government-foi-statistics

Background notes

1. Details of the policy governing the release of new data are available by visiting www.statisticsauthority.gov.uk/assessment/code-of-practice/index.html or from the Media Relations Office email: media.relations@ons.gsi.gov.uk

Copyright

References

1. EB,2013 - Eurobarometer

2. BSAS,2013 - British Social Attitudes

3. IIDEA,2010 - www.idea.int/

4. MORI,2010 - www.ipsos-mori.com/

About Understanding Society, the UK Household Longitudinal Study

Understanding Society is a unique and valuable academic study that captures important information every year about the social and economic circumstances and attitudes of people living in 40,000 UK households. It also collects additional health information from around 20,000 of the people who take part.

Information from the longitudinal survey is primarily used by academics, researchers and policy makers in their work, but the findings are of interest to a much wider group of people including those working in the third sector, health practitioners, business, the media and the general public.

Key facts

- 40,000 households – 2,640 postcode sectors in England, Scotland and Wales – 2,400 addresses from Northern Ireland.
- £48.9 million funding (until 2015).
- Approximately 3 billion data points of information.
- Innovation Panel of 1,500 respondents.
- Participants aged 10 and older.
- Building on 18 years of British Household Panel Survey.
- 35 to 60 minutes: the average time to complete each face to face interview.

How does it work?

Interviews began in 2009 with all eligible members of the selected households.

- Adults are interviewed every 12 months either face to face or over the phone using Computer Assisted Interviewing.
- 10 to 15 year olds fill in a paper self-completion questionnaire.

From 2010 some 20,000 participants aged over 16 also received nurse visits and provided a blood sample and some basic physical measurements (height, weight, blood pressure, grip strength).

For more information about the UKHLS see Understanding Society

About the ONS Measuring National Well-being Programme

NWB logo 2

This article is published as part of the ONS Measuring National Well-being Programme.

The programme aims to produce accepted and trusted measures of the well-being of the nation - how the UK as a whole is doing. It is about looking at 'GDP and beyond' and includes:

- Greater analysis of the national economic accounts, especially to understand household income, expenditure and wealth.
- Further accounts linked to the national accounts, including the UK Environmental Accounts and valuing household production and 'human capital'.
- Quality of life measures, looking at different areas of national well-being such as health, relationships, job satisfaction, economic security, education environmental conditions.
- Working with others to include the measurement of the well-being of children and young people as part of national well-being.
- Measures of 'personal well-being' - individuals' assessment of their own well-being.
- Headline indicators to summarise national well-being and the progress we are making as a society.

The programme is underpinned by a communication and engagement workstream, providing links with Cabinet Office and policy departments, international developments, the public and other stakeholders. The programme is working closely with Defra on the measurement of 'sustainable development' to provide a complete picture of national well-being, progress and sustainable development.

Find out more on the Measuring National Well-being website pages.

Office for
National Statistics

Measuring National Well-being: Children's Well-being, 2014

Coverage: **UK**
Date: **06 March 2014**
Geographical Area: **Country**
Theme: **Children, Education and Skills**
Theme: **Crime and Justice**
Theme: **Health and Social Care**
Theme: **People and Places**

Introduction

This article proposes a draft set of measures of national well-being for children aged 0 to 15. The measures are the latest output from the ONS Measuring National Well-being (MNW) programme and are released alongside a draft set of measures of national well-being for young people aged 16 to 24. The aim of these measures is to provide information on key sub-groups of the population to supplement the existing 41 experimental measures of national well-being which are published by the MNW Programme twice a year.

This publication outlines a first draft set of 24 headline measures of children's well-being and reasons for their selection for seven of the ten domains used in the national set. These domains are Personal Well-being, Our Relationships, Health, What We Do, Where We Live, Personal Finance and Education & Skills. The remaining three domains (Governance, Natural Environment and Economy) are more relevant to all age groups and have not been included here.

The full list of proposed headline measures can be found in the data section (213.5 Kb Excel sheet) of this article. Other potential measures have been included which reflect possible additional or alternatives to the proposed headline measures.

Findings from the MNW Children and Young People's project have been used to inform this work[1]. Where new measures have been proposed, the criteria to determine the original set of broader measures has been used. As outlined in the criteria, UK data has been used where available, in cases where there is not a measure for the UK, England or England and Wales has been used[2].

ONS would appreciate any feedback on these measures by 17 April 2014. ONS will continue to develop the measures for children and young people taking account of ongoing feedback from users and experts. An update of the measures will be published taking into account data availability and further work needed to fill gaps in measurement. ONS will also undertake more in-depth analysis of the measures to provide further insight into what the data and measures tell us about children and young people's well-being in the UK.

Why measure Children's Well-being?

Children's well-being is an important aspect of the well-being of the nation. In 2012 there were 12 million children, representing nearly a fifth of the total UK population[3]. Research from the Children's Society has shown that a significant minority of children in the UK suffer from low well-being and this impacts on their childhood and life chances as well as for the families and communities around them (Children's Society, 2013).

Notes for Introduction

1. ONS, 2013 Review of available sources and measures for children and young people's well-being (712.7 Kb Pdf); ONS, 2012 Measuring National Well-being - Children's Well-being, 2012.
2. Where England and / or England and Wales data has been used as a proxy for the UK, information on similar sources for the rest of the UK has been included in the data section of this report.
3. ONS UK population estimates.

Personal Well–being

Proposed headline measures

Measure	Geographic coverage	Age group	Source	Latest year	Latest data
Proportion of children with medium / high level of life satisfaction	GB	10-15	Children's Society	February/ March 2013	77%
Proportion of children with medium / high level of happiness yesterday	GB	10-15	Children's Society	February/ March 2013	74%
Proportion of children with medium / high level of worthwhileness	GB	10-15	Children's Society	February/ March 2013	75%

Download table

XLS XLS format
(26.5 Kb)

Personal well-being of children refers to subjective measures of what children feel and think about different aspects of their lives, and is clearly associated with objective measures such as health, education and housing (Bradshaw et al, 2013). It has been suggested that positive personal well-being is associated with a range of positive social, economic and health outcomes in the present as well as in the future (Lyubomirsky et al, 2005).

Personal well-being measures

The Children's Society has investigated children's personal well-being since 2005 through various surveys, individual or group discussions and statistical testing (Children's Society, 2013). The proposed measures use The Children's Society survey data[1]. The three questions used are:

- Overall, how satisfied are you with your life nowadays?
- Overall, how happy did you feel yesterday?
- Overall, to what extent do you think the things you do in your life are worthwhile?

These questions have been developed by the Office for National Statistics in its work with adults (ONS, 2011). Children are asked to give their answers on a scale of 0 to 10 where 0 is 'not at all' and 10 is 'completely'. The questions allow children to make an assessment of their life overall, as well as providing an indication of their day-to-day emotions[2].

Notes

1. Aspects of children's personal well-being have been incorporated in some other surveys in the UK and internationally, but much less than for adults. The Health Behaviour of School-aged Children (HBSC) for example (a cross-national survey of children aged 11-13 and 15-years old, conducted every four years since 1983) includes a question on life satisfaction. The British Household Panel Survey (BHPS) (part of the Understanding Society survey since 2009) has asked children aged 11-15 how they feel about their life as a whole, about their appearance, family, friends, school, school work and self-esteem every year since 1994.

2. These reflect three approaches to measuring personal well-being. The 'evaluative' approach is used when children are asked to make a cognitive assessment of how their life is going overall or of how specific aspects of their life are going, such as family or school. The "eudemonic" approach, sometimes referred as the psychological approach, measures children's degree of self-acceptance, their sense of meaning and purpose in life, the degree of autonomy and personal growth in their lives, positive connections with family and friends, as well as their sense of control and management of everyday life (Ryff's model, 1989). The 'experience' approach which measures children's positive and negative experiences (or affect) over a short timeframe to capture their personal well-being on a day-to-day basis. Only questions about positive affect have been used so far as testing found that children were less comfortable with answering

questions about negative affect (such as feeling anxious). Further information is available in <ins>The Good Childhood report 2013</ins>.

Our Relationships

Proposed headline measures

Measure	Geographic coverage	Age group	Source	Latest year	Latest data
Proportion of children who quarrel with a parent more than once a week (mother/ father)	UK	10-15	Understanding Society	2011–12	28% (mother) 20% (father)
Proportion of children who talk to a parent about things that matter more than once a week (mother/father)	UK	10-15	Understanding Society	2011–12	63% (mother) 40% (father)
Proportion of children who eat a meal with family 3 or more times in the last week	UK	10-15	Understanding Society	2011–12	75%
Proportion of children who have been bullied at school either physically or in other ways or both, 4 or more times in the last 6 months	UK	10-15	Understanding Society	2011–12	12%

Download table

XLS <ins>XLS format</ins>
(28 Kb)

Our relationships looks at the quality of personal relationships children have with those in their lives. The quality of these social connections is important to their well-being as it can affect their experiences, emotions and health (Helliwell and Putnam, 2004).

Relationship with parents

The quality of family relationships has been shown to be an important contributor to children's personal well-being (Rees et al, 2010). Proposed headline measures aim to capture whether children's communication with their parents is harmonious and meaningful. Whereas earlier research focused more on the quality of the children's relationships with their mother, latest research has highlighted the importance of children's relationships with their father leading to the government to acknowledge the need for fathers to be recognised in children's policies (Tim Loughton speech to Fatherhood Commission, 2010). Therefore both mother and father have been included for the quarrelling and talking with parents measures.

Family meal times

Eating regular meals with family is also thought to be an important factor accounting for happiness of children with family life (Ermish et al, 2011) and can strengthen children's family bonds, sense of belonging and cultural identity (Wolin and Bennett, 1984). The benefits of eating meals together as a family are also associated with better eating habits, nutritional intake and decreased risk of obesity (Gillman et al, 2000).

Being Bullied

Peer victimisation has been associated with a large number of short-term and long-term adverse outcomes in children, including lower levels of personal well-being (Wolke and Skew, 2011; Rees et al, 2010) and increased risk of behavioural, physical and mental health problems in childhood as well as in adulthood (Kim and Leventhal, 2008; Wolke and Skew, 2011; Wolke et al, 2013). Bullying can include a range of acts, from psychological and physical abuse to theft and social exclusion, either mild or severe, and can occur at school or at home. The proposed headline measures focuses on the percentage of children frequently bullied at school.

Over the past 10 years, the issue of cyber bullying (where children are bullied through the Internet or other technologies such as smartphones) has been brought to public attention due to the reporting of high profile cases in the media. Cyber bullying has been described as particularly harmful for the well-being of children, as it is a type of bullying that can follow the child everywhere and at anytime. There is currently no survey data available for cyber bullying of children but this will be kept under review. However, a measure has been included on social networking usage in the What We Do domain.

Other potential measures

Other proposed measures which could help provide further context for this domain are how happy children are with their family life, how happy children are with their friends and how supported they feel by their family (available from Understanding Society). Relationships with friends is important for children's personal well-being, self-esteem and sense of own identity (Chanfreau et al, 2008; Currie et al, 2012).

Health

Proposed headline measures

Measure	Geographic coverage	Age group	Source	Latest year	Latest data
Proportion of term babies with low birthweight	England and Wales	Gestational age between 37 and 42 weeks	ONS	2011	3%
Conception rates for girls aged 13–15	England and Wales	13-15	ONS	2012	5.6 per 1000 girls
Proportion of children who are overweight including obese	England	2-15	HSE	2012	28%
Proportion of children who have a relatively high level of happiness with their appearance	UK	10-15	Understanding Society	2011–12	74%

Download table

 XLS format
(27 Kb)

Health is very important for children. The independent report "Fair Society, Healthy Lives" (Marmot review, 2010) states that policy objectives to reduce health inequalities in the UK are required to "give every child the best start in life" and to ensure "healthy standard of living for all". A healthy experience through a child's life cycle from before birth to the teenage years is therefore of paramount importance for the future prospect of the child as an adult[1,2]

The headline measures proposed are related to different aspects of health and the life cycle: low birth weight, conception rates, obesity and subjective measures of happiness with appearance.

Low birth weight

Low birth weight is closely associated with disability and mortality in infants and children, with additional long-term health consequences in adulthood. Low birth weight is directly linked to the health and health behaviours of the mother before and during pregnancy (Bakeo and Clarke, 2006; Bradshaw, 2011; Chomitz et al, 1995). However, the relationship between birth weight and mortality is complex and varies within different ethnic groups (Kerry et al, 2009).

The measure for low birth weight of term babies refers to babies born after 36 weeks gestation with a weight of less than 2, 500 g. This measure is in line with the English Public Health Outcomes Framework.

Under 16 conception rates

Early child-bearing can lead to a wide range of health problems for under-16 mothers and their children (Joseph Rowntree Foundation, 2006). The Teenage Pregnancy Strategy was set out by the Department of Health in 1999, and renewed in 2010[3]. The aim of the Strategy is to halve the rate of teenage pregnancy that existed in 1998.

Obesity

Obesity in children has become an important public health issue in the turn of the 21st century. Research has suggested that being overweight or obese in childhood is linked to immediate and long-term physical and mental health risks. Mental health risks can arise from body dissatisfaction, social discrimination, low self-esteem and low quality of life (Griffiths et al, 2010; Xavier and Mandal, 2005). Obese children rate their personal well-being low, because of problems such as bullying at school, fatigue and difficulties in doing physical activities (Schwimmer et al, 2003).

Happiness with appearance

Children's satisfaction with their appearance has been highlighted as a key aspect of their overall well-being (Children's Society, 2013). Lower levels of satisfaction with appearance could potentially be linked to the high importance of image in the current culture (Dohnt and Tiggemann,2006). It has been suggested that exaggerated preoccupation or feelings of unhappiness about personal appearance (or dysmorphia) could cause mental health problems, such as depression, social isolation or intense self-consciousness leading to distress.

Other potential measures

Other proposed measures which could help provide further context for the Health domain include physical / mental health and subjective measures of health.

Healthy life expectancy:

Healthy life expectancy is a whole population measure which is included in the national well-being measures. These figures are widely used at a local, national and international level to monitor health inequalities and target resources effectively. Healthy life expectancy[4] is defined as the number of years an individual can expect to spend in very good or good general health.

Perinatal Health:

The measure for low birth weight was chosen to be consistent with the English Public Health Outcome Framework. But there are several other important measures of perinatal health. These include the proportion of babies born weighing less than 2,500g irrespective of gestational age[5] and the proportion of babies who are small for gestational age (SGA)[6]. The prevalence of pre-term births, rates of stillbirth (babies born without any signs of life on or after 24 weeks of gestation), prevalence of major congenital anomalies, neonatal death rates and the infant mortality rates have also been highlighted as important (European Perinatal Health Report, 2010).

Physical Health:

Important aspects of physical health for children include a measure for the percentage of children with long-standing health conditions as reported by parents (using Understanding Society data) and measures of the prevalence of asthma and type-I diabetes.

Health-related behaviours:

Some health behaviours (such as eating at least five portions of fruits and vegetables a day) are positive health behaviours, with positive outcomes. On the other hand, smoking, drinking and drug use[7] are negative health behaviours, with negative health outcomes and very well documented health consequences[8]. These are important contextual measures but have not been selected as headline measures.

Self-reported health:

The national well-being measures include a self-reported health measure. Various surveys including questions on self-assessed health for children[9], where children aged 10-15 are asked whether they would say that their health is excellent, very good, good, fair or poor.

Mental health:

ONS is undertaking further work to explore the available measures of mental health in children. One option is the Strengths and Difficulties Questionnaire (SDQ) (Goodman et al., 2000) to assess the percentage of children with mental health disorders. The SDQ consists of five sets of five questions, relating to emotional symptoms, conduct problems, hyperactivity/inattention, peer relationships problems and pro-social behaviours[10]. The Health Behaviour in School-aged Children survey, on the other hand, uses a measure called the KDSCREEN-10 Mental Health Index, consisting of a set of 10 questions exploring different aspects such as the child experience of depressive moods or stressful feelings, the quality of their relationships with family and friends or their self-perception of their cognitive abilities.

Notes

1. The current Public Health Outcomes Framework 2013 to 2016 in England and the Welsh Public Health Framework Our Healthy Future aim to improve health of children and young

people through healthier lifestyles and reduction of health inequalities. In Scotland, an Action Framework for Children and Young People's Health was set up in 2007 as a structured programme of actions to foster and safeguard the health and well-being of children and young people.

2. In February 2014, the Department of Health (DH) has published a series of factsheets on why wellbeing is important to health at different life stages.

3. Teenage Pregnancy Strategy, Department of Health.

4. Healthy life expectancy at birth is also used as a measure of well-being for adults: http://www.ons.gov.uk/ons/publications/re-reference-tables.html?edition=tcm%3A77-323390

5. This measure is used by WHO and OECD.

6. Refers to babies whose birth weight lies below the tenth percentile for their gestational age.

7. Data are available from Health Survey for England.

8. A summary of the health harms of drugs, Department of Health, 2011

9. Understanding Society: The Children's Society survey; The British Household Panel survey; The Health Behaviour of School-aged children.

10. A self-reported SDQ was included in the Understanding Society Survey. However, the SDQ is not directly comparable to the GHQ-12 measure used for adults in the ONS framework.

What we do

Proposed headline measures

Measure	Geographic coverage	Age group	Source	Latest year	Latest data
Proportion of children who have participated in any sport in the last week	England	11-15	DCMS	2012–13	89%
Proportion of children who have engaged with, or participated in, arts or cultural activity at least 3 times in the last year	England	5-15	DCMS	2012–13	94%
Proportion of children who belong to social networking sites (such as Facebook, Bebo and MySpace)	UK	10-15	Understanding Society	2011–12	86%

Download table

 XLS format
(27 Kb)

What We Do refers to how a person spends their time in work and non work activities such as leisure time and the balance between them. In the case of a child's well-being only the latter will be explored.

Leisure time

Leisure time is spent doing non-compulsory activities such as engaging in physical activity, culture and arts, according to preferences and lifestyles and can form part of a child's identity.

Physical activity[1] can be an organised activity such as playing football with a club or riding a bike.

Participation in arts and culture[2] can be reading and writing at home, or visiting a theatre / museum. Both physical activity and participation in arts and culture has been attributed to improving a child's short and long term well-being, for example health and mental health benefits(Children's Society, 2013; Department of Health, 2007).

Social media

Using social media sites such as Bebo, Facebook or MySpace is growing. While it can have positive advantages of helping children connect with friends and family, make communication easier for shy children and improve technical computer skills, it has also been associated with aspects of lower well-being in children such as depression and social isolation. In addition, social media creates opportunities for cyber bullying, sexting and exposure to risky situations (Holder et al 2009; O'Keeffe GS 2011; ONS, 2012,).

Other potential measures

Other potential measures which can help provide further context for the 'What we do' domain include technology and social media usage, volunteering activities, subjective measures and caring.

Technology and social networking usage:

While playing on computers, games consoles and chatting on social media sites can enhance children's recreational and networking experiences there are risks with excessive usage, lack of physical activity, exposure to negative influences and experiences. Research has highlighted a connection between well-being and the length of time children use technology and social networking - well-being decreased as time spent on computer games, games consoles and internet etc increased (Skew et al, 2011).

Volunteering:

Volunteering is time spent doing an unpaid activity that benefits another person (or group) or society. Volunteering can give people an increased sense of well-being, for example, by meeting new people and gaining new skills.

Subjective measures:

A subjective measure of children's views about what they do could be included. Potential areas could be satisfaction with how they use their time and / or satisfaction with the amount of choice they have in their life (Children's Society).

Young carers:

The population of England and Wales is ageing, and in response the provision of unpaid care by family members, friends, and neighbours has increased. While those who provide unpaid care make a valuable contribution to society, for young carers it can have a negative effect on future careers employment, social and leisure activities (ONS 2013a).

Criminal behaviour:

Engaging in criminal behaviour is an example of children participating in risky behaviour which is detriment to their well-being. Recorded data of criminal behaviour aspects such as rate of offending for those aged 10-15, types of offences and changes in reoffending rates could be examined.

Notes

1. Participants from the Taking Part Survey were asked if they had engaged in a sport activity, an example of some of the eligible sports activities included was: riding a bike, football; snooker; swimming; skating, athletics and walking. See the full Taking Part report for a full list of sports activities. Interviews for children aged 5-10 are conducted with the adult respondent by proxy and, due to this, the 5-10 survey is limited to asking about activities undertaken out of school. For 11-15 year olds, the questions are asked directly to the child and cover both in and out of school activities.

2. Excludes reading and writing.

Where We Live

Proposed headline measures

Measure	Geographic coverage	Age group	Source	Latest year	Latest data
Proportion of children who have been victims of a crime at least once in the last year	England & Wales	10-15	ONS	2012–13	13%
Proportion of children who have a bit or big worry about being a victim of crime	UK	10-15	Understanding Society	2011–12	16%
Proportion of children who feel a bit or very unsafe walking alone in neighbourhood after dark	UK	10-15	Understanding Society	2011–12	44%
Proportion of children who like living in their neighbourhood	UK	10-15	Understanding Society	2011–12	88%

Download table

XLS XLS format
(27 Kb)

Where we live is about an individual's dwelling, their local environment and the type of community in which they live, all of which can have an impact on a child's well-being.

Crime

In order to explore a child's perception of their neighbourhood it is important to understand a child's experience of crime. The Crime Survey in England and Wales (ONS 2013b) produces a victimisation rate for children (10-15 years) based on their experiences of crime in the 12 months prior to interview. It is important to note that victimisation rates do not simply translate into the number of incidents, as some children may have experienced more than one crime over the 12 months. Being a victim of crime can be a traumatic experience for the victim and their family and friends. This can present itself emotionally or through behaviour changes (such as taking precautions to avoid becoming a victim again).

Neighbourhood

It is important to note that the likelihood of being a victim of crime and the fear of crime are not always related. Nevertheless, studies have shown that parents will restrict outside play if they have concerns over crime and safety (Kalish et al, 2010).

Children who live in an area they consider safe will be confident to go outside and play. If they consider the neighbourhood to be friendly they will also be able to go and make friends with other children in the neighbourhood, all of which can contribute to a child's levels of happiness with life in general.

Other potential measures

Another potential measure which can help provide further context for the 'Where we live' domain includes whether children live in overcrowded or under-occupied houses[1.]

Notes

1. Levels of overcrowding and under-occupation are measured using the Department of Communities and Local Government's English Household Survey 'bedroom standard' (occupation density).This is the number of bedrooms required by the household to avoid undesirable sharing (given the number, ages and relationships of the household members). This is then compared with the number of bedrooms actually available to the household.

Personal Finance

Proposed headline measures

Measure	Geographic coverage	Age group	Source	Latest year	Latest data
Proportion of children living in households with less than 60% of median income	UK	0-19	DWP	2011/12	17%
Proportion of children living in workless households	UK	0-15	ONS	2013	14%

Table notes:

1. A child in the HBAI (Households Below Average Income) is defined as as an individual under 16 or anyone aged 16 to 19 who is not married, in a civil partnership or living with a partner, who is living with parents and who is in full-time non-advanced education or unwaged Government training.

Download table

 XLS format
(26 Kb)

Personal finance can have a significant impact on people's sense of well-being and the financial situation of the population is an important aspect of National Well-being. It is also important for the well-being of children.

The headline measures proposed within this domain include children living in relative poverty and workless households.

Children Living in Poverty

While on average, children living in low income families do not report low levels of well-being, poverty in childhood has very strong associations with children's outcomes in life (Bradshaw, 2011). Household income is important because of the impact it has on whether children themselves feel materially deprived, that they 'have enough' or 'fit in' (Children's Society, 2012a).

The chosen measure of relative low income is one of four income related targets set out in the Child Poverty Act 2010. This measures the proportion of children living in households where income is less than 60% of median household income, Before Housing Cost using the Households Below Average Income data[1].

Other income-based measures are available for children living in absolute low income, combined low income and material deprivation and persistent poverty (see DWP Statistical First Release, Low income and Material Deprivation in the UK).

Workless households

Children whose parents are in employment are at a reduced risk of poverty and its effects. Children in workless households are much more likely to live in low income households than those families with at least one adult in work[2].

Other potential measures

Other potential measures for this domain include subjective measures based on children's views. The Good Childhood Index (Children's Society, 2013) identified satisfaction with money and possessions as one of 12 important aspects of children's lives. The Children's Society and the University of York have also undertaken research to develop an index of child-centred and child-reported measures of material well-being (The Children's Society, 2012b).

Notes

1. The preferred measure of low income for children is based on incomes measures Before Housing Costs, as After Housing Costs measures can underestimate the true standard of living of families who choose to spend more on housing to attain a higher standard of accommodation. Households Below Average Income (HBAI) uses household disposable incomes, after adjusting for the household size and composition, as a proxy for material living standards. Changes in relative low-income measures depend on how changing incomes at the lower end of the distribution compare with income growth for the rest of the population.

2. DWP Statistical Release on Households Below Average Income, June 2013.

Education and Skills

Proposed headline measures

Measure	Geographic coverage	Age group	Source	Latest year	Latest data
Proportion of 3 and 4 year olds participating in funded early years education places	England	3-4	Department for Education	2013	96%
Proportion of children who achieved 5 or more GCSEs or equivalent A*-C including English and Maths	England/ Wales/Northern Ireland	In last year of compulsory education	Department for Education	2010–11	59%
Proportion of children with relatively high level of happiness with their school	UK	10-15	Understanding Society	2011–12	83%
Proportion of children who would like to go on to full-time education at a college or university	UK	10-15	Understanding Society	2011–12	62%

Download table

XLS XLS format
(19.5 Kb)

Children's education and development of skills are important for their well-being and for that of the nation as a whole. Learning ensures that children develop the knowledge and understanding, skills, capabilities and attributes which they need for mental, emotional, social and physical well-being now and in the future (ONS, 2012).

This domain includes participation in early years education, achievements in formal qualifications and measures of how school children feel about their well-being at school and future aspirations.

Early years education

The importance of early education for an individual's future well-being has been emphasised and supported by the provision of funded part-time nursery places and the associated inspection of the quality of provision for these children. The aim of early education is to promote personal, social and emotional development; physical development; and communication and language.

Compulsory Education

In line with national well-being measures, a measure of pupils' academic performance is included as measured by achievement in their last year of compulsory education. Children's circumstances affect how well a child does in school and examinations. Data on qualifications by pupil characteristics are available (for example, those eligible for Free School Meals, looked after children and SEN(see ONS paper 2012 for an overview). Other potential measures are also available for education attainments at different key stages[2].

Feelings about school

It is not just children's attendance at school but also children's experience within the school that is important to their overall well-being. A study of the ALSPAC (Avon Longitudinal Study of Parents and Children) of pupil and school effects during primary school found that different children have different experiences even at the same school and that for well-being, 'child-school' fit is as important as attending a particular school (Gutman and Feinstein, 2008).

A measure of happiness with school has been included as a headline measure. A further potential measure of school engagement – happiness with school work – is also available from Understanding Society.

Aspirations for the future

Expectations for the future is one of the ten aspects of children's well-being identified by the Children's Society in the Good Childhood Index. The future aspirations of children can be measured by what children hope to do when they leave school.

Other potential measures

There are several other potential measures available for the 'Education and skills' domain which include school readiness, parental involvement and school absenteeism / exclusion:

School readiness:

School readiness includes the Early Years Foundation Stage Profile in England which provides assessment against 17 early learning goals (ELG). An individual is deemed to have reached a good level of development if they have achieved the expected level in 12 of these ELGs in the key areas of learning and in the specific areas of mathematics and literacy.

Parental involvement:

Data from Understanding Society is available on parental involvement in education.

School absenteeism and exclusion:

Children who are persistently absent from school lose out on learning and may fail to catch up with their peers.

Notes

1. In England all 4-year-olds have been entitled to a funded early education place since 1998 and in 2004 this was extended to all 3-year-olds.

2. Further information about the results at Key Stages 1 and Key Stages 2 in England.

About the ONS Measuring National Well-being Programme

National well-being

This article is published as part of the ONS Measuring National Well-being Programme.

The programme aims to produce accepted and trusted measures of the well-being of the nation - how the UK as a whole is doing. It is about looking at 'GDP and beyond' and includes:

*   Greater analysis of the national economic accounts, especially to understand household income, expenditure and wealth.
*   Further accounts linked to the national accounts, including the UK Environmental Accounts and valuing household production and 'human capital'.
*   Quality of life measures, looking at different areas of national well-being such as health, relationships, job satisfaction, economic security, education environmental conditions.
*   Working with others to include the measurement of the well-being of children and young people as part of national well-being.

- Measures of 'personal well-being' - individuals' assessment of their own well-being.
- Headline indicators to summarise national well-being and the progress we are making as a society.

The programme is underpinned by a communication and engagement workstream, providing links with Cabinet Office and policy departments, international developments, the public and other stakeholders. The programme is working closely with Defra on the measurement of 'sustainable development' to provide a complete picture of national well-being, progress and sustainable development.

Find out more on the Measuring National Well-being website pages.

References

Bakeo and Clarke., (2006) Risks factors for low birthweight based on birth registration and census information, England and Wales, 1981-2000. Health Stat Q (30): 15-21.

Bradshaw, J. and Keung, A., (2011) Trends in child subjective well-being in the UK, Journal of Children's Services, 6, 1, 4-17.

Bradshaw J (2011)., Child poverty and deprivation, in J. Bradshaw (ed.) The Well-being of Children in the UK, 3rd ed, The Policy Press, Bristol, pp.27-52.

Bradshaw, J., B. Martorano, L. Natali and C. de Neubourg (2013). Children's Subjective Well-being in Rich Countries, Child Indicators Research, 6, 4, 619–635.

Chanfreau J., Lloyd C., Byron C et al., (2008) Predicting wellbeing. NatCen Prepared for the Department of Health.

Childrens Society., (2012a) Promoting positive well-being for children.

Children's Society., (2012b) Missing out: A child centred analysis of material deprivation and subjective well-being.

Children's Society., (2013) The Good Childhood Report.

Chomitz V.R., Cheung L.W.Y., Lieberman E., (1995) The Future of Children. Vol. 5, No. 1, Low Birth Weight, pp. 121-138.

Currie C et al., eds. Social determinants of health and well-being among young people. Health Behaviour in School-aged Children (HBSC) study: international report from the 2009/2010 survey. Copenhagen, WHO Regional Office for Europe, 2012 (Health Policy for Children and Adolescents, No. 6).

Department of Communities and Local Government., (2013) Taking Part 2012/13 Annual Child Report.

Department of Health., (2007) Report of the Review of Arts and Health Working Group.

Dohnt H and Tiggemann M., (2006) The contribution of peer and media influences to the development of body satisfaction and self-esteem in young girls: a prospective study. Developmental psychology; 42(5): 929-36

Ermish J., Iacovou M. And Skew A.J. Family relationships. McFall, S. L. & Garrington, C. (Eds.)., (2011) Understanding Society: Early findings from the first wave of the UK's household longitudinal study. Colchester: Institute for Social and Economic Research, University of Essex.

Euro-Peristat., (2010) European Perinatal Health Report (2010).

Gillman M.W., Rifas-Shiman S.L., Frazier A.L., Rockett H.R.H., Camargo C.A., Field A.E., Berkey C.S., Colditz G.A., (2000) Family Dinner and Diet Quality Among Older Children and Adolescents. Arch Fam Med. 2000; 9:235-240.

Goodman R., Ford T., Simmons H., Gatward R., Meltzer H., (2000) Using the Strengths and Difficulties Questionnaire (SDQ) to screen for child psychiatric disorders in a community sample. The British Journal of Psychiatry; 177: 534-539.

Griffiths LJ., Parsons TJ., Hill AJ., (2010) Self-esteem and quality of life in obese children and adolescents: a systematic review. Int J Pediatr Obese; 5(4):282-304.

Gutman and Feinstein., (2008) Children's Well-Being in Primary School: Pupil and School Effects. Wider Benefits of Learning Research Report No.25. Centre for Research on the Wider Benefits of Learning.

Helliwell, J.F., Putnam, R.D., (2004) The Social Context of Wellbeing.

Holder, M.D., Coleman, B.,& Sehn, Z.L., (2009) The contribution of active and passive leisure to children's well-being, Journal of Health Psychology, 14(3),pp.378-386.

Joseph Rowntree Foundation's report by Bradshaw J., (2006) Teenage births.

Kalish M., Banco L., Burke G and Lapidus G., (2010) Outdoor play: A survey of parent's perceptions of their child's safety J Trauma. 201; 69(4 Suppl):S218-22.

Kim and Leventhal., (2008) Bullying and suicide. International Journal of Adolescent Medicine and Health. Volume 20, Issue 2, Pages 133–154.

Lyubomirsky S., King L., and Diener E., (2005) The benefits of frequent positive affect: does happiness lead to success? . Psychological Bulletin. 131(6):803-55.

Marmot M., (2010) The Marmot Review "Fair Society, Healthy Lives", A strategic review of health inequalities in England and post-2010"

O'Keeffe GS., Clarke-Pearson K., (2011) Council on Communications and Media. Clinical Report - The impact of social media on children, adolescents, and families. Pediatrics;127(4):800-804.

Office for National Statistics., (2011) Initial investigation into Subjective Well-being from the Opinions Survey

Office for National Statistics., (2012) Measuring National Well-being - Children's Well-being, 2012

Office for National Statistics., (2013) Review of available sources and measures for children and young people's well-being

Office for National Statistics., (2013a) Providing unpaid care may have an adverse affect on young carers' general health

Office for National Statistics., (2013b) 'Crime in England and Wales, Year Ending March 2013'

Rees G, Goswami H., and Bradshaw J., (2010) Developing an index of children's subjective well-being in England. The Children's Society, available at:

Ryff, C. D., (1989) Happiness is everything, or is it? Explorations on the meaning of psychological well-being. Journal of Personality and Social Psychology, 57, 1069-1081.

Schwimmer J.B., Burwinkle T.M., Varni J.W., (2003) Health-related quality of life of severely obese children and adolescents. Journal of American Medical Association. Vol. 289 Nb 14.

Skew A, et al., (2011). Young People and Well-Being, Presentation to children and young people as part of the 2011 Festival of Social Science, London, 3 November 201

Tim Loughton., speech to Fatherhood Commission, 2010

Tucker C.J., Finkelhor D., Turner H. and Shattuck A., (2013). Association of Sibling Aggression With Child and Adolescent Mental Health. Pediatrics Vol. 132, Nb 1.

Wolke D., and Skew A.J., (2011) Bullied at home and at school: relationship to behaviour problems and unhappiness. McFall, S. L. & Garrington, C. (Eds.).Understanding Society: Early findings from the first wave of the UK's household longitudinal study. Colchester: Institute for Social and Economic Research, University of Essex.

Wolke D., Copeland W.E., Angold A.and Costello E.J., (2013) Impact of Bullying in Childhood on Adult Health, Wealth, Crime, and Social Outcomes. Journal of the Association for Psychological Science(10):1958-70.

Xavier S, Mandal S. The psychosocial impacts of obesity in children and young people: A future health perspective. Public Health Medicine 2005;6(1):23-27.

Background notes

1. Authors: Sian Bradford, Rachel O'Brien and Veronique Siegler

2. Understanding Society is a unique and valuable academic study that captures important information every year about the social and economic circumstances and attitudes of people

living in 40,000 UK households. It also collects additional health information from around 20,000 of the people who take part.

Information from the longitudinal survey is primarily used by academics, researchers and policy makers in their work, but the findings are of interest to a much wider group of people including those working in the third sector, health practitioners, business, the media and the general public.

The data in this analysis is from the youth self-completion questionnaire module of Waves 1-3 of the Survey and has been weighted using the combined cross-sectional youth interview weight.

More information about the UKHLS.

3. The Children's Society has been running a regular online well-being survey since July 2010 with a sample of 2,000 children and their parents, which uses a household panel that is run by the research agency Research Now. The survey was run every quarter until 2013 and then every six months since January 2013. Each wave has so far covered a representative sample of approximately 2,000 children, initially in UK, but in GB since wave 3 of the survey. The survey includes quota sampling for age, gender and family socio-economic status (i.e. occupation of the main income earner, information provided by parent). Waves 1 to 9 included children aged 8 to 15, while Wave 10 included children aged 10 to 17. Each wave of the survey has included a standard set of questions that make up "The Good Childhood Index" together with questions covering additional topics which have varied for each wave. The three ONS questions were added as additional questions for the first time in wave 7 and repeated them in waves 8, 9 and 10. For more information about these surveys, see: http://www.childrenssociety.org.uk/what-we-do/research/well-being/background-programme-0

4. The age range for the proposed headline measure for the proportion of children living in households with less than 60% of median income has been amended from 0-15 to 0-19 and now includes the full definition of a child used in the HBAI for clarification.

5. Details of the policy governing the release of new data are available by visiting www.statisticsauthority.gov.uk/assessment/code-of-practice/index.html or from the Media Relations Office email: media.relations@ons.gsi.gov.uk

Copyright

Office for
National Statistics

Measuring National Well-being - Young People's Well-being, 2014

Coverage: **UK**
Date: **06 March 2014**
Geographical Area: **Country**
Theme: **Children, Education and Skills**
Theme: **Crime and Justice**
Theme: **Economy**
Theme: **Health and Social Care**
Theme: **People and Places**

Abstract

This publication proposes a draft set of measures of national well-being for young people aged 16 to 24. The measures are the latest output from the ONS Measuring National Well-being (MNW) programme and are released alongside a draft set of measures of national well-being for children aged 0 to 15. The aim of these measures is to provide information on key sub-groups of the population to supplement the existing 41 experimental measures of national well-being which are published by the MNW Programme twice a year.

Introduction

This article outlines a first draft set of 29 headline measures of young people's well-being and the reasons for their selection across seven of the ten domains used in the national set. These domains are Personal Well-being, Our Relationships, Health, What We Do, Where We Live, Personal Finance and Education & Skills. The remaining three domains (Governance, Natural Environment and Economy) are more relevant to all age groups and have not been included here.

The full list of headline measures can be found in the data section (369.5 Kb Excel sheet) of this article. Other potential measures have been included which reflect possible additional or alternatives to the proposed headline measures.

Findings from the MNW Children and Young People's project have been used to inform this work[1]. Where new measures have been proposed, the criteria to determine the original set of broader measures have been used. As outlined in the criteria, UK data has been used where available; in cases where there is not a measure for the UK, England or England and Wales has been used.

ONS would appreciate any feedback on these measures by 17 April 2014. ONS will continue to develop the measures for children and young people taking account of ongoing feedback from users and experts. An update of the measures will be published taking into account data availability and further work needed to fill gaps in measurement. ONS will also undertake more in-depth analysis of the measures to provide further insight into what the data and measures tell us about children and young people's well-being in the UK.

Why measure young people's well-being?

There were around 7.5 million young people aged 16 to 24 in the UK in 2010 according to the Office for National Statistics (ONS) mid-year population estimates (ONS, 2013a). This age is important as it is a time of transition from childhood to adulthood, and the ways in which this transition is negotiated may affect well-being. Arnett (2004) coined the phrase 'emerging adulthood' to describe this stage of life. He explained how it is different from 'late adolescence' as it is a period of life "much freer from parental control [and] much more a period of independent exploration." Furthermore, Arnett argues this period of life is different from 'young adulthood' as many 18-24 year olds have yet to make "the transitions historically associated with adult status" such as marriage and parenthood.

Notes

1. For further information see: ONS, 2013 Review of available sources and measures for children and young people's well-being (712.7 Kb Pdf); ONS, 2012 Measuring National Well-being - Children's Well-being, 2012

Personal Well-being

Personal well-being proposed measures

Measure	Geographic coverage	Source	Latest year	Latest data
Proportion of young people with a medium-high level of life satisfaction*	UK	ONS	2012–13	81%
Proportion of young people with a medium-high level of feeling their activities are worthwhile*	UK	ONS	2012–13	79%
Proportion of young people with a medium-high level of happiness yesterday*	UK	ONS	2012–13	72%
Proportion of young people with a medium-low level of anxiety yesterday*	UK	ONS	2012–13	64%
Mental well-being (mean score out of 35)*	UK	Understanding Society	2009–10	25 out of 35

Table notes:

1. *Measure also included in the National Measures of Well-being

Download table

XLS XLS format
(27 Kb)

An important component of national well-being is the subjective well-being of all individuals, including young people. It is measured by finding out how people think and feel about their own lives. Subjective well-being measures are grounded in individuals' preferences and take account of what matters to people by allowing them to decide what is important. By looking at young people as a separate sub-group, we can see if they differ from the general population. While subjective well-being is important, it is just one component of national well-being.

Personal Well-being

Since April 2011, the Annual Population Survey, which samples people from age 16, has included four questions which are used to monitor personal wellbeing in the UK:

1. Overall, how satisfied are you with your life nowadays?

2. Overall, to what extent do you feel the things you do in your life are worthwhile?

3. Overall, how happy did you feel yesterday?

4. Overall, how anxious did you feel yesterday?

Responses are on a scale of 0 to 10 where 0 is 'not at all' and 10 is 'completely'. Higher levels of personal well-being for life satisfaction, worthwhile and happiness are defined as 7 or more out of 10. However, for anxiety 3 or less out of 10 is used because lower levels of anxiety indicate better personal well-being.

Young people are more likely to report higher levels of satisfaction with their life and lower levels of anxiety compared with all adults. This may relate to the increase in freedom, independence and self-focus associated with the 'emerging adulthood' lifestage. Similar proportions of young people have higher levels of happiness yesterday and feel that the things they do are worthwhile as all adults.

Mental Well-being

The mental well-being measure is the shortened version of the Warwick-Edinburgh Mental Well-being Scale (SWEMWBS). This was developed to measure the mental well-being of populations and groups over time. As such, we can compare young people as a sub-group with the general population. The SWEMWBS provides a mean score (out of 35) of mental well-being for the population and changes over time can be assessed by examining differences in the mean score; however, it cannot be used to categorise good, average or poor mental well-being[1]. "WEMWBS has been validated for use in the UK with those aged 16 and above. Validation involved both student and general population samples, and focus groups" (Health Scotland).

Notes

1. As well as not being designed to identify people who have or probably have a mental illness, WEMWBS does not have a 'cut off' level to divide the population into those who have 'good' and those who have 'poor' mental well-being in the way that scores on other mental health measures, for example the GHQ 12.

Our Relationships

Our relationships proposed measures

Measure	Geographic coverage	Age group	Source	Latest year	Latest data
Proportion of young people with someone to rely on when there is a serious problem*	UK	16 to 24	Understanding Society	2010–11	82%
Proportion of young people who quarrel with a parent more than once a week (mother/father)	UK	16 to 21 only	Understanding Society	2011–12	25% Mother 16% Father
Proportion of young people who talk to a parent about things that matter more than once a week (mother/father)	UK	16 to 21 only	Understanding Society	2011–12	58% Mother 36% Father
Proportion of young people who eat an evening meal with their family three or more times a week	UK	16 to 21 only	Understanding Society	2011–12	60%

Table notes:

1. * Measure also included in the National Measures of Well-being

Download table

XLS XLS format
(27 Kb)

A person's relationships with family and friends can affect their well-being in a number of ways. "People who have close friends and confidants, friendly neighbours and supportive co-workers are less likely to experience sadness, loneliness, low self-esteem and problems with eating and sleeping...Subjective well-being is best predicted by the breadth and depth of one's social connections" (Helliwell and Putnam, 2004). An analysis of experimental data from the Annual Population Survey found that overall life satisfaction and personal relationships are related; those who reported a higher level of life satisfaction were more likely to report higher satisfaction with their personal relationships than those with lower levels of life satisfaction (ONS 2012a).

Good communication is important to healthy relationships, so the proposed headline measures include both quarrelling with parents and talking to parents about things that matter. Whereas earlier research focused more on the quality of the children's relationships with their mother, latest research has highlighted the importance of children's relationships with their father (Tim Loughton speech to Fatherhood Commission, 2010). These relationships are still vital during the transition to adulthood.

The proportion of young people who eat an evening meal with their family three or more times a week provides an indication of family cohesion. The data for these measures comes from the young adults module of the Understanding Society Survey which was asked of all 16 to 21 year olds, living in the parental home[1]. Having someone to rely on, be it a partner or spouse, another family member, or a friend, when there is a serious problem shows the importance of a support network.

Someone to rely on

Using data from Understanding Society, in 2010-11 82% of 16 to 24 year olds had someone to rely on. This is less than the proportion of all adults, where 87% had someone to rely on. The difference may be accounted for by the higher levels of marriage and partnerships in older age groups compared with 16 to 24 year olds. Young people may also have other role models and confidants that they can rely on for support, such as teachers, which may not be captured by this measure.

Relationship with parents

The measures 'quarrelling with mother/father' and 'talking to mother/father about things that matter' are proposed to reflect young people's perceptions of the quality of their relationships with their family.

The differences in some of these measures, when compared with children aged 10 to 15 years old, illustrate the 'emerging adulthood' life stage, where young people are developing more self-reliance, self-awareness and preparing to become independent adults. Children, especially as they move through adolescence, are still trying to establish their independence and will often challenge their parents to do this. Arnett (2004) claims that emerging adulthood is a time when parental supervision has diminished and young people are more self-focused.

Other potential measures

Living with parents

The Office for National Statistics recently published an analysis of Labour Force Survey data, which showed that in 2013, 49% of 20 to 24 year olds lived with their parents, compared with 42% in 2008 (ONS, 2014a). It shows that men are more likely than women (at all ages) to live with their parents and that amongst 20 to 34 year olds, the percentage of those living with their parents who are unemployed (13%) is more than twice that of those who don't (6%). As expected, the proportion of 16 to 19 year olds living at home is similar in 2008 to the proportion living at home in 2013, with 84% compared with 86% respectively. This measure is important but these data do not allow us to determine whether living with parents after the age of 20 has a positive or negative effect on a person's well-being.

Relationships with friends

Friendships are also important to a person's well-being. Time may be spent on social websites, chatting to friends online, or going out socially with friends. Data from Understanding Society in 2011-12 show that nearly 91% of young people belong to a social website compared with less than 50% of all adults. Furthermore, nearly 40% of young people spent between 1 and 3 hours chatting to friends online a day, and nearly 15% spent over 4 hours online with friends. Despite all the time spent online, young people still spend time with their friends in person, as over 90% of 16 to 21 year olds went out socially with their friends in 2011-12. These measures have not been included as headline measures as people are able to choose their friends and so are more likely to be happy with their friends and have good, supportive relationships.

Notes

1. It is important to note that this is a specific sub-group of young people. The questions about relationships with parents could also be relevant to young people living away from the parental home, either temporarily (e.g. students) or permanently; however, they will have a qualitatively different meaning in this context.

Health

Health proposed measures

Measure	Geographic coverage	Source	Latest year	Latest data
Proportion of young people with a disability or long-term illness*	UK	ONS	Mar-13	11%
Proportion of young people with a relatively high level of satisfaction with their health*	UK	Understanding Society	2011–12	66%
Proportion of young people with some symptoms of anxiety or depression*	UK	Understanding Society	2011–12	21%
Under 18 conception rate	England and Wales	ONS	2011	30.9 per 1,000 women aged 15–17
Proportion of young people who are overweight, including obese	England	Health and Social Care Information Centre	2012	36%

Table notes:

1. * Measure also included in the National Measures of Well-being

Download table

XLS XLS format
(27 Kb)

Data from the Annual Population Survey showed that amongst adults in the UK, self-reported health was the most important factor associated with subjective well-being (ONS 2013b). A person's health is affected by the social and economic environment, the physical environment and personal characteristics and behaviours. People reporting very bad health reported lower levels of life satisfaction and higher levels of anxiety than people in good health.

Disability and long-term illness

A measure which is used in national well-being and is also available for young people is the proportion of the population with a long term limiting illness or disability. Most children with physical disabilities or chronic illness will live to adulthood. The transition into adulthood for children with long-term illnesses and disabilities can be difficult and frightening. During adolescence problems can occur such as social isolation, a lack of daily-living skills, difficulties in finding work and additional problems in family relationships, such as over-protectiveness by parents and low parental expectations. They will experience change in a number of areas: from paediatric to adult health services, school to higher education or work and childhood dependence to adult autonomy. How this transition is negotiated may determine whether it has a positive or negative impact on their future well-being.

Satisfaction with health

Health problems develop with age, as can be seen in the proportions of adults with long-term illnesses or disabilities, so it is reasonable to expect young people to be more satisfied with their health than older people. Analysis by ONS identified that young people were more likely to report satisfaction with their health than any other age group (ONS, 2013c). It is important to maintain or improve people's health and their satisfaction with their health as they age to ensure positive well-being in later life.

Mental health

Another measure used in national well-being which is also available for the 16 to 24 age group is the proportion with some symptoms of anxiety or depression, measured using the General Health Questionnaire (GHQ) scores. An illustration of how GHQ scores differ by age group can be found in "Measuring National Well-being – Health" (ONS 2013c). Poor mental health is often a direct response to what is happening in young people's lives. The emotional well-being of young people is just as important as their physical health. Good mental health allows young people to develop resilience and grow into well-rounded, healthy adults.

"An important part of growing up is working out and accepting who you are. Some young people find it hard to make this transition to adulthood and may experiment with alcohol, drugs or other substances that can affect mental health" (Mental Health Foundation).

Teenage Pregnancy

Both teenage motherhood and being a child of a young mother can affect individuals' future well-being across several domains of national well-being including health, the economy and personal finance. Some of the problems associated with becoming a teenage mother include disrupted schooling, which may lead to the mother and child living in relative poverty and becoming a low socio-economic household. In addition, children born to teenage mothers are twice as likely to become teenage parents themselves (ONS 2013d).

Obesity

The Health Survey for England[1] uses objective measurements of height and weight to calculate Body Mass Index. It shows that the proportion of young people who are overweight or obese had increased between 2003 and 2012. Obesity at a younger age can increase the risk of developing serious diseases, can damage a person's quality of life and may trigger depression in later life.

Other potential measures

Life expectancy
Life expectancy for both men and women at age 16 has increased over the decade 2002 to 2012. "The length and quality of people's lives differ substantially. Some of these differences are unavoidable (e.g., genetic differences) or random (e.g., accidents). However, factors that are amenable to change, such as socio-economic status, education and quality of one's immediate living environment, also play a significant part, leading to large inequalities in life expectancy" (The Kings Fund). Women have a longer life expectancy than men, but the difference between life expectancy for men and women at age 16 is becoming smaller. Figures from ONS show that in 2002 there was a difference of 4.5 years, whereas in 2012 the difference was 3.8 years. Life expectancy is important but is more affected by mortality and morbidity at older ages. As such, the other headline measures are considered more relevant to young people.

Lifestyle behaviours
A person's health is affected by the social and economic environment, the physical environment and personal characteristics and behaviours (World Health Organisation). Risky behaviours such as smoking, drinking alcohol and taking drugs are known to affect a person's short and long-term health and will therefore have an effect on well-being. However, as there is not one overall measure of how healthy people's lifestyles are this has not been included as a headline measure.

Causes of death
The leading cause of death in England and Wales in 2012 amongst 16 to 24 year olds was suicide. Suicide has recently overtaken land transport accidents (LTAs) as the leading cause of death amongst young people in England and Wales, as there has been a decline in the rate of LTA deaths for both men and women aged 16 to 24. Suicide rates can be used as an indication of acute mental health problems.

Notes

1.   Heath Survey for England

What We Do

What we do proposed measures

Measure	Geographic coverage	Source	Latest year	Latest data
Unemployment rate for young people*	UK	ONS	Apr–June 2013	21%
Proportion of young people with a relatively high level of satisfaction with the amount of leisure time they have*	UK	Understanding Society	2011–12	62%
Proportion of young people who have volunteered in the last 12 months*	UK	Understanding Society	2011–12	17%
Proportion of young people who participate in at least one session of moderate activity a week*	England	Sport England	Oct 2012 – Oct 2013	54%
Proportion of young people who have engaged with or participated in an arts or cultural activity at least three times in the last year*	England	Department for Culture Media and Sport	2012–13	83%

Table notes:

1.   * Measure also included in the National Measures of Well-being

Download table

XLS XLS format
(27 Kb)

This domain aims to capture the diversity of activities in which people engage and the levels of commitment and involvement that they bring to them. It considers the balance between leisure and non-leisure time and the well-being derived from leisure activities including engaging with culture and sport.

Unemployment Rate

The unemployment rate is the proportion of economically active people who are not currently working but who have been looking for work in the last four weeks and are available to start within the next two weeks. People may be economically inactive for a number of reasons; for example they are full-time carers, profoundly disabled, or in full-time education. Due to the economic downturn resulting in fewer jobs[1] young people may decide to continue in full-time education.

Data from the Office for National Statistics Labour Force Survey shows that the unemployment rate for young people has increased substantially over the last decade, from 12.5% in April-June 2003 to 21.4% in April-June 2013. Young people may be unemployed due to a lack of experience, education, qualifications, training or jobs available. The article "Young People in the Labour Market" published by ONS (2014c) presents a fuller analysis of these changes.

A lack of money due to unemployment may increase feelings of social isolation in young people as they cannot afford to socialise or go out and meet other people as often as they may like. Young unemployed people may also experience symptoms of mental illness.

The Prince's Trust claims that "the longer people are out of work, the more likely they are to feel a lapse in confidence. Those who are long-term unemployed are significantly more likely to feel this way than those out of work for less than six months" (The Prince's Trust Macquarie Youth Index 2014).

Leisure time

The Understanding Society survey asks respondents to say how satisfied they are with the amount of leisure time they have. As a subjective measure, this is important to understand how people's time-use can affect their well-being. "The amount and quality of leisure time is important for people's well-being for the direct satisfaction it brings. Additionally leisure, taken in certain ways, is important for physical and mental health. Leisure also contributes to the well-being of people other than the person directly enjoying leisure." (OECD, 2009)

Volunteering

Being a volunteer has been shown to be related to better well-being. "We define volunteering as any activity that involves spending time, unpaid, doing something that aims to benefit the environment or someone (individuals or groups) other than, or in addition to, close relatives. Central to this definition is the fact that volunteering must be a choice freely made by each individual." (Volunteering England).

Volunteering can help develop new skills and it is an opportunity to gain experience and meet new people. A young person can make a difference by volunteering. The New Economics Foundation's

Five Ways to Well-being states "Seeing yourself, and your happiness, linked to the wider community can be incredibly rewarding and creates connections with the people around you."

Participation in at least one session of moderate activity a week

According to Sport England, participation in physical activity and sport has been shown to be effective in reducing depression, anxiety, psychological distress and emotional disturbance. Low-to-moderate physical exercise can reduce anxiety and have both short and long-term beneficial effects on psychological health. Taking part in sport and spectating can have a positive impact on the well-being and happiness of young people.

Engagement or participation in an arts or cultural activity

Arts and culture can have a positive impact on well-being. Access to arts and culture also feeds into the domains of health, where we live and education.

 "Creative activity has long been known to have tangible effects on health and quality of life. The arts, creativity and the imagination are agents of wellness: they help keep the individual resilient, aid recovery and foster a flourishing society" (National Alliance for Arts Health and Wellbeing).

Notes

1. Vacancies statistics produced by ONS

Where We Live

Where we live proposed measures

Measure	Geographic coverage	Source	Latest year	Latest data
Proportion of young people who have been victims of crime at least once in the last year	England and Wales	ONS	2012–13	26%
Proportion of young people who feel safe walking alone in their local area after dark*	England and Wales	ONS	2012–13	72%

Table notes:

1. * Measure also included in the National Measures of Well-being

Download table

XLS XLS format
(26.5 Kb)

There is a disparity between levels of recorded crime and people's perceptions of crime in their neighbourhoods. Young people are more likely to be a victim of crime and this can affect what they do and when they do it, and how they feel about their community.

Victims of crime

A person's well-being can be affected in many ways if they have been a victim of crime. There can be short or long term effects of crime and some people cope well with horrific crimes while others can be distressed by a minor incident (Victim Support). Crime can also affect family and friends, and people's lifestyle can change by taking precautions if they do not feel safe. Age can be a factor in determining whether someone becomes a victim of personal crime: the percentage of both men and women who were victims of personal crime decreases with age.

Feeling safe walking alone in their local area after dark

This measure can help us to understand people's perceptions of crime. A person may not feel they are safe walking alone after dark if they fear they are at a higher risk of being a victim of crime.

Other potential measures

Belonging to the neighbourhood
Belonging to the neighbourhood leads to a greater sense of community and feelings of security. Positive feelings of belonging to the neighbourhood as a community and a member of that community is a key factor in achieving economic and civil well-being. It may also be associated with positive mental health.

Young people experience their neighbourhoods differently from both children and the older adult population. They may be in them temporarily and so be less likely to feel strong bonds with the area.

Personal Finance

Personal finance proposed measures

Measure	Geographic coverage	Source	Latest year	Latest data
Proportion of young people living in households with less than 60% of median income*	UK	Eurostat	2011	20%
Proportion of young people with a relatively high level of satisfaction with household income*	UK	Understanding Society	2011–12	52%
Proportion of young people finding their financial situation difficult or very difficult*	UK	Understanding Society	2011–12	11%

Table notes:

1. * Measure also included in the National Measures of Well-being

Download table

XLS XLS format
(27 Kb)

Respondents to the National Debate on 'What matters to you' (ONS 2012b) identified the importance of having adequate income or wealth to cover basic needs such as somewhere to live and food on the table. A lack of finances can affect a person's health, their access to community resources and their own contribution to that community. During emerging adulthood, personal finance becomes important as young people become independent, expect to move out of the parental home and take on financial responsibilities such as rent or mortgages. Being unable to do the things you would like to do because of a lack of money can reduce your level of life satisfaction, make life seem less worthwhile and affect how happy you may be; furthermore, worrying about finances could make you more anxious. Seddon (ONS, 2012c) illustrates the relationship between personal well-being and income. Using experimental data from the Opinions Survey, she found that the lowest two income groups had the lowest life satisfaction, worthwhile and happiness yesterday scores, and the highest anxiety scores.

Household income

This is a measure which is frequently used to indicate households which are in relative poverty and being poor can affect an individual's well-being. While this may be used as the headline measure for well-being, other thresholds of measurement may be used in analysis of this domain, together with different household structures and the number of young people living in households within these thresholds. Analysis by ONS illustrated the changes to median household income[1] before and after housing costs since 1994/95 (ONS 2012c). It explains that the fall in median income between 2009/10 and 2010/11 was mainly due to earnings increasing by less than the relatively high inflation rate over the period. The recent decrease in the proportion of households with less than 60% of median income is due not to these households' incomes increasing, but as a result of the fluctuations in the median income threshold. Further analysis can be found in "The Effects of Taxes and Benefits on Household Income, 2011/12" (ONS 2013e).

Subjective measures

These measures were chosen to reflect whether household income is perceived as sufficient. The questions about satisfaction with household income and how people find their financial situation were asked of all individuals aged 16 and over, regardless if they lived in their own household or with their parents. There is debate around whether the relationship between income and well-being is absolute or relative. Income may relate to subjective well-being because it aids individuals in meeting basic needs. However, it may also relate to well-being because people compare themselves to other people around them based on income (Diener, E, et al 1993).

Other potential measures

Debt

Debt is a large and important factor which influences a person's life choices. In a recent analysis of a survey of those who are in debt, the Money Advice Service (MAS) suggested that 21% of those in debt were aged 18-24. They classified 11.3% of the over-indebted population as 'Struggling Students'. The survey found that for over half of 'struggling students,' keeping up with bills is a heavy burden and nearly three-quarters have fallen behind with credit commitments in the last three months. The MAS classified a further 9.8% of the over-indebted population as 'First Time Workers'. The survey found that for half of first time workers, keeping up with bills is a heavy burden and nearly four in five have fallen behind with credit commitments in the last three months. No measure of indebtedness which meets the criteria for measures of national well-being has been identified.

Notes

1. Median household income is the middle point of the range of household income in the UK. Half of UK households have less than the median and half have more. Household income is equivalised to take account of the different sizes and composition of households.

Education and Skills

Education and skills proposed measures

Measure	Geographic coverage	Source	Latest year	Latest data
Proportion who have attained National Qualifications Framework level 2 qualifications by age 19	England	Department for Education	2012	85%
Proportion who have attained National Qualifications Framework level 3 qualifications by age 19	England	Department for Education	2012	58%
Proportion of young people not in education, employment or training (NEET)	England	ONS	July–Sept 2013	15%

Download table

 XLS format
(26.5 Kb)

Education and skills were highlighted in the National Debate as being important to well-being. Having a good education and a strong skills set equips you for the future, and is associated with a higher income, greater emotional resilience, and better physical health (Sabates, R and Hammond, C, 2008), all of which may have an impact upon personal well-being.

For many 16 to 24 year olds, the 'emerging adult' lifestage is a period of continued education, which should be a route to increasing one's personal well-being. "Learning encourages social interaction and increases self-esteem and feelings of competency. Behaviour directed by personal goals to achieve something new has been shown to increase reported life satisfaction" (Michaelson, J., et al, New Economics Foundation, 2009). Most 16 year olds will have completed compulsory education and many will aspire to pursue higher and further education qualifications. By the age of 24, studies will be, on the whole, completed and the learning and skills obtained during this period will be put to use. There is contradictory evidence about the effects of education on personal well-being, with some studies suggesting that middle-level education is related to the highest levels of well-being. Although there is a positive association between education and life satisfaction, Sabates and Hammond suggest that "Maybe education has negative as well as positive impacts, for example through raising expectations that are not met and by leading to occupations that carry high levels of stress."

Qualifications

The proportion of young people achieving the equivalent of five GCSEs graded A*-C (National Qualifications Framework Level 2) or the equivalent of 2 or more A-levels by age 19 are key measures in the Department for Education's business plan[1] and the Government Social Mobility Strategy[2]. In recent years there has been much debate around 'grade-inflation'; that exams are getting easier and the threshold for a passing grade is lower. Baird et al (2013) at the Oxford University Centre for Educational Assessment found that there is no definitive evidence for grade inflation. They argue that, "rises in grades might be explained by harder work, better teaching, more support for learning and higher aspirations. But examinations could be easier, or they could be testing the wrong kind of learning in a target-driven education system."

Not in Education, Employment or Training

Being not in education, employment or training – NEET – is a measure specific to young people and can impact upon many areas of their well-being. "Young People in the Labour Market" (ONS 2014c) explains the main reasons for inactivity among young people no longer in full time education. The Princes Trust Macquarie Youth Index 2014 states "Young people's confidence in their qualifications remained at its lowest ever point for the second year running." Furthermore, it found that young people with fewer than five GCSEs graded A*-C were less happy with their work or employment than young people overall and young people classified as NEET ranked lowest in terms of happiness and confidence.

Other potential measures

Aspirations

Aspirations are important for young people to provide them with goals and a direction in life. Research has found that young people from disadvantaged backgrounds often have the same aspirations as those from more well-off backgrounds but lack the mechanisms and support to achieve those aspirations. Croll and Fuller (2010) found that "at all levels of ability, young people from disadvantaged backgrounds are less likely to believe that they can be successful educationally and in the world of work". Having and achieving aspirations is important to a number of areas of well-being but to understand the full picture we would also have to measure whether young people have the opportunities to achieve their aspirations.

University entrants

Going to university and achieving a degree is often a key aspiration for young people. As well as being a step towards their future career, university life helps young people to gain new experiences become self-aware and independent.

Notes

1. Department for Education business plan, 2012

2. Cabinet Office, Government Social Mobility Strategy, 2011

About the ONS Measuring National Well-being Programme

National well-being

This article is published as part of the ONS Measuring National Well-being Programme.

The programme aims to produce accepted and trusted measures of the well-being of the nation - how the UK as a whole is doing. It is about looking at 'GDP and beyond' and includes:

*   Greater analysis of the national economic accounts, especially to understand household income, expenditure and wealth.
*   Further accounts linked to the national accounts, including the UK Environmental Accounts and valuing household production and 'human capital'.
*   Quality of life measures, looking at different areas of national well-being such as health, relationships, job satisfaction, economic security, education environmental conditions.
*   Working with others to include the measurement of the well-being of children and young people as part of national well-being.
*   Measures of 'personal well-being' - individuals' assessment of their own well-being.
*   Headline indicators to summarise national well-being and the progress we are making as a society.

The programme is underpinned by a communication and engagement workstream, providing links with Cabinet Office and policy departments, international developments, the public and other stakeholders. The programme is working closely with Defra on the measurement of 'sustainable development' to provide a complete picture of national well-being, progress and sustainable development.

Find out more on the Measuring National Well-being website pages.

References

Arnett, J.J, (2004) Emerging Adulthood; The Winding Road from Late Teens through the Twenties, New York, Oxford University Press

Beaumont, J., Lofts, H., (2013c) Measuring National Well-being - Health, ONS.

Croll, P and Fuller, C., (2012) Understanding Young People's Aspirations.

Department for Education (2012) Business plan key measures.

Deputy Prime Minister's Office (2011) Social Mobility Strategy.

Diener, E., Sandvik, E., Seidlitz. L., Diener, M. (1993) The relationship between income and subjective well-being: Relative or absolute?

Donovan, R., (2014c) Young People in the Labour Market ONS

Health Scotland (2008) Warwick-Edinburgh Mental Well-being Scale.

Health Survey for England (2012) Trend tables.

Helliwell, J.F., Putnam, R.D., (2004) The Social Context of Wellbeing.

Humby, P., (2013d) An Analysis of Under 18 Conceptions and their Links to Measures of Deprivation, England and Wales, 2008-10 ONS

Jackson, C., (2007) The General Health Questionnaire.

Loughton, T. (2010) Speech to the Fatherhood Institute.

Marks, N. (2008) The New Economics Foundation's Five Ways to Well-being.

Mental Health Foundation: Children and Young People.

Michaelson, J., Abdullah, S., Steuer, N., Thompson, S., and Marks, N., (2009) National Accounts of Well-being - bringing real wealth onto the balance sheet, London, NEF.

Money Advice Service (2013) Indebted lives: the complexities of life in debt.

National Alliance for Arts Health and Wellbeing (2012) A Charter for Arts, Health and Wellbeing.

OECD (2009) Special Focus: Measuring Leisure in OECD Countries.

Oguz, S., Merad, S., Snape, D., (2013b) Measuring National Well-being – What matters most to Personal Well-being? ONS 2013.

ONS (2012b) Consultation on proposed domains and measures of national well-being: responses received.

ONS (2013a) Population Estimates for UK, England and Wales, Scotland and Northern Ireland, Mid-2001 to Mid-2010 Revised.

ONS (2014a) Statistical Release: Young adults living with parents.

ONS (2014b) Vacancies and Unemployment.

ONS (2013e) Statistical Release: The Effects of Taxes and Benefits on Household Income 2011/12.

Oxford University Centre for Educational Assessment (2013) Research evidence relating to proposals for reform of the GCSE.

Randall, C., (2012a) Measuring National Well-being – Our Relationships ONS.

Sabates, R., Hammond, C., (2008) The Impact of Lifelong Learning on Happiness and Well-being.

Seddon, C., (2012c) Measuring National Well-being – Personal Finance, ONS.

Sport England Sport and Health.

The Prince's Trust (2014) The Prince's Trust Macquarie Youth Index 2014.

The King's Fund Life Expectancy.

Victim Support How crime can affect you.

World Health Organisation Health Impact Assessment.

Background notes

1. Authors: Rachel Beardsmore and Helen Lofts

2. The four main estimates of personal well-being are based on data from the Annual Population Survey (APS) which includes responses from around 165,000 people. This provides a large representative sample of adults aged 16 and over who live in residential households in the UK. These questions allow people to make an assessment of their life overall, as well as providing an indication of their day-to-day emotions. Although 'yesterday' may not be a typical day for any one individual, the large sample means that these differences 'average out' and provide a reliable assessment of the anxiety and happiness of the adult population in the UK over the year.

3. **Understanding Society, the UK Household Longitudinal Study**

    Understanding Society is a unique and valuable academic study that captures important information every year about the social and economic circumstances and attitudes of people living in 40,000 UK households. It also collects additional health information from around 20,000 of the people who take part.

Information from the longitudinal survey is primarily used by academics, researchers and policy makers in their work, but the findings are of interest to a much wider group of people including those working in the third sector, health practitioners, business, the media and the general public.

Key facts

- 40,000 households – 2,640 postcode sectors in England, Scotland and Wales – 2,400 addresses from Northern Ireland
- £48.9 million funding (until 2015)
- Approximately 3 billion data points of information
- Innovation Panel of 1,500 respondents
- Participants aged 10 and older
- Building on 18 years of British Household Panel Survey
- 35-60 minutes: the average time to complete each face to face interview

How does it work?

Interviews began in 2009 with all eligible members of the selected households.

- Adults are interviewed every 12 months either face to face or over the phone using Computer Assisted Interviewing.
- 10 to15 year olds fill in a paper self-completion questionnaire.

    From 2010 some 20,000 participants aged over 16 also received nurse visits and provided a blood sample and some basic physical measurements (height, weight, blood pressure, grip strength).

Data used in this analysis

The data in this analysis is from the adult self completion questionnaire of Waves 1-3 of the Survey and has been weighted using the cross-sectional adult main interview weight.

More information about the UKHLS.

4. Art and cultural activities include: heritage, museums, galleries, libraries and arts (includes attending e.g. theatre, and participating, e.g. painting).

5. Details of the policy governing the release of new data are available by visiting www.statisticsauthority.gov.uk/assessment/code-of-practice/index.html or from the Media Relations Office email: media.relations@ons.gsi.gov.uk

Copyright

National Well-being Measures, March 2014

Author Name(s): **Tammy Powell, Office for National Statistics**

Abstract

This article is published as part of the ONS Measuring National Well-being Programme. The programme aims to produce accepted and trusted measures of the well-being of the nation - how the UK as a whole is doing. The article outlines the latest changes to the measures of national well-being and is part of the ongoing refinement of measures. Also published today is an updated National Well-being Wheel of Measures and National Well-being interactive charts. Get all the tables for this publication in the data section of this publication.

Introduction

The aim of the MNW programme is to 'develop and publish an accepted and trusted set of National Statistics which help people to monitor national well-being'. Critical to achieving this aim is the development of an agreed set of domains and measures.

The initial list of national well-being domains and measures was developed based on responses to the National Debate (which took place between November 2010 and April 2011), existing research and international initiatives.

The measures were the subject of a public consultation which ran between October 2011 and January 2012. A summary and discussion of responses received was published in July 2012, Measuring National Well-being: Report on consultation responses on proposed domains and measures. (524.4 Kb Pdf) No significant changes were made to the set of measures at that time.

In May 2013 Measuring National Well-being – Review of domains and measures, 2013 was published. This honoured a commitment made in November 2012 in Measuring National Well-being: Life in the UK, 2012 that ONS would 'review and further refine domains and measures of well-being and the criteria used to select them'. Feedback was invited on the changes made in this review, resulting in the further refined set of measures published in September 2013.

Updated national well-being measures data will be published in Spring and Autumn each year.

ONS seek and welcome feedback about the national well-being domains and measures. Please send comments to nationalwell-being@ons.gov.uk

Summary of changes to measures

This section summarises the changes made to national well-being measures since the last publication in September 2013.

- The calculation for 'Has a spouse, family member or friend to rely on if they have a serious problem' has changed.
- The calculation for 'Real net national income per head' measure in the Economy domain has changed.

No measures have been added or deleted since the publication in September 2013.

Explanation of changes to measures

This section explains the changes made to national well-being measures since the last publication in September 2013.

1. The calculation for 'Has a spouse, family member or friend to rely on if they have a serious problem' has changed.

The calculation used for the September 2013 release included non respondents. The figure that is being published for March 2014 will now exclude the non responders.

2. The calculation for 'Real net national income per head' measure in the Economy domain has changed.

On advice from ONS National Accounts who provide the data, we have used a different population estimate for calculating this measure.

Details of which measures data has been updated since the September 2013 publication can be found in the National Well-being Measures, March 2014 (1.58 Mb Excel sheet) spreadsheet.

Where to find national Well-being measures data

There are 41 measures of national well-being split across 10 domains. Information and data for the latest release of domains and measures is available in various formats:

- National Well-being Measures Excel file (1.58 Mb Excel sheet) containing the latest and time series data plus links to data sources.
- Interactive wheel of measures which includes data for the latest and previous periods plus time series charts.
- Wheel of measures PDF (2.8 Mb Pdf) 'print and keep' version showing the latest data.
- Interactive charts showing the latest data for selected measures by region and country.

About the ONS Measuring National Well-being Programme

NWB logo 2

This article is published as part of the ONS Measuring National Well-being Programme.

The programme aims to produce accepted and trusted measures of the well-being of the nation - how the UK as a whole is doing. It is about looking at 'GDP and beyond' and includes:

- Greater analysis of the national economic accounts, especially to understand household income, expenditure and wealth.
- Further accounts linked to the national accounts, including the UK Environmental Accounts and valuing household production and 'human capital'.
- Quality of life measures, looking at different areas of national well-being such as health, relationships, job satisfaction, economic security, education environmental conditions.
- Working with others to include the measurement of the well-being of children and young people as part of national well-being.
- Measures of 'personal well-being' - individuals' assessment of their own well-being.
- Headline indicators to summarise national well-being and the progress we are making as a society.

The programme is underpinned by a communication and engagement workstream, providing links with Cabinet Office and policy departments, international developments, the public and other stakeholders. The programme is working closely with Defra on the measurement of 'sustainable development' to provide a complete picture of national well-being, progress and sustainable development.

Find out more on the [Measuring National Well-being](#) website pages.

Background notes

2. Details of the policy governing the release of new data are available by visiting www.statisticsauthority.gov.uk/assessment/code-of-practice/index.html or from the Media Relations Office email: media.relations@ons.gsi.gov.uk

18 March 2014

Copyright

Office for
National Statistics

Measuring National Well-being: Life in the UK, 2014

Author Name(s): Chris Randall, Ann Corp and Abigail Self, Office for National Statistics

Abstract

Measuring National Well-being: Life in the UK, 2014 provides the latest overview of well-being in the UK today. A snapshot of well-being is provided across the 10 domains of well-being (for example, 'Health', 'Where we live', 'What we do'); together with a brief overview of international comparisons. The report is the second summary of life in the UK to be delivered by the Measuring National Well-being programme and will be updated annually.

Introduction

The Measuring National Well-being programme began in November 2010 with the aim to 'develop and publish an accepted and trusted set of National Statistics which help people understand and monitor well-being'.

The Programme has developed a set of 41 headline measures, organised by ten 'domains' including topics such as 'Health', 'What we do' and 'Where we live'. The measures include both objective data (for example, number of crimes against the person per 1,000 adults) and subjective data (for example, percentage who felt safe walking alone after dark). Measures are updated with latest data in March and September each year. The 'Life in the UK' report accompanies the March update and takes a closer look at measures within each domain.

This report summarises well-being in each of the ten domains. Latest data are provided for each measure, with more detailed commentary focused on one measure per domain. The final section provides an overview of European comparability.

Where possible, data are presented for the UK. Where this is not the case, the best available geography is used. Data are the latest available at February 2014.

Feedback is welcome at nationalwell-being@ons.gov.uk

Also released today

- National Well-being Measures Excel file (1.58 Mb Excel sheet) containing the latest data and time series data and links to data sources.

- [Interactive wheel of measures](#) which includes data for the latest and previous periods plus time series charts.
- [Wheel of measures PDF (2.8 Mb Pdf)](#) 'print and keep' version showing the latest data.
- [Interactive charts](#) showing the latest data for selected measures by region and country.

Overview

In May 2013, the Measuring National Well-being programme highlighted that the factors most strongly associated with personal well-being are self-reported health (which had the strongest association), employment status and relationship status[1]. The 'Life in the UK 2014' report shows that since 2010 the proportion satisfied with their health has fallen (from 68.3% in 2009/10 to 58.6% in 2011/12), a smaller proportion of the economically active are unemployed (7.2% in October to December 2013 down from 7.8% in October to December 2010) and most have someone to rely on in a crisis (87.0% in 2010/11).

The Measuring National Well-being national debate highlighted a range of other things that 'mattered', for example, economic security and job satisfaction, work-life balance, education and training, and local and natural environment.

Life in the UK 2014 shows that the majority (77.0%) were satisfied with their lives in the UK in 2012/13, an increase from 75.9% in 2011/12.

In 2011–12 median household income in Great Britain was £23,208. Between 2010/11 and 2011/12 the proportion in the UK satisfied with their income fell (from 57.3% to 52.9%) and around 1 in 10 (10.9% in 2011/12) reported finding it difficult to get by financially. Over the same period, the proportion satisfied with their job remained around 77% while the proportion satisfied with the amount of leisure time fell from 60.9% to 58.8%.

In England the proportion engaging with the arts or cultural activities remained at around 8 in 10 (83.2% in 2012/13) and participation in sport at 35.7% in 2012–13. The proportion volunteering more than once in the last 12 months in the UK in 2010/11 was 16.7%.

In the UK in 2011/12, around 6 in 10 (59%) had 5 or more GCSEs Grade A* to C including English and Maths and in 2013 nearly 1 in 10 (9.3%) had no formal educational qualifications. Human Capital – which is the value of individuals, skills, knowledge and competences in the labour market fell between 2011 and 2012 from £18.0 trillion to £17.9 trillion.

The number of crimes against the person in England and Wales - fell between 2011/12 and 2012/13 (from 83 to 76 per 1,000 adults) and in 2011/12, fewer of us (62.9%) in the UK felt a sense of belonging to our neighbourhood, compared with 66.0% in 2009/10. The proportion of household waste recycled in England remained at around 43% between 2011/12 and 2012/13 but this represents a large growth since 2000/01 where only 11.2% was recycled.

The proportion who trust in Government was 1 in 4 (24%) in the UK in Autumn 2013. Voter turnout in UK general elections, though higher in 1950, has remained at around 6 in 10 for the last two General Elections (61.1% in 2010).

Internationally, the report shows that the UK ranks above the EU average in areas such as life satisfaction, recycling rates, trust in Government and satisfaction with accommodation. The UK are below the EU average in households making ends meet, perceived health status, and support if needed advice about a serious personal or family matter.

The Commission on the Measurement of Economic Performance and Social Progress (Stiglitz, Sen, Fitoussi, 2009)[2] stimulated interest in well-being and highlighted the need to acknowledge that people value things differently. In keeping with this, the priority or weight placed on any one measure or domain, or 'what matters' and what this means for UK well-being overall has not been included at this stage. The Measuring National Well-being programme is developing methods to aid users to interpret changes to National Well-being.

Notes

1. Measuring National Well-being - What matters most to Personal Well-being?

2. www.stiglitz-sen-fitoussi.fr/en/index.htm

Key points

Life satisfaction

- In the UK, 77.0% adults aged 16 and over rated their life satisfaction as 7 or more out of 10 in 2012/13, an increase from 75.9% in 2011/12.
- In 2012/13 the average rating of life satisfaction by UK adults aged 16 and over was 7.5 out of 10, with the lowest average rating in the 45 to 54 age group (7.1 out of 10) and the highest in the 16 to 19 and 65 to 79 age groups (both 7.8 out of 10).

Someone to rely on

- In the UK, 87% of adults aged 16 and over in 2010/11 had a spouse, family member or friend to rely on if they have a serious problem.
- In the UK in 2010/11 those aged 65 to 74 had the highest proportion with a spouse, family member or friend to rely on if they have a serious problem (92.3%) and those aged 16–24 had the lowest proportion (82.2%).

Satisfaction with health

- In the UK, 58.6% of adults aged 16 and over were somewhat, mostly or completely satisfied with their general health in 2011/12, a decrease from 65.6% in 2010/11 and 68.3% in 2009/10.
- In the UK in 2011/12 those aged 45 to 54 were most likely to report dissatisfaction with their general health (38.3%), a higher proportion than all older age groups - 55 to 64 (37.3%), 65 to 74 (33.3 %) and 75 and over (35.1%).

Volunteering

- In the UK, 16.7% of people aged 16 and over volunteered more than once in the 12 months prior to interview in 2010/11.
- Among the UK countries in 2010/11 England had the highest proportion who volunteered more than once in the last 12 months (17.0%) and Wales had the lowest (13.3%).

Satisfaction with accommodation

- 91.2% were very or fairly satisfied with their accommodation in England in 2011–12, an increase from 90.8% in 2010–11 and 90.2% in 2008–09.
- In England in 2011–12 owner occupiers were most satisfied with their accommodation at 95.7%, compared with 83.1% of private renters and 80.7% of all social renters.

Getting by financially

- In the UK, 10.9% of people found it very or quite difficult to get by financially in 2011/12, a decrease from 11.6% in 2010/11 and 12.3% in 2009/10.
- In the UK in 2011/12, those aged 25 to 44 were more likely to report finding it very or quite difficult to get by financially (14.6%), while those aged 75 were least likely (2.7%).

Real Net National Income per head

- Real National Net income per head was £20,725 in the UK in 2012, a decrease of £747 from £21,472 in 2011.

No educational qualifications

- The proportion of UK residents aged 16–64 who had no educational qualification in 2013 was 9.3%, an increase from 2012 (9.2%) and an overall decrease from 2008 (13.1%).
- Among the UK countries in 2012–2013, England had the lowest proportion with no qualifications (9.2%) and Northern Ireland had the highest (17.3%) in 2013.

Trust in government

- In the UK, 24% of people aged 15 and over reported that they 'tended to trust' the government in the autumn of 2013 – an increase from 22% in spring 2013 and a decrease from 25% in Autumn 2012.

Recycling

- In England, 43.2% of household waste was recycled in 2012/13 – an increase from 43.0% in 2011/12 and 11.2% in 2000/01.

European comparisons

- Over 6 in 10 people (62.7%) aged 16 and over in the UK rated their health status as very good or good, just behind the EU–28 average of 64.0% in 2011.

- Just over 8 in 10 (80.2%) of people aged 16 and over in the UK rated their satisfaction with their accommodation as 7 or more out of 10, higher than the EU–28 average of 76.9% in 2011.

Next steps

The Measuring National Well-being programme will continue to develop and deliver a suite of outputs covering well-being across the economy, society and the environment. Upcoming development work includes:

- Analysis of inequalities in personal well-being.
- Continued work to assess change in measures of national well-being.
- Report on international comparisons of well-being.
- Report on economic well-being.
- Development of Natural Capital Statistics.
- Development of household satellite accounts including transport and housing.
- Estimates of Human Capital.

Personal well-being

Domain overview and importance

Personal (or subjective) well-being concerns peoples' self-reported assessment of their own well-being, for example, by asking about their life satisfaction, happiness, and psychological wellbeing.

The importance of measuring subjective well-being has gained momentum internationally. The report of the Commission for the Measurement of Economic Performance and Social Progress stated in 2009 that 'it is possible to collect meaningful and reliable data on subjective as well as objective well-being. Subjective well-being encompasses different aspects (cognitive evaluations of one's life, happiness, satisfaction, positive emotions such as joy and pride, and negative emotions such as pain and worry).

Table 1: Measures included in the 'Personal well-being' domain

United Kingdom

	2011/12	2012/13
Medium/high (7 to 10 out of 10) rating of satisfaction with their lives overall[1]	75.9%	77.0%
Source: Annual Population Survey, Office for National Statistics		

	2011/12	2012/13
Medium/high (7 to 10 out of 10) rating of how worthwhile the things they do are[1]	80.0%	80.7%
Source: Annual Population Survey, Office for National Statistics		

	2011/12	2012/13
Rated their happiness yesterday as medium/high (7 to 10 out of 10)[1]	71.1%	71.6%
Source: Annual Population Survey, Office for National Statistics		

	2011/12	2012/13
Rated their anxiety yesterday as low (0 to 3 out of 10)[1]	60.1%	61.5%
Source: Annual Population Survey, Office for National Statistics		

	2008	2009/10
Population mental well-being (average rating out of 35)	24.3	25.2

Source: Understanding Society,
the UK Household Longitudinal
Study

Table notes:

1. Adults aged 16 and over were asked 'Overall, how satisfied are you with your life nowadays?', 'Overall, to what extent do you feel the things you do in your life are worthwhile?', 'Overall, how happy did you feel yesterday?' and 'Overall, how anxious did you feel yesterday?' where 0 is 'not at all' and 10 is 'completely'.

Download table

 XLS format
(61.5 Kb)

The full list of 41 National Well-being measures is available in various formats: an Excel file with time series data, an interactive wheel of measures which includes time series charts, and a PDF 'print and keep' version showing the latest data. Interactive graphs are also available showing selected measures by region and country. All are available at www.ons.gov.uk/well-being

Focus on 'Life satisfaction'

Why this measure?

Life satisfaction measures how people evaluate their life as a whole rather than their current feelings. It captures a reflective assessment of which life circumstances and conditions are important for personal well-being.

Has it changed over time?

Between 2011/12 and 2012/13 there was an overall improvement in life satisfaction. The proportion of people rating their life satisfaction as 7 or more out of 10 rose from 75.9% to 77.0%. Over the same period there was a decrease in people rating their life satisfaction as 4 or less out of 10. This fell from 6.6% to 5.8%.

Breakdown by distribution of responses

Figure 1: Distribution of responses for life satisfaction (1), 2012/13

United Kingdom

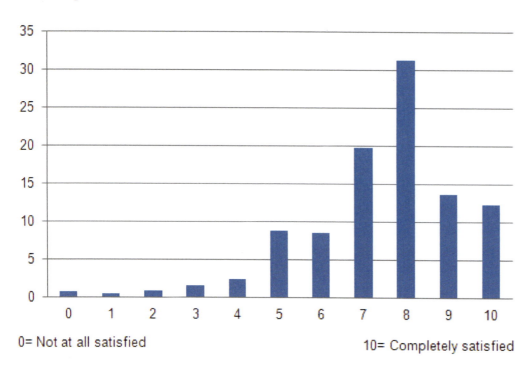

0= Not at all satisfied   10= Completely satisfied

Source: Annual Population Survey (APS) - Office for National Statistics

Notes:

1. Adults aged 16 and over were asked 'Overall, how satisfied are you with your life nowadays?' where 0 is 'not at all' and 10 is 'completely'. All data is weighted. Non-respondents are not included.

Download chart

 XLS format
(26 Kb)

Additional breakdowns

In 2012/13:

-   The average rating of life satisfaction for all adults aged 16 and over was 7.5 out of 10.
-   On average, women have higher life satisfaction than men (7.5 and 7.4 out of 10 respectively).
-   People aged 16 to 19 and 65 to 79 rated their life satisfaction higher than any other age group at 7.8 out of 10.
-   People aged 45 to 54 rated their life satisfaction lower than any other age at 7.1 out of 10.
-   The White and Indian respondents are on average the most satisfied with their lives (7.5 out of 10) while the Black/African/Caribbean/Black British respondents are the least satisfied (6.9 out of 10).

- Northern Ireland had proportionately more people than any other country in the UK rating their life satisfaction as very high (9 or 10 out of 10) (33.1%).
- Wales had proportionately more people than any other country in the UK rating their life satisfaction as very low (0-4 out of 10) (6.7%).
- Among the English regions, the South West had the highest proportions of people giving the highest ratings of 9 or 10 out of 10 for life satisfaction (27.9%).
- Among the English regions, the North East had proportionately more people who rated their life satisfaction as 4 or less out of 10 (7.0%).

Our relationships

Domain overview and importance

The amount and quality of social connections with people around us are an essential part of our well-being. This was highlighted in the Office for National Statistics National Debate on Measuring National Well-being. When people were asked what mattered most for the measurement of National Well-being, nearly 9 in 10 (89%) reported 'having good connections with friends and relatives'.

Table 2: Measures included in the 'Our relationships' domain

United Kingdom

	2003	2007	2011
Average rating of satisfaction with family life (average rating out of 10)	7.9	8.2	8.2
Source: Eurofound, European Quality of Life Survey			

	2003	2007	2011
Average rating of satisfaction with social life (average rating out of 10)	7.0	8.0	7.0
Source: Eurofound, European Quality of Life Survey			

	2010/11
Has a spouse, family member or friend to rely on if they have a serious problem	87.0%
Source: Understanding Society, the UK Household Longitudinal Study	

Download table

 XLS format
(26.5 Kb)

The full list of 41 National Well-being measures is available in various formats: an Excel file with time series data, an interactive wheel of measures which includes time series charts, and a PDF 'print and keep' version showing the latest data. Interactive graphs are also available showing selected measures by region and country. All are available at www.ons.gov.uk/well-being

Focus on 'Have a spouse, family member or friend to rely on if they have a serious problem'

Why this measure?

Social relationships with family and friends are an important part of life which in turn may affect individual well-being.

'Social connections, including marriage, of course, but not limited to that, are among the most robust correlates of subjective well-being. People who have close friends and confidants, friendly neighbours and supportive co-workers are less likely to experience sadness, loneliness, low self-esteem and problems with eating and sleeping', Helliwell and Putnam, 2004.

Breakdown by age

Figure 2: Percentage of people that have a spouse, family member or friend to rely on if they have a serious problem (1): by age 2010/11

United Kingdom

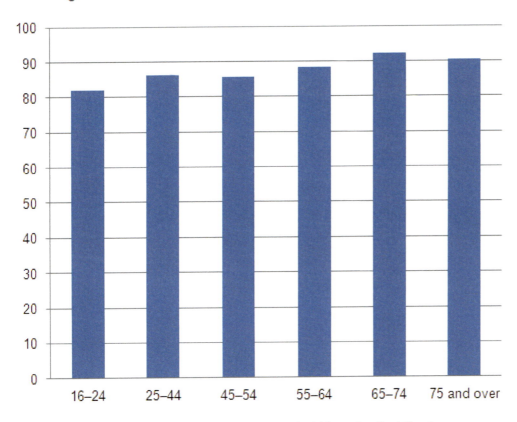

Percentages

Source: Understanding Society, the UK Household Longitudinal Study

Notes:

1. Respondents aged 16 and over were asked 'Do you have a spouse, family member or friend to rely on if you have a serious problem?'

Download chart

 XLS format

(28 Kb)

In the UK in 2010/11, just over 9 in 10 people (92.3%) aged 65 to 74 had a spouse, family member or friend to rely on if they had a serious problem. This compared with just over 8 in 10 (82.2%) of those aged 16 to 24.

Additional breakdowns

In 2010/11:

- 85.9% of men and 88.0% of women aged 16 and over had a spouse, family member or friend to rely on if they had a serious problem.
- Among the UK countries, 88.5% of people aged 16 and over had a spouse, family member or friend to rely on if they had a serious problem compared with 86.9% in England, 86.8% in Northern Ireland and 86.2% in Wales.
- Among the English regions, 82.7% of people aged 16 and over in London had a spouse, family member or friend to rely on if they had a serious problem, compared with 88.5% in the South West.

Health

Domain overview and importance

When people were asked what mattered most for the measurement of National Well-being, in the Office for National Statistics National Debate on Measuring National Well-being, 'Health' was the most common response with 89% of respondents.

The World Health Organisation defines health as 'a state of complete physical, mental and social well-being and not merely the absence of disease or infirmity'.

Table 3: Measures included in the 'Health' domain

United Kingdom

	2000–02	2005–07	2008–10
Healthy life expectancy at birth (male)	60.7	61.4	63.5
Healthy life expectancy at birth (female)	62.4	62.9	65.7
Source: Office for National Statistics			

	Jan to Mar 2000	Jan to Mar 2012	Jan to Mar 2013
Reported a long term illness and a disability	18.5%	20.0%	19.7%
Source: Labour Force Survey, Office for National Statistics			

	2009/10	2010/11	2011/12
Somewhat, mostly or completely satisfied with their health	68.3%	65.6%	58.6%
Source: Understanding Society, the UK Household Longitudinal Study			

	2009/10	2010/11	2011/12
Some evidence indicating probable psychological disturbance or mental ill health	18.0%	18.4%	18.6%
Source: Understanding Society, the UK Household Longitudinal Study			

Download table

XLS XLS format
(29 Kb)

The full list of 41 National Well-being measures is available in various formats: an Excel file with time series data, an interactive wheel of measures which includes time series charts, and a PDF 'print and keep' version showing the latest data. Interactive graphs are also available showing selected measures by region and country. All are available at www.ons.gov.uk/well-being

Focus on 'Satisfaction with health'

Why this measure?

People's own assessment of their health is associated with their assessment of their overall life satisfaction.

'How people view their health was the most important factor related to personal well-being... People who reported very bad health had much lower ratings of life satisfaction, feelings that things were worthwhile, levels of happiness and higher ratings of anxiety on average than those who said their health was good', What matters most to personal well-being? Office for National Statistics, 2013.

Has it changed over time?

Between 2009/10 and 2011/12, people aged 16 and over in the UK who reported that they were somewhat, mostly or completely satisfied with their health had fallen by 9.7 percentage points from 68.3% to 58.6%. The proportion of people that reported that they were mostly dissatisfied with their health more than doubled from 6.3% to 13.5% over the same period.

Breakdown by age

Figure 3: Satisfaction with health (1): by age, 2011–12

United Kingdom

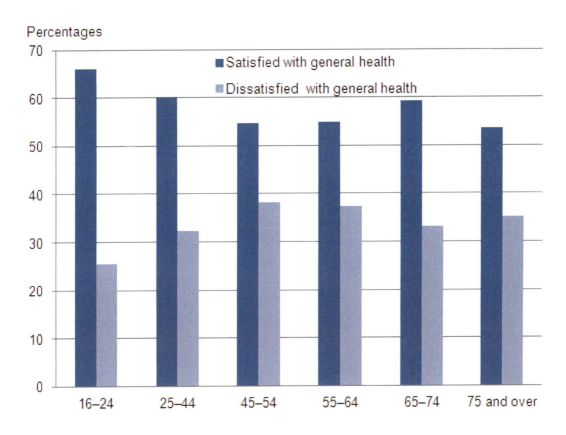

Source: Understanding Society, the UK Household Longitudinal Study

Notes:

1. Those who reported that they were either 'somewhat, mostly or completely satisfied' or 'somewhat, mostly or completely dissatisfied' with their general health. This chart does not include those who were neither satisfied nor dissatisfied.

Download chart

 XLS format
(28 Kb)

Satisfaction with health varied by age group in the UK. Two-thirds (66.1%) of people aged 16 to 24 reported that they were somewhat, mostly or completely satisfied with their general health in 2011–12. This compares with 54.7% of those aged 45 to 54, 55.0% of those aged aged 55 to 64 and 53.7% of those aged 75 and over. Those aged 45 to 54 and 55 to 64 were more likely to have reported that they were somewhat, mostly or completely dissatisfied with their general health at 38.3% and 37.3% respectively.

Additional breakdowns

In 2011/12:

- Around 6 in 10 men and women aged 16 and over that reported they were somewhat, mostly or completely satisfied with their general health at 60.0% and 57.4% respectively.
- Among the UK countries, people aged 16 and over in Northern Ireland were more likely to be somewhat, mostly or completely satisfied with their general health at 62.4%. This compares to 58.9% in England, 57.0% in Scotland and 55.4% in Wales.

What we do

Domain overview and importance

Across the UK people live many different lifestyles based on individual choices, characteristics, personal preferences and circumstances. Individuals divide their time between various tasks and activities, including paid or unpaid employment, volunteering and various leisure activities. What we do in life shapes our lifestyles, our relationships with others and our overall well-being.

Table 4: Measures included in the 'What we do' domain

United Kingdom (unless specified)

	Oct-Dec 2010	Oct-Dec 2012	Oct-Dec 2013
Unemployment rate	7.8%	7.8%	7.2%
Source: Labour Force Survey, Office for National Statistics			
	2009/10	**2010/11**	**2011/12**
Somewhat, mostly or completely satisfied with their job	77.8%	78.5%	77.3%
Source: Understanding Society, the UK Household Longitudinal Study			
	2009/10	**2010/11**	**2011/12**
Somewhat, mostly or completely satisfied with their amount of leisure time	62.3%	60.9%	58.8%
Source: Understanding Society, the UK Household Longitudinal Study			
		2010/11	

			16.7%
Volunteered more than once in the last 12 months			

Source: Understanding Society, the UK Household Longitudinal Study

	2008/09	2011/12	2012/13
Engaged with/ participated in arts or cultural activity at least 3 times in last year (England)	80.8%	83.9%	83.2%

Source: Department for Culture, Media and Sport

	2005-06	2011–12	2012–13
Adult participation in 30 minutes of moderate intensity sport, once per week (England)	34.2%	36.0%	35.7%

Source: Sport England

Download table

 XLS format

(28 Kb)

The full list of 41 National Well-being measures is available in various formats: an Excel file with time series data, an interactive wheel of measures which includes time series charts, and a PDF 'print and keep' version showing the latest data. Interactive graphs are also available showing selected measures by region and country. All are available at www.ons.gov.uk/well-being

Focus on 'Volunteered more than once in the last 12 months'

Why this measure?

Volunteering may have benefits for both health and well-being and can make a difference to the lives of other people, the community or the environment.

'Volunteering is vital to charities and civil society, helps to strengthen local communities, and improves the wellbeing of individuals who participate' - Daniel Fujiwara, Paul Oroyemi and Ewen McKinnon, Wellbeing and Civil Society.

Breakdown by UK country and region

In 2010/11, 16.7% of people aged 16 and over in the UK did some sort of unpaid help or worked as a volunteer for an organisation or charity more than once in the 12 months prior to interview. In England 17.0% of people volunteered more than once a year compared to 15.7% in Scotland, 15.6% in Northern Ireland and 13.3% in Wales.

Figure 4: Volunteering more than once in the last 12 months (1): by UK country and region, 2010/11

United Kingdom

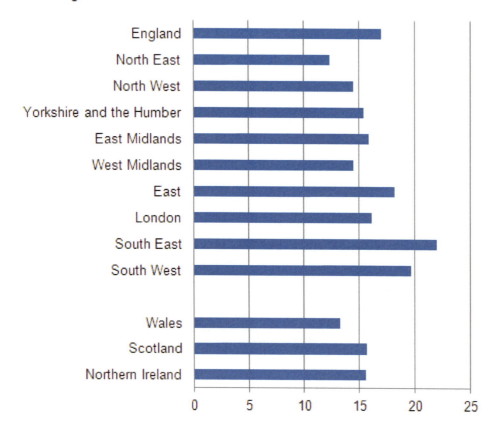

Source: Understanding Society, the UK Household Longitudinal Study

Notes:

1. Respondents who had in the last 12 months, given any unpaid help or worked as a volunteer for any type of local, national or international organisation or charity were asked 'Including any time spent at home or elsewhere, about how often over the last 12 months have you generally done something to help any of these organisations?' The chart includes those who volunteered more than once a in the year prior to interview as a proportion of all adults and does not include those who stated a one-off activity or those who helped or worked on a seasonal basis.

Download chart

XLS XLS format
(27.5 Kb)

Among the English regions, a higher proportion of people living in the South East (22.0%), the South West (19.7%) and the East of England (18.2%) volunteered more than once a year. People living in the North East were less likely to volunteer (12.3%).

Additional breakdowns

In 2010/11:

- Nearly 1 in 10 (9.0%) people aged 16 and over volunteered at least once a week, while 3.4% volunteered at least once a month.
- Women were more likely than men to volunteer more than once a year (17.6% and 15.6% respectively).
- Those aged 65 to 74 were more likely to volunteer more than once a year (22.3%), while those aged 25 to 44 were less likely (14.1%).

Where we live

Domain overview and importance

Where we live can have a significant impact on our sense of well-being. Homes which meet our individual needs and provide us with shelter and security are made all the better by having easy access to local shops and services, and safe and green spaces to walk or play in, which in turn can help people to live healthier and happier lives.

Table 5: Measures included in the 'Where we live' domain

United Kingdom (unless specified)

	2003/04	2011/12	2012/13
Crimes against the person (per 1,000 adults) (England and Wales)	107	83	76
Source: Crime Survey for England and Wales, Office for National Statistics			

	2009/10	2011/12	2012/13
Accessed natural environment at least once a week in the last 12 months (England)	54%	55%	55%
Source: Natural England			

		2009/10	2011/12
Agreed/agreed strongly they felt they belonged to their neighbourhood		66.0%	62.9%
Source: Understanding Society, the UK Household Longitudinal Study			

	2006/07	2011/12	2012/13
Felt fairly/very safe walking alone after dark (men)	82.9%	87.0%	84.8%
Felt fairly/very safe walking alone after dark (women)	56.0%	64.6%	56.8%
Source: Crime Survey for England and Wales, Office for National Statistics			

	2007	2010	2011

Households with good transport access to key services or work (2010 = 100) (England)	110	100	97
Source: Department for Transport			

	2008–09	2010–11	2011–12
Satisfaction with accommodation (England)	90.2%	90.8%	91.2%
Source: Department for Communities and Local Government			

Download table

 XLS format
(30.5 Kb)

The full list of 41 National Well-being measures is available in various formats: an Excel file with time series data, an interactive wheel of measures which includes time series charts, and a PDF 'print and keep' version showing the latest data. Interactive graphs are also available showing selected measures by region and country. All are available at www.ons.gov.uk/well-being

Focus on 'Satisfaction with accommodation'

Why this measure?

Satisfaction with our accommodation is important. Our homes are a place of refuge, entertainment and relaxation.

Shelter stated in their response to the Office for National Statistics consultation 'Proposed Domains and Headline Indicators for Measuring National Wellbeing' 'Housing is a key component of well-being... it is also linked to every aspect that has been identified by the ONS as key to measuring national well-being'.

Has it changed over time?

This measure has not changed significantly over the last four years, with the proportion of households that are satisfied with their accommodation being consistently high at around 90% to 91%.

Breakdown by tenure

Figure 5: Satisfaction with accommodation (1): by tenure, 2011–12

England

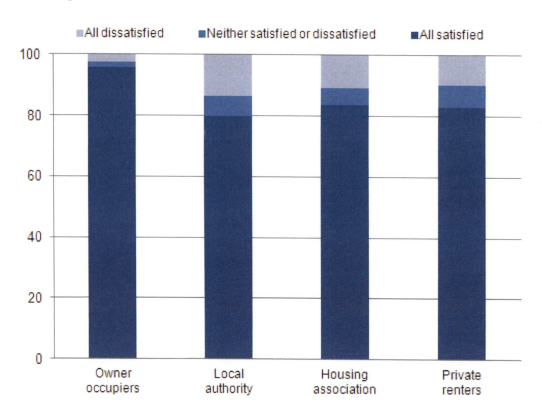

Source: English Housing Survey - Communities and Local Government

Notes:

1. Households were asked to rate their levels of satisfaction with their accommodation using a five-point scale where 1 = very satisfied and 5 = very dissatisfied.

Download chart

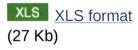 XLS format

(27 Kb)

In 2011–12, dissatisfaction with accommodation was more likely among households that rented. Local authority renters were the most likely to be dissatisfied (13.6%), followed by housing association renters (10.7%) and private renters (10.0%). Just 2.4% of owner occupiers were dissatisfied with their accommodation. Conversely, owner occupiers were most satisfied with their accommodation at 95.7%, compared with 83.1% of private renters and 80.7% of all social renters. However it must be noted that social renters reported on the English Housing Survey that there were more problems in their local area than other tenures, which may influence their overall satisfaction with the accommodation.

Additional breakdowns

In 2011–12:

- Older people are more likely to be satisfied with their accommodation. For example, 97.1% of people (household reference person[1]) aged 75 and over were satisfied with their accommodation compared to 79.7% of those aged 16 to 24.
- Satisfaction with accommodation varied by the ethnic group of the household reference person[1] from 74.1% of those in the black ethnic group to 88.4% in the Indian ethnic group to 92.3% in the white ethnic group in 2011–12.
- Satisfaction varied by household type with 94.7% of couples with no dependent children satisfied with their accommodation compared with 88.8% of couple households with dependent children.

Notes

1. Household reference person (HRP): The person in whose name the dwelling is owned or rented or who is otherwise responsible for the accommodation. In the case of joint owners and tenants, the person with the highest income is taken as the HRP. Where incomes are equal, the older is taken as the HRP. This procedure increases the likelihood that the HRP better characterises the household's social and economic position. The English Housing Survey definition of HRP is not consistent with the Census 2011, in which the HRP is chosen on basis of their economic activity. Where economic activity is the same, the older is taken as HRP, or if they are the same age, HRP is the first listed on the questionnaire.

Personal finance

Domain overview and importance

Personal finance refers to individuals and household consumption possibilities, both now and in the future, and is therefore driven by both income and wealth. It can have a significant impact on people's sense of well-being and the financial situation of the population is an important aspect of national well-being.

Table 6: Measures included in the 'Personal finance' domain

United Kingdom (unless specified)

	2002/03	2010/11	2011/12
Individuals in households with less than 60% of median income after housing costs	22%	21%	21%
Source: Department for Work and Pensions			

		2006/08	2008/10
Median wealth per household, including pension wealth (Great Britain)		£210,300	£232,400
Source: Wealth and Assets Survey, Office for National Statistics			

	2002–03	2010–11	2011–12
Median household income	£17,829	£22,671	£23,208
Source: Office for National Statistics			

	2009/10	2010/11	2011/12
Somewhat, mostly or completely satisfied with the income of their household	57.2%	57.3%	52.9%
Source: Understanding Society, the UK Household Longitudinal Study			

	2009/10	2010/11	2011/12
Report finding it quite or very difficult to get by financially	12.3%	11.6%	10.9%

Source: Understanding
Society, the UK
Household Longitudinal
Study

Download table

XLS XLS format
(19.5 Kb)

The full list of 41 National Well-being measures is available in various formats: an Excel file with time series data, an interactive wheel of measures which includes time series charts, and a PDF 'print and keep' version showing the latest data. Interactive graphs are also available showing selected measures by region and country. All are available at www.ons.gov.uk/well-being

Focus on 'Finding it quite or very difficult to get by financially'

Why this measure?

To have the financial means to comfortably attain a gratifying lifestyle is an important factor to many people's sense of well-being.

'Economic resources enhance people's freedom to choose the lives that they want to live and protect them against economic and personal risks' How's Life? 2013: Measuring Well-being, OECD.

Has it changed over time?

The proportion of people aged 16 and over in the UK who reported that they were finding it quite or very difficult to get by financially fell from 12.3% in 2009/10 to 10.9% in 2011/12. The proportion of people that reported that they were 'doing alright' increased from 32.9% to 34.9% over the same period.

Breakdown by age-group

Figure 6: Finding personal financial situation quite or very difficult: by age group (1), 2011/12

United Kingdom

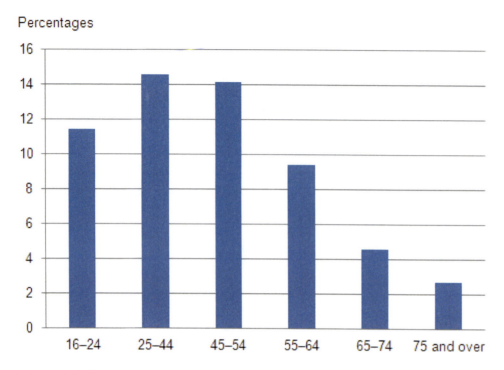

Source: Understanding Society, the UK Household Longitudinal Study

Notes:

1. Respondents were asked how well they were managing financially these days with responses 'living comfortably, doing alright, just about getting by, finding it quite difficult or finding it very difficult'.

Download chart

 XLS format

(26.5 Kb)

In 2011/12, 10.9% of those aged 16 and over in the UK reported that they were finding their financial situation quite or very difficult. The proportion finding their financial situation quite or very difficult varied considerably between the age groups. A higher percentage of those aged 16 to 24 (11.4%), 25 to 44 (14.6%) and 45 to 54 (14.1%) reported finding their financial situation quite or very difficult than the average for all aged 16 and over. For those aged 55 and above, a smaller proportion of each age group reported that they were finding their financial situation quite or very difficult, with the lowest proportion among those aged 75 and over (2.7%).

Additional breakdowns

In 2011/12:

- 10.5% of men reported finding their financial situation quite or very difficult compared with 11.3% of women.

- 11.0% of people aged 16 and over living in England reported finding their financial situation quite or very difficult. This compares with 10.5% in Scotland, 10.4% in Wales and 9.6% in Northern Ireland.
- Across the English regions, the proportion of people aged 16 and over who reported finding their financial situation quite or very difficult was highest in London (14.6%) and lowest in East Midlands (9.6%) and the North West (9.8%).

Economy

Domain overview and importance

The economy is the set of activities related to the production and distribution of goods and services. Its performance will impact everyone financially and has a direct role in people's material conditions, for example, housing, wealth, jobs and earnings.

Table 7: Measures included in the 'Economy' domain

United Kingdom

	2002	2011	2012
Real net national income per head	£20,347	£21,472	£20,725
Source: Office for National Statistics			

	2002/03	2011/12	2012/13
UK public sector net debt as a percentage of Gross Domestic Product	31.4%	70.9%	73.8%
Source: Office for National Statistics			

	Jan 2012	Jan 2013	Jan 2014
Inflation rate (as measured by the Consumer Price Index)	3.6%	2.7%	1.9%
Source: Office for National Statistics			

Download table

XLS XLS format
(27.5 Kb)

The full list of 41 National Well-being measures is available in various formats: an Excel file with time series data, an interactive wheel of measures which includes time series charts, and a PDF 'print and keep' version showing the latest data. Interactive graphs are also available showing selected measures by region and country. All are available at www.ons.gov.uk/well-being

Focus on 'Real net national income per head'

Why this measure?

'Material living standards are more closely associated with measures of NNI and consumption than with GDP' (Stiglitz, Sen and Fitoussi, 2009).

Gross Domestic Product (GDP) is often used for judging how well an economy is doing, however, it was not designed as a measure of individual or national well-being. Living standards are more closely aligned with net national income (NNI) (the total income available to residents of that country) as GDP can grow at the same time as incomes decreases and vice versa. For example, multinational firms can produce goods and services in the UK contributing to GDP, but then repatriate some or all of the profits back to their home country. Equally, individuals could work in the UK (contributing to GDP) but live in another country (this is more common in countries that share land boarders). In both of these cases, there is a contribution to GDP but the income is not available to residents of the UK. NNI takes account of these flows of income between countries (amongst other differences) and therefore better represents the total income available to residents of a country.

Has it changed over time?

Figure 7: Real net national income per head (1)

United Kingdom

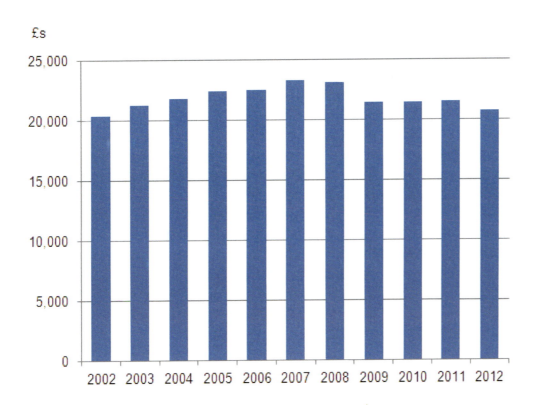

Source: Office for National Statistics

Notes:

1. 2010 prices.

Download chart

XLS XLS format
(28.5 Kb)

Prior to the recession that started in 2008, real Net National Income (NNI) per head grew steadily from £20,347 in 2002 to £23,253 in 2007. During 2008 and 2009, NNI per head fell to £23,125 and £21,380 respectively. In 2010 and 2011 NNI per head remained broadly unchanged at £21,408 and £21,472, before falling again in 2012 to £20,725.

Notes

1. These are examples of the difference between GDP and NNI, for a full description of the differences refer to Measuring National Well-being: The Economy 2012 Measuring National Well-being - The Economy.

Education and skills

Domain overview and importance

'Learning encourages social interaction and increases self-esteem and feelings of competency. Behaviour directed by personal goals to achieve something new has been shown to increase reported life satisfaction', New Economics Foundation 2009.

When people were asked what mattered most for the measurement of National Well-being, in the Office for National Statistics National Debate on Measuring National Well-being, nearly 7 in 10 people (69%) said 'Education and skills' were important.

Table 8: Measure included in the ' Education and skills' domain

United Kingdom

	2001	2011	2012
Human capital - the value of individuals' skills, knowledge and competences in labour market (£ trillion - figures in 2010 prices)	14.46	18.00	17.90
Source: Office for National Statistics			

	2008/09	2010/11	2011/12
Five or more GCSEs A* to C including English and Maths	49.8%	58.5%	59.0%
Source: Department for Education; Welsh Government; Scottish Government; Northern Ireland Department of Education			

	2008	2012	2013
UK residents aged 16 to 64 with no qualifications	13.1%	9.2%	9.3%
Source: Labour Force Survey, Office for National Statistics			

Download table

 XLS format
(28 Kb)

The full list of 41 National Well-being measures is available in various formats: an Excel file with time series data, an interactive wheel of measures which includes time series charts, and a PDF 'print and keep' version showing the latest data. Interactive graphs are also available showing selected measures by region and country. All are available at www.ons.gov.uk/well-being

Focus on 'UK residents aged 16 to 64 with no qualifications'

Why this measure?

People with qualifications may have a higher chance of securing employment or continuing their education through higher education establishments such as universities than those without any qualifications.

'Educational attainment not only affects employability, but also has an impact on income from employment', Education at a Glance 2013: OECD Indicators.

'Learning was associated with higher wellbeing after controlling for a range of other factors. We found evidence that informal learning was associated with higher wellbeing. There was also some evidence that obtaining qualifications was also linked to higher wellbeing', Department for Business, Innovation and Skills. Research Paper 92, Learning and Wellbeing Trajectories among Older Adults in England, November 2012.

Has it changed over time?

Figure 8: Percentage of UK residents aged 16 to 64 with no qualifications (1)

United Kingdom

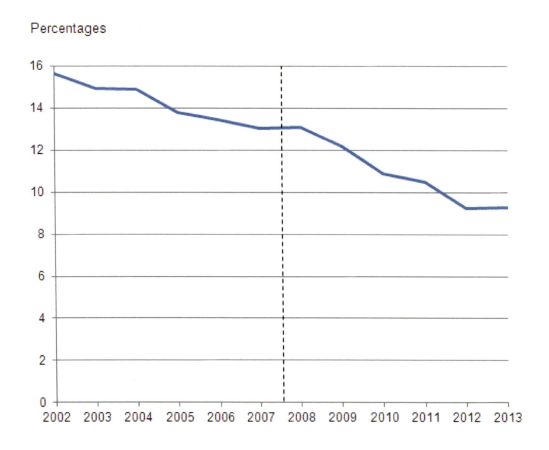

Source: Labour Force Survey - Office for National Statistics

Notes:

1. Men aged 16-64 and women aged 16-59 between 2002 and 2007 and men and women aged 16 to 64 from 2008 onwards.

Download chart

 XLS format
(28 Kb)

The proportion of people in the UK with no educational qualifications has been falling since 2002. In 2002, 15.7% of UK residents had no qualifications, by 2007 this had fallen to 13.0%. In 2013 under 1 in 10 (9.3%) reported that they had no educational qualifications, 6.4 percentage points lower than in 2002.

Breakdown by region

Figure 9: Percentage of UK residents aged 16 to 64 with no qualifications: by region, 2012–13 (1)

United Kingdom

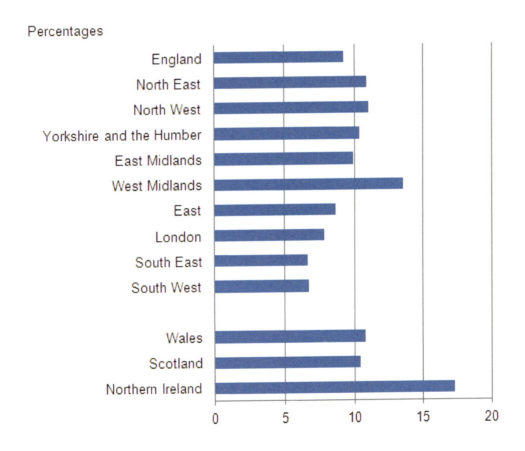

Source: Annual Population Survey (APS) - Office for National Statistics

Notes:

1. Data is for October 2012 to September 2013.

Download chart

 XLS format
(29 Kb)

Just under 1 in 10 residents (9.2%) aged 16 to 64 in England had no educational qualifications in 2012–13. This compares with 10.5% in Scotland, 10.8% in Wales and 17.3% in Northern Ireland. Among the English regions the highest proportion of people aged 16 to 64 without any educational qualifications were in the West Midlands (13.6%), while the lowest proportion were in the South East (6.7%) and the South West (6.8%).

Governance

Domain overview and importance

A fundamental part of the work of government is to support a better life for its citizens and help build strong and resilient communities which in turn may improve the well-being of individuals. This was highlighted in the Office for National Statistics National Debate on Measuring National Well-being. When people were asked what mattered most for the measurement of National Well-being, 'Governance' was one aspect that people considered important.

Table 9: Measures included in the 'Governance' domain

United Kingdom

Measures	Autumn 2003	Spring 2013	Autumn 2013
Those who have trust in national Government	24%	22%	24%
Source: Eurobarometer			
	1950	**2005**	**2010**
Voter turnout (in UK General Elections)	81.6%	58.3%	61.1%
Source: The International Institute for Democracy and Electoral Assistance			

Download table

XLS XLS format
(26.5 Kb)

The full list of 41 National Well-being measures is available in various formats: an Excel file with time series data, an interactive wheel of measures which includes time series charts, and a PDF 'print and keep' version showing the latest data. Interactive graphs are also available showing selected measures by region and country. All are available at www.ons.gov.uk/well-being

Focus on 'trust in national Government'

Why this measure?

'Citizens look to governments to lead the way. Without strong leadership, supported by effective policies, trust is easily eroded. Good governance means putting the needs of people at the centre of policy-making', Secretary-General Angel Gurría, The Organisation for Economic Co-operation and Development.

In the simplest sense, government accountability means that the Government is answerable for its performance or results. Much of the public's trust rests upon the Government being openly accountable for its decisions, actions and mistakes.

Has it changed over time?

Figure 10: Percentage of those who have trust in national Government (1)

United Kingdom

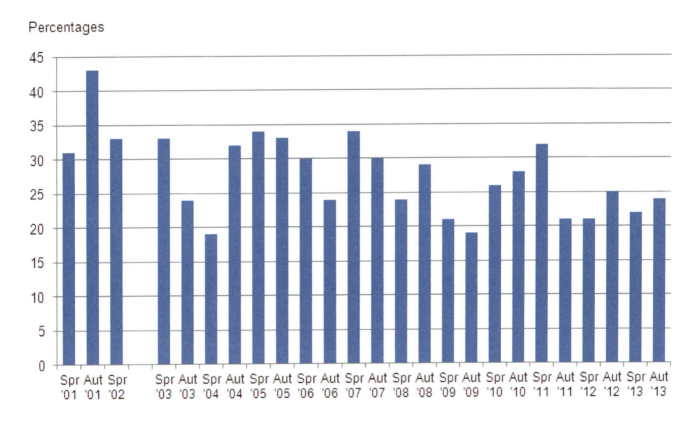

Percentages

Source: Eurobarometer

Notes:

1. Respondents aged 15 and over were asked if they 'tend to trust' or 'tend to not trust' the UK government. Percentages are for those who answered 'tend to trust'. Fieldwork was carried out in Spring (Spr) and Autumn (Aut) of each year. Data not available for Autumn 2002.

Download chart

XLS XLS format
(29 Kb)

Nearly a quarter of people (24%) aged 15 and over in the UK reported that they 'tended to trust' the government in the autumn of 2013. This was a rise of two percentage points from 22% in spring

2013 and a fall of one percentage point from 25% in Autumn 2012. Between 2001 and 2013, the proportion of people who trusted in government peaked in autumn 2001 at 43% but has remained below 35% since then. In the autumn of 2009, trust in government fell to a low of just under a fifth (19%).

Natural environment

Domain overview and importance

In the Office for National Statistics National Debate on Measuring National Well-being, 73% of respondents mentioned the environment, including local green space and nature, as an important factor in well-being. The natural environment has a role to play to ensure sustainable supply of natural goods like food, water, minerals, raw materials, and to maintain critical ecosystem services that provide benefits for human welfare.

Table 10: Measures included in the 'Natural environment' domain

United Kingdom (unless specified)

	2004	2011	2012
Energy consumed within the UK from renewable sources	1.1%	3.8%	4.2%
Source: Department for Energy and Climate Change			

	2000/01	2011/12	2012/13
Household waste that is recycled (England)	11.2%	43.0%	43.2%
Department for Environment, Food and Rural Affairs			

	1980	2012	2013
Protected areas in the UK (million hectares)	4,888	14,466	14,467
Department for Environment, Food and Rural Affairs			

	1990	2011	2012

Total green house gas emissions (million tonnes carbon dioxide equivalent)	769.7	552.6	571.5

Source: Department for Energy and Climate Change

Download table

XLS XLS format
(26.5 Kb)

The full list of 41 National Well-being measures is available in various formats: an Excel file with time series data, an interactive wheel of measures which includes time series charts, and a PDF 'print and keep' version showing the latest data. Interactive graphs are also available showing selected measures by region and country. All are available at www.ons.gov.uk/well-being

Focus on 'Household waste that is recycled'

Why this measure?

Recycling was the most commonly cited proposed addition to the 'Natural Environment' domain in the Office for National Statistics consultation on 'Proposed Domains and Headline Indicators for Measuring National Wellbeing'. The measure gives an indication of the priority that households are now giving to protecting the natural environment. It also shows how we are making best use of the natural resources and minimising the use of landfill sites.

Has it changed over time?

Figure 11: Percentage of household waste that is recycled (1)

England

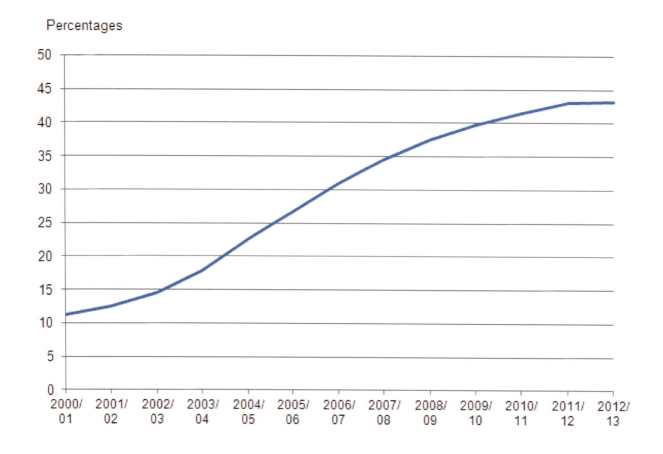

Source: Department for Environment, Food and Rural Affairs

Notes:

1. Includes composting and reused waste.

Download chart

 XLS format
(26.5 Kb)

Since 2000/01 there has been a steady increase in household waste that is recycled. The household waste recycling rate was 43.2% in England in 2012/13, 32 percentage points higher than in 2000/01 (11.2%) and 0.2 percentage points higher than 2011/12 (43.0%). In the last couple of years, the recycling rate has remained relatively stable, however, between 2003/04 and 2008/09 there were year on year changes of between 3.0 and 4.7 percentage points. This was mainly due to local authorities introducing and expanding their recycling collection schemes.

Breakdown by region

Figure 12: Household waste recycling rate (1): by English region, 2012/13

England

Percentages

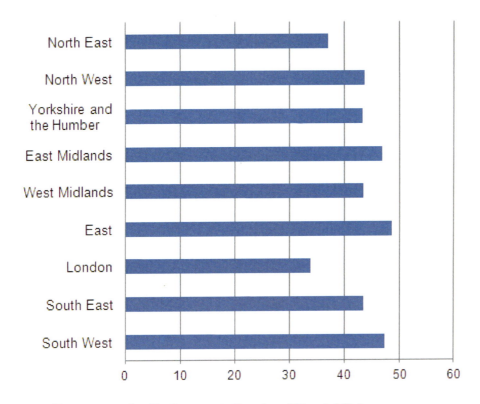

Source: Department for Environment, Food and Rural Affairs

Notes:

1. Includes composting and preparation for reuse.

Download chart

`XLS` XLS format
(27.5 Kb)

Among the English regions, the highest recycling rate was in the East (48.5%), while London had the lowest recycling rate (34.0%). Across the waste disposal authorities or councils in England, the highest recycling rates were in Rochford District Council (66.8%) while the lowest was in Ashford Borough Council (11.9%).

In Wales over half (52.6%) of household waste was recycled or composted in 2012/13, this compares with 36.3% in 2008/09[1]. In Scotland 41.2% of household waste was recycled in 2012/13. The waste authority with the highest recycling rate was in Clackmannanshire (58.9%) and the lowest in the Shetland Isles (13.5%). In Northern Ireland 39.7% of household waste was recycled, with the highest recycling rate in Magherafelt (56.1%) and the lowest in Derry (26.8%).

Additional breakdowns

- Total household waste in England in 2012/13 has fallen by 12.2% since 2006/07 to 22.6 million tonnes, amounting to 423kg per person per year.
- 9.8 million tonnes of waste was recycled in England in 2012/13 equivalent to 183kg per person per year.
- About 40% of waste collected for recycling, compost and reuse in England in 2012/13 was green waste for compost.

Notes

1. In Wales, 2008/09 includes household waste 'collected' for reuse, recycling or composted, 2012/13 includes household waste 'sent' for reuse, recycling or composted.

European comparisons

Overview

European data are available for seven out of ten measures of National Well-being that were focused on earlier in this article and are highlighted here. Direct comparable data is only available for one of these measures (trust in Government), therefore the remaining six measures have proxy comparisons as detailed in **Table 11**.

Table 11: European comparable measures

ONS Measures	European comparison measures
Personal well-being	
Satisfaction with their lives overall (7 or more out of 10)	How satisfied would you say you are with your life these days (7 or more out of 10)
Source: Annual Population Survey, Office for National Statistics (2012/13)	Source: Third European Quality of Life Survey (2011)
Our relationships	
Has a spouse, family member or friend to rely on if they have a serious problem	From whom would you get support if you needed advice about a serious personal or family matter? (Family member, a friend, neighbour, or someone else)
Source: Understanding Society, the UK Household Longitudinal Study (2010/11)	Source: Third European Quality of Life Survey (2011)
Health	
Somewhat, mostly or completely satisfied with their health	Perceived health status (Very good or good)
Source: Understanding Society, the UK Household Longitudinal Study (2011/12)	Source: Third European Quality of Life Survey (2011)
Where we live	
Fairly/very satisfied with their accommodation	Your accommodation/Could you please tell me on a scale of 1 to 10 how satisfied you are with it
Source: Department for Communities and Local Government (2011–12)	Source: Third European Quality of Life Survey (2011)
Personal finance	
Report finding it quite or very difficult to get by financially	Households making ends meet with difficulty and great difficulty
Source: Understanding Society, the UK Household Longitudinal Study (2011/12)	Eurostat (2012)
Governance	
Those who have trust in national Government	Those who have trust in national Government
Source: Eurobarometer (Autumn 2013)	Source: Eurobarometer (Autumn 2013)
Natural environment	
Household waste that is recycled	Municipal waste that is recycled/composted/digested

ONS Measures	European comparison measures
Department for Environment, Food and Rural Affairs (2012/13)	Source: Eurostat (2011)

Download table

XLS [XLS format](#)
(27 Kb)

Table 12 shows that of the seven measures, the UK ranked above the EU average in four of the measures and below the EU average in three of the measures. The remainder of this section will describe this in more detail and further highlight the countries that ranked highest and lowest in each of the measures.

Table 12: European comparisons summary

	UK	EU average	Top ranked country	Bottom ranked country
Life satisfaction	71.8%	69.3%	Denmark (91.0%)	Bulgaria (38.3%)
Support if needed advice about a serious personal or family matter	88.7%	93.0%	Slovakia (98.8%)	France (86.1%)
Perceived health status	62.7%	64.0%	Ireland (75.3%)	Latvia/Lithuania (41.1%)
Satisfaction with accommodation	80.2%	76.9%	Finland (90.9%)	Latvia (55.2%)
Households making ends meet with difficulty and great difficulty	20.2%	27.7%	Greece (73.1%)	Sweden (6.8%)
Trust in national government	24%	23%	Sweden (57%)	Spain (9%)
Municipal waste that is recycled/ composted/ digested[1]	46% (est.)	41%	Germany (65%)	Romania (1% est.)

Table notes:

1. 'est.' is estimated data

Download table

 XLS format
(27 Kb)

Personal well-being

Life satisfaction

Figure 13: Life satisfaction (1), 2011

EU comparison

Percentages

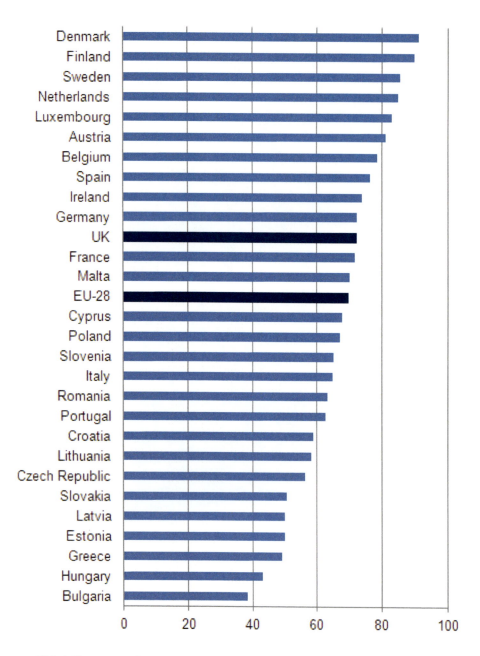

Source: Third European Quality of Life Survey

Notes:

1.   Adults aged 16 and over rating their life satisfaction between 7 and 10 out of 10.

Download chart

XLS XLS format
(27 Kb)

Over 7 in 10 (71.8%) adults aged 16 and over in the UK rated their satisfaction with life as 7 or more out of 10 in 2011. This was higher than the EU–28 average of 69.3%. The proportion of those reporting a life satisfaction of 7 or more out of 10 was highest in Denmark (91.0%) and Finland (89.8%) and lowest in Bulgaria (38.3%) and Hungary (43.2%).

Our relationships

Support from family, friends, neighbours or someone else if you needed advice about a serious personal or family matter

In 2011, just under 9 in 10 (88.7%) of people in the UK aged 16 and over reported that they had support from family, friends, neighbours or someone else if they needed support or advice about a serious personal or family matter. This was lower than the EU–28 average of 93.0%. People in the UK along with France (86.1%) and Denmark (88.1%) were least likely to have this support. Slovakia had the highest proportion of people reporting they had support from family, friends, neighbours or someone else (98.8%).

Health

Perceived health status

Over 6 in 10 people (62.7%) aged 16 and over in the UK rated their health status as very good or good, just behind the EU–28 average of 64.0% in 2011. The highest proportion of people who rated their health status as very good or good were in Ireland (75.3%) and Greece (75.0%). The lowest proportions were in Lithuania and Latvia (both 41.1%).

Where we live

Satisfaction with accommodation

Just over 8 in 10 (80.2%) of people aged 16 and over in the UK rated their satisfaction with their accommodation as 7 or more out of 10 in 2011, higher than the EU–28 average of 76.9%. Finland had the highest proportion of people who rated their satisfaction with their accommodation as 7 or more out of 10 (90.9%), followed by Denmark and Malta (both 89.7%). Latvia had the smallest proportion of people rating their satisfaction with their accommodation as 7 or more out of 10 (55.2%).

Personal finance

Households making ends meet with difficulty or great difficulty

Figure 14: Households making ends meet with difficulty or great difficulty, 2012

EU comparison (1)

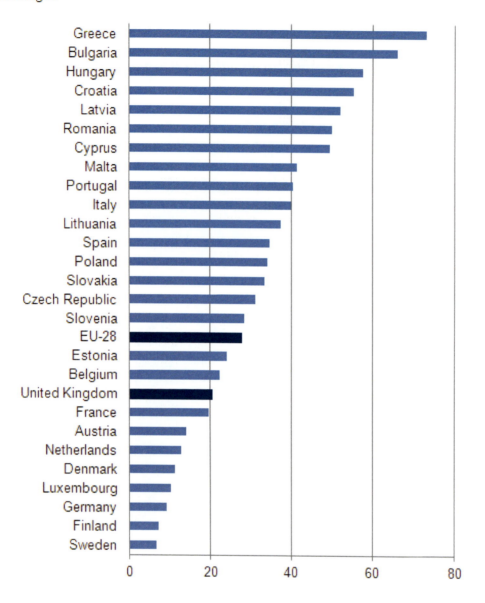

Percentages

Source: Eurostat

Notes:

1. Data not available for Ireland.

Download chart

XLS XLS format

(18.5 Kb)

Just over 2 in 10 (20.2%) households in the UK reported that they had difficulty or great difficulty making ends meet in 2012 which was below the EU–28 average of 27.7%. The highest proportion of households who reported a difficulty in making ends meet was in Greece (73.1%) and Bulgaria

(65.9%) in 2012. The lowest proportion of households that reported difficulty was in Sweden (6.8%), Finland (7.1%) and Germany (9.2%).

Governance

Trust in national Government

Just under a quarter (24%) of people aged 15 and over in the UK reported that they tended to trust their national government in the autumn of 2013, just over the EU–28 average of 23%. The highest proportions of trust were in Sweden (57%) and Luxembourg (51%). The lowest proportions of trust were in Spain (9%) and Greece, Italy and Slovenia (all 10%).

Natural environment

Municipal waste which is recycled, composted or digested [1,2]

Figure 15: Percentage of municipal waste which is recycled, composted or digested, 2012 (1)

EU comparison

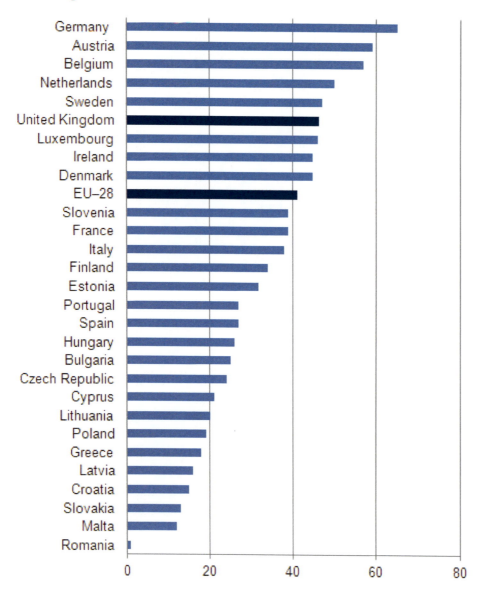

Source: Eurostat

Notes:

1.   Data is estimated for Slovakia, Lithuania, Czech Republic, Spain, Ireland, Luxembourg and the UK.

Download chart

 XLS format
(18.5 Kb)

An estimated 46% of the UK's municipal waste was recycled, composted or digested in 2012, above the EU–28 average of 41%. Germany had the highest proportion of recycled waste at 65%. The countries with the lowest proportions of recycled, composted or digested municipal waste were Romania (estimated at 1%), Malta (12%) and Slovakia (13%).

Notes

1. Municipal waste is mainly produced by households, though similar wastes from sources such as commerce, offices and public institutions are included.

2. Anaerobic digestion is a collection of processes by which microorganisms break down biodegradable material in the absence of oxygen. The process is used for industrial or domestic purposes to manage waste and/or to produce fuels.

Background notes

1. Details of the policy governing the release of new data are available by visiting www.statisticsauthority.gov.uk/assessment/code-of-practice/index.html or from the Media Relations Office email: media.relations@ons.gsi.gov.uk

Copyright

© Crown copyright 2014

You may use or re-use this information (not including logos) free of charge in any format or medium, under the terms of the Open Government Licence. To view this licence, visit www.nationalarchives.gov.uk/doc/open-government-licence/ or write to the Information Policy Team, The National Archives, Kew, London TW9 4DU, or email: psi@nationalarchives.gsi.gov.uk.

This document is also available on our website at www.ons.gov.uk.

Sources, reports and surveys related to 'Life in the UK, 2014'

Personal well-being

Personal well-being accross the UK - SB - Personal Well-being Across the UK, 2012/13

Personal well-being in the UK - SB - Personal Well-being in the UK, 2012/13

Understanding Society, the UK Household Longitudinal Survey - Understanding Society

Our relationships

Eurofound, European Quality of Life Survey - European Quality of Life Survey (2012)

Understanding Society, the UK Household Longitudinal Survey - Understanding Society

Health

Life expectancies - Life Expectancies

Understanding Society, the UK Household Longitudinal Survey - Understanding Society

What we do

Labour market statistics - Labour Market Statistics

Understanding Society, the UK Household Longitudinal Survey - Understanding Society

Department for Culture, Media and Sport - DCMS - Taking Part Survey

Sport England - www.sportengland.org/research/about-our-research/active-people-survey/

Where we live

Crime Survey for England and Wales - Crime in England and Wales

Natural England - Natural England

Understanding Society, the UK Household Longitudinal Survey - Understanding Society

Department for Transport - www.gov.uk/government/publications/accessibility-statistics-2012

Department for Communities and Local Government - www.gov.uk/government/collections/english-housing-survey

Personal Finance

Department for Work and Pensions - DWP: Households Below Average Income

Wealth and Assets Survey - Wealth and Assets Survey

Understanding Society, the UK Household Longitudinal Survey - Understanding Society

Economy

National accounts - National Accounts - all releases

Educations and skills

Human capital - Human Capital Estimates index

Department for Education - Department for Education

Governance

Eurobarometer - Eurobarometer

The International Institute for Democracy and Electoral Assistance - www.idea.int/

Natural environment

Department for Energy and Climate Change - Digest of UK Energy Statistics (DUKES)

Department for Environment, Food and Rural Affairs - DEFRA website

European comparisons

Eurostat - Eurostat

Eurofound, European Quality of Life Survey - European Quality of Life Survey (2012)

Eurobarometer - Eurobarometer

About the ONS Measuring National Well-being Programme

NWB logo 2

This article is published as part of the ONS Measuring National Well-being Programme.

The programme aims to produce accepted and trusted measures of the well-being of the nation - how the UK as a whole is doing. It is about looking at 'GDP and beyond' and includes:

- Greater analysis of the national economic accounts, especially to understand household income, expenditure and wealth.
- Further accounts linked to the national accounts, including the UK Environmental Accounts and valuing household production and 'human capital'.
- Quality of life measures, looking at different areas of national well-being such as health, relationships, job satisfaction, economic security, education environmental conditions.
- Working with others to include the measurement of the well-being of children and young people as part of national well-being.
- Measures of 'personal well-being' - individuals' assessment of their own well-being.
- Headline indicators to summarise national well-being and the progress we are making as a society.

The programme is underpinned by a communication and engagement workstream, providing links with Cabinet Office and policy departments, international developments, the public and other stakeholders. The programme is working closely with Defra on the measurement of 'sustainable development' to provide a complete picture of national well-being, progress and sustainable development.

Find out more on the Measuring National Well-being website pages.

Office for
National Statistics

Measuring National Well-being: Economic Well-being

Author Name(s): **Jawed Khan and James Calver; Office for National Statistics**

Abstract

This article considers ways to measure the economic well-being of the UK. It reaffirms the importance of Gross Domestic Product (GDP) as the central and indispensable measure of economic activity. But it also considers ways in which GDP falls short as a measure of economic well-being. It proposes a set of seven additional indicators, which with GDP could constitute a "dashboard" for the purpose of assessing changes in the various dimensions of economic well-being.

Background

In recent years, there has been substantial discussion about the best way to measure national well-being. The Commission on the Measurement of Economic Performance and Social Progress Report (Stiglitz et al. 2009) crystallised many of these issues and its recommendations led to subsequent work to refine and implement these, around the world. In the United Kingdom, the National Statistician set up the Measuring National Well-being programme in 2010 to take this agenda forward.

This article considers the measurement of economic or material well-being. This is a subset of the overall issue of measuring well-being and recognises that many dimensions of well-being are outside the material sphere (see, for example, the ONS "Wheel of Well-being"). Nevertheless, as the Stiglitz Commission recognised, measuring changes in economic well-being is important in its own right.

In the UK, the National Accounts, and Gross Domestic Product (GDP) in particular, currently have the highest profile in regard to changes in the economy and the measurement of economic progress. In its own terms, this prominence is fully warranted. GDP measures the sum total of the final output that the economy produces. Equivalently, it measures the income that, as a nation, we earn from that production. Similarly, it measures what is available to spend – either to consume or to invest in capital for the future.

Given that it measures aggregate activity in the economy, GDP, supported by other information, inevitably and correctly plays a central role in discussion about monetary and fiscal policy and about the state of the economy generally. It is therefore of vital importance.

At the same time, GDP has long known weaknesses as a measure of economic welfare or well-being. The founding fathers of national accounting, Hicks, Kuznets, Samuelson, Tinbergen, were well aware of this, and explicit about it. The System of National Accounts (SNA) - the international convention that governs national accounting in most countries - recognises the limitations of GDP as a measure of well-being[1]:

"Movements of GDP cannot be expected to be good indicators of changes in total welfare unless all the other factors influencing welfare happen to remain constant, which history shows is never the case".

This should not be taken, however, as a counsel of despair. The approach adopted in this article is as follows:

- Diagnose the ways in which GDP is defective in measuring changes in economic well-being.
- Propose additional measures that deal with these issues.
- In this way, construct a dashboard of a small number of indicators that together give a more rounded and comprehensive basis for assessing changes in material well-being.

The rest of this article takes this procedure forward.

Notes

1. Source: OECD (2013)

Problems With Using GDP as a Measure of Economic Well-being

The issues concerning the use of GDP as a measure of welfare can be broadly considered in two groups:

- Some apply generally to the way GDP is defined and constructed. One point here is that GDP is defined without reference to the number of people in the population that produce the output it covers and benefit from the income generated. If GDP increases but the population producing it rises by the same percentage, there would be no reason to suppose the well-being of individuals would have increased. One obvious adjustment to make therefore is to consider, instead, measures defined in per capita terms. There are, however, other issues related to GDP's ability to function as a measure of well-being, as set out below.
- A further set of issues relate to what the Stiglitz Commission called the need to emphasise the household dimension. Its observation was that only people actually experience well-being, rather than companies or other legal institutions. The implication is that alongside looking at what is happening to the economy as a whole, attention should be paid to what is happening specifically to households. It is also important, in this context, that GDP and, for that matter aggregate household measures of income give only an aggregate picture. There is also a need to consider who is benefiting from that income, as well as the total position.

The following sections discuss and address these issues in turn.

A. General Issues

1. Adjusting for population change

The first issue under the general heading is to adjust Gross Domestic Product (or other relevant aggregates) for population change. This can be done straightforwardly and the following chart compares the path in recent years of Gross Domestic Product (GDP) per capita with the more familiar GDP profile.

Figure 1: GDP and GDP per capita, 1997 - 2013

United Kingdom

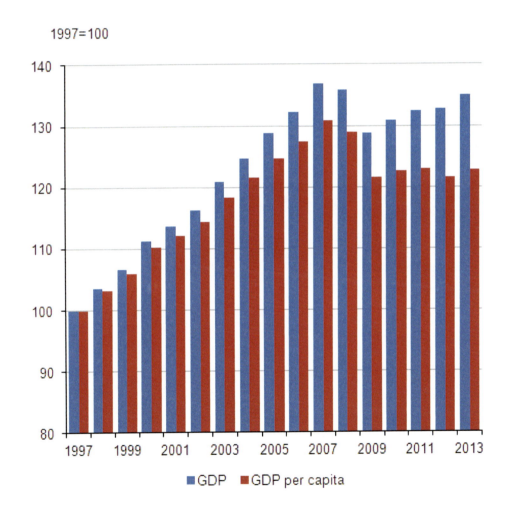

Source: Office for National Statistics

Download chart

XLS XLS format
(9.7 Kb)

Figure 1 shows that there had been little recovery in GDP per capita as compared with 2008, whereas GDP had recovered significantly from the low point reached in 2009. Underlying this conclusion is the fact that the slow recovery in GDP itself since 2009 had been matched by an increase in population of roughly the same order.

2. Adjusting for capital consumption

GDP is "gross" in the sense that it includes depreciation or capital consumption. It treats such consumption of capital as no different from any other form of consumption. But most people would not regard depreciation of their cars or houses, for example, as adding to their material well-being. On this basis, looking at Net Domestic Product (NDP), as the Stiglitz Commission suggested, is liable to have a closer relationship with economic well-being than GDP. Figure 2 below compares the behaviour of GDP per head with NDP per head in recent years. The figure shows that the trend in the UK NDP per capita closely mirrored the trend in GDP per capita, increasing during the pre-crisis period and falling during and after the recession.

Figure 2: GDP and NDP per capita (2010 prices), 1997 - 2012

United Kingdom

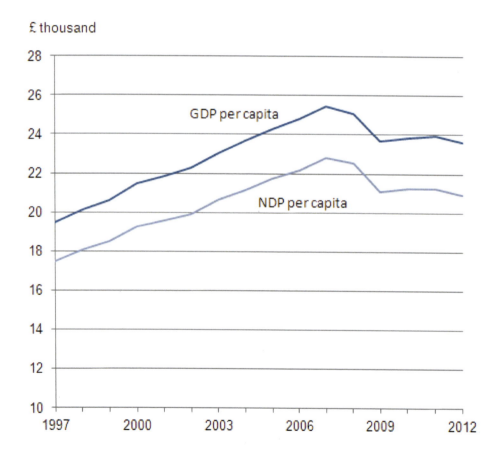

Source: Office for National Statistics

Download chart

XLS XLS format
(10.2 Kb)

3. Real Net National Disposable Income (RNNDI)

GDP measures the production in a country and, correspondingly, the income generated from that production. However from the viewpoint of assessing well-being, it is more likely to be the total income of the resident population that is relevant, including that from other sources. Three adjustments can be made to address this issue.

First, not all income generated by production in the UK will be payable to UK residents. Some of the capital employed will be owned by non-residents and they will be entitled to the return on that investment. Conversely, the UK's residents receive income from production activities taking place elsewhere, based on their investments overseas. These offsetting flows of income are increasingly important in a progressively globalising world. When NDP is adjusted for these income flows to and from the rest of the world, the statistic known as Net National Income (NNI) is the resulting income measure.

Second, adjustments need to be made for net current transfers (for example, current international co-operation or remittances between households) from and to other countries. Making this adjustment to NNI gives Net National Disposable Income (NNDI).

Third, changes in standards of living are also determined by prices of products that can be acquired with a given sum of money. One factor here is the domestic price level itself. In addition, there will be an effect from the relative price of foreign products - the rate at which exports may be traded against imports from the rest of the world, also known as terms of trade. When UK export prices rise more quickly than the prices of it imports, UK citizens are better off and vice versa. Real Net National Disposable Income (RNNDI) results from adjusting NNDI for changes in the price level that income recipients face. RNNDI might be expected to have a close correlation with economic well-being.

Figure 3 below compares the behaviour of RNNDI per capita with GDP per capita. Unlike the GDP per capita measure which has been broadly flat since 2009, the RNNDI per capita measure has been continuing to fall gently to the end of 2013.

Figure 3: GDP and RNNDI per capita (2010 prices), 1997 - 2012

United Kingdom

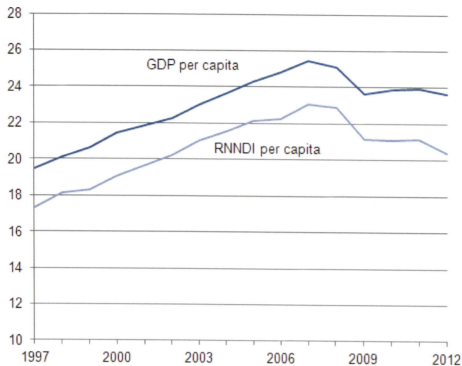

Source: Office for National Statistics

Download chart

 XLS format
(10.3 Kb)

4. Wealth

GDP measures the flows of output or income but not the corresponding stock of wealth and net assets. Thus, it is possible that a nation might be increasing its output and consumption while running down its assets, but this output and consumption would not be sustainable. Or the reverse might be the case and GDP would then underestimate the true position in regard to sustainable future consumption and thus well-being. In principle, a wide range of assets and liabilities might be appropriate to this calculation, including for example, natural capital, so-called human capital and social capital. However, this article takes into account only physical and financial capital, where data are readily available and published regularly.

Figure 4: Net financial and produced assets (2010 prices), 1997 - 2012

United Kingdom

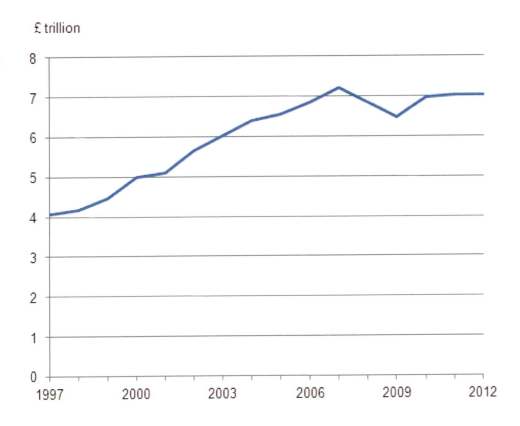

Source: Office for National Statistics

Download chart

XLS XLS format
(8.8 Kb)

Figure 4 shows that wealth defined in this way rose fairly steadily in real terms in the years to 2007. It then fell under the influence of the financial crisis and the recession. Thereafter, there was some recovery but to 2012 it had not yet resumed its upward trend.

B. Emphasising the Household Dimension

5. Real Adjusted Household Disposable Income

As discussed earlier, on the basis of it being people, not institutions, who experience well-being, looking at developments within the household sector may be at least as important as looking at the economy overall. Both OECD (2011) and Stiglitz (2009) argued that when assessing well-being, it is better to look particularly at developments from the perspective of households and individuals, as well as at the aggregate condition of the economy.

In this context, it is natural to have regard to Real Household Disposable Income (RHDI). This has long been published as part of the National Accounts and represents the income received by the household sector, adjusted for taxes paid and benefits received and also taking account of changes in the price level.

In addition, regard needs to be taken of the fact that households receive some material benefits via free public services such as the NHS and schools which would otherwise have to be paid for directly. Real Adjusted Household Disposable Income (RAHDI) is a statistic regularly published in the UK Economic Accounts, which includes the value of these social benefits. It seems directly relevant to assessment of households' economic well-being.

Figure 5 below compares RAHDI per capita with the path for GDP per capita. It suggests that households did not experience the full effects of the recession in 2008 and 2009. Indeed, household incomes held up during the first part of the recession. However, RAHDI per capita continued to fall gently thereafter to the end of 2013.

Figure 5: RAHDI and GDP per capita (2010 prices), 1997 - 2013

United Kingdom

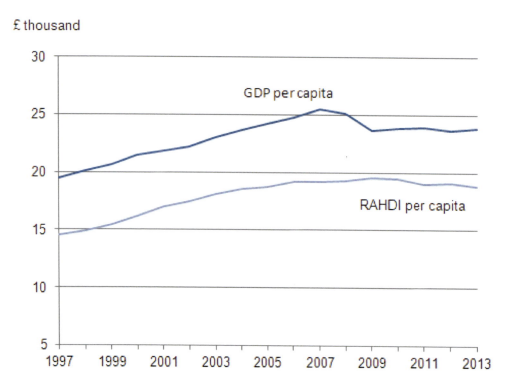

Source: Office for National Statistics

Download chart

6. Median real household income

Average measures of household income per person are helpful but give no indication about how available resources are distributed across people and households. For example, average income per capita might remain unchanged while the distribution of income also changed, with implications for the typical household.

One indicator which is helpful in this respect is median real household income, that is, the income that the middle household receives if all households are ranked from highest to lowest (or the reverse) in terms of the income they receive. If, for example, household incomes per capita were rising but only because high income households were enjoying large further increases in income, this would not be reflected in the median household income series.

Figure 6: Median real household income(1), GDP and RHDI per capita, 1997 - 2011

United Kingdom

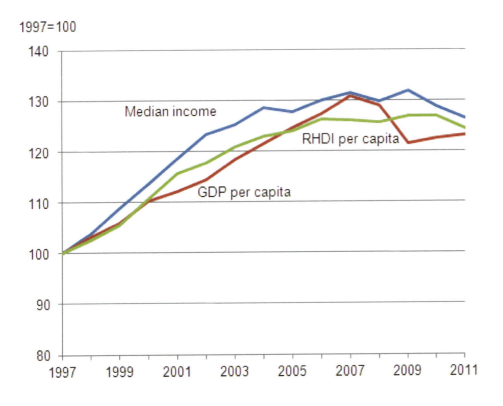

Source: Office for National Statistics

Notes:

1.   Income has been equivalised using the modified-OECD scale to account for differences in the size and composition of households.

Download chart

 XLS format
(8.8 Kb)

Figure 6 suggests that median real household income and real household disposable income per head grew broadly in line with each other over this period. In particular, both held up during the first phase of the recession as measured by GDP overall. However, both of them have shown a decline since GDP itself began a sluggish recovery.

7. Household Wealth

Just as for the economy overall, income provides only a partial view of the economic resources available to households to support consumption. What is happening to their wealth is also important in assessing whether current consumption is sustainable or whether, per contra, higher levels of wealth mean more consumption could be sustained and well-being thus raised, with no change in income.

As for the economy overall, there are a number of different dimensions of wealth. But this article concentrates on physical and financial assets and liabilities, where regular statistics are already published.

Figure 7 below shows household wealth on this basis in real terms, using the GDP deflator to correct for changes in the price level. The figure shows that there was an increase in household wealth from 1997 to 2007, driven mainly by rising house prices. However, the onset of the recession in 2008 saw the net worth of households dropped significantly, but in 2012 it recovered and was almost at the pre-crises level.

Figure 7: Real household wealth (2010 prices), 1997 - 2012

United Kingdom

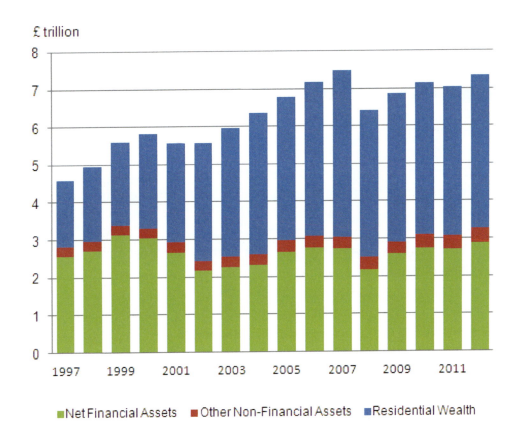

Source: Office for National Statistics

Download chart

`XLS` XLS format
(10.3 Kb)

Summary and Further Work

This article has examined the limitations of GDP as a measure of economic well-being, while acknowledging its central importance as a measure of economic activity. On the basis of this consideration, the article suggests a dashboard of seven regularly published indicators to give the means for a more rounded and complete assessment of changes in economic well-being.

The dashboard outlined covers both economy wide statistics and also some more specifically focused on the household sector.

Economy wide

- Gross Domestic Product (GDP) per capita.
- Net Domestic Product (NDP) per capita.
- Real Net National Disposable Income (RNNDI) per capita.
- Real Net Financial and Physical Assets.

Households

- Real Adjusted Household Disposable Income (RAHDI) per capita.
- Median Real Household Income.
- Real Household Net Financial and Physical Assets.

As is widely agreed, economic well-being has a number of dimensions and any assessment needs to take these various dimensions into account. However, several points seem apparent from the above indicators:

- Unlike GDP, which has now recovered substantially from the falls in the recent recession, GDP per capita has recovered only a little of the fall seen during the recession.
- Real Net National Disposable Income per capita has continued to fall gently.
- Real Adjusted Household Disposable Income per capita held up well during the deepest phase of the recession. However, it has been falling gently in the subsequent period.
- Median real household income and real household disposable income have grown broadly in line with each other in recent years, suggesting there have not been major distributional factors at work.

As the article has suggested at various points, there are ways in which the dashboard could be developed further, for example by considering a wider range of capital, such as natural capital and human capital. Work is proceeding to generate better estimates of these aggregates. That, in turn, would allow broader estimates of capital consumption to be taken into account when measuring variants of Net Domestic Product. When the results of such work are available, consideration could be given to updating the dashboard accordingly.

The ONS is also currently updating the Household Satellite Accounts (HHSA) which measures household production in the UK. This provides benefits which themselves should be taken into account in assessing material well-being. The HHSA provide a means by which the influence of changing patterns of unpaid work on the economy can be measured. This activity is divided into several principal functions providing housing, transport, nutrition, clothing, laundry services, adult care, child care and voluntary work. In 2013, ONS published estimates of Informal Childcare in the UK, Informal Adult Care in the UK and Valuing voluntary activity in the UK. Over the coming year, ONS plans to update the remaining sections of the household satellite account.

References

OECD (2011), How's life? Measuring Well-Being, OECD Publishing, Paris

OECD (2013), OECD Framework for Statistics on the Distribution of Household Income, Consumption and Wealth

ONS (2013) United Kingdom National Accounts

ONS (2013), United Kingdom Economic Accounts Stiglitz et al. (2009) Report by the Commission on the Measurement of Economic Performance and Social Progress

Background notes

1. Details of the policy governing the release of new data are available by visiting www.statisticsauthority.gov.uk/assessment/code-of-practice/index.html or from the Media Relations Office email: media.relations@ons.gsi.gov.uk

Copyright

Income, Expenditure and Personal Well-being, 2011/12

Author Name(s): **James Lewis, Office for National Statistics**

Abstract

This article presents new findings on the relationship between personal well-being and household income and expenditure using regression analysis. It looks at how income, the distribution of income across society, source of income and spending affect life satisfaction, a sense that the things we do in life are worthwhile, and levels of happiness and anxiety.

1. Introduction

This article analyses the relationship between personal well-being and household income and expenditure.

Previous analysis by ONS (2013a, b) has used the Annual Population Survey (APS) to study the factors related to personal well-being, for example, the link between commuting and well-being. These articles did not look at relationships between personal well-being and household income or household expenditure, as this data is not recorded by the APS. The relationships between household finances and personal well-being in this article have been explored using household income and expenditure data available from the Effects of Taxes and Benefits on Household Income dataset.

This article looks at how personal well-being varies in relation to household finances, after taking account of a range of possible influences on well-being. Specifically, the analysis examines the relationships between different aspects of personal well-being and:

- household income,
- the proportion of total household income that is received in cash benefits from the state, while controlling for the total level of household income,
- household expenditure.

2. Key Points

- Individuals in households with higher incomes report higher life satisfaction and happiness, and lower anxiety, holding other factors fixed. Higher household income is not significantly related to people's sense that the things they do in life are worthwhile.

- An increase in the proportion of household income from cash benefits such as Housing Benefit and Jobseeker's Allowance is associated with lower well-being across all four measures, with the effects strongest for men. This effect remained even when taking differences in household income into account.

- Household expenditure appears to have a stronger relationship with people's life satisfaction, sense that the things they do in life are worthwhile and happiness, than household income. There is no significant relationship between higher household expenditure and lower anxiety.

- The biggest differences in well-being between people in neighbouring fifths of both the income and expenditure distributions are between those in the bottom and second-lowest fifths of the distributions, holding other factors fixed. This suggests that well-being increases fastest in relation to increases in income and expenditure from the lower levels of income and expenditure.

3. Research methods

This article presents results obtained from regression analysis, a statistical technique which enables analysis of how responses to personal well-being questions vary by specific characteristics and circumstances of individuals while holding all other characteristics equal. The key benefit of regression analysis is that it provides a better method of identifying those factors which matter most to personal well-being than by analysing the relationship between only two characteristics at a time.

The analysis is based on a special version of the Effects of Taxes and Benefits on Household Income dataset (which included the four standard ONS personal well-being questions) and covers the period April 2011 to March 2012. The Effects of Taxes and Benefits on Household Income is an annual article produced by ONS using data from the Living Costs and Food Survey (LCF).

3.1 Key definitions

Over 8,000 adults (aged 16 and over) answered the following four standard ONS personal well-being questions which were included in all Living Costs and Food Survey interviews conducted in Great Britain during this period:

- Overall, how satisfied are you with your life nowadays?
- Overall, to what extent do you feel the things you do in your life are worthwhile?
- Overall, how happy did you feel yesterday?
- Overall, how anxious did you feel yesterday?

People answer these questions on a scale of 0 to 10 where 0 is 'not at all' and 10 is 'completely'. Further information about the distribution of responses for each measure is available in section 7.10 Personal well-being questions.

Household income

The measure of income used in this analysis is equivalised disposable household income. Disposable income is the total income a household has from 'original' sources (primarily employment and investment income) plus cash benefits received from the state, minus direct taxes.

This measure of income is 'equivalised' to adjust for differences in household composition, in order to give a measure that can be used to meaningfully compare incomes between households of different sizes and types.

Household, as opposed to personal income, is used in this analysis as typically all members of a household can benefit economically from an increase in income. In addition, certain taxes and benefits are paid or received by the household as a whole, such as Council Tax and Housing Benefit.

Cash benefits

This article also analyses the relationship between personal well-being and the proportion of a household's gross income (their total income from both original and cash benefit sources) which is made up of cash benefits received from the state, such as Housing Benefit and Jobseeker's Allowance.

The Effects of Taxes and Benefits on Household Income publication provides further information on definitions of income and equivalisation and covers a comprehensive range of cash benefits.

Household expenditure

Household expenditure in this analysis includes all expenditure defined by ONS as consumption expenditure (See: ONS Family Spending Chapter 1), plus a number of additional items and adjustments which make expenditure more comparable across households. These include expenditure abroad, on mortgage interest and employer-paid expenditure on company cars. Further information on the definition of expenditure used in this article can be found in the Supporting Information section.

As with income, household expenditure has been equivalised using the modified-OECD scale, in order to make the expenditure of households of different sizes and types comparable.

3.2 The regression models

In order to isolate the relationship between income or expenditure and personal well-being, other factors which could potentially influence well-being are held equal in the analysis:

- employment status,
- sex,
- age,
- whether there are dependent children in the household,
- relationship status,
- housing tenure,
- region of Great Britain (including urban/rural differences),
- personal receipt of a disability benefit (this is included as a substitute for self-reported health or disability, which are not available from the LCF. Further information on what is contained in this variable can be found in the section Supporting Information),
- highest qualification obtained,
- ethnicity.

The relationships between many of these variables and personal well-being are explored in detail in ONS (2013a) using data from the APS.

Two different regression analysis techniques were used in this analysis: ordered probit and ordinary least squares (OLS). Further information about these techniques can be found in section 7 Technical Appendix.

Ordered probit was used to specify the models as it is the technique best suited to the ordered nature of the responses to the personal well-being questions (ie, with responses on a scale from 0 to 10), while OLS is generally used for continuous data. However, the results of ordered probit analysis are not straightforward to interpret and explain to a wide audience in an accessible way. Due to the two methods often yielding similar results when there are more than four categories for ordered responses, it is considered acceptable to undertake the analysis using either ordered probit or OLS (Ferrer-i-Carbonell and Frijters 2004; Stevenson and Wolfers 2008; Fleche et al., 2011).

In this analysis, the relative coefficient sizes and statistical significance levels produced using the two techniques are very similar. As a result, this analysis has used the ordered probit method to specify the models (including control variables) and the estimated models produced by the OLS method to report the results.

Results from both ordered probit and OLS models are included in the reference tables.

3.3 Interpreting the numbers

For the regression models in this article, a natural logarithmic transformation has been applied to income and expenditure (see 7.7 Key analysis variables). This enables the findings to be presented as the difference in each aspect of personal well-being measured on a 0 to 10 scale, associated with a percentage difference in income or expenditure.

Looking at the absolute difference in well-being resulting from a percentage difference in income reflects the widely held notion that a percentage difference in income is likely to have similar effects on people of different income levels; whereas an absolute increase in income of, say £500 per year, is likely to have a larger impact on people with a low income than on people with a high income (see Kahneman and Deaton, 2010, for an example of how this relates to personal well-being).

The article also looks at the differences in well-being associated with differences in the percentage of household income derived from cash benefits. The results can be interpreted as the difference in reported well-being between people living in a household where 0% of the income is derived from cash benefits and people living in a household where 100% of income is derived from benefits.

It is important to note that the results should not be interpreted as the difference in well-being experienced immediately before and immediately after a change in income, expenditure, or the proportion of income derived from cash benefits. Previous studies (Di Tella et al., 2003, Brickman et al, 1978) have shown that an increase in economic prosperity can lead to a large increase in well-being immediately after the change occurs. However, over time people can "adapt" to their new level of prosperity, and their reported well-being appears to fall over time, closer to the original pre-change level.

This analysis is based on responses made at a one point in time and cannot differentiate between an impact on well-being that is recent, for example, a change in income last month, or one to which the individual has had time to adapt, such as a change in income a year ago.

More information on the caveats around inferring causality from regression analysis is in the section 7.6 Causality.

Overall, the analysis has been able to explain just over 12% of the differences between individuals in reported levels of life satisfaction and just over 4% of the differences in reported anxiety. For more information on the explanatory power of the models, see 7.3 The explanatory power of the models.

4. How much does household income matter to personal well-being?

Key findings:

- Those in households with higher incomes report higher life satisfaction and happiness, and lower anxiety on average, but do not give significantly different ratings to their sense that the things they do in life are worthwhile, holding other factors equal.
- Comparing this analysis to previous ONS findings suggests that household income has a relationship with a wider range of measures of personal well-being than personal earnings.
- The aspect of well-being most strongly associated with household income is life satisfaction, with a doubling of income associated with life satisfaction 0.17 points higher on the 0 to 10 scale. The scale of this difference is considerably smaller than that between employees and the unemployed or that between people who are married and those who are widowed.
- Holding all else equal, the biggest differences in well-being between neighbouring fifths of the income distribution are between the lowest and second-lowest income groups, suggesting that increases in income are most strongly related to increases in well-being for those at the bottom of the income distribution.

4.1 Income and well-being

There is an argument that more income allows people to satisfy more preferences, resulting in increased well-being (see OECD, 2013). The importance of income in determining people's ability to satisfy their preferences suggests that a relationship should be expected between higher household income and higher personal well-being.

On average, those living in households in the poorest fifth (or quintile) of the income distribution rated their life satisfaction at 6.9 on the 0 to 10 scale. Those in the richest fifth of households rated their life satisfaction at an average of 7.7. This is a similar result to that recently found between life satisfaction and earnings for employees in the EU as a whole (Eurofound, 2013). While these figures show that average life satisfaction is higher for individuals at the top than the bottom of the income distribution, this does not take into account other factors (such as employment status, age and region). For example, there is a large increase in life satisfaction between individuals in the bottom fifth and the second fifth of the income distribution. However, there are also more retired people in the second fifth of the income distribution and, as life-satisfaction is known to increase between middle-age and old-age (Blanchflower and Oswald, 2007, ONS, 2013a), this may also have some impact on the difference in life satisfaction between these two groups.

Using regression analysis, these additional factors can be taken into account in order to isolate the relationship between income and personal well-being. This article looks at the absolute difference in personal well-being on a scale of 0 to 10 associated with a percentage difference in income.

Table 1: Relationship between household income and personal well-being, after controlling for individual characteristics (1)

Great Britain

	Life satisfaction	Worthwhile	Happy yesterday	Anxious yesterday
Log of equivalised disposable household income (coefficients)	0.249*	0.079	0.114*	-0.164*
Difference in well-being associated with a doubling of equivalised disposable household income (points on the 0–10 scale)	0.173*	0.055	0.079*	-0.114*

Table source: Office for National Statistics

Table notes:
1. * Shows that the relationship is statistically significant at the 5% level.

Download table

XLS XLS format
(27 Kb)

Table 1 shows that higher income appears to be associated with higher well-being across all four measures of well-being, that is: higher levels of life satisfaction, people's sense that the things they do in life are worthwhile and happiness, and lower levels of anxiety. The relationship between income and people's sense that the things they do in life are worthwhile is not strong enough to be considered statistically significant.

The findings show that the aspect of well-being most strongly associated with household income is life satisfaction. A doubling of income is associated with an average life satisfaction rating which is 0.17 points higher on the 0 to 10 scale, holding other factors equal. The size of this difference is roughly comparable to the difference in life satisfaction between individuals renting social (Local Authority and Housing Association) accommodation compared with those renting privately. This difference is small relative to the average 1.15 point difference observed in life satisfaction between individuals in employment compared with those who are unemployed when holding other factors equal.

The impact of a doubling of income is smaller on happiness and anxiety than on life satisfaction. Table 1 shows that, on average, a doubling of income is associated with people rating their happiness 0.08 points higher and their anxiety 0.11 points lower on the 0 to 10 scale.

It is important to note that these results cannot be interpreted as the change in personal well-being immediately before and after a doubling of income as, over time, people's well-being can 'adapt' to changes in prosperity. More information on adaption can be found in 3.3 Interpreting the numbers.

4.2 Distribution of household income

To analyse the distribution and (in)equality of income, the Effects of Taxes and Benefits on Household Income dataset ranks households from poorest to richest in terms of their equivalised disposable income to split them into five equally-sized groups known as quintiles or fifths. For these allocations:

- the bottom fifth contains the poorest 20% of households, by equivalised disposable income,
- the second fifth contains households with incomes between the 20th and 40th percentile of the distribution,
- the middle fifth contains households with incomes between the 40th and 60th percentile of the distribution,
- the fourth fifth contains households with incomes between the 60th and 80th percentile of the distribution,
- the top fifth contains the richest 20% of households by equivalised disposable income.

These income groups were used to analyse the relationship between an individual's personal well-being and where they are in the income distribution.

Image 1: Allocation of households into income fifths

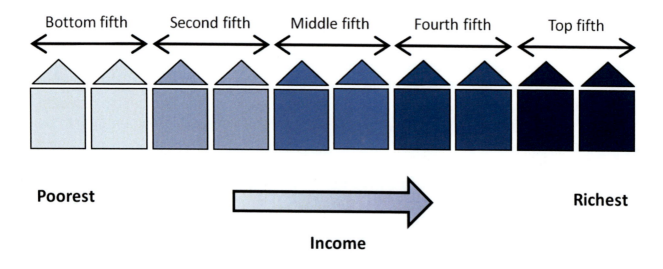

Figure 1: Relationship between personal well-being and different income fifths, compared to the middle fifth, after controlling for individual characteristics

Great Britain

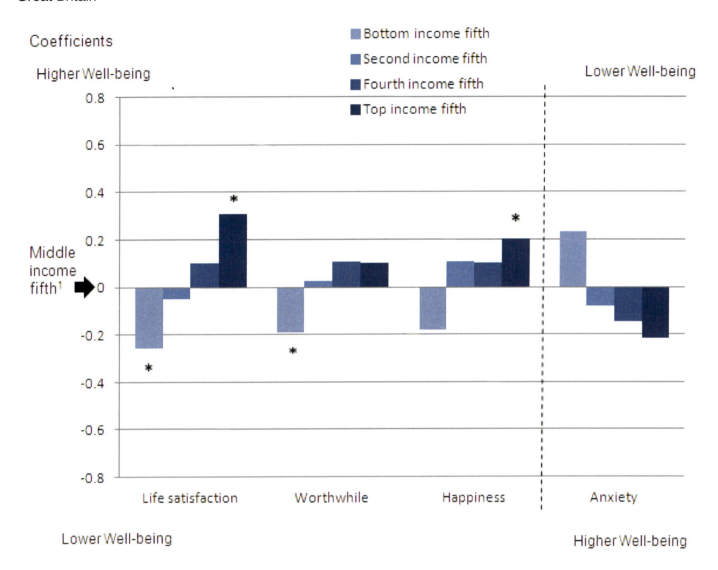

Source: Office for National Statistics

Notes:

1. People in households in the middle fifth of the income distrubution are represented at the baseline (zero).
2. * Shows that the difference from the middle fifth is statistically significant at the 5% level.

Download chart

 XLS format

(29 Kb)

Figure 1 shows the difference in personal well-being associated with living in a household in the middle fifth of the income distribution compared to living in a household in one of the other income groups. The difference in life satisfaction estimated for individuals in households in the bottom and top fifths of the income distribution is 0.56 points. This is roughly comparable to the difference in life satisfaction between individuals in married couples and those who are single, when other factors are taken into account. Relative to those in households in the bottom fifth, being in the top of the income distribution is associated with a perception that the things one does in life are worthwhile and happiness respectively 0.29 and 0.38 points higher, and anxiety 0.45 points lower, holding all else equal.

Figure 1 shows that the biggest difference in all four measures of personal well-being between individuals in neighbouring fifths of the income distribution, is between the bottom and second fifths. Between households in the second, middle, fourth and top fifths of the income distribution, there are no statistically significant differences in perceptions that the things they do in life are worthwhile or in anxiety. This suggests that, as income increases, the largest differences in people's perceptions that the things they do in life are worthwhile and anxiety are at the lower levels of income.

Life satisfaction differs from the other three well-being measures in its relationship with the different income groups, with individuals in the top fifth of the income distribution having significantly higher life satisfaction than those in any other fifth. This suggests that greater household incomes may be associated with higher life satisfaction, even for people in households which are near the top of the income distribution.

An interactive version of Figure 1 is also available.

4.3 Taking the household perspective

The finding that household income is more strongly associated with life satisfaction than other measures of well-being is consistent with previous findings from ONS (2013a) on the relationship between earnings from employment and well-being.

The results of this new analysis also show that, unlike higher personal earnings, higher household income is related to lower anxiety. This may be due to people living in households with high incomes, many of whom may not personally have high earnings, experiencing lower anxiety as a result of finding it easier to meet financial obligations. This reinforces the idea that the total income available to a household is generally more important to personal well-being than individual earnings.

5. How important is the source of household income?

Key findings:

- A higher proportion of household income obtained from cash benefits (for example Jobseeker's Allowance) is associated with lower well-being across all four measures, even after holding equal the total amount of household income.
- Anxiety is the aspect of personal well-being most strongly associated with differences in the proportion of household income derived from cash benefits.
- The relationship between personal well-being and the proportion of household income derived from cash benefits is stronger for men than for women, affecting both happiness and a sense that the things one does in life are worthwhile.

- The relationship between personal well-being and the proportion of income derived from cash benefits is significant even after taking employment status into account, suggesting that the source of income matters to well-being beyond its connection to employment status.

5.1 Income from cash benefits

Having seen a positive relationship between income and life satisfaction, it is helpful to analyse whether the source of a households' income also has an effect on personal well-being in addition to the amount. In the Effects of Taxes and Benefits on Household Income data and report, a distinction is made between the original income that households obtain from employment and investments (including private pensions), and cash benefits received from the state, such as Housing Benefit and Jobseeker's Allowance. This section looks at the association between personal well-being and the proportion of a household's gross (ie. pre-tax) income that is derived from cash benefits, while holding other factors equal, including the total amount of equivalised disposable household income.

A large proportion of households that receive the majority of their income from cash benefits (including the State Pension) are retired households. To distinguish potential effects of the proportion of income coming from cash benefits from the effects of being in a retired household, this part of the analysis looks at non-retired households only.

Table 2: Relationship between the proportion of household income derived from cash benefits and well-being, and household income and well-being, after controlling for individual characteristics (1,2)

Great Britain, Individuals in non-retired households only

Coefficients

	Life satisfaction	Worthwhile	Happy yesterday	Anxious yesterday
Proportion of household income derived from cash benefits (coefficients)	-0.477*	-0.346*	-0.488*	0.655*
Log of equivalised disposable household income (coefficients)	0.240*	0.099	0.084	-0.112

Table source: Office for National Statistics

Table notes:

1. * shows that the relationship is statistically significant at the 5% level.
2. Non-retired households are households which receive less than half their income from retired members.

Download table

XLS XLS format
(27 Kb)

Table 2 shows that, both the household income and the proportion of this income that comes from cash benefits have a statistically significant relationship with life satisfaction, with a higher proportion of income coming from cash benefits being associated with lower life satisfaction.

After taking the proportion of income from cash benefits into account, only life satisfaction is significantly related to household income while all four measures of personal well-being are significantly related to the proportion of income from cash benefits.

A higher proportion of income being derived from cash benefits is significantly related to lower life satisfaction, lower ratings for the perception that the things one does in life are worthwhile, lower happiness and higher anxiety. The largest of these relationships appears to be for anxiety. All else being equal, including the amount of household income, an individual living in a household receiving all its income from cash benefits would rate their anxiety 0.66 points higher on the 0 to 10 scale than someone living in a household receiving no income from cash benefits.

5.2 Differences in the relationship between the source of income and personal well-being for men and women

In contrast to the relationship between well-being and income alone, which does not appear to show large disparities between men and women, there appear to be some differences between the sexes when the relationship between both the level of household income and the proportion of income derived from cash benefits are analysed together.

Table 3: Relationship between the proportion of household income derived from cash benefits and well-being, and household income and well-being, and after controlling for other factors, for men and women (1,2,3)

Great Britain, Individuals in non-retired households only

Coefficients

	Life satisfaction	Worthwhile	Happy yesterday	Anxious yesterday
Proportion of household income derived from cash benefits (coefficients)				
Men	-0.561*	-0.661*†	-0.774*†	0.873*
Women	-0.395*	-0.065†	-0.229†	0.461
Log of equivalised disposable household income (coefficients)				
Men	0.200*	0.053	0.025	-0.080
Women	0.286*	0.146*	0.148	-0.146

Table source: Office for National Statistics

Table notes:

1. * Shows that the relationship is statistically significant at the 5% level.
2. † Difference between the sexes is statistically significant at the 5% level. This has been calculated by "interacting" the income and proportion of income derived from cash benefits with the variables for sex.
3. Non-retired households are households which receive less than half their income from retired members.

Download table

XLS XLS format
(29.5 Kb)

Table 3 shows that men's well-being is, on average, more negatively affected by the proportion of household income derived from cash benefits than women's, particularly the sense that the things they do in life are worthwhile and happiness. All else being equal, a man living in a household in which all of the income is derived from cash benefits would rate his sense that the things he does in life are worthwhile 0.66 points lower and his happiness 0.77 points lower on average than a man living in a household with the same amount of income, none of which is from cash benefits. The findings show this is not the case for women for whom only life satisfaction is significantly affected by the proportion of income from cash benefits.

5.3 Interpretation of relationship between well-being and source of income

Much research has been carried out on the effects of unemployment on personal well-being. McKee-Ryan et al. (2005) and Sen (1997) summarise a variety of reasons that unemployment may impact on well-being, including a lack of structure and purpose to people's lives, lowered social status and sense of self-esteem and a reduced sense of freedom and financial control. Very little research has previously been carried out on the relationship between receipt of cash benefits as a proportion of income and personal well-being.

The findings here show a strong relationship between a higher proportion of household income being derived from cash benefits and lower well-being across all four aspects of personal well-being. Potential reasons may relate to those which link unemployment and low well-being, such as a loss of financial control. However, over 80% of adults living in non-retired households where more than half of income was derived from cash benefits were not unemployed. Employment status was controlled for in the models looking at the proportion of income coming from cash benefits, and both of these variables are highly significant. This suggests both unemployment and the source of household income are related to personal well-being.

6. Does household spending matter to personal well-being?

Key findings:

- Those in households with higher expenditures report higher life satisfaction, sense that the things one does in life are worthwhile and happiness, but do not give significantly different ratings for anxiety, holding other factors equal.
- The relationship between household expenditure and life satisfaction, a sense that the things one does in life are worthwhile and happiness appears to be stronger than the relationship between these aspects of personal well-being and household income.
- As with household income, the largest differences in personal well-being between people in neighbouring fifths of the expenditure distribution, while holding other factors equal, is between people in the lowest and second-lowest expenditure groups.

6.1 Expenditure and well-being

Recent research has highlighted the importance to well-being of economic factors other than income, such as wealth, debt and expenditure. Stiglitz, Sen and Fitoussi (2009) and OECD (2013) emphasise the importance of looking at income, consumption and wealth, when measuring a society's material standard of living.

The availability of detailed expenditure data on the Living Costs and Food Survey has enabled analysis of the relationship between expenditure and well-being. As with household income, expenditure has been equivalised in order to account for differences in household size and composition.

Table 4: Relationship between household expenditure and personal well-being, after controlling for individual characteristics (1)

Great Britain

	Life satisfaction	Worthwhile	Happy yesterday	Anxious yesterday
Log of equivalised household expenditure (coefficients)	0.364*	0.210*	0.254*	-0.112
Difference in well-being associated with a doubling of equivalised household expenditure (points on the 0–10 scale)	0.252*	0.146*	0.176*	-0.077

Table source: Office for National Statistics

Table notes:

1.   * Shows that the relationship is statistically significant at the 5% level.

Download table

XLS XLS format
(28.5 Kb)

Table 4 shows that, holding all else equal, people in households with higher levels of expenditure have significantly higher life satisfaction, give higher ratings for the sense that the things they do in life are worthwhile and rate their happiness higher as well. As with household income, the strongest of these relationships is between household expenditure and life satisfaction. While the results in section 4 showed a doubling of household income being associated with life satisfaction 0.17 points higher on the 0 to 10 scale, the relationship is larger for expenditure, with a doubling in household expenditure associated with life satisfaction 0.25 points higher on average.

Unlike with household income, there is a statistically significant relationship between household expenditure and the sense that the things one does in life are worthwhile. A doubling of household expenditure is associated with people rating the things they do in life as worthwhile 0.15 points higher on the 0 to 10 scale on average.

Looking at the relationship between happiness and household expenditure, holding all else equal, a doubling of expenditure is associated with reported happiness 0.18 points higher on the 0 to 10 scale on average. This suggests there is a larger positive effect on happiness associated with a doubling of household expenditure than with a doubling of household income.

In contrast to the household income findings, the data do not show a significant relationship between household expenditure and levels of anxiety. This could suggest that while the experiences that expenditure bring appear to increase peoples' enjoyment of life, it is higher income that appears to have a larger effect on their feelings of financial security and therefore their levels of anxiety.

Comparing the overall results, the regression models which included household expenditure rather than household income were able to explain more of the differences in people's life satisfaction, sense that the things they do in life are worthwhile and happiness. This suggests that household expenditure may be a more accurate predictor of these aspects of personal well-being than household income. For example, the model which included household expenditure was able to explain 12.5% of the variance in individual life satisfaction compared to 12.1% for the model with household income. Similarly, the models with household expenditure explained 8.8% of the variance in individual ratings of the extent to which the things they do in life are worthwhile and 6.6% of the variance in happiness ratings compared to 8.5% and 6.4% respectively for the household income models.

6.2 Expenditure and well-being in different types of households

When comparing across different types of households, expenditure can often be a more helpful measure of a household's material standard of living than income, as people may fund expenditure from different sources during different periods of their lives. For example, income is the most important determinant of expenditure for most non-retired households, while savings are more likely to play a part in the expenditure of retired households.

The ability of people to draw on savings and loans and to accumulate savings means that their expenditure level maybe more stable over their lifetime than their income level (Friedman, 1957, OECD, 2013). Looking at expenditure data enables us to see if the relationship between people's well-being and the economic resources of their household differs for people of different ages, something which is not possible in studies on only income and personal well-being.

This analysis looks at whether there are differences in the relationship between household expenditure and personal well-being for retired households and for non-retired households with and without children. These household groupings are the same as those used in the annual ONS publication, the Effects of Taxes and Benefits on Household Income, and further definitions of how they are comprised can be found in the Background Notes section.

Table 5: Relationship between household expenditure and personal well-being, after controlling for individual characteristics, by household type (1,2)

Great Britain

	Life satisfaction	Worthwhile	Happy yesterday	Anxious yesterday
Log of equivalised household expenditure (coefficients)				
Retired households	0.206*†	0.175*	0.170	-0.175
Non-retired households with children	0.306*	0.068†	0.166	-0.013
Non-retired households without children	0.499*	0.320*	0.361*	-0.136
Difference in well-being associated with a doubling of equivalised household expenditure (points on the 0–10 scale)				
Retired households	0.143*†	0.122*	0.118	-0.121
Non-retired households with children	0.212*	0.047†	0.115	-0.009
Non-retired households without children	0.346*	0.222*	0.250*	-0.094

Table source: Office for National Statistics

Table notes:

1. * Shows that the relationship is statistically significant at the 5% level.
2. Non-retired households are households which receive less than half their income from retired members.

Download table

XLS XLS format
(29.5 Kb)

Table 5 suggests a stronger relationship between household expenditure and life satisfaction, a sense that the things one does in life are worthwhile and happiness for non-retired households without children than for other household types. Only two of these differences are large enough to be considered statistically significant: the association of household expenditure and life satisfaction is significantly stronger for non-retired households without children than for retired households; and the association of household expenditure with the sense that the things one does in life are worthwhile is significantly stronger for non-retired households without children than non-retired households with children.

These results suggest that the well-being of people in non-retired households without children may be more strongly related to household spending than among those in other types of household.

6.3 Importance of expenditure in addition to income

The findings confirm the importance of household expenditure to personal well-being, although the relative strength of association between expenditure and the four well-being measures differs substantially.

It is important to remember that it is through expenditure that households are able to obtain the necessities required to maintain an acceptable standard of living, as well as the non-essential goods and services which may add to their enjoyment of life. Headey, Mufflels and Wooden (2004) describe expenditure as 'the most valid measure of current living standards' in their analysis of household finances and well-being.

The strength of the relationships found here between expenditure and the three positive aspects of well-being, particularly happiness and the sense that the things one does in life are worthwhile, suggests that higher expenditure, through increasing the household's purchases of goods and services resulting in positive experiences, may increase people's enjoyment of life. Hudders and Pandelaere (2011) list numerous mechanisms through which expenditure may impact well-being from the purely functional benefits of purchasing more and higher-quality goods to the enjoyment resulting from purchases of luxury goods, and also mention that the benefits from increasing expenditure appear to differ depending on personality type. Truglia (2013) proposes that increases in 'conspicuous' expenditure result in higher well-being as a result of enabling individuals to signal a higher socio-economic status to others.

The absence of a strong relationship between higher expenditure and lower anxiety, however, suggests that higher expenditure is not closely associated with an increased sense of financial security. This is in contrast to the income model, which showed a relationship between higher household income and lower anxiety.

It is possible that many households with high levels of expenditure relative to their income run a risk of falling into debt. Brown, Taylor and Price (2005) have studied the link between well-being and wealth and debt, with their results suggesting a strong negative effect on well-being from debt, but a much smaller positive effect from saving. Information on wealth and debt are not available from the Living Costs and Food Survey, on which this analysis is based. However ONS intends to examine the links between wealth, debt and personal well-being later in the year, using data from the Wealth and Assets Survey.

6.4 Distribution of expenditure

As with household income, this article also looks at the relationship between an individual's personal well-being and the fifth of the expenditure distribution that their household is in, holding all else equal. Figure 2 shows that some of the patterns observed in the relationship between income fifths and personal well-being can also be observed in the relationship between expenditure fifths and personal well-being.

Figure 2: Relationship between personal well-being and different expenditure fifths, compared to the middle fifth, after controlling for individual characteristics

Great Britain

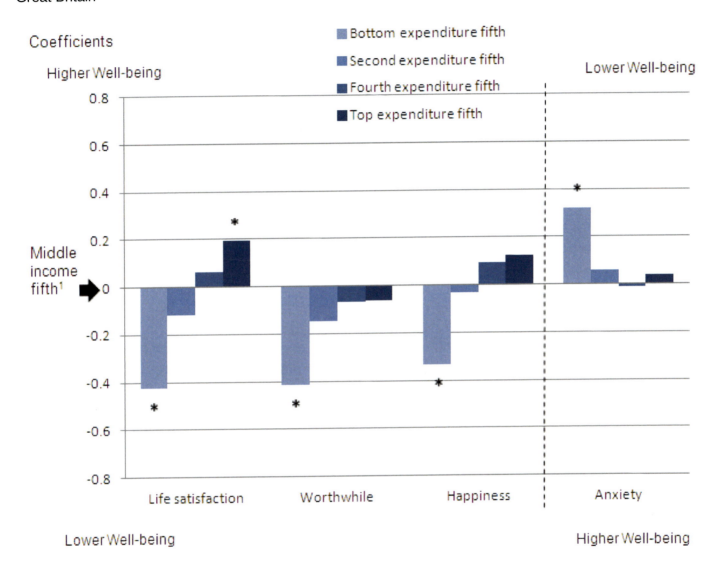

Source: Office for National Statistics

Notes:
1.   People in households in the middle fifth of the expenditure distribution are represented at the baseline (zero).
2.   * Shows that the difference from the middle fifth is statistically significant at the 5% level.

Download chart

 XLS format
(28.5 Kb)

As with household income, the largest differences for all four measures of personal well-being between individuals in neighbouring fifths of the expenditure distribution, are between the bottom and second fifth, which are statistically significant for all measures except anxiety. There are smaller differences in well-being between individuals in the second, middle, fourth and top fifths of the income distribution, particularly for anxiety and people's sense that the things they do in life are worthwhile. The largest differences between individuals in different fifths of the expenditure distribution are in life satisfaction, with individuals in the top fifth rating their life satisfaction 0.62 points higher than those in the bottom fifth of the income distribution, all other factors held equal.

An interactive version of Figure 2 is also available.

7. Technical Appendix

7.1 Why undertake a regression analysis?

In analysis which looks at the relationship between two variables, it can be tempting to infer that one variable is directly related to the other. For example, life satisfaction is higher for households in the top fifth of the income distribution than those in the bottom, but does this mean we can assume that the differences observed in relation to life satisfaction ratings are primarily about differences in income? This conclusion would only be justified if we could show there were no other important differences between high- and low-income households which might affect the findings, such as differences in age or region of residence in the UK.

Regression analysis allows us to do this by holding all the variables in the model equal while measuring the size and strength of the relationship between two specific variables. If the regression results show a significant relationship between income and life satisfaction, then this means that two people who have identical characteristics apart from their income are very highly likely to rate their anxiety levels differently. This implies a direct relationship between income and life satisfaction even when the other variables included in the analysis are taken into account. Therefore, the key benefit of regression analysis is that it provides a better method of isolating the factors which matter most to personal well-being than looking at the relationship between only two variables without controlling for differences in others.

However, every analytical method has its limitations and regression analysis is no exception. The following sections summarise some key considerations which should be borne in mind in terms of the statistical assumptions underlying the techniques used here, and the types of inference which can be drawn from the findings.

7.2 Using OLS for ordered responses and the robustness of the OLS estimates

A key implicit assumption in ordinary least squares (OLS) regression is that the dependent variable (the outcome we are trying to explain, such as the personal well-being rating) is continuous. Continuous data is data that can take any value (usually within a range). For example, the height of two individuals would be within the range of human heights, but could differ by a tiny fraction of a millimetre. The personal well-being survey responses, however, are discrete, that is, they can only take on a relatively small number of whole integer values, between 0 and 10 with no other values possible, such as halves, in between.

OLS regression also assumes that the values of the dependent variable (e.g., personal well-being ratings) are cardinal. This means that the interval between any pair of categories such as between 2 and 3 is assumed to be of the same magnitude as the interval between any other similar pair such as between 6 and 7. As the personal well-being responses are based on subjective ratings, it is not possible to say with certainty that the distance between 2 and 3 is the same as the distance between 6 and 7 on the 0 to 10 response scale. For example, it may be that only small changes in circumstances are required to move people from 2 to 3 in their rating of life satisfaction, but it may take a lot more for them to jump from 6 to 7. This suggests that the OLS regression approach may not be ideally suited to modelling this kind of dependent variable.

There are a number of alternatives to OLS for modelling discrete response variables, such as logit or probit regression. In these models the categories of the responses are treated separately which means there is no implied order of the categories, for example 4 is not necessarily higher than 3. An important disadvantage of these methods is that the information contained in the ordering of the personal well-being ratings is lost. A way of overcoming this issue is to create two categories, for example ratings of life satisfaction above or below 7 on the 0 to 10 scale, but the resulting categories are artificial and do not capture people's actual ratings of their well-being.

An alternative method is to treat the response variable as ordinal and use regression techniques, such as ordered logit or ordered probit that are developed to deal with ordinal data. Ordinal data values can be ranked or ordered on a scale such as from 0 to 10 with each higher category representing a higher degree of personal well-being (or lower personal well-being in the case of anxiety) and unlike the OLS method, ordered probit or ordered logit regression does not assume that the differences between the ordinal categories in the personal well-being rankings are equal. They capture the qualitative differences between different scores. It is important to note that ordinal probit/logistic performs several probit/logistic regressions simultaneously, assuming that the models are identical for all scores. The latter assumption can be relaxed but the interpretation of the results becomes more difficult.

In common with much of the existing literature modelling subjective well-being, this analysis has used ordered probit models to explore the factors contributing to a person's personal well-being. As Greene (2000) points out, the reasons for favouring one method over the other (such as ordered probit or ordered logit) is practical and in most applications it seems not to make much difference to the results.

The major advantage of such models is that it takes the ordinal nature of the personal well-being ratings into account without assuming equality of distance between the scores. Similarly to OLS, it identifies statistically significant relationships between the explanatory variables, for example age, disability, and relationship status, and the dependent variable which in this case is the rating of personal well-being. A difficulty that remains is that the estimated coefficients are difficult to explain clearly to a wide audience.

The existing literature also suggests that OLS may still be reasonably implemented when there are more than four levels of the ordered categorical responses, particularly when there is a clear ordering of the categories as is the case for the personal well-being questions which have response scales from 0 to 10 (Larrabee 2009). Several studies applied both methods to personal well-being data and found that the results are very similar between the OLS models and the theoretically preferable methods such as ordered probit. For example, see Ferrer-i-Carbonell and Fritjers (2004) for a detailed discussion of this issue.

The main advantage of OLS is that the interpretation of the regression results is more simple and straightforward than in alternative methods.

For the sake of completeness, the analysis was conducted in both OLS and probit regression methods. This also acts as a sensitivity check for the robustness of the OLS results as the key assumptions for the OLS regression may not hold for the ordered personal well-being data.

It should be noted that this does not imply that the OLS regression estimates were completely 'robust'. Post regression diagnostics identified some violations of the OLS regression assumptions such as model specification and the normality of residuals. However, as some studies (for example see Osborne and Waters, 2002), suggest that several assumptions of OLS regression are 'robust' to violation, such as normal distribution of residuals, and others are fulfilled in the proper design of the study such as the independence of observations. In this analysis, using the survey design controlled for the potential dependence of the individual observations with each other and applying the survey weights provided some protection against model misspecification.

SAS, the computer program in which the analysis was conducted, automatically computes Huber-White standard errors that are robust to heteroskedasticity when the regressions are estimated incorporating survey design.

Additionally, estimating the models using different specifications as well as two methods (OLS and ordered probit) confirmed that the magnitude and the statistical significance of the parameter estimates did not notably change and the general inferences from the analysis remained the same.

7.3 The explanatory power of the models

It is important to note that the explanatory power of the regression models used in this analysis are similar to that of other reported regression analyses undertaken on personal well-being. As with these previous studies, there are substantial differences in the ability of the models as a whole to explain different aspects of well-being.

The lowest proportion of variance explained by the statistical models was for anxiety, at between 4-5%. A higher proportion of the variance in individuals' happiness and their sense that the things they do in life are worthwhile was explained by the models at 6-7% and 8-9% respectively. As is consistent with previous studies (Kahneman and Deaton, 2010 and ONS, 2013a, b), a much larger proportion of the variation in individual's life satisfaction was explained, at 12-13%. On the whole the levels of explanatory power observed in this analysis are very similar to those found on other analyses of sample surveys, such as ONS (2013a, b) and Headey, Muffels and Wooden (2004).

The limited explanatory power of the model could be due to leaving out important factors which contribute to personal well-being. For example, genetic and personality factors are thought to account for about half of the variation in personal well-being. It has not been possible to include variables relating to personality or genes in the models as the LCF does not include data of this type.

The subjective nature of the outcome variable also means that it is probably measured with some imperfect reliability. The lower the reliability of the outcome variable, the more unclear its correlations with other variables will tend to be.

7.4 Omitted variable bias

In an ideal world, a regression model should include all the relevant variables that are associated with the outcome (i.e. variable being analysed such as personal well-being). In reality, however, we either cannot observe all the potential factors affecting well-being (such as personality) or are limited by whatever information is collected in the survey data used in the regression analysis.

If a relevant factor is not included in the model, this may result in the effects of the variables that have been included being mis-estimated. When the omitted variables are correlated with the included variables in the model, the coefficient estimates of those variables will be biased and inconsistent. However, the estimated coefficients are less affected by omitted variables when these are not correlated with the included variables (i.e. the estimates will be unbiased and consistent). In the latter case, the only problem will be an increase in the estimated standard errors of the coefficients which are likely to give misleading conclusions about the statistical significance of the estimated parameters.

7.5 Multi-collinearity-dependence (or correlations) among the variables

If two or more independent variables in the regression model are highly correlated with each other, the reliability of the model as a whole is not reduced but the individual regression coefficients cannot be estimated precisely. This means that the analysis may not give valid results either about individual independent variables, or about which independent variables are redundant with respect to others. This problem becomes increasingly important as the size of correlations between the independent variables (i.e. multi-collinearity) increases.

As there is no formal statistical test that can be used to identify excessive multi-collinearity when the covariates in the model are dummy variables, an informal method of cross-tabulating each pair of variables can be used, along with analysis of the Pearson correlation coefficients between variables and the Variance Inflation Factors (VIFs) of each of explanatory variables. When very high correlations between the variables were observed, the explanatory regressions were rationalised by removing the variable with the weaker relationship with well-being.

It would be reasonable to expect there to be a degree of correlation between equivalised disposable household income and the proportion of gross household income which comes from cash benefits. Indeed, the data show that higher income households often receive a lower proportion of their income from cash benefits. However the Pearson correlation coefficient between equivalised disposable household income and the proportion of gross household income which comes from cash benefits is closer to 0 (indicating no correlation) than to -1 (indicating perfect correlation), while the VIFs for these two variables are also low (under 3). This indicates that the relationship between these two variables is not strong enough to adversely affect our ability to draw inferences from these models.

7.6 Causality

Regression analysis based on cross-sectional observational data cannot establish with certainty whether relationships found between the independent and dependent variables are causal. This is particularly the case in psychological contexts where there may be a reciprocal relationship between the independent and the dependent variables. For example, the usual assumption is that individual characteristics or circumstances like marital or employment status are independent variables which may affect personal well-being (viewed here as a dependent variable). However, some of the association between employment and well-being may be caused by the impact of personal well-being on employment.

Furthermore, as the data used in the regression analysis here are collected at one point in time (i.e. cross-sectional), they are not able to capture the effect of changes over time and identify which event preceded the other. For example, it is not possible to tell from this data whether movement out of employment precedes a drop in well-being or whether a drop in well-being precedes movement out of employment. We can only definitely say that unemployment is significantly related to lower levels of well-being compared to people who are employed. Therefore, while the regression analysis here can demonstrate that a relationship between two variables exists even after holding other variables in the model equal, these findings should not be taken to infer causality.

The coefficients reported in this article cannot be taken as the difference in well-being experienced immediately before and immediately after a change in income, expenditure, or the proportion of income being derived from cash benefits. Previous studies (such as Di Tella et al., 2003) have suggested that an increase in economic prosperity can lead to a large increase in well-being immediately after the change occurs. However, over time people can "adapt" to their new level of prosperity, and their reported well-being appears to fall over time back to a level closer to that before the change. Brickman et al. (1978) appear to find this even in the case of extreme changes in prosperity, by observing the well-being of lottery winners.

As households with a low income in a particular year are likely to have had a low income in the previous year, and households with a high income are likely to have had a high income in the previous year (Jenkins, 2011), many individuals in this analysis will have had time to fully adapt to their current income levels. However, many individuals in this data source will have experienced recent changes in their incomes, and so the coefficients reported in this analysis cannot be assumed to be the effect on well-being of different income levels after individuals have fully adapted to these changes.

It should also be noted that the data used in this analysis are from responses to the Living Costs and Food Survey between April 2011 and March 2012. This was a period of low economic growth, and it cannot necessarily be assumed that the relationships during this time will be representative of the relationship between income and expenditure in different economic conditions.

7.7 Key analysis variables

7.7.1 Income and expenditure

For the regression models in this article, a natural logarithmic transformation has been applied to income and expenditure.

Looking at the absolute difference in well-being resulting from a percentage difference in income reflects the widely held notion that an absolute increase in income of, for example £500 per year, is likely to have a larger impact on the individual if they have a low income than if they have a high income; but that a percentage difference in income is likely to have similar effects on people of different income levels. This is an application of Weber's Law, which states that the size of a just noticeable difference in a stimulus (such as a sound), is generally a fixed proportion of the intensity of the original stimulus. Evidence from the United States (Kahneman and Deaton, 2010) suggests that this may apply to responsiveness of personal well-being to differences in income.

In addition to helping the models better fit the relationship between personal well-being and income and expenditure, applying a logarithmic transformation reduces the skewness of the income distribution due to very high income and expenditure cases, reducing the influence of these outliers and helping to "normalise" the income and expenditure distributions.

Use of a logarithmic transformation does, however, necessitate further calculations in order to work out the difference in personal well-being associated with a percentage difference in income. In the following formulae, β is the regression coefficient produced for log income or log expenditure, Δ is the percentage difference in income or expenditure for which an associated difference in well-being is sought, and ln is the natural logarithmic function.

The difference in well-being from a $\Delta\%$ increase in income or expenditure $= \beta \times \ln(1 + (\Delta/100))$

The difference in well-being from a $\Delta\%$ decrease in income or expenditure $= \beta \times \ln(1 - (\Delta/100))$

As a result of the calculations required to interpret the regression coefficients, additional figures have been provided in the article showing the difference in well-being, measured on a 0 to 10 scale, between two individuals with identical circumstances except that one has a household income or expenditure double that of the other.

7.7.2 Proportion of income from cash benefits

This article also looks at the differences in well-being associated with differences in the percentage of gross household income derived from cash benefits. Unlike with household income and expenditure, no logarithmic term has been applied to the cash benefit term and this relationship is modelled as being linear.

The coefficients for this relationship can be interpreted as the difference in reported well-being between someone living in a household where 0% of the income is derived from cash benefits and someone living in a household where 100% of income is derived from benefits. As this relationship is linear, the difference in well-being associated with a one percentage point increase in the proportion of household income derived from cash benefits is assumed to be one-hundredth the size of the difference in well-being associated with a one hundred percentage point increase in this measure. Likewise, the difference in well-being associated with a fifty percentage point increase in proportion of household income derived from cash benefits (for example an increase from 25% to 75% of income being derived from cash benefits) can be assumed to be half the size of the regression coefficient.

The logarithm of equivalised disposable household income was also included in the proportion of gross income from cash benefits models, to control for the average income of households which get most of their income from cash benefits being lower than the average income of households with little income from cash benefits. As a large proportion of the households receiving the majority of their income from cash benefits (which includes the State Pension) are retired households, the cash benefits models used data from non-retired households only, to isolate any potential effects of the proportion of income coming from cash benefits from the effects of being in a retired household.

7.7.3 Income and expenditure quintiles

In order to analyse how well-being differs across the income and expenditure distributions, while holding other factors equal, further regression models were produced with the log of income or expenditure variables replaced with the quintile of the income or expenditure distribution a person is in.

This approach is less appropriate for calculating the statistical significance of the relationship between income and well-being than analysing the relationship between the logarithm of income and well-being, as information about differences in well-being associated with small differences in income within fifths of the income distribution is lost. However, including the fifth of the income distribution that a household occupies in the regressions can provide some interesting insights into the implications of the distribution of income for personal well-being.

The figures in the quintile charts in this article can simply be interpreted as the difference in personal well-being between an individual in any quintile relative to the personal well-being of an individual in the middle quintile, holding other factors equal.

7.8 Interpreting the reference tables

In addition to the coefficients discussed above, the reference tables included in this analysis also report the standard errors, confidence intervals and statistical significance of all the variables included in the regression analysis.

The level used to determine statistical significance throughout this article is the 5% level. This means that a variable is considered statistically significant where the probability of observing a relationship between the variable in question and personal well-being as strong as that found in the model, by pure chance, is less than .05 (or less than one in twenty).

Statistical significance is displayed in the reference tables using p-values (P > |t|). Smaller p-values indicate higher statistical significance, so a p value of <.0001 indicates that the probability of observing a relationship as strong as has been found by pure chance is less than one in ten thousand.

The reference tables also give the 95% confidence intervals around the coefficient estimate. These show the range of possible values which the coefficient lies within with 95% probability.

The proportion of the variance in each aspect of personal well-being which is explained by the model as a whole is also given in the reference tables for each OLS model as the R-square.

7.9 Taking the design of the LCF sample into account in the analysis

Regression analysis normally assumes that each observation is independent of all the other observations in the dataset. However, members of the same household are likely to be more similar to each other on some or all of the measures of personal well-being than they are to members of different households. If the analysis ignores this within-household correlation, then the standard errors of the coefficient estimates will be biased, which in turn will make significance tests invalid.

Therefore, to correctly analyse the data and to make valid statistical inferences, the regressions are estimated in SAS with the specification of the survey design features – the clusters that are formed by the households and the strata that the survey was drawn from. The survey weights were also used in the estimation of the model as these allow for more consistent estimation of the model coefficients, reduce the effects of any biases due to non-response and provide some protection against model misspecification.

Unlike some ONS surveys, such as the Annual Population Survey, which may be conducted both in person and via telephone, the Living Costs and Food Survey is only conducted in person. This means that there are no modal effects that need to be controlled for in this analysis.

7.10 Personal well-being questions

Four personal well-being questions were included in all Living Costs and Food Survey interviews conducted in Great Britain between April 2011 and March 2012:

- Overall, how satisfied are you with your life nowadays?
- Overall, to what extent do you feel the things you do in your life are worthwhile?
- Overall, how happy did you feel yesterday?
- Overall, how anxious did you feel yesterday?

These are the four ONS questions on personal well-being, and interviewees give answers to these questions on a scale of 0 to 10. Figure 3 shows how these responses are distributed for each measure.

Figure 3: Distribution of responses for personal well-being in the Living Costs and Food Survey, 2011/12

Great Britain

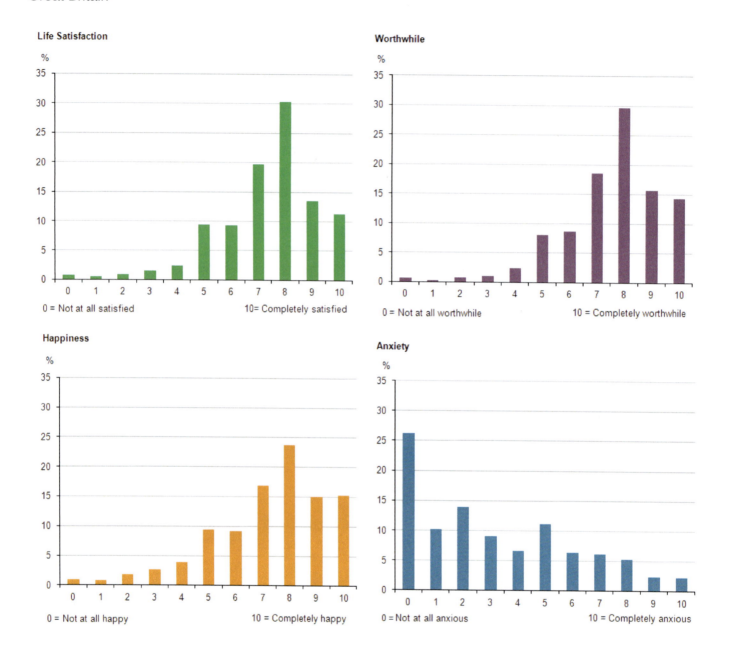

Source: Office for National Statistics

Notes:

1. Adults aged 16 and over were asked 'Overall, how satisfied are you with your life nowadays?', 'Overall, to what extent do you feel the things you do in your life are worthwhile?', 'Overall, how happy did you feel yesterday?' and 'Overall, how anxious did you feel yesterday?'. Answers were given on a 0 to 10 scale where 0 meant 'not at all' and 10 meant 'completely'.

Download chart

 XLS format
(28 Kb)

This distribution of responses is generally very similar to that from the Annual Population Survey (ONS, 2013e). The large proportion of the population rating their life satisfaction, the sense that the things they do in life are worthwhile and happiness between 8 and 10 and their anxiety between 0 and 2, suggests the majority of individuals have high levels of personal well-being.

There are slight differences between the distributions from the two surveys, with slightly fewer respondents to the Living Costs and Food Survey reporting the highest level of personal well-being. This could be due to a number of reasons including differences in the mode of interview. Regression analysis of the APS ONS (2013a) showed that, on average, respondents to telephone interviews gave higher ratings for their personal well-being than respondents to face-to-face interviews. As the APS is conducted both by telephone and face-to-face, while the LCF is only conducted face-to-face, the additional 1-2% of people giving the top rating to their personal well-being in the APS relative to the LCF is consistent with these modal effects.

Due to the personal nature of these well-being questions, respondents only gave ratings for their own personal well-being, and not for other household members who were absent when the interview took place. This meant that, while there were 10,500 eligible people living in households covered by the LCF, nearly 2,500 did not give ratings for their personal well-being, resulting in a final sample of just over 8,000 individuals.

Of those who gave ratings for their personal well-being, just over half were considered to be the Household Reference Person for their household (typically the person responsible for the accommodation, or if there is joint responsibility, the householder with the higher personal income). In order to account for potential non-response bias, data from each interview was weighted by the age, sex and region of the respondent.

7.11 Development of the regression models

Overall, 7 regression models have been published for each well-being measure, using both ordinary least squares and ordered probit techniques:

- Household income.
- Household income quintiles (fifths).
- Household income and the proportion of income received from cash benefits.
- Household income and the proportion of income received from cash benefits by sex.
- Household expenditure.
- Household expenditure by different household types.
- Household expenditure quintiles (fifths).

Each of these was analysed first using OLS and then using ordered probit. All of these results are available in the Reference Tables, as follows:

Reference Table 1 (351 Kb Excel sheet) contains the results for the household income and household income quintile models.

Reference Table 2 (229.5 Kb Excel sheet) contains the results for the proportion of income received from cash benefits and proportion of income received from cash benefits by sex models.

Reference Table 3 (297 Kb Excel sheet) contains the results for the household expenditure, household expenditure by household type and household expenditure quintile models.

Reference Table 4 (52 Kb Excel sheet) contains details of the sample sizes for each of the variables used in the regression models.

8. About the ONS Measuring National Well-being Programme

NWB logo 2

This article is published as part of the ONS Measuring National Well-being Programme.

The programme aims to produce accepted and trusted measures of the well-being of the nation - how the UK as a whole is doing.

Measuring National Well-being is about looking at 'GDP and beyond'. It includes headline indicators in areas such as health, relationships, job satisfaction, economic security, education, environmental conditions and measures of personal well-being (individuals' assessment of their own well-being).

Find out more on the Measuring National Well-being website pages.

Background notes

1. The Effects of Taxes and Benefits on Household Income is an annual ONS publication. The most recently published edition is for 2011/12 and can be found here. Should users have any queries on household income or expenditure they can email ONS at hie@ons.gov.uk.

2. The data analysed in this report are derived from a customised weighted 12 month Living Costs and Food Survey/Effects of Taxes and Benefits on Household Income microdataset produced specifically for the analysis of personal well-being. ONS plans to make this microdata available to approved researchers to allow them to undertake further analysis on personal well-being.

3. A list of the job titles of those given pre-release access to the contents of this article is available on the website.

4. Details of the policy governing the release of new data are available by visiting the UK Statistics Authority or from the Media Relations Office.

5. © Crown copyright 2014

   You may use or re-use this information (not including logos) free of charge in any format or medium, under the terms of the Open Government Licence, write to the Information Policy Team, The National Archives, Kew, London TW9 4DU, or email: psi@nationalarchives.gsi.gov.uk.

6. Details of the policy governing the release of new data are available by visiting www.statisticsauthority.gov.uk/assessment/code-of-practice/index.html or from the Media Relations Office email: media.relations@ons.gsi.gov.uk

Copyright

References

1. Blanchflower, D., and Oswald, A. (2007). 'Is well-being U-shaped over the life cycle?', IZA Discussion Papers, No. 3075.

2. Brickman, P., Coates, D. And Janoff-Bulman, R., (1978). 'Lottery Winners and Accident Victims: Is Happiness Relative?', Journal of Personality and Social Psychology, Vol. 36, No. 8, 917-927.

3. Brown, S., Taylor, K. and Price, S. (2005). 'Debt and distress: Evaluating the psychological cost of credit', Journal of Economic Psychology 26 (2005) 642–663.

4. Di Tella, R., New, J.H.-D. and MacCulloch, R., (2010). 'Happiness Adaptation to Income and to Status in an Individual Panel', Journal of Economic Behavior and Organization, doi:10.1016/j.jebo.2010.09.016.

5. Eurofound (2013), 'Third European Quality of Life Survey – Quality of life in Europe: Subjective well-being', Publications Office of the European Union, Luxembourg.

6. Ferrer-i-Carbonell, A. and Frijters, P. (2004). 'How important is methodology for the estimates of the determinants of happiness', The Economic Journal, 114, 641-659.

7. Fleche, S., Smith, C. and Sorsa, P. (2011), 'Exploring determinants of subjective wellbeing in OECD countries – evidence from the World Value Survey', OECD Economics Department Working Paper, No. 921.

8. French, M. and Dunlap, L. (1998), 'Compensating wage differentials for job stress', Applied Economics, 30, 1067-1075.

9. Greene, W. H. (2000) 'Econometric Analysis', Upper Saddle River, NJ: Prentice-Hall, fourth edition.

10. Friedman, M. (1957) 'A Theory of the Consumption Function', Princeton University Press.

11. Headey, B., Muffels, R. and Wooden, M. (2004) 'Money Doesn't Buy Happiness ... Or Does It? : A Reconsideration Based on the Combined Effects of Wealth, Income and Consumption', IZA Discussion paper series, No. 1211.

12. Hudders, L. and Pandelaere (2011) 'The Silver Lining of Materialism: The Impact of Luxury Consumption on Subjective Well-Being', Journal of Happiness Studies, 13:411–437.

13. Jenkins, S. (2011), 'Changing Fortunes: Income Mobility and Poverty Dynamics in Britain', Oxford University Press.

14. Kahneman, D. and Deaton, A. (2010) 'High income improves evaluation of life but not emotional well-being'. Proceedings of the National Academy of Sciences of the United States of America, Vol.107, No.38, 16489–16493.

15. Larrabee, B. (2009), 'Ordinary Least Squares Regression of Ordered Categorical Data: Inferential Implications for Practice' Kansas State University.

16. Layard, R. (2005) 'Happiness: Lessons from a New Science', Penguin, London, UK. ISBN 9780141016900.

Supporting Information

Glossary

Retired and non-retired persons and households

A retired person is defined as anyone who describes themselves (in the Living Costs & Food Survey) as 'retired' or anyone over minimum National Insurance pension age describing themselves as 'unoccupied' or 'sick or injured but not intending to seek work'. A retired household is defined as one where the combined income of retired members amounts to at least half the total gross income of the household. Non-retired individuals are simply those who do not meet the criteria of retired individuals. A non-retired household is one where combined income of non-retired members amounts to more than half the total gross income of the household. By no means are all retired people in retired households and all non-retired people in non-retired households. For example, households comprising one retired and one non-retired adult are often classified as non-retired. Around one in five households comprising three or more adults contains retired people.

Original Income

Original income is all income that households receive from non-government sources, including earnings from employment and income from private pensions, annuities and other investments.

Gross Income

Gross income is the total income households receive from original income plus cash benefits provided by the state, including the State Pension.

Disability Benefit

The Living Costs and Food Survey does not ask respondents to rate their health or disability. Instead, disability has been controlled for in the model by including a variable for receipt of one of the following benefits: Industrial Injury Disablement Benefit, Disability Living Allowance (either self-care or mobility), Severe Disablement Allowance, Attendance Allowance or Employment and Support Allowance (either contribution or income-based)).

Disposable Income

Disposable income is the amount of money that households have available for spending and saving. It is equal to gross income minus direct taxes (such as income tax and council tax).

Expenditure

The definition of household expenditure used in this article includes all expenditure defined by ONS as consumption expenditure (See: ONS Family Spending Chapter 1), plus a small number of additional items and adjustments which make expenditure more comparable across households. These include expenditure abroad, on duty free goods bought in the UK, on mortgage interest (but not capital repayments), interest payments on credit cards, and on TV licences. Adjustments are made for uprating of expenditure on items where underreporting in surveys is known to occur (such as alcohol, tobacco and confectionary, see The Effects of Taxes and Benefits on Household Income

- ONS 2013c, OECD 2013) and employer-paid expenditure on company cars and fuel (which can be considered a form of household income which is immediately spent – ONS 2013c). Money obtained from gambling winnings and the onward sale of used vehicles are subtracted from the expenditure figure, as these can be considered forms of negative expenditure (OECD, 2013).

Equivalisation

Equivalisation is a process that makes adjustments to disposable incomes, so that the standard of living of households with different compositions can be compared. When applying an equivalence scale, the values for each household member are added together to give the total equivalence number for that household. This number is then used to divide disposable income for that household to give equivalised disposable income. The equivalence scale which has been applied to the LCF income data in order to divide the sample into the fifths (also known as income quintiles) used in this article is the modified-OECD scale where a two-adult household has an equivalence value of one:

Modified–OECD Equivalence Scale

Type of household member	Modified-OECD Equivalence value
First adult	0.67
Second and subsequent adults	0.33 (each)
Child aged 14 and over	0.33 (each)
Child aged 13 and under	0.2 (each)

Download table

XLS XLS format
(25 Kb)

Statistical Contacts

Dawn Snape   +44 (0)1633 455674   Measuring National Well-being   personal.well-being@ons.gsi.gov.uk

Richard Tonkin   +44 (0)1633 456082   Household Income and Expenditure Analysis
hie@ons.gsi.gov.uk

Exploring Personal Well-being and Place

Author Name(s): **Sebnem Oguz, Analysis and Data Access**

Abstract

This article presents the findings of new analysis by ONS on the connections between personal well-being and place. Using data from the APS Personal Well-being dataset (2012/13), regression analysis is used to look at the contributions of the place and the people who live there in shaping the level of personal well-being across different areas of the UK.

2. Introduction

Previous publications by ONS (October 2013) have shown how people rate aspects of their personal well-being, such as life satisfaction, a sense that daily activities are worthwhile, and their levels of happiness and anxiety varies across different areas of the UK. Personal well-being also appears to vary in relation to the specific characteristics of where we live. For example, personal well-being is higher on average in rural areas than in urban areas and in the least deprived areas compared to the most deprived (ONS, May 2013). However, it was noted that these results only reflected the average personal well-being ratings between relatively large geographical areas and this may mask important differences between smaller or local areas within them.

Just looking at the aggregated average personal well-being ratings in different areas, it may be tempting to conclude that differences between places (for example, differences in physical, environmental, social and cultural factors) are the drivers of individual differences in personal well-being outcomes. However, where an individual lives is just one aspect that may influence an individual's response to the personal well being questions and the differences between people living within these areas could be larger than the differences between areas.

The main purpose of this working paper is to use regression analysis to investigate the relationship between personal well-being and where we live, in particular, the degree to which regression analysis of the Annual Population Survey (APS) data can help us understand the relationship between personal well-being and the 'place' where an individual lives. In doing so, the paper is a follow up to the previous ONS "What matters most to personal well-being" article (ONS, May 2013), that used similar regression techniques to examine which factors matter most to well-being but that only gave limited consideration to the effect of place. This article particularly focuses on the following questions:

- Are some parts of the Great Britain associated with higher personal well-being than others?
- Are some types of areas associated with higher personal well-being than others?

- To what extent the place where we live is associated with our personal well-being?
- To what extent the differences in average personal well-being between the areas are driven by the characteristics of people who live in these areas compared with the other characteristics of the areas themselves?

The knowledge that to fully understand differences in average personal wellbeing across places it is necessary to consider the characteristics of the people living there in addition to the other (e.g., physical) characteristics of the place itself is important when determining policy. The final section of this article discusses this issue.

Overall, the paper is aimed mostly at an audience of researches in academia and policy researchers in government. The paper aims to stimulate further debate on the subject of the relationship between personal well-being and place among these audiences. However, the results and findings are also likely to be of interest to those engaged in personal well-being issues at the local level.

2.1 Explaining differences in personal well-being between areas

The differences in observed average personal well-being ratings between areas can be due to:

- the effects relating to people with different characteristics living in different areas (individual effects).
- the effects relating to differences between the areas themselves (rather than the people who live there). This is called area effects.

It is important to note that people may choose to live in a particular area for many different reasons, but their reasons may be similar to those of other people who have opted to live in the same area. For example, they may have similar preferences for the types of schools in the area, access to the countryside and to local amenities. They may also have similar levels of household income which influence their choices of neighbourhood and home. All of this would lead to people with similar characteristics or incomes clustering together in particular areas, which can be described as a 'sorting' process. Because people tend to 'sort' into areas alongside people of similar characteristics, we may find that the average characteristics of people in one area may differ quite substantially from the average characteristics of people in a different area. Meanwhile, a wide range of studies have established that peoples' individual characteristics are related to how they rate their personal well-being (ONS May 2013). For example, people who are unemployed rate their well-being much lower than people in employment and those who rate their health as poor also tend to rate their well-being this way. Taken together, these issues may suggest that personal well-being is really about the people in the place rather than the place itself.

However, it is also likely that personal well-being can be influenced by the characteristics of places where people live. The types of local features which could influence personal well-being are likely to be those things which relate to perceived quality of life, such as the local environment[1], social and cultural life, the local labour market and economic conditions, access to health care and schools and geographical features such as green space. If differences in personal well-being levels across areas relates primarily to characteristics of the place, then people with similar individual characteristics would be expected to rate their personal well-being differently across areas because of different features of the places where they live.

This article explores the differences in personal well-being between local areas and types of areas and investigates using regression analysis to what extent these differences occur because of differences in the types of people in different areas (individual effects) versus different outcomes for the similar types of people in different areas (area effects). The article also describes some important methodological and conceptual challenges associated with examining this topic that need to be borne in mind when reviewing the results. The article concludes by placing the results of the regression work in context.

2.2 Methodological challenges

It is important to be aware that several methodological challenges arise in attempting to understand the relationship between personal well-being and where we live. Some of these challenges are summarised below.

- **Difficulty in disentangling the individual and area effects.** The two explanations proposed above (i.e. individual versus area effects) suggest that the effects of each can be isolated to provide a clear understanding of their separate contributions to personal well-being. However, as many researchers such as Cummins et al (2007) have noted, there may be a 'mutually reinforcing and reciprocal relationship between people and place'. For example, the place may contribute to or undermine the health of those living there- so place may have an effect on health which in turn has an effect on personal well-being (Macintyre et al 2002). Indeed a recent research from Imperial College London found that environmental factors, such as air pollution, accounted for roughly 5-10% of a person's risk of disease, which was significant in terms of a population. As such, in this example the 'area effect' is influencing wellbeing via its impact on an individual effect (health). In other words, there is not always a clear separation between area and individual effects (see also the discussion of sorting below).
- **Lack of clarity about the most appropriate geographical level at which to capture any 'area' effects on personal well-being.** As people vary significantly in their choices of where to live and why, it is not clear at what geographical level (e.g., region, local authority or neighbourhood), differences between areas matter most to personal well-being. Also, some aspects of where we live, such as sense of community, may not coincide neatly with established geographical boundaries so may be difficult to detect in analysis using standard geographical definitions.
- **Difficulty in establishing which aspects of the 'place' are most important to personal well-being.** There are often strong correlations between different factors related to a 'place'. For example, previous analysis (ONS, May 2013) found a positive relationship between living in a rural area and personal well-being after holding equal individual characteristics, but many factors that differ between rural and urban areas are correlated to each other. Rural areas are likely to have more green space and less air pollution and several studies (White et al 2013, Douglas 2014 or Ferreira et al 2013) have found a significant relationship between access to green spaces or pollution and personal well-being. Isolating the separate effects of each on personal well-being is very challenging.

2.2.1 Effect of 'Sorting'

It is worth focusing on how sorting links to individual or area effects. It can be observed that different types of people are clustered into different areas. The fact that this has occurred makes it important that individual effects are examined when seeking to explain differences in average personal wellbeing across areas, (for example, when an area is home to many people who possess individual characteristics usually associated with high wellbeing, that area will likely have a high average wellbeing rating). However, it should be noted that area effects can also be influenced by the sorting of people, because the characteristics of your neighbours can act as an area effect that influences personal well-being.

There is also a separate, but related, question of why this sorting occurs in the first place, and the role of area effects to influence it. This question is not examined in this report. Evidence on this would be found in literature on factors influencing the location choice of households, these factors may include area effects such as the characteristics of neighbours, physical environment, pollution levels etc. As mentioned, this is not within the scope of this article. This article takes the observed distribution of households and individuals across areas as a starting point to the analysis, and examines to what extent the observed differences in average personal well-being between the areas are driven by the characteristics of people who live in these areas compared with the other characteristics of the areas themselves.

Notes

1. The characteristics of the people living in the area are also part of the local environment.

3. Methodology and Data

3.1 How personal well-being is measured

The research is based on data from the Annual Population Survey (APS) from April 2012 to March 2013. The survey provides a representative sample of people living in residential households in the UK and includes about 165,000 respondents.

Since April 2011, ONS have included four questions on the APS which focus on different aspects of personal wellbeing: how we assess our life satisfaction; whether we feel our lives have meaning and purpose; and our recent experiences of positive and negative emotions. These are measured by asking people aged 16 and over four questions:

*   Overall, how satisfied are you with your life nowadays?
*   Overall, to what extent do you feel the things you do in your life are worthwhile?
*   Overall, how happy did you feel yesterday?
*   Overall, how anxious did you feel yesterday?

Those taking part in the survey are asked to give their answers on a scale of 0 to 10 where 10 is 'completely' and 0 is 'not at all'. For the first three questions which are about positive aspects of personal well-being, a higher score indicates higher personal well-being. However, the fourth question asks about anxiety which is a negative emotion so a higher score here indicates lower personal well-being. In this report the abbreviations 'life satisfaction', 'worthwhile' 'happiness' and 'anxiety' are used to refer to the findings in relation to these four questions.

3.2 'Area' data used in the analysis

The APS dataset provides detailed geographical information on individuals which potentially allows analysis at lower geographical levels. Due to sample sizes, the smallest spatial units at which personal well-being data in the APS can be analysed robustly are local authority districts. However, 'place' may have an effect on personal well-being at a more local level than this. In order to overcome sample size problems and to explore the relationship between personal well-being and neighbourhoods, smaller area groupings were used in this analysis as well. These areas were classified together on the basis of similar environmental or socio-economic characteristics and are based on Census output areas. The data used for grouping areas together were derived from various sources such as Census, Index of Multiple Deprivation and small area income estimates. These datasets were all merged into a single data file and then used in the analysis.

A limitation of this approach is that, although the groups are based on smaller areas, they are 'types' of small areas and as such are spread out across Great Britain. As a result they may not capture differences associated with a specific location in the country. Also, an important but untested assumption is that all of the characteristics of these areas are identical.

Note that some of the place related variables, such as rural/urban identification could not be created for all of the UK. As such, the analysis reported in this article does not include respondents from Northern Ireland. Additionally, in some cases it excludes respondents from Scotland; these cases are referred to clearly in the text.

Areas, area groupings and the geographical levels included in the analysis:

- Local authority counties
- Local authority districts
- Weekly average net household income after housing costs in the area - equivalised for household composition (MSOA)
- Weekly average net household income in the area (MSOA)
- Index of multiple deprivation (LSOA)
- Green space (LSOA)
- Rural urban areas (OA)
- Built up areas (OA)
- Population density (OA)
- Output area classification (OA)

Information on these areas and the datasets used can be found in the Technical Annex.

3.3 Regression analysis

First, the differences between individuals were ignored and regressions were run for each of the four personal well-being questions using only a set of area indictors (dummy variables that indicate where the person lives) for each area or area type considered.

The coefficients (b) represent the difference between the average personal well-being rating in a given area and the average personal well-being in the reference area. These regressions, referred to as 'the basic model', show how different areas were related to personal well-being without differentiating between area and individual effects.

Then, a second set of regressions were run including both the area-related and the individual-related variables in the model. These regressions show both the effect of individual characteristics and the additional effects of areas on personal well-being.

$$PWB_i = a + bP_i + e_i$$

where

PWB = individual i's rating for one of the personal well-being outcomes such as life satisfaction (on a scale of 0 to 10)

P = variables (dummy) that indicates where the individual i lives

b = unstandardised coefficients showing area effects

e = an error term that represents unobserved factors associated with personal well-being but that are uncorrelated with area effects.

In these regressions, the coefficients (b) show the effect of areas on personal well-being after accounting for individual characteristics and circumstances. Similarly, the coefficients (g) show the impact of individual characteristics and circumstances on their personal well-being after controlling for the effects of the areas.

Note that, it is not possible to control for all the individual characteristics and circumstances that are associated with personal well-being. If some of these unobserved characteristics also influence sorting into areas, then these factors would be attributed incorrectly to area effects. Because of this as well as the other methodological challenges noted earlier, the estimated area effects in this analysis can best be understood as an approximation of the 'true' area effects. Finally, the estimates are based on a sample and there is the possibility that different samples can give different results.

At each stage, the regressions were carried out using the Ordinary Least Squares (OLS) technique. Although ordered probit is the regression technique which is usually considered best suited to the ordered nature of the responses to the personal well-being questions (i.e., with responses on a scale from 0 to 10), they were not suitable to use for the variance analysis. As in our previous regression analysis (ONS May 2013, ONS February 2014) we also estimated the regressions in ordered probit to test the robustness of OLS results. The statistical significance, the signs and the relative sizes of the regression coefficients between the two methods were very similar, however, the findings from the ordered probit regressions are not reported in this article. The findings in this report are based on the results of the OLS regressions not only for the sake of simplicity and ease of interpretation, but also to enable the variance analysis to be undertaken.

3.3.1 Variables included in the regression models

As an extension of previously published regression findings (ONS, May 2013), the same variables were included in this analysis but more variables were added focusing particularly on aspects of the areas where people live. The following is the full list of variables included in the models:

- Age
- Sex
- Ethnicity
- Migration status
- Relationship status
- Economic activity status
- Housing tenure
- Self-reported health
- Self-reported disability
- Highest qualification held
- Socio-economic status
- Presence of dependent and non-dependent children in the household
- Religious affiliation
- Mode of interview (telephone or personal interview)
- Day of the week of the survey
- Month of the survey
- Length of time at the current address[1]
- A 'place' indicator

The development of the regression models is described more fully in ONS (May 2013).

3.4 Analysis of variance

The extent of the individual or area effects on overall personal well-being, or on the differences in average personal well-being between the areas, can be examined via the coefficients of the regressions before and after accounting for individual characteristics and circumstances. However, to assess the extent to which differences in personal well-being between areas are due to individual or area effects formally and also the extent to which areas matter for individual outcomes of personal well-being , a method called variance decomposition analysis has been used. This involves the use of estimates from the regressions to calculate the variation in personal well-being ratings attributable to either area differences or to differences in the people living in the area.

This technique has also been used in other contexts such as labour economics to explore whether and to what extent sorting on the basis of individual characteristics influences wages (Gibbons et al 2010 or Combes et al 2007). This article used the methods developed by Gibbons et al (2010) to decompose the variation in individual personal well-being ratings into individual and group (or area) specific components. This method gives an estimate of the extent that the observed differences in average personal well-being between the areas reflect differences in the people living in them and/or whether it reflects differences in the areas themselves.

The detailed methodology of the variance decomposition method with an application to area disparities can be found in the paper by Gibbons et al 2010.

In brief, the regression analyses produced three different estimates of the amount of variance which were used to estimate how much of the observed differences in average personal well-being across the areas could be attributed either to the characteristics of the people living in each area (individual effects) or to differences in the areas themselves and the extent to which areas matter for individual outcomes of personal well-being. The following provides a brief description of the estimates which indicate the extent to which areas matter for individual outcomes of personal well-being:

- The **'raw variance share'**, or **RVS** which is derived from the basic model[2], shows how much of the variation in overall personal well-being ratings can be explained by the area, regardless of whether the differences relate to the area itself or to the people living there.

- The **'correlated variance share'**, or **CVS**, shows how much of the variation in overall personal well-being ratings can be explained by the area, after accounting for the characteristics of the people living there. This measure excludes the direct contribution of individual effects on the average personal well-being of the area, however, it includes any indirect effect that the people living in the area may have on the area effects[3].

- The **'uncorrelated variance share**, or **UVS**, also shows how much of the variation in overall personal well-being ratings can be explained by the area, after accounting for the characteristics of the people living there. However, it focuses only on the contribution of area effects that are uncorrelated with the observed individual characteristics and circumstances of the people living in the area, therefore it can be interpreted as the 'net' effects of the area.

These variance estimates are then used to provide some indication on the contribution of individual or area effects to observed differences in average well-being between areas.

3.5 Interpreting the numbers

Two types of results are reported in the sections which follow. These are findings from:

1. the variance analysis; and
2. the regression analysis.

3.5.1 Understanding the variance analysis results

The numbers in Table 1 and Table 2 represent:

- the proportions of overall personal well-being ratings that can be explained by area-related variables:

  - before individual characteristics and circumstances are taken into account (RVS), and

  - after individual characteristics and circumstances are taken into account, either directly by area effects (UVS), or additionally including the indirect effect that the individuals living in the area may have on the area effects (CVS)
- the proportion of the area share of the area differences in observed average personal well-being. That is the contribution of area effects (versus individual effects) to the differences in average personal well-being between areas (CVS or UVS / RVS).

3.5.2 Understanding the regression analysis results

The numbers included throughout the text and in the tables in section 5 are the unstandardised coefficients for each variable included in the regression models. This shows the size of the effect that the variable has on the specific aspect of personal well-being considered.

In interpreting the findings, it is important to remember that these numbers represent the difference between two groups when all other variables in the model have been held equal. The comparisons are therefore between two people who are otherwise the same in every respect apart from the particular characteristic, circumstance or area being considered. This helps to isolate the effect of any specific characteristic, circumstance or area on personal well-being.

Under the tables, when results are referred to as 'significant at the 5% level', this means there is a probability of less than .05 (or less than one in twenty) that the result could have occurred by chance.

Notes

1. This is an individual level variable but it is potentially related with 'place'

2. It is the R-squared from the basic model

3. Because the estimated area effects are potentially correlated with individual characteristics/ circumstances

4. Results - Variance Analysis

This section reports the results of the variance analysis. It focuses on the extent to which average differences in personal well-being between areas arise because of differences in the characteristics of people who live in these areas (individual effects) or differences in characteristics of the areas (area effects). Variance analysis also provides an estimate on the extent to which areas matter for individual outcomes of personal well-being.

To assess the role of individual versus area effects in understanding the differences in observed average personal well-being between areas, first, the differences between individuals were ignored and separate regressions were run for each of the four personal well-being questions and for each set of area indictors (dummies). These regressions, referred to as 'the basic model', showed how different areas were related to personal well-being without differentiating between area and individual effects. The results showed that there are statistically significant and occasionally sizeable differences in average personal well-being between areas[1]. These are represented by RVS in Table 1 which show that:

- Life satisfaction had strongest association with area.
- The weakest associations were found between daily emotions such as anxiety and happiness and area.

- Among the area variables included in the analysis, areas grouped on the basis of the output area classification contributed most to the explanation of the differences in overall personal well-being ratings;
- Local authorities contributed most to the explanation of the differences in overall anxiety yesterday ratings.

The analysis also found areas based on one common characteristic such as rural-urban, or green space were only able to explain a small amount of the differences in overall personal well-being even though these characteristics are derived from small geographies. However, this should not mean that these characteristics are not important for personal well-being. As mentioned before, it is implicitly assumed that area characteristics or the issues faced by the people living in that particular type of area are identical. While this is likely to be the case for IMDs and OACs it is less likely to be so for the rural-urban or built up areas. For example, among the urban places even within the same city there are large differences in terms of economic wealth, quality of life and character of the area. Similarly, in rural areas there may be differences in terms of access to public transport or differences in living costs relative to incomes.

Table 1: Variance decomposition of areas - proportion of the overall personal well-being ratings explained by the area before and after accounting for the characteristics and circumstances of people

Area	Life satisfaction	Worthwhile	Happy yesterday	Anxious yesterday
Local Authority County				
RVS	0.56%	0.45%	0.36%	0.46%
CVS	0.20%	0.18%	0.15%	0.37%
UVS	0.19%	0.17%	0.15%	0.35%
Local Authority District				
RVS	1.14%	1.08%	0.85%	1.07%
CVS	0.57%	0.59%	0.53%	0.93%
UVS	0.56%	0.57%	0.52%	0.91%
Equivalised net weekly household income after housing costs in the area				
RVS	0.60%	0.44%	0.36%	0.03%
CVS	0.01%	0.01%	0.01%	0.04%
UVS	0.01%	0.01%	0.01%	0.04%
Net weekly household income in the area				
RVS	0.54%	0.43%	0.37%	0.03%
CVS	0.01%	0.02%	0.01%	0.04%
UVS	0.01%	0.02%	0.01%	0.03%
Index of Multiple Deprivation				
RVS	1.27%	0.87%	0.72%	0.14%
CVS	0.03%	0.01%	0.03%	0.01%
UVS	0.03%	0.00%	0.02%	0.01%
Green space per hectare				
RVS	0.46%	0.36%	0.20%	0.11%
CVS	0.06%	0.03%	0.02%	0.03%

Area	Life satisfaction	Worthwhile	Happy yesterday	Anxious yesterday
UVS	0.05%	0.03%	0.02%	0.03%
Built up areas				
RVS	0.42%	0.33%	0.21%	0.15%
CVS	0.07%	0.04%	0.03%	0.06%
UVS	0.06%	0.04%	0.03%	0.05%
Rural-Urban				
RVS	0.45%	0.35%	0.21%	0.16%
CVS	0.08%	0.04%	0.04%	0.07%
UVS	0.07%	0.04%	0.03%	0.06%
Population density				
RVS	0.63%	0.49%	0.31%	0.17%
CVS	0.06%	0.03%	0.05%	0.04%
UVS	0.06%	0.03%	0.04%	0.04%
Output Area Classification				
RVS	1.80%	1.48%	1.01%	0.38%
CVS	0.12%	0.15%	0.08%	0.15%
UVS	0.10%	0.13%	0.07%	0.13%

Table source: Office for National Statistics

Download table

XLS XLS format
(29.5 Kb)

The regressions were then run including both the area-related and the individual-related variables in the model. Again, separate regressions were run for each of the four personal well-being questions for each of set of area indictors. These regressions show how each personal characteristic is associated with personal well-being and the **additional** effects of areas on personal well-being after controlling for individual characteristics[1].

Analysis of variation represented by CVSs and UVSs in Table 1 shows how much each area related variable considered in the analysis contributed to the overall differences in average personal well-being after taking account of individual characteristics and circumstances. It shows that the area related variables were only able to explain a small amount of the differences in personal well-being. For example, only about 0.10% of the variance in life satisfaction can be attributed exclusively to living in different OAC areas. The variable representing local authority districts explained more of the variance in personal well-being than any other area variable considered in the analysis.

Table 1 showed that, in general area effects (as shown by CVS or UVS) only explain a small variation in overall personal well-being after accounting for individual characteristics of the people. For details of the overall explanatory power of the regression models see technical appendix section 1.3).

Table 2 shows how much of the observed differences in average personal well-being between the areas could be attributed to the 'area' effects only (as opposed to individual effects).

Table 2 shows that for the positive measures of personal well-being, different attributes of the people living in each place (or sorting effects) accounted for most of the area differences in well-being. For example, individual characteristics and circumstances accounted for around 90% of the area differences in personal well-being between the OAC groups, with the areas accounting for the remaining 10% approximately (i.e. 6%,7%,9% for life satisfaction, happy yesterday and 'worthwhile' measures). However, for local authorities, area effects appeared to matter more than the other places considered here. For the local authority districts in particular, individual effects accounted approximately for half of the area differences in average personal well-being leaving area effects to account for the other half.

In contrast, area effects appeared to have a larger influence on the feelings of anxiety. For local authorities particularly, most of the observed variation in anxiety could not be attributed to the individual characteristics and circumstances of the people living in these areas. However, note the variation in 'anxiety yesterday' explained by the areas (as shown by RVS) were generally lower than the other personal well-being outcomes (even before accounting for individual characteristics and circumstances). Therefore, the proportions presented in Table 2 refer to an already small variation explained by the areas.

Table 2: Contribution of 'area' effects to area differences in average personal well-being

Area	Life satisfaction	Worthwhile	Happy yesterday	Anxious yesterday
Local Authority County				
CVS/RVS	36%	40%	42%	80%
UVS/RVS	34%	38%	42%	76%
Local Authority District				
CVS/RVS	50%	55%	63%	87%
UVS/RVS	49%	53%	61%	85%
Equivalised net weekly household income after housing costs in the area				
CVS/RVS	2%	2%	3%	100%
UVS/RVS	2%	2%	3%	100%
Net weekly household income in the area				
CVS/RVS	2%	5%	3%	100%
UVS/RVS	2%	5%	3%	100%
Index of Multiple Deprivation				
CVS/RVS	2%	1%	4%	7%
UVS/RVS	2%	0%	3%	7%
Green space per hectare				
CVS/RVS	13%	8%	10%	27%
UVS/RVS	11%	8%	10%	27%
Built up areas				
CVS/RVS	17%	12%	14%	40%
UVS/RVS	14%	12%	14%	33%
Rural-Urban				
CVS/RVS	18%	11%	19%	44%
UVS/RVS	16%	11%	14%	37%

Area	Life satisfaction	Worthwhile	Happy yesterday	Anxious yesterday
Population density				
CVS/RVS	10%	6%	16%	24%
UVS/RVS	10%	6%	13%	24%
Output Area Classification				
CVS/RVS	7%	10%	8%	39%
UVS/RVS	6%	9%	7%	34%

Table source: Office for National Statistics

Download table

XLS XLS format
(20 Kb)

Note that, it is not possible to control for all the individual characteristics and circumstances that are associated with personal well-being. If some of these unobserved characteristics also influence sorting into areas, then these factors would be attributed incorrectly to area effects.

Note also that areas grouped as rural/urban, household income, built-up and population density cover England and Wales, IMD, OAC and local authorities cover Great Britain, and green space covers England only, therefore, the results within Tables 1 and 2 are not directly comparable. However, to test whether the higher variation in average personal well-being in the areas covering Great Britain was influenced by relatively higher well-being ratings in Scotland, we estimated IMD, OAC and local authorities without including the respondents from Scotland. The results were similar.

Notes

1. The findings from these regressions are presented in section 5

5a. Results - Administrative Areas

The previous section on variance analysis provided a formal method of examining the extent to which area effects as opposed to individual effects accounted for differences in average personal wellbeing across areas. It showed that individual effects were generally more important than area effects for explaining the differences in observed average personal well-being between the areas (but that this result was not so strong for local authorities and did not apply for all the regressions explaining anxiety yesterday). Estimates of area effects can also be examined via the estimated coefficients of the regressions before and after controlling for individual characteristics. This section focuses on the size of the regression coefficients for the different area variables included in this analysis to both reconfirm the results from the previous section but also to provide additional detail.

There are three types of tables included in this section. The first of these (for example, table 3) compares the regression results for a) the 'basic' regression model without individual effects and b) the regression model after accounting for individual characteristics and circumstances by summarising the spread between the area with the highest and the area with the lowest average personal well-being in each case.

The second type of table shows the unstandardised coefficients for each of the areas considered in that section before controlling for individual characteristics and circumstances (for example, table 7) whilst the third type of table does the same but this time for the regression results after controlling for individual characteristics and circumstances (for example, table 9). Note that for local authorities and for the areas grouped by output area classifications these latter tables are not included in the article due to size considerations. However, the results are available in the reference tables.

The full results of each regression model are provided in the accompanying reference tables. The discussion in this section focuses on the size of identified area effects. However, the full results also include coefficients for each of the individual effects included in the model. In brief the results for the individual effects in each of the regressions were very similar and the key points were that:

- Amongst the observed individual characteristics and circumstances included in the analysis, people's self-reported health made the largest contribution to their levels of personal well-being, followed by their work situation and relationship status.
- Other observed individual characteristics such as age, sex, ethnic group, migration status, religious affiliation, level of qualification, presence of children, reasons for economic inactivity, occupation or housing tenure were also associated in different ways to personal well-being, but none to the same extent as self-reported health, unemployment and relationship status.

5. 1 'Area' effects among administratively defined areas

5.1.1 Local authority counties (Great Britain)

Differences in average personal well-being levels between local authority counties were reported in the ONS publication "Personal wellbeing across the UK (ONS, October 2013)". The publication showed that there was some (statistically significant) variation between the average personal well-being levels of the people living in different local authority across the UK.

The results of the regression analysis can be found in Reference tables 1. They show, for example, before controlling for individual effects, the average life satisfaction in Stoke-on-Trent and in Inner London were 0.43 and 0.42 points respectively lower than average life satisfaction in York which is the reference region in the analysis. At the high end, the average life satisfaction was 0.36 points higher in the county of Eilean Siar, Orkney and Shetland than in York.

Table 3 shows that before accounting for individual characteristics, the difference between the local authority with the lowest coefficient for average life satisfaction and the local authority with the highest coefficient for life satisfaction is 0.79 points (on a scale of 0–10). The table also shows the spread was largest for the anxiety yesterday question[1].

Table 3: Distribution of area effects before and after controlling for individual characteristics: Local Authority Counties

Points on the 0–10 point scale

	Minimum to maximum (before)	Minimum to maximum (after)
Life satisfaction	0.79	0.60
Worthwhile	0.91	0.65
Happy yesterday	0.93	0.65
Anxious yesterday	1.21	1.23

Table source: Office for National Statistics

Table notes:

1. Data for Great Britain from April 2012 to March 2013

Download table

XLS XLS format
(25.5 Kb)

It should be noted that whilst Table 3 is illustrating the maximum extent of the spread between the highest and lowest values, the full results in the accompanying reference tables 1 show that average well-being ratings between most of the local authorities were similar to each other. For example, results for 77 of the 139 local authorities were not statistically significantly different from the reference local authority of York.

After accounting for individual effects, with the exception of anxiety yesterday, the spread between the local authorities with the lowest and highest average well-being was less than the one found in the basic model (with no individual characteristics). For example, the difference in the observed average life satisfaction between the local authority with the lowest average life satisfaction and the local authority with the highest life satisfaction is now 0.60 points (on a scale of 0-10) as shown in Table 3. Additionally, the results in reference tables 1 show that the number of local authorities with statistically significantly different results to the reference local authority of York was much lower at just 13 out of 139.

These findings imply that some of the differences in average personal well-being between the local authorities can be mainly explained by the individual characteristics of the people living in them. For example, after accounting for individual effects, the average life satisfaction in inner London was no longer significantly different to average life satisfaction in York. By contrast, living in the county of Eilean Siar, Orkney and Shetland was still associated with higher average life satisfaction than living in York (0.30 points higher on average) suggesting the possible existence of positive area effects within this local authority.

Note that for anxiety, the results and implications were different. As shown by the variance shares previously in Table 2, for local authorities, individual effects accounted for a smaller proportion in the observed average anxiety ratings between the areas than the area effects.

Note that the estimates are based on a sample, therefore, there is a possibility that different samples give different results.

5.1.2 Local authority districts (Great Britain)

To examine the association between where we live and our personal well-being at a more localised level a similar analysis has also been carried out for the 407 local authority districts of Great Britain.

Table 4 shows the distribution of area effects. For example, before controlling for the individual characteristics the difference in the observed average life satisfaction between the local authority with the lowest average life satisfaction to the local authority with the highest life satisfaction is 1.35 points (on a scale of 0-10). The largest difference was observed for anxiety yesterday outcomes. The distribution of area effects after accounting for individual characteristics indicate that individual effects only accounted for some of the differences in average personal well-being between the local authority districts. The spread between the lowest and highest areas remained relatively large.

Table 4: Distribution of area effects before and after controlling for individual characteristics: Local Authority Districts

Points on the 0–10 point scale

	Minimum to maximum (before)	Minimum to maximum (after)
Life satisfaction	1.35	1.12
Worthwhile	1.52	1.08
Happy yesterday	1.53	1.21
Anxious yesterday	2.20	2.42

Table source: Office for National Statistics

Table notes:

1. Data for Great Britain from April 2012 to March 2013

Download table

XLS XLS format
(17 Kb)

The full results of the regressions are presented in Reference tables 2. For example, in the basic models when taking the district of York as the reference area, London district of Harlow had the lowest average ratings for life satisfaction, happiness yesterday and feelings doings things that are worthwhile (0.84, 0.79 and 0.87 point lower than the average ratings observed in York, respectively), while the respondents living in the Horsham district reported the highest anxiety yesterday levels compared to the residents of York (1.14 points higher than York).

After accounting for individual effects, the average ratings for the positive personal well-being measures in Harlow district were still one of the lowest among the local authorities and statistically different from York. They were now 0.45, 0.50 and 0.56 points lower than the average ratings observed in York for life satisfaction, happy yesterday and 'worthwhile', respectively. The respondents living in the district of Horsham still had the highest average anxiety yesterday rating compared to the average anxiety levels observed in the district of York.

The tables also show after accounting for individual effects a larger number of local authorities had average well-being ratings which are not statistically significant from the reference local authority of York (only 41 local authorities were statistically significantly different from York after taking into account individual effects compared to 124 local authorities before taking individual effects into account). Again, these findings imply that some of the differences in average personal well-being between the local authorities can be explained by the individual characteristics of the people living in them. Similarly, for anxiety levels, the results and implications were different. As shown by the variance shares previously in Table 2, among local authorities, individual effects accounted for a smaller proportion in the observed average anxiety ratings between the areas than the area effects.

Note that the estimates are based on a sample, therefore, there is a possibility that different samples give different results. Also, for local authority districts, sample sizes are relatively small which increases the size of confidence intervals and reduces the chances of finding statistically significant difference between areas.

Notes

1. The coefficients in the regression as shown in reference tables are relative to a reference area and would change if a different reference area were chosen. However, the minimum to maximum spread is not affected by the choice of reference area.

5b. Results - LSOA/MSOA Area Groups

This section focuses on the findings for small area groupings classified together on the bases of similar environmental or socio-economic characteristics. As noted earlier, although the groupings are derived from smaller geographies, they are spread out across the Great Britain. As a result they may not capture differences associated with a specific location in the country. Also, it is implicitly assumed that the area characteristics including the issues faced by the residents of the same type of area are identical and this is a limitation of using these groupings.

5.2.1 Middle Layer Super Output Area (MSOA) level groups

Average household incomes in the area

Average household income of a neighbourhood[1] is one of the contextual factors of an area which is potentially associated with personal well-being. Average income in an area could affect personal well-being in a number of ways. For example, several researchers such as, Diener et.al (1993), Ferrer-i-Carbonell (2005) or Lutmer (2004) found that a person's or household's income relative to their neighbours is one of the factors associated with personal well-being. Average income of an area could also be viewed as an indicator of the desirability of the area. For example, high income areas are generally associated with desirable characteristics, such as low crime, good resources and public services and stable communities living in the area which are all potentially related positively to personal well-being.

The MSOAs are the smallest geographical level for which income information is available. In this section we classified MSOAs on the basis of the average household income in the area to explore how living in relatively rich or poor MSOAs was associated with personal well-being.

Two sets of deciles of the average net weekly household income in the MSOAs were created; average net household income and average equivalised[2] net household income after housing costs to adjust for differences in household composition. The information on average income estimates were derived from the small area income estimates[3] for England and Wales. The income refers to the income a household receives from wages and salaries, self-employment, benefits, pensions, plus any other sources of income. The figures have been produced using a modelling methodology that combines survey, census and administrative data. Note that these estimates generally have large confidence intervals (i.e. they are subject to variability) and the estimates of average income do not reflect the spread of income (i.e. income inequality) in the areas. Indeed a number of deprived neighbourhoods (indicated by IMD) within the MSOAs with relatively high average household incomes in the APS dataset were found.

Looking only at the differences in average personal well-being across areas without controlling for personal characteristics and circumstances, personal well-being was found to be higher on average in the areas with higher incomes and lower in the areas with lower incomes compared to the areas with the lowest average household incomes. People living in the richer MSOAs also reported slightly lower anxiety levels yesterday than people living in the poorest MSOAs. The findings are shown in Tables 5 to 8.

Table 5: Distribution of area effects before and after controlling for individual characteristics: Deciles of net household weekly income in an area after housing costs

Points on the 0–10 point scale

	Minimum to maximum (before)	Minimum to maximum (after)
Life satisfaction	0.41	0.05
Worthwhile	0.35	0.05
Happy yesterday	0.38	0.07
Anxious yesterday	0.19	0.17

Table source: Office for National Statistics

Table notes:

1. Net household weekly income is equivalised for household composition
2. Data for England and Wales from the Annual Population Survey (April 2012 to March 2013) and the Small Area Income Estimates (2007/08)

Download table

XLS XLS format
(17.5 Kb)

Table 6: Distribution of area effects before and after controlling for individual characteristics: Deciles of average weekly net household income in an area

Points on the 0–10 point scale

	Minimum to maximum (before)	Minimum to maximum (after)
Life satisfaction	0.33	0.06
Worthwhile	0.25	0.05
Happy yesterday	0.31	0.09
Anxious yesterday	0.17	0.17

Table source: Office for National Statistics

Table notes:

1. Data for England and Wales from the Annual Population Survey (April 2012 to March 2013) and the Small Area Income Estimates (2007/08)

Download table

XLS XLS format
(17 Kb)

Table 7: Effects of relative net household weekly income in an area after housing costs on personal well-being before controlling for individual characteristics

Coefficients

	Life satisfaction	Worthwhile	Happy yesterday	Anxious yesterday
2nd income decile	0.078*	0.089*	0.021	-0.037
3rd income decile	0.124*	0.115*	0.115*	-0.021
4th income decile	0.232*	0.201*	0.196*	-0.108*
5th income decile	0.284*	0.227*	0.247*	-0.116*
6th income decile	0.325*	0.268*	0.245*	-0.071
7th income decile	0.367*	0.315*	0.341*	-0.191*
8th income decile	0.391*	0.348*	0.325*	-0.116*
9th income decile	0.397*	0.341*	0.378*	-0.093*
10th income decile	0.407*	0.317*	0.368*	-0.097*

Table source: Office for National Statistics

Table notes:

1. The reference group for area net household weekly income is the bottom income decile
2. * shows that the relationship is statistically significant at the 5% level
3. Data for England and Wales from the Annual Population Survey (April 2012 to March 2013) and the Small Area Income Estimates (2007/08)

Download table

XLS XLS format
(19.5 Kb)

Table 8: Effects of relative net household weekly income in the area on personal well-being before controlling for individual characteristics

Coefficients

	Life satisfaction	Worthwhile	Happy yesterday	Anxious yesterday
2nd income decile	0.163*	0.173*	0.182*	-0.139*
3rd income decile	0.276*	0.25*	0.271*	-0.129*
4th income decile	0.235*	0.235*	0.233*	-0.093*
5th income decile	0.318*	0.27*	0.297*	-0.107*
6th income decile	0.322*	0.293*	0.341*	-0.16*
7th income decile	0.367*	0.34*	0.37*	-0.132*
8th income decile	0.395*	0.382*	0.364*	-0.129*
9th income decile	0.409*	0.347*	0.422*	-0.132*
10th income decile	0.493*	0.419*	0.496*	-0.172*

Table source: Office for National Statistics

Table notes:

1. The reference group for relative income is the bottom income decile
2. * shows that the relationship is statistically significant at the 5% level
3. Data for England and Wales from the Annual Population Survey (April 2012 to March 2013) and the Small Area Income Estimates (2007/08)

Download table

XLS XLS format
(19.5 Kb)

After accounting for individual characteristics and circumstances the average household income in the MSOA did not appear to matter additionally to the life satisfaction, feelings of worthwhile and happiness of the respondents living in these areas. The findings are shown in Tables 9 and 10 where it can be seen there are hardly any results which are statistically significantly different to the reference group (bottom decile). These results are in line with those reported in Table 2 in section 4 which showed that individual characteristics and circumstances were able to explain almost all of the differences in average life satisfaction, and 'worthwhile' and 'happiness yesterday' between these areas.

Table 9: Effects of relative net household weekly income in an area after housing costs on personal well-being after controlling for individual characteristics

Coefficients

	Life satisfaction	Worthwhile	Happy yesterday	Anxious yesterday
2nd income decile	-0.022	-0.003	-0.051	0.0263
3rd income decile	-0.041	-0.033	-0.016	0.0975*
4th income decile	-0.005	-0.007	0.005	0.0460
5th income decile	0.009	-0.016	0.020	0.0663
6th income decile	-0.018	-0.038	-0.047	0.1550*
7th income decile	-0.012	-0.028	0.019	0.0520
8th income decile	-0.003	-0.009	-0.012	0.1384*
9th income decile	-0.018	-0.032	0.023	0.1701*
10th income decile	-0.011	-0.055	-0.001	0.1548*

Table source: Office for National Statistics

Table notes:

1. The reference group for area net household weekly income is the bottom income decile
2. * shows that the relationship is statistically significant at the 5% level
3. Data for England and Wales from the Annual Population Survey (April 2012 to March 2013) and the Small Area Income Estimates (2007/08)

Download table

XLS XLS format
(27 Kb)

Table 10: Effects of relative net household weekly income in the area on personal well-being after controlling for individual characteristics

Coefficients

	Life satisfaction	Worthwhile	Happy yesterday	Anxious yesterday
2nd income decile	0.000	0.029	0.060	-0.031
3rd income decile	0.046	0.053	0.085*	0.031
4th income decile	-0.012	0.014	0.029	0.074
5th income decile	0.034	0.013	0.057	0.084
6th income decile	-0.005	0.004	0.065	0.062
7th income decile	-0.005	0.002	0.047	0.116*
8th income decile	0.009	0.029	0.03	0.111*
9th income decile	-0.012	-0.032	0.061	0.143*
10th income decile	0.028	-0.001	0.094*	0.111*

Table source: Office for National Statistics

Table notes:
1. The reference group for relative income is the bottom income decile
2. * shows that the relationship is statistically significant at the 5% level
3. Data for England and Wales from the Annual Population Survey (April 2012 to March 2013) and the Small Area Income Estimates (2007/08)

Download table

XLS XLS format
(19 Kb)

The results were different for the feelings of anxiety yesterday data. After accounting for individual characteristics, living in higher income areas appeared to be associated with higher anxiety yesterday than living in the lower income areas. Those living in MSOAs with the top 30% of income had higher anxiety levels on average than those living in MSOAs with lowest average incomes. For example, respondents living in the MSOAs with the highest equivalised average net household incomes after housing costs reported their anxiety levels yesterday 0.15 points higher than the respondents living in the lowest income areas after controlling for individual effects.

The Reference Tables 3 and 4 provide the results for all the variables in the regression model for the MSOA areas grouped by average household incomes.

5.2.2 Lower Layer Super Output Area (LSOA) level groups

Social theories suggest that people are affected by neighbourhood context in a number of ways. For example, there are empirical studies showing that unemployment, besides having adverse effects on personal well-being of those who actually have no job, can also affect the well-being of other individuals such as their families, colleagues and neighbours. However, Many of the contextual factors that may have a potential influence on personal well-being at an area (or neighbourhood) level are highly correlated. For example, neighbourhoods with poor housing conditions may have high unemployment. This in turn makes it very difficult to identify exactly which contextual factor(s) may have an association with wellbeing. Therefore, instead of looking at neighbourhoods based just on one characteristic, such as average unemployment rate, this article utilised a number of composite indices that condense key information on the characteristics of the areas and its neighbourhood composition, namely the Output Area Classification (OAC) and the Index of Multiple Deprivation (IMD).

Deciles of Index of Multiple Deprivation (IMD) (Great Britain)

Previously published regression analysis by ONS (May 2013) considered how the relative level of deprivation in the area may affect personal well-being. In this section small LSOA level areas were analysed by comparing a standard ranking system based on how deprived they are relative to other areas. The ranking system, called the Index of Multiple Deprivation (IMD), takes into account a number of different aspects of the local area (economic, social, housing and environmental issues) and combines them into a single deprivation score for each area.

Table 11 indicates that individual characteristics and circumstances accounted for most of the differences in observed average well-being between these types of areas (also shown in Table 2).

Table 11: Distribution of area effects before and after controlling for individual characteristics: Indices of Multiple Deprivation (IMD)

Points on the 0–10 point scale

	Minimum to maximum (before)	Minimum to maximum (after)
Life satisfaction	0.69	0.08
Worthwhile	0.64	0.13
Happy yesterday	0.55	0.05
Anxious yesterday	0.33	0.09

Table source: Office for National Statistics

Table notes:

1. Data for England and Wales from the Annual Population Survey (April 2012 to March 2013), English IMD (2010), Scottish IMD (2012) and Welsh IMD (2013)

Download table

XLS XLS format
(25.5 Kb)

Table 12 shows that before accounting for individual characteristics and circumstances the reported average well-being increases as the deprivation of the local area decreases.

Table 12: Effects of relative deprivation in the area on personal well-being before controlling for individual characteristics

Coefficients

	Life satisfaction	Worthwhile	Happy yesterday	Anxious yesterday
2nd decile	0.157*	0.134	0.171*	-0.104*
3rd decile	0.243*	0.212*	0.216*	-0.122*
4th decile	0.333*	0.291*	0.332*	-0.172*
5th decile	0.372*	0.317*	0.367*	-0.187*
6th decile	0.463*	0.361*	0.428*	-0.229*
7th decile	0.518*	0.439*	0.5*	-0.319*
8th decile	0.586*	0.483*	0.532*	-0.330*
9th decile	0.602*	0.479*	0.511*	-0.299*
10th decile (least deprived)	0.691*	0.546*	0.641*	-0.324*

Table source: Office for National Statistics

Table notes:
1. The reference group for deprivation is the bottom decile (most deprived)
2. * shows that the relationship is statistically significant at the 5% level
3. Data for England and Wales from the Annual Population Survey (April 2012 to March 2013), English IMD (2010), Scottish IMD (2012) and Welsh IMD (2013)

Download table

XLS XLS format
(19 Kb)

The individual characteristics and circumstances accounted for most of the differences in the feelings of 'worthwhile' between the areas. However, those living in relatively less deprived areas rated their levels of life satisfaction and 'happiness yesterday' on average somewhat higher than those living in the most deprived areas after their individual characteristics were taken into account, however, on the average no difference was found in anxiety levels between the respondents living in the most and the least deprived areas. The findings are shown in Table 13.

Table 13: Effects of relative deprivation in the area on personal well-being after controlling for individual characteristics

Coefficients

	Life satisfaction	Worthwhile	Happy yesterday	Anxious yesterday
2nd decile	0.026	0.032	0.063	-0.018
3rd decile	0.004	0.023	0.02	0.03
4th decile	0.015	0.034	0.077*	0.025
5th decile	-0.007	0.008	0.057	0.056
6th decile	0.031	0.005	0.075*	0.039
7th decile	0.039	0.04	0.106*	-0.016
8th decile	0.075*	0.053	0.11*	-0.008
9th decile	0.056*	0.016	0.062	0.044
10th decile (least deprived)	0.077*	0.026	0.129*	0.068

Table source: Office for National Statistics

Table notes:

1. The reference group for deprivation is the bottom decile (most deprived)
2. * shows that the relationship is statistically significant at the 5% level
3. Data for England and Wales from the Annual Population Survey (April 2012 to March 2013), English IMD (2010), Scottish IMD (2012) and Welsh IMD (2013)

Download table

XLS XLS format
(19 Kb)

Reference table 5 provides the results for all the variables in this version of the regression model.

Relative concentration of green space in LSOA areas (England)

A considerable body of research (for example, Ambrey et.al (2012 and 2013) suggests that proximity to green space is associated with personal well-being through its effects on health. This may relate either to increased opportunities for physical activity in areas with more green space or to other health related issues that differ between areas with more or less green space, such as air pollution. The accessibility of local green spaces was also found to be valued more by urban residents than by those living in non-urban areas.

The findings in this section show the relationship between the amount of green space in local areas and personal well-being. For this analysis, deciles were created based on the green space per square metre in the LSOA areas.

Table 14 indicates that individual characteristics and circumstances accounted for some of the differences in observed average well-being between these types of areas (also shown in Table 2).

Table 14: Distribution of area effects before and after controlling for individual characteristics: Deciles of green space per metre squared

Points on the 0–10 point scale

	Minimum to maximum (before)	Minimum to maximum (after)
Life satisfaction	0.38	0.15
Happy yesterday	0.32	0.11
Worthwhile	0.32	0.10
Anxious yesterday	0.30	0.15

Table source: Office for National Statistics

Table notes:

1. Data for England from April 2012 to March 2013

Download table

XLS XLS format
(17.5 Kb)

The results shown in Table 15 indicate that a statistically significant relationship exists between the amount of the green space in the local area where a person lives and his/her personal well-being before accounting for the composition of the area. Residents living in areas where the amount of green space per square metre is relatively large reported higher ratings for all the measures of positive personal well-being (and lower anxiety levels yesterday) than people living in areas with smaller amounts of green space per square metre.

Table 15: Effects of the amount of green space in the area on personal well-being before controlling for individual characteristics

Coefficients

	Life satisfaction	Worthwhile	Happy yesterday	Anxious yesterday
2nd decile	0.01	0.017	-0.033	-0.033
3rd decile	0.024	0.041	-0.053	-0.076
4th decile	0.023	0.051	-0.038	-0.094
5th decile	0.011	0.023	-0.03	-0.075
6th decile	0.064	0.037	-0.025	-0.125*
7th decile	0.094*	0.092*	0.028	-0.175*
8th decile	0.156*	0.125*	0.048	-0.222*
9th decile	0.264*	0.24*	0.138*	-0.244*
10th decile	0.376*	0.323*	0.263*	-0.296*

Table source: Office for National Statistics

Table notes:

1. The reference group for green space is the 'bottom decile'
2. * shows that the relationship is statistically significant at the 5% level
3. Data for England from April 2012 to March 2013

Download table

 XLS format

(27 Kb)

Table 16 shows after accounting for personal characteristics and circumstances the amount of green space in the area appeared to have some additional association with personal well-being. People living in the areas with the largest amount of green space (top 20%) rated their life satisfaction and 'happiness yesterday' higher on average than people living in the areas with the least amount of green space (the bottom decile). Consistent with literature, our results also found that green space appeared to matter more for 'anxiety yesterday' ratings than other well-being ratings. Results show that reported average levels of anxiety decreases as the amount of the green space in the local areas increases and the coefficients showing the association between personal well-being and green space were generally larger than the ones found for the other measures of personal well-being.

Table 16: Effects of the amount of green space in the area on personal well-being after controlling for individual characteristics

Coefficients

	Life satisfaction	Worthwhile	Happy yesterday	Anxious yesterday
2nd decile	0.021	0.024	-0.016	-0.025
3rd decile	0.044	0.057*	-0.026	-0.066
4th decile	0.047	0.064*	-0.005	-0.085
5th decile	0.012	0.019	-0.012	-0.054
6th decile	0.044	0.013	-0.025	-0.083
7th decile	0.055	0.047	0.014	-0.116*
8th decile	0.062*	0.028	-0.01	-0.146*
9th decile	0.107*	0.086*	0.022	-0.126*
10th decile	0.152*	0.098*	0.083*	-0.135*

Table source: Office for National Statistics

Table notes:
1. The reference group for green space is the 'bottom decile'
2. * shows that the relationship is statistically significant at the 5% level
3. Data for England from April 2012 to March 2013

Download table

XLS XLS format
(26.5 Kb)

Reference table 6 provides a summary of the results for all the variables in the regression model.

Notes

1. This section only examines the relationship between the average household income in the area and personal well-being. For the relationship between household income and personal well-being see the recently published ONS article.

2. Equivalisation adjusts for differences in household composition in order to give a measure that can be used meaningfully to compare incomes between different sizes and types of households.

Further information on definitions of income and equivalisation can be found in the 2012 Family Spending Edition.

3. The latest available data was 2008 small area income estimates. It is assumed that the average household incomes in these areas did not change significantly since then.

5c. Results - Output Area Groups

5.3 'Area' effects based on Output Area groups

Rural-Urban (England and Wales)

Previously published regression analysis findings (ONS, May 2013) showed that after taking into account individual and household characteristics, the average well-being of people living in rural areas was higher than the average well-being of people living in urban areas. However, it was also shown that the size of the relationship between living in an urban or rural area and personal well-being was generally small. It was also noted that these results only reflected the average personal well-being ratings between relatively large geographical areas and this may mask important differences between smaller or local areas within them.

To explore this further, this analysis used the 2001 census rural urban classification which splits urban areas into three different groups and rural areas into five different groups. Due to its vastly large size, a separate category was created for London.

Table 17 indicates that (with the exception of anxiety yesterday outcomes) individual characteristics and circumstances accounted for most of the differences in observed average well-being between these types of areas (also shown in Table 2).

Table 17: Distribution of area effects before and after controlling for individual characteristics: Rural and urban areas

Points on the 0–10 point scale

	Minimum to maximum (before)	Minimum to maximum (after)
Life satisfaction	0.52	0.31
Worthwhile	0.39	0.21
Happy yesterday	0.43	0.11
Anxious yesterday	0.66	0.53

Table source: Office for National Statistics

Table notes:

1. Data for England and Wales from April 2012 to March 2013

Download table

 XLS format
(17 Kb)

Table 18 shows that before accounting for individual characteristics, in general rural areas are associated with higher well-being than urban areas. Examining urban areas alone, people living in other types of urban areas also reported higher average life satisfaction and lower average levels of anxiety yesterday than people living in London.

Table 18: Effects of living in types of rural and urban areas on personal well-being before controlling for individual characteristics

Coefficients

	Life satisfaction	Worthwhile	Happy yesterday	Anxious yesterday
Urban (Less Sparse)	0.157*	0.095*	0.031	-0.227*
Urban (Sparse)	0.306*	0.174*	0.084	-0.08
Town and Fringe (Sparse)	0.366*	0.166*	0.316*	-0.657*
Village (Sparse)	0.519*	0.389*	0.316*	-0.376*
Hamlet and Isolated Dwellings (Sparse)	0.49*	0.373*	0.316*	-0.405*
Town and Fringe (Less Sparse)	0.318*	0.26*	0.316*	-0.341*
Village (Less Sparse)	0.455*	0.372*	0.316*	-0.411*
Hamlet and Isolated Dwellings (Less Sparse)	0.479*	0.386*	0.316*	-0.457*

Table source: Office for National Statistics

Table notes:
1. The reference group for the rural and urban type areas is London – a very large urban area
2. * shows that the relationship is statistically significant at the 5% level
3. Data for England and Wales from April 2012 to March 2013

Download table

 XLS format
(27 Kb)

Table 19 shows that after accounting for individual characteristics and circumstances, generally there remains a positive association between personal well-being and living in rural areas compared with living in London. The coefficients were largest for life satisfaction and 'happy yesterday' for sparse villages whilst anxiety yesterday levels were lowest relative to London in the Sparse Town and Fringe category.

Examining urban areas alone, the average life satisfaction ratings in the other urban areas were still higher than the average ratings in London. However, for the 'happy yesterday' measure, London was no different from either the urban (sparse) or urban (less sparse) areas, however, London was lower on this measure than the Town and Fringe areas.

Table 19: Effects of living in types of rural and urban areas on personal well-being after controlling for individual characteristics

Coefficients

	Life satisfaction	Worthwhile	Happy yesterday	Anxious yesterday
Urban (Less Sparse)	0.088*	0.062*	0.024	-0.178*
Urban (Sparse)	0.213*	0.147	0.061	-0.012
Town and Fringe (Sparse)	0.186*	0.027*	0.21*	-0.527*
Village (Sparse)	0.309*	0.211	0.283*	-0.249*
Hamlet and Isolated Dwellings (Sparse)	0.234*	0.123	0.246*	-0.248*
Town and Fringe (Less Sparse)	0.128*	0.108*	0.057	-0.222*
Village (Less Sparse)	0.186*	0.131*	0.126*	-0.252*
Hamlet and Isolated Dwellings (Less Sparse)	0.186*	0.119*	0.107*	-0.275*

Table source: Office for National Statistics

Table notes:
1. The reference group for the rural and urban type areas is London – a very large urban area
2. * shows that the relationship is statistically significant at the 5% level
3. Data for England and Wales from April 2012 to March 2013

Download table

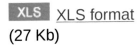 XLS format
(27 Kb)

Reference table 7 provides the results for all the variables in the regression model.

Built up areas (England and Wales)

Another way of investigating differences between types of areas is to use the ONS Built-Up Areas categorisation. This data provides information on the villages, towns and cities where people live, and allows comparisons between people living in built-up areas and those living elsewhere. Similar to disaggregated rural and urban analysis, London is included as a separate category.

Table 20 indicates that individual characteristics and circumstances generally accounted for most of the differences in observed average well-being between these types of areas (also shown in Table 2).

Table 20: Distribution of area effects before and after controlling for individual characteristics: Built-up areas

Points on the 0–10 point scale

	Minimum to maximum (before)	Minimum to maximum (after)
Life satisfaction	0.45	0.19
Happy yesterday	0.35	0.15
Worthwhile	0.35	0.12
Anxious yesterday	0.43	0.28

Table source: Office for National Statistics

Table notes:
1. Data for England and Wales from April 2012 to March 2013

Download table

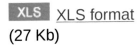 XLS format
(17 Kb)

Table 21 suggests that, before accounting for individual effects, average well-being ratings generally increase as the size of the built up area reduces. As these groupings are highly correlated with the green space and rural urban groupings analysed before, the findings were very similar.

Table 21: Effects of living in types of built-up areas on personal well-being before controlling for individual characteristics

Coefficients

	Life satisfaction	Worthwhile	Happy yesterday	Anxious yesterday
Major (1 million -3 million)	0.098*	0.04	-0.018	-0.228*
Large (500,000 - 999,999)	0.16*	0.063*	-0.011	-0.199*
Medium (100,000-499,999)	0.143*	0.1*	0.009	-0.202*
Small (10,000-99,999)	0.214*	0.15*	0.103*	-0.265*
Minor (<10,000)	0.37*	0.299*	0.228*	-0.375*
non-Built Up	0.452*	0.346*	0.336*	-0.431*

Table source: Office for National Statistics

Table notes:

1. The reference group for built-up areas is London
2. * shows that the relationship is statistically significant at the 5% level
3. Data for England and Wales from April 2012 to March 2013

Download table

 XLS format
(18.5 Kb)

Table 22 shows that there remains an association with personal well-being and living in relatively less built-up areas, compared with living in London, even after controlling for individual characteristics and circumstances. For example, reported average life satisfaction, the feelings of doing things that are worthwhile and happiness yesterday were 0.19, 0.15 and 0.10 points respectively higher for those living in the least built up areas than those living in the most built up areas (London). Similarly, the reported anxiety yesterday levels of the people living in the least built-up areas were 0.28 points lower on average than those living in London.

Table 22: Effects of living in types of built-up areas on personal well-being after controlling for individual characteristics

Coefficients

	Life satisfaction	Worthwhile	Happy yesterday	Anxious yesterday
Major (1 million -3 million)	0.06*	0.03	-0.004	-0.191*
Large (500,000 - 999,999)	0.118*	0.061*	0.011	-0.177*
Medium (100,000-499,999)	0.08*	0.074*	0.01	-0.161*
Small (10,000-99,999)	0.093*	0.068*	0.056	-0.178*
Minor (<10,000)	0.154*	0.118*	0.089*	-0.235*
non-Built Up	0.191*	0.099*	0.148*	-0.277*

Table source: Office for National Statistics

Table notes:
1. The reference group for built-up areas is London
2. * shows that the relationship is statistically significant at the 5% level
3. Data for England and Wales from April 2012 to March 2013

Download table

XLS XLS format
(26.5 Kb)

Reference table 8 provides the results for all the variables in the regression model.

Population density (England and Wales)

Research suggests that population density is another potential factor which may influence personal well-being. Studies have generally shown an inverse relationship between the two (i.e. personal well-being increases as population density decreases). A high level of urbanisation (high density) has also been shown by some studies to be associated with higher levels of psychosis and depression (Cramer et. al 2004 or Sundquist et. al 2004).

There are several ways in which population density may be related to personal well-being, including:

- Air and noise pollution- it increases with density and this in turn leads to health problems both physical and mental.
- Restricted physical activity.

- Social stress – for example, Lederborgen et.al (2013) found that brain area activity differences associated with urbanisation may be linked to the higher incidence of schizophrenia in urban areas compared to non-urban areas. They interpret their findings as showing a causal relationship.
- Lack of trust or fear of crime.

To explore the association between personal well-being and population density in the local area, 13 groups were created based on the 2011 Census population per hectare in the output areas.

Table 23 indicates that individual characteristics and circumstances generally accounted for most of the differences in observed average well-being between these types of areas (also shown in Table 2).

Table 23: Distribution of area effects before and after controlling for individual characteristics: Population Density per Hectare

Points on the 0–10 point scale

	Minimum to maximum (before)	Minimum to maximum (after)
Life satisfaction	0.63	0.22
Happy yesterday	0.45	0.18
Worthwhile	0.53	0.12
Anxious yesterday	0.6	0.38

Table source: Office for National Statistics

Table notes:
1. Data for England and Wales from April 2012 to March 2013

Download table

XLS XLS format
(25.5 Kb)

Table 24 shows before accounting for individual effects, reported average well-being ratings generally reduce as the population density increases.

Table 24: Effects of population density per hectare in the output area on personal well-being before controlling for individual characteristics

Coefficients

	Life satisfaction	Worthwhile	Happy yesterday	Anxious yesterday
1 person per hect	0.031	0.055	-0.023	-0.138
2-3 people per hect	-0.077	-0.061	-0.079	0.063
4-13 people per hect	-0.141*	-0.118*	-0.152*	0.045
14-25 people per hect	-0.179*	-0.140*	-0.207*	0.154*
26-35 people per hect	-0.232*	-0.191*	-0.275*	0.113
36-45 people per hect	-0.253*	-0.171*	-0.25*	0.108
46-54 people per hect	-0.322*	-0.251*	-0.359*	0.216*
55-65 people per hect	-0.374*	-0.298*	-0.396*	0.256*
66-80 people per hect	-0.39*	-0.328*	-0.39*	0.278*
81-112 people per hect	-0.403*	-0.324*	-0.342*	0.273*
113-250 people per hect	-0.522*	-0.436*	-0.454*	0.349*
251+ people per hect	-0.596*	-0.477*	-0.407*	0.463*

Table source: Office for National Statistics

Table notes:
1. The reference group is an average of zero person per Hectare
2. * shows that the relationship is statistically significant at the 5% level
3. Data for England and Wales from April 2012 to March 2013

Download table

XLS XLS format
(27.5 Kb)

Table 25 shows that population density of the local area has no additional association with a person's feelings that the things they do in their lives are 'worthwhile'. However, there was still an association between other measure of personal well-being and living in relatively less dense areas. For example, people living in the most populated output areas rated their life satisfaction on average 0.22 points lower than those living in the least dense areas. Their reported average anxiety yesterday was also 0.27 points higher than those living in the least populated areas. For 'happy yesterday' measure, least dense areas were no different from the most populated areas.

Table 25: Effects of population density per hectare in the output area on personal well-being after controlling for individual characteristics

Coefficients

	Life satisfaction	Worthwhile	Happy yesterday	Anxious yesterday
1 person per hect	0.001	0.06	-0.038	-0.108
2-3 people per hect	-0.033	0.004	-0.034	0.044
4-13 people per hect	-0.08*	-0.021	-0.081*	0.015
14-25 people per hect	-0.078*	-0.003	-0.105*	0.107
26-35 people per hect	-0.111*	-0.034	-0.155*	0.057
36-45 people per hect	-0.116*	-0.004	-0.116*	0.038
46-54 people per hect	-0.144*	-0.053	-0.183*	0.111
55-65 people per hect	-0.155*	-0.061	-0.178*	0.13*
66-80 people per hect	-0.126*	-0.05	-0.139*	0.134*
81-112 people per hect	-0.096*	-0.01	-0.066	0.095
113-250 people per hect	-0.17*	-0.057	-0.138*	0.131*
251+ people per hect	-0.219*	-0.062	-0.089	0.268*

Table source: Office for National Statistics

Table notes:

1. The reference group is an average of zero person per hectare

2. * shows that the relationship is statistically significant at the 5% level

3. Data for England and Wales from April 2012 to March 2013

Download table

XLS **XLS format**
(19.5 Kb)

Again these groupings were highly correlated with the green space, rural urban and built-up area groupings analysed before, therefore the findings were very similar.

Reference Table 9 provides the results for all the variables in the regression models.

Output Area Classifications (Great Britain)

The Output Area Classification (OAC) is another composite index that condenses key information on the characteristics of the areas and its neighbourhood composition: The Output Area Classification (OAC) distils key results from the 2001 Census for the whole of the UK at a fine grain to indicate the character of local areas. The classification groups areas into clusters based on similar characteristics: demographic, household composition, housing, socio-economic, employment and industry sector.

Table 26 shows that there is quite a large difference between the OAC area with the highest and lowest average personal wellbeing before accounting for individual characteristics. However, once individual characteristics are considered, the difference in average personal well-being between OAC areas reduces considerably. This is consistent with the results reported in Table 2.

Table 26: Distribution of area effects before and after controlling for individual characteristics: Output Area Classification

Points on the 0–10 point scale

	Minimum to maximum (before)	Minimum to maximum (after)
Life satisfaction	0.93	0.22
Happy yesterday	0.93	0.35
Worthwhile	0.84	0.28
Anxious yesterday	0.77	0.55

Table source: Office for National Statistics

Table notes:

1. Data for Great Britain from April 2012 to March 2013

Download table

XLS **XLS format**
(17.5 Kb)

There are 52 OAC areas so it is not possible to display all the coefficients in a table in this article. However, the regression results can be found in the accompanying Reference Tables 10. These show that among the 52 neighbourhood types, the highest average personal well-being ratings were found in the areas located in the countryside and in the prospering suburbs. The lowest average personal well-being was observed in the relatively deprived areas (neighbourhood types 5 and 7).

After controlling for individual characteristics and circumstances, (with the exception of anxiety yesterday levels) individual effects were able to explain most of the differences in average personal well-being between these areas and there was very little additional association with personal well-being and living in most of these areas. For example, only 6 out of 51 OAC area groupings were statistically significantly different from the reference group. Neighbourhoods with a negative association with personal well-being were located in relatively deprived city areas in England, especially in London and some around Birmingham (area types 7). People living in some of these areas (e.g. area types 7b) also reported higher anxiety levels on the average than people living the reference area, however, reported anxiety yesterday levels was also found to be higher in more affluent and educated parts of the cities mainly in London and Scotland (area types 2a2, 2b2) than in some of the deprived neighbourhoods. Similar to the findings in previous sections, neighbourhoods with a positive association with well-being were located in the rural areas.

Note in Reference Table 10, the areas are identified by their OAC codes. Full explanations of each of the OAC subgroups can be found in the OAC summary document.

6. Discussion and Policy Implications

This article has extended earlier ONS research on the relationships between personal well-being and place and offers a further step in understanding the relationship between where we live and personal well-being. The main findings of the regression and the variance analysis are summarised below:

- Before accounting for individual characteristics and circumstances, the data showed that areas or types of areas have considerable associations with **individual** personal well-being outcomes.
- After accounting for individual characteristics and circumstances, the data showed that areas or types of areas have much lower associations with **individual** personal well-being outcomes.
- Observed differences in average life satisfaction, happiness yesterday and peoples' feelings that the things they do in their lives that are 'worthwhile' **between the areas or area types** mainly reflected the different characteristics of people living in them.
- Local authority districts had the largest amount of variation in average personal well-being unexplained by individual effects.
- Area effects appeared to matter more for the feelings of anxiety **between the areas or area types** than for the other measures of personal well-being for some of the areas and area types.
- Among the individual characteristics and circumstances considered, people's self-reported health was the most important factor associated with personal well-being, followed by their work situation and then their relationship status. Other factors such as people's age, sex, ethnic group, migration status, religious affiliation, level of qualification, presence of children, reasons for inactivity, occupation and home ownership were also associated in different ways to personal well-being, but none to the same extent as health, unemployment and relationship status.

It should be noted, however, that the regression technique applied to the personal well-being data cannot be considered to give definitive answers to the issue of the importance of place on personal wellbeing. The results above are important indications of the likely impact of place on personal well-being but they are only part of the story. To understand this, it is necessary to consider both a number of caveats to the regression work and also to look at the subject in a slightly wider context.

A key caveat is that it is more difficult to disentangle the individual effects and the area effects than the above suggests. The two aspects cannot be entirely separated. For example, air pollution may negatively impact on an individual's health which is a case where the area effect is influencing personal well-being via its impact on an individual effect (health). It is difficult for regression, in particular a cross-sectional type regression analysis, to disentangle these impacts. It is also difficult to know at what geographical level different factors might influence personal well-being and to ensure that all the possibilities are covered. More advanced statistical techniques and additional data (such as panel data) may be required to explore this further.

Similarly, it is difficult for regression work to establish which aspects of place may impact on personal well-being. This is because there are often strong correlations between different factors related to place. For example, rural areas will typically have low noise pollution, low crime, low air pollution, more scenic views etc. relative to urban areas and isolating which of these is actually the important factor(s) in influencing personal well-being is very challenging.

In terms of providing a wider context, it needs to be borne in mind that individuals are not randomly distributed across the country. Individuals have choices about where to live, and in making their choices they will weigh up many issues, some of which will include the characteristics of the local area. Typically, it is found that people of similar characteristics (in terms of income etc.) tend to be clustered together in similar areas. When examining differences in personal well-being across areas it is the existence of this clustering of individuals that explains much of the difference in observed average personal well-being across areas.

Why this sorting and clustering takes place, and the degree to which aspects of the local area influence this process are not in the scope of this article, but are clearly interesting topics for anyone wishing to consider the average personal well-being differences across areas and how they change over time.

So what conclusions should be taken away from this working paper?

- A key finding was that the analysis largely confirmed that individual characteristics are usually key to personal well-being and also to the average personal well-being differences between areas (subject to the caveats).
- Area effects were found to exist to some degree by the regression work. However, it is difficult to isolate exactly what the key determinants of area effects may be. Additionally, the process of isolating individual compared to area effects is not clear cut with some overlap likely to exist. Finally, the analysis did not examine the degree to which 'area effects' may influence individuals housing location choice – yet it is this clustering that is one of the key influences in why average personal well-being across two different areas will often be different.
- In terms of policy, the relative importance of individual effects may suggest that people based policies would have greater potential for well-being improvements than area-based policies.

However, this finding needs to be balanced against the respective costs of the different policies whilst the uncertainties around the analysis discussed above would also need to be considered. In reality, the mix of appropriate place- versus individual-based policies is likely to differ depending on policy aims.

- Although this analysis found relatively little direct area effects on personal well-being, further research on area effects should be encouraged. This could involve examination of additional aspects of local areas beyond those included here. More consideration could also be given to neighbourhoods and the factors that encourage people to choose one neighbourhood over another, drawing on the body of literature on 'residential location choice'.

Background notes

1. Details of the policy governing the release of new data are available by visiting www.statisticsauthority.gov.uk/assessment/code-of-practice/index.html or from the Media Relations Office email: media.relations@ons.gsi.gov.uk

Copyright

References

1. Ambrey, C.L. and Fleming, C.M. (2012). 'Valuing Australia's Protected Areas: A Life Satisfaction Approach', New Zealand Economic Papers, vol. 46, no. 3, 191–209

2. Ambrey, C.L., Fleming, C.M., (2013). 'Public Greenspace and Life Satisfaction in Urban Australia', Urban Studies, vol. 51, no. 6, 1290-1321

3. Balas, D. (2013). 'What makes a happy city?', Cities 32 (2013) S39-S50

4. Combes, P.P., Duranton, G. and Gobillon, L. (2007). ' Spatial wage disparities: Sorting matters!', Journal of Urban Economics, Volume (Year): 63 (2008), Issue (Month): 2 (March), 723-742

5. Cramer, V., Torgersen, S. and Kringlen, E. (2004). ' Quality of Life in a City: The Effect of Population Density', Social Indicators Research, Vol. 69, No. 1 (Oct., 2004), pp. 103-116

6. Cummins, S. Curtis, S. Diez-Roux, A.V. and Macintyre, S. (2007). ' Understanding and representing 'place' in health research: A relational approach, Social Science & Medicine 65 (2007) 1825–1838

7. Diener, E., Sandvik, E., Seidlitz, L., & Diener, M. (1993). The relationship between income and subjective well-being: Relative or absolute? Social Indicators Research 28, 195–223

8. Dorling,D., Smith, G., Noble, M., Wright, G., Burrows, R., Bradshaw, J., Joshi, H., Pattie, C., Mitchell, R., Green, A. E., McCulloch, A. (2001). 'How much does place matter?', E&PA, Volume 33, No. 8., 1335-1369

9. Douglas, I. (2004). 'Urban green space and mental health'. UK MAB Urban Forum

10. Ferreira, S., Akay, A., Brereton, F., et al. (2013). 'Life satisfaction and air quality in Europe', Ecological Economics. 88:1-10

11. Ferrer-i-Carbonell, A. (2005). ' Income and well-being: an empirical analysis of the comparison income effect', Journal of Public Economics 89 (2005) 997–1019

12. Ferrer-i Carbonell, A. and Frijters, P. (2004). 'How important s methodology for the estimates of the determinants of happiness?', The Economic Journal, 114 (July), 641-659

13. Gibbons, S, Overman, H.G. and Pelkonen, P. (2010). 'Wage disparities in Britain: People or Place?', SERC Discussion Paper, 60

14. Greene, W.H. (2000). 'Econometric Analysis', Upper Saddle River, NJ: Prentice Hall, fourth edition

15. Larrabee. B.R. (2009). 'Ordinary least squares regression of ordered categorical data: Inferential implications for practice', A Report submitted in partial fulfilment of the requirements for the degree of Master of Science, Kansas State University

16. Lederbogen, F, Haddad,L. and Meyer-Lindenberg, A (2013). 'Urban social stress – Risk factor for mental disorders. The case of schizophrenia', Environmenal Pollution (2013), 1-5

17. Lutmer, E.F.P. (2004). 'Neighbours as negatives: Relative earnings and well-being', NBER Working Paper No. 10667

7. Technical Annex

7.1 Why undertake a regression analysis?

In analysis which looks at the relationship between two variables, it can be tempting to infer that one variable is directly related to the other. For example, people in one ethnic group may have higher life satisfaction than those in another ethnic group, but can we assume that the differences observed in relation to life satisfaction ratings are primarily about ethnic differences? This conclusion would only be justified if we could show there were no other important differences between the ethnic groups which might affect the findings such as differences in health or employment status.

Regression analysis allows us to do this by holding all the variables in the model equal while measuring the size and strength of the relationship between two specific variables. If the regression results show a significant relationship between ethnicity and life satisfaction, then this means that two people who are identical in every way apart from their ethnicity would indeed rate their life satisfaction differently. This implies a direct relationship between ethnicity and life satisfaction even when the other variables included in the analysis are taken into account. Therefore, the key benefit of regression analysis is that it provides a better method than analysis looking at the relationship between only two variables at a time of indentifying those factors which matter most to personal well-being.

However, every analytical method has its limitations and regression analysis is no exception. The following sections summarise some key considerations which should be borne in mind in terms of the statistical assumptions underlying the techniques used here and the types of inference which can be drawn from the findings.

7.1.1 Using OLS for ordered responses and the robustness of the OLS estimates

A key implicit assumption in OLS regression is that the dependent variable (the outcome we are trying to explain, such as the personal well-being ratings) is continuous. Continuous data is data that can take any value (usually within a range). For example, a person's height could be any value within the range of human heights or time in a race which could even be measured to fractions of a second. The personal well-being survey responses, however, are discrete, i.e., they can only take on a relatively small number of integer values, such as 6 or 10 with no other values such as halves in between.

OLS regression also assumes that the values of the dependent variable (e.g., personal well-being ratings) are cardinal, i.e. the interval between any pair of categories such as between 2 and 3 is of the same magnitude as the interval between any other similar pair such as between 6 and 7. As the personal well-being responses are only rankings we cannot know whether for example the distance between 2 and 3 is the same as the distance between 6 and 7. For example, it may be the case that it doesn't take much for people to move from 2 to 3 in life satisfaction ranking, but it may take a lot more for them to jump from 6 to 7. Therefore, the OLS regression approach may not be well suited for modelling this kind of dependent variable.

There are a number of alternatives to OLS for modelling discrete response variables, such as logit or probit regression. In these models the categories of the responses are treated separately (i.e. there is no order to the categories, for example, 4 is not higher than 3). The disadvantage of these methods is that the information contained in the ordering of the personal well-being ratings is lost.

However, a way of overcoming this issue is to create two categories, for example rankings below 7 and above 7, but the categories will be artificial.

An alternative method is to treat the response variable as ordinal and use regression techniques, such as ordered logit or ordered probit that are developed to deal with ordinal data. Ordinal data values can be ranked or ordered on a scale such as from 0 to 10 with each higher category representing a higher degree of personal well-being (or lower personal well-being in the case of anxiety) and unlike the OLS method, ordered probit or ordered logit regression does not assume that the differences between the ordinal categories in the personal well-being rankings are equal.

They capture the qualitative differences between different scores. It is important to note that ordinal probit/logistic performs several probit/logistic regressions simultaneously, assuming that the models are identical for all scores. The latter assumption can be relaxed but the interpretation of the results becomes more difficult. The major advantage of such models is that it takes the ordinal nature of the response variable (i.e. personal well-being rankings) into account without assuming equality of distance between the scores. Similarly to OLS, it identifies statistically significant relationships between the explanatory variables (e.g. age, health, etc) and the dependent variable (personal well-being ranking); however, the estimated coefficients have no direct interpretation.

The existing literature also suggests that OLS may still be reasonably implemented when there are more than five levels of the ordered categorical responses, particularly when there is a clear ordering of the categories e.g. levels of happiness with 0 representing the lowest category and 10 representing the highest category (for example see Larrabee, 2009). Indeed, several studies including our regression analysis (May 2013 and February 2014) applied both methods to personal well-being data and found that there is little difference between the OLS and the theoretically preferable methodologies such as ordered probit. For example, see Ferrer-i-Carbonell and Fritjers (2004) for a detailed discussion of this issue. Also, Greene (2000) points out, the reasons for favouring one method over the other (such as ordered probit or ordered logit) is practical and in most applications it seems not to make much difference to the results. The main advantage of OLS is that the interpretation of the regression results is more simple and straightforward than in alternative methods.

Because the ordered probit regressions were not suitable for the variance analysis only the findings from the OLS regressions are reported in this article. However, we have estimated the regressions in ordered probit to test the robustness of the OLS results. As before, the statistical significance, the signs and the relative sizes of the regression coefficients were similar between the two methods were very similar.

7.1.2 Diagnostic checks of the OLS regressions

Post regression diagnostics identified some violations of the OLS regression assumptions such as model specification and the normality of residuals. However, as some studies (for example see Osborne and Waters, 2002), suggest that several assumptions of OLS regression are 'robust' to violation such as normal distribution of residuals and others are fulfilled in the proper design of the study such as the independence of observations. In this analysis, using the survey design controlled for the potential dependence of the individual observations with each other (see section 7.2) and applying the survey weights provided some protection against model misspecification.

As there is no formal statistical test that can be used to identify multi-collinearity when the covariates in the model are dummy variables, an informal method of cross-tabulating each pair of dummy variables can be used. When cross-tabulations showed very high correlation between the variables they were not used in the regression. An example where this was the case is between the variables "reported being a Muslim" and "reported being Pakistani"; to get around this problem in this example, the dummy variables for the individual religions from the model were replaced with a single dummy variable "reported a religion".

Stata automatically computes standards errors that are robust to heteroskedasticity when the regressions are estimated incorporating survey design.

Additionally, estimating the models using different specifications as well as two methods (OLS and ordered probit) confirmed that the magnitude and the statistical significance of the parameter estimates did not significantly change and the general inferences from the analysis remained the same.

7.1.3 The explanatory power of the models

It is important to note that the explanatory power of the regression models used here is relatively low. Indeed, the amount of variance that has been explained by the model is similar to that of other reported regression analyses undertaken on personal well-being. For the 'happy yesterday', 'anxious yesterday' and 'worthwhile' questions, around 10% - 14% of the variation between individuals is explained by the variables included in the model. By contrast, a much higher proportion (19%) of the individual variation in ratings for life satisfaction was explained by the model.

The lower explanatory power of the model could be due to leaving out important factors which contribute to personal well-being. For example, genetic and personality factors are thought to account for about half of the variation in personal well-being. It has not been possible to include variables relating to personality or genes in the models as the APS does not include data of this type.

The subjective nature of the outcome variable also means that it is probably measured with some imperfect reliability. The lower the reliability of the outcome variable, the more unclear its correlations with other variables will tend to be.

7.1.4 Omitted variable bias

In an ideal world, a regression model should include all the relevant variables that are associated with the outcome (i.e. variable being analysed such as personal well-being). In reality, however, we either cannot observe all the potential factors affecting well-being (such as personality) or are limited by whatever information is collected in the survey data used in the regression analysis.

If a relevant factor is not included in the model, this may result in the effects of the variables that have been included being mis-estimated. When the omitted variables are correlated with the included variables in the model, the coefficient estimates of those variables will be biased and inconsistent. However, the estimated coefficients are less affected by omitted variables when these are not correlated with the included variables (i.e. the estimates will be unbiased and consistent).

In the latter case, the only problem will be an increase in the estimated standard deviations of the coefficients which are likely to give misleading conclusions about the statistical significance of the estimated parameters.

7.1.5 Causality

Regression analysis based on cross-sectional observational data cannot establish with certainty whether relationships found between the independent and dependent variables are causal. This is particularly the case in psychological contexts where there may be a reciprocal relationship between the independent and the dependent variables. For example, the usual assumption is that individual characteristics or circumstances like health or employment status are independent variables which may affect personal well-being (viewed here as a dependent variable). However, some of the association between health and well-being may be caused by the impact of personal well-being on health.

Furthermore, as the data used in the regression analysis here are collected at one point in time (i.e. cross-sectional), they are not able to capture the effect of changes over time and which event preceded another. For example, it is not possible to tell from this data whether the perception of being in bad health precedes a drop in well-being or whether a drop in well-being precedes the perception that one is in bad health. We can only definitely say that the perception of being in bad health is significantly related to lower levels of well-being compared to people who say they are in good health. Therefore, while the regression analysis here can demonstrate that a relationship between two variables exists even after holding other variables in the model constant, these findings should not be taken to infer causality.

7.1.6 Multi-collinearity- dependence (or correlations) among the variables

If two or more independent variables in the regression model are highly correlated with each other, the reliability of the model as a whole is not reduced but the individual regression coefficients cannot be estimated precisely. This means that the analysis may not give valid results either about individual independent variables, or about which independent variables are redundant with respect to others. This problem becomes increasingly important as the size of correlations between the independent variables (i.e. multi-collinearity) increases.

7.2 Taking the design of the APS sample into account in the analysis

The primary sampling unit in the Annual Population Survey is the household. That is, individuals are grouped into households and the households become units in sample selection.

Regression analysis normally assumes that each observation is independent of all the other observations in the dataset. However, members of the same household are likely to be more similar to each other on some or all of the measures of personal well-being than they are to members of different households. If the analysis ignores this within-household correlation, then the standard errors of the coefficient estimates will be biased, which in turn will make significance tests invalid. Therefore, to correctly analyse the data and to make valid statistical inferences, the regressions are estimated in Stata with the specification of the survey design features. The survey weights were also used in the estimation of the model as these allow for more consistent estimation of the model coefficients and provide some protection against model misspecification.

7.3 Analysis of variance

The detailed methodology of the variance decomposition method with an application to area disparities can be found in the paper by Gibbons et al 2010.

7.4 Areas and area groupings used in the analysis

All the area related variables were constructed using 2001 Census geographies.

7.4.1 Administrative geographies

Administrative geography concerns itself with the hierarchy of areas relating to national and local government in the UK. The analysis considered two types of administrative geographies: Local Authority County and Local Authority District.

7.4.2 Geographies used in the construction of area groupings

Areas are classified together on the basis of similar environmental or socio-economic characteristics and are based mainly on Census 2001 output areas and super output areas.

Output areas (OAs) are created for Census data, specifically for the output of census estimates. 2001 Census OAs were built from clusters of adjacent unit postcodes but as they reflected the characteristics of the actual census data they could not be generated until after data processing. They were designed to have similar population sizes and be as socially homogenous as possible based on tenure of household and dwelling type (homogeneity was not used as a factor in Scotland).

In constructing the areas, urban/rural mixes were avoided where possible; OAs preferably consisted entirely of urban postcodes or entirely of rural postcodes. They had approximately regular shapes and tended to be constrained by obvious boundaries such as major roads. OAs were required to have a specified minimum size to ensure the confidentiality of data.

In England and Wales 2001 Census OAs were based on postcodes as at Census Day and fit within the boundaries of 2003 statistical wards and parishes. If a postcode straddled an electoral ward/division or parish boundary, it was split between two or more OAs.

The minimum OA size was 40 resident households and 100 resident people but the recommended size was rather larger at 125 households. These size thresholds meant that unusually small wards and parishes were incorporated into larger OAs.

In Scotland OAs were based on postcodes as at December 2000 and related to 2001 wards. However, the OAs did not necessarily fit inside ward boundaries where confidentiality issues made it more appropriate to straddle boundaries. The minimum OA size was 20 resident households and 50 resident people, but the target size was 50 households.

Super output areas were designed to improve the reporting of small area statistics and are built up from groups of output areas (OAs). Statistics for lower layer super output areas (LSOAs) and middle layer super output areas (MSOAs) were originally released in 2004 for England and Wales. Scotland also released statistics for data zones (equivalent to LSOAs) in 2004 and intermediate geographies (equivalent to MSOAs) in 2005.

LSOAs in England and Wales have a minimum population of 1,000 and 400 households and a maximum population of 3,000 and 1,200 households. MSOAs in England and Wales have a minimum population of 5,000 and 2,000 households and a maximum population of 15,000 and 6,000 households.

Data zones (DZs) and Intermediate zones (IZs) in Scotland in Scotland are smaller in population size than their LSOA and MSOA counterparts in England and Wales. DZs have a minimum population of 500 and IGs have a minimum population of 2,500.

Further information is available on ONS geographies.

7.4.3 Socio-economic and environmental characteristics of areas

Index of Multiple Deprivation

The Indices of Deprivation measure relative deprivation for small areas (LSOAs). Deprivation is a wider concept than poverty, and so the indices are constructed from a number of different types, or domains, of deprivation. These domains are combined into a single index, the Index of Multiple Deprivation (IMD), which ranks the areas in order of deprivation. A rank of 1 identifies the most deprived area.

The IMD deciles in this analysis are created by treating the most-deprived 10% of these areas as a single (non-adjacent) area, named Decile 1. The next most-deprived 10% are then grouped into a single area, named Decile 2, and so on.

Each of the four Nations of the UK produces its own Index. These Indices are not directly comparable because they use different domains and indicators, reflecting the priorities in the individual countries, and are published on different timescales covering different time periods.

However, the two domains – income and employment- are common to all four national IMDs and they contribute around half the weight of each IMD. They also use similar indicators such as simple percentage of individuals receiving one or more income or employment benefits. This implies they are relatively comparable across countries. For this analysis, the IMD deciles are created separately for each GB nation and then it is matched with the individual data. Although the values of the IMD deciles variable are not comparable across different nations, the variable can be considered a fairly good proxy for the relative deprivation of the area where an individual lives.

The deciles are based on the latest publications of the IMD Indices. These were: the English IMD Index - 2010, Scottish IMD Index - 2012 and the Welsh IMD Index - 2011.

Output Area Classifications

The 2001 Area Classification are used to group together geographic areas according to key characteristics common to the population in that grouping. These groupings are called clusters, and are derived using census data.

The largest cluster is the supergroup, of which there are seven. Each supergroup is further split into groups (21 in total) and further into subgroups (52 in total). This analysis is based on 52 subgroups.

Detailed information on these groups can be found in output area classifications.

For this analysis, output area classifications were matched with the individual data in the APS.

Rural - Urban Classification

The Rural/Urban Definition and LA Classification were developed following the 2001 Census and defines the rurality of very small 2001 Census based geographies.

Four settlement types are identified and assigned to either a 'sparse' or 'less sparse' regional setting to give eight classes of Output Areas.

Information on the rural-urban classification was available in the APS.

For further information please see the Rural-Urban Definition page.

Built-up areas classification

Built-up areas (BUAs) are a new geography, created as part of the 2011 Census outputs.

This data provides information on the villages, towns and cities where people live, and allows comparisons between people living in built-up areas and those living elsewhere. Census data for these areas (previously called urban areas) has been produced every 10 years since 1981.

For this analysis, output area classifications were matched with the individual data in the APS.

For further information please see ONS geography built-up areas.

Average household income in the MSOA areas

For this analysis, we classified MSOAs on the basis of the average household income in the area to explore how living in relatively rich or poor MSOAs was associated with personal well-being. Middle Layer Super Output Areas (MSOAs) are the smallest geographical level for which income information is available.

Small area (Middle Layer Super Output Area) income estimates covers MSOA areas in England and Wales. The estimates are calculated using a model based method to produce four estimates of average weekly income. The income refers to the income a household receives from wages and salaries, self-employment, benefits, pensions, plus any other sources of income. The figures have been produced using a modelling methodology that combines survey, census and administrative data.

Two sets of deciles of the average new weekly household income in the MSOAs were created; average net household income and equivalised net household income after housing costs to adjust for differences in household composition.

The deciles in this analysis are created by treating the areas with the lowest average household income as 10% and grouping these areas as a single (non-adjacent) area, named Decile 1. The next 10% are then grouped into a single area, named Decile 2, and so on.

For this analysis, the average household income deciles were created separately and then it was matched with the individual data in APS.

Further information on small area income estimates is available in small area model-based income estimates.

Green space

Deciles of the amount of green space per square metre in the output areas were created using the data from 'Land Use Statistics (Generalised Land Use Database)'.

The deciles in this analysis are created by treating the areas with the lowest amount of green space per square metre as 10% and grouping these areas as a single (non-adjacent) area, named Decile 1. The next 10% are then grouped into a single area, named Decile 2, and so on.

For this analysis, the green space deciles were created separately and then it was matched with the individual data in APS.

Population density

For this analysis 13 groups were created based on the 2011 population per square metre in the output areas. The groups were created separately and then it was matched with the individual data in APS.

Office for
National Statistics

Measuring National Well-being: European Comparisons, 2014

Author Name(s): **Chris Randall and Ann Corp, Office for National Statistics**

Abstract

This article is published as part of the Office for National Statistics (ONS) Measuring National Well-being programme. The programme aims to produce accepted and trusted measures of the well-being of the nation – how the UK as a whole is doing. This article explores how the UK is faring in key areas of well-being compared to the European Union and the countries within it.

Introduction

The Measuring National Well-being programme began in November 2010 with the aim to 'develop and publish an accepted and trusted set of National Statistics which help people understand and monitor well-being'.

The Office for National Statistics (ONS) publishes 41 measures of National well-being , organised by ten 'domains' including topics such as 'Health', 'What we do' and 'Where we live'. The measures include both objective data (for example, the unemployment rate) and subjective data (for example, percentage who felt safe walking alone after dark). More information is available at www.ons.gov.uk/well-being

This article explores how key areas of well-being in the UK compare with those in the European Union and the countries within it. The article uses comparable or similar European data where available from five sources, Eurostat, the European Quality of Life Survey, Eurobarometer, the Programme for International Students Assessment (PISA) and the World Gallup Poll.

Key points

- In 2011, 71.8% of adults aged 16 and over in the UK rated their life satisfaction as 7 or more out of 10, higher than the EU–28 average of 69.3%.
- The average rating of satisfaction with family life by people aged 16 and over in the UK in 2011 was 8.2 out of 10, higher than the EU–28 average of 7.8 out of 10.
- Over 6 in 10 people (62.7%) aged 16 and over in the UK rated their health status as very good or good in 2011, lower than the EU–28 average of 64.0%.
- In 2011, 58.4% of people aged 16 and over in the UK reported that they felt close to other people in the area where they lived, lower than the EU–28 average of 66.6%.
- A fifth (20.2%) of households in the UK in 2012 reported great difficulty or difficulty in making ends meet, lower than the estimated EU–28 average of 27.7%.
- In 2013, 79% of adults aged 15 and over in the UK scored very high, high or medium on an index of cultural practice (measuring frequency of cultural participation), higher than the EU–27 average of 66%.

Personal well-being

An important component of measuring national well-being is the personal well-being of individuals, which is measured by finding out how people think and feel about their own lives.

There are five measures in the National Well-being 'Personal well-being' domain. Directly comparable European data are not available from the same sources for these measures, but for three of the measures comparisons are made using proxy measures from different sources. For more information see Table 2 at the end of this section.

Summary

Table 1 shows that the UK was above the EU average in all three measures being compared - 'life satisfaction', 'worthwhile' and 'rating of happiness'. The rest of this section will describe this in more detail and highlight the countries that ranked highest and lowest in each of the measures.

Table 1: European comparisons summary - Personal well-being

	UK	EU average	Highest ranked country	Lowest ranked country
How satisfied are you with your life these days? (7 or more out of 10) Source: Third European Quality of Life Survey (2011)	71.8%	69.3%	Denmark (91.0%)	Bulgaria (38.3%)
I generally feel that what I do in life is worthwhile (strongly agree or agree) Source: Third European Quality of Life Survey (2011)	81.9%	78.5%	Denmark, Netherlands (91.4%)	Greece (47.8%)
Taking all things together, how happy would you say you are? (7 or more out of 10) Source: Third European Quality of Life Survey (2011)	77.9%	74.1%	Finland (90.6%)	Bulgaria (48.0%)

Download table

XLS XLS format
(26.5 Kb)

Life satisfaction

According to the European Quality of Life Survey in 2011, 71.8% of adults aged 16 and over in the UK rated their satisfaction with life as 7 or more out of 10[1] **(Figure 1)**. This was slightly higher than the EU–28 average of 69.3% and was similar to both Germany (72.3%) and France (71.6%).

The highest-ranking countries were Denmark and Finland, where 91.0% and 89.8% rated their satisfaction with life as 7 or more out of 10 respectively. The lowest-ranking country was Bulgaria with 38.3% rating their satisfaction with life as 7 or more out of 10.

Figure 1: Life satisfaction (1), 2011

EU comparison

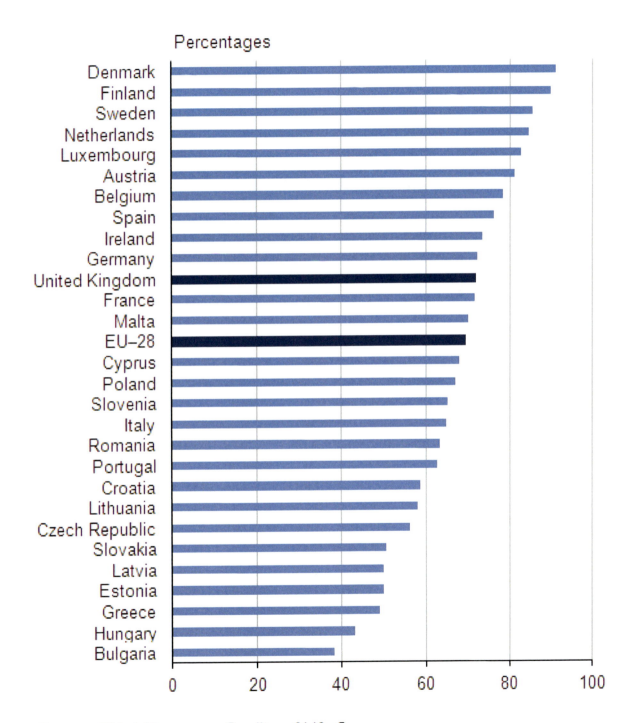

Source: Third European Quality of Life Survey

Notes:

1. Adults aged 16 and over rating their life satisfaction between 7 and 10 out of 10.

Download chart

Feeling worthwhile

The European Quality of Life Survey in 2011 also found that over 8 in 10 (81.9%) of adults aged 16 and over in the UK strongly agreed or agreed they generally felt that what they did in life was worthwhile. This was higher than the EU–28 average of 78.5%, and was similar to both Spain (81.5%) and Belgium (81.1%). The highest-ranking countries were Denmark and the Netherlands, where over 9 in 10 (91.4%) strongly agreed or agreed that they generally felt that what they did in life was worthwhile, while the lowest-ranking country was Greece (47.8%).

Happiness

According to the European Quality of Life Survey in 2011, when asked to rate on a scale of 1 to 10 how happy people thought they were, 77.9% adults aged 16 and over in the UK rated their happiness as 7 or more out of 10[2]. This was higher than the EU–28 average of 74.1% and was similar to Cyprus (76.8%). The highest-ranking countries were Finland (90.6%) and Denmark (90.2%), while the lowest-ranking country was Bulgaria (48.0%).

Table 2: Comparison of National Well-being measures and European measures - Personal well-being

National Well-being measures (UK)	European comparison measures
Medium/high (7 or more out of 10) rating of satisfaction with their lives overall	How satisfied would you say you are with your life these days? (7 or more out of 10)
Source: Annual Population Survey, Office for National Statistics (2012/13)	Source: Third European Quality of Life Survey (2011)
Medium/high (7 or more out of 10) rating of how worthwhile the things they do are	I generally feel that what I do in life is worthwhile (strongly agree or agree)
Source: Annual Population Survey, Office for National Statistics (2012/13)	Source: Third European Quality of Life Survey (2011)
Rated their happiness yesterday as medium/high (7 or more out of 10)	Taking all things together, how happy would you say you are? (7 or more out of 10)
Source: Annual Population Survey, Office for National Statistics (2012/13)	Source: Third European Quality of Life Survey (2011)
Rated their anxiety yesterday as low (0 to 3 out of 10)	No comparable or similar data
Source: Annual Population Survey, Office for National Statistics (2012/13)	
Population mental well-being (average rating out of 35)	No comparable or similar data
Source: Understanding Society, the UK Household Longitudinal Study (2009/10)	

Download table

XLS XLS format
(60 Kb)

Notes

1. Respondents were asked 'All things considered, how satisfied would you say you are with your life these days? Where 1 means very dissatisfied and 10 means very satisfied.

2. Respondents were asked 'Taking all things together on a scale of 1 to 10, how happy would you say you are? Where 1 means you are very unhappy and 10 means you are very happy'.

Our relationships

The quality of social connections with people around us and a correct balance between working and social life may be beneficial to an individual's overall well-being.

There are three measures in the National Well-being 'Our relationships' domain. Directly comparable European data are available for two of these measures from the same source but for the remaining measure a comparison is made using a proxy measure from a different source. For more information see Table 4 at the end of this section.

Summary

Table 3 shows that the UK was above the EU average for 'satisfaction with family life' and below the EU average for 'satisfaction with social life' and 'having support when needed'. The rest of this section will describe this in more detail, and highlight the countries that ranked highest and lowest in each of the measures.

Table 3: European comparisons summary - Our relationships

	UK	EU average	Highest ranked country	Lowest ranked country
Average rating of satisfaction with family life (out of 10)	8.2	7.8	Cyprus (8.9)	Bulgaria (6.7)
Source: Third European Quality of Life Survey (2011)				
Average rating of satisfaction with social life (out of 10)	7.0	7.3	Denmark (8.3)	Bulgaria (5.9)
Source: Third European Quality of Life Survey (2011)				
Support if needed advice about a serious personal or family matter	88.7%	93.0%	Slovakia (98.8%)	France (86.1%)
Source: Third European Quality of Life Survey (2011)				

Download table

XLS XLS format
(26.5 Kb)

Satisfaction with family life

According to the European Quality of Life Survey in 2011, people aged 16 and over were asked to rate their satisfaction with their family life out of 10. In the UK, the average rating of satisfaction was 8.2 out of 10. This was higher than the EU–28 average of 7.8 out of 10, and the same as Spain and Luxembourg. The country with the highest average rating was Cyprus (8.9 out of 10), while the country with the lowest average was Bulgaria (6.7 out of 10).

Satisfaction with social life

On the same European Quality of Life Survey in 2011, people aged 16 and over were asked to rate their satisfaction with their social life out of 10. In the UK the average rating of satisfaction was 7.0 out of 10. This was lower than the EU–28 average of 7.3 out of 10 and similar to Ireland and Greece (both 7.1 out of 10) and Estonia and Croatia (both 6.9 out of 10). The country with the highest average rating was Denmark (8.3 out of 10), while the country with the lowest average was Bulgaria (5.9 out of 10).

Support if needed advice about a serious personal or family matter

On the European Quality of Life Survey in 2011, people aged 16 and over were asked who would give them support if they needed advice about a serious personal or family matter. In the UK, 88.7% people said that they had support from family, friends, neighbours or someone else **(Figure 2)**. This was lower than the EU–28 average of 93.0%. The highest-ranking country was Slovakia (98.8%), while the lowest-ranking countries were France (86.1%) and Denmark (88.1%).

Figure 2: Support if needed advice about a serious personal or family matter (1), 2011

EU comparison

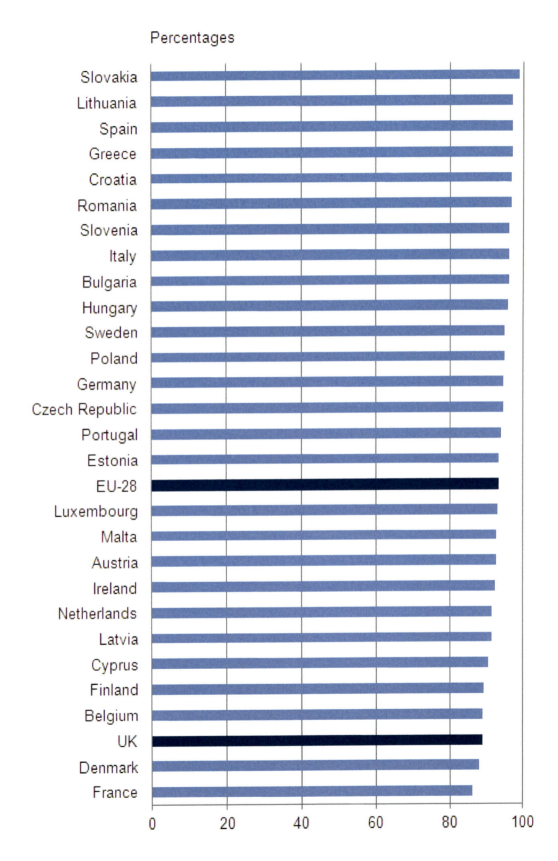

Percentages

Source: Third European Quality of Life Survey

Notes:

1. Respondents aged 16 and over who reported they got support from a member of their family, a relative, a friend, neighbour, or someone else if they needed advice about a serious personal or family matter.

Download chart

 XLS format
(27.5 Kb)

Table 4: Comparison of National Well-being measures and European measures - Our relationships

National Well-being measures (UK)	European comparison measures
Average rating of satisfaction with family life (out of 10)	Average rating of satisfaction with family life (out of 10)
Source: Third European Quality of Life Survey (2011)	Source: Third European Quality of Life Survey (2011)
Average rating of satisfaction with social life (out of 10)	Average rating of satisfaction with social life (out of 10)
Source: Third European Quality of Life Survey (2011)	Source: Third European Quality of Life Survey (2011)
Has a spouse, family member or friend to rely on if they have a serious problem	Support if needed advice about a serious personal or family matter
Source: Understanding Society, the UK Household Longitudinal Study (2010/11)	Source: Third European Quality of Life Survey (2011)

Download table

 XLS format
(59 Kb)

Health

According to the Department of Health[1], there is a two way relationship between well-being and health: health influences well-being and well-being influences health.

There are four measures in the National Well-being 'Health' domain. Directly comparable European data are not available from the same sources for these measures, but for three of the measures comparisons are made using proxy measures from different sources. For more information see Table 6 at the end of this section.

Summary

Table 5 shows that the UK was above the EU average for 'healthy life years' and below the EU average for 'perceived health status', while 32.9% of people in the UK reported 'having a long standing illness or health problem' compared to the EU average of 31.5%. The rest of this section will describe this in more detail, and highlight the countries that ranked highest and lowest in each of the measures.

Table 5: European comparisons summary - Health

	UK	EU average	Highest ranked country	Lowest ranked country
Healthy life years (male)	64.5	61.3	Malta (71.8)	Estonia (53.1)
Healthy life years (female)	64.5	61.9	Malta (72.4)	Slovakia (53.1)
Source: Eurostat (2012)				
Having a long-standing illness or health problem	32.9%	31.5%	Bulgaria (18.6%)	Finland (46.7%)
Source: Eurostat (2012)				
Perceived health status (very good or good)	62.7%	64.0%	Ireland (75.3%)	Latvia, Lithuania (41.1%)
Source: Third European Quality of Life Survey (2011)				

Download table

XLS XLS format
(27 Kb)

Healthy life years

Healthy life years are the years that a person at birth is still expected to live in a healthy condition. According to data from Eurostat, both males and females in the UK had an estimated 64.5 healthy life years in absolute value at birth in 2012. This is higher than the estimated EU–28 average of 61.3 years for males and 61.9 years for females. It was similar to Belgium for males (64.4 years) and the same as Croatia for females (64.5 years). The countries with the highest healthy life years were Malta (71.8 years for males and 72.4 years for females) and Sweden (70.9 years for males and 70.7 years for females). The country with the lowest healthy life years for males was Estonia (53.1 years) and for females was Slovakia (53.1 years).

Long standing illness or health problem

According to data from Eurostat, nearly a third (32.9%) of people aged 16 and over in the UK had a long-standing illness or health problem in 2012. This is slightly higher than the estimated EU–28 average of 31.5%, and is similar to Austria (33.1%) and Cyprus (32.6%). The highest proportion of people with a long-standing illness or health problem was in Finland (46.7%), while the lowest proportion was in Bulgaria (18.6%). The proportion of people in the UK with a long-standing illness or health problem has decreased over the years since 2005 when it was 37.4%. Over the same period the EU average has remained stable at around 31%.

Perceived health status

Over 6 in 10 people (62.7%) aged 16 and over in the UK rated their health status as very good or good in 2011 **(Figure 3)**. This was lower than the EU–28 average of 64.0% and similar to Germany (63.3%). The highest proportion of people who rated their health status as very good or good were in Ireland (75.3%) and Greece (75.0%). The lowest proportions were in Lithuania and Latvia (both 41.1%).

Figure 3: Perceived health status (1), 2011

EU comparison

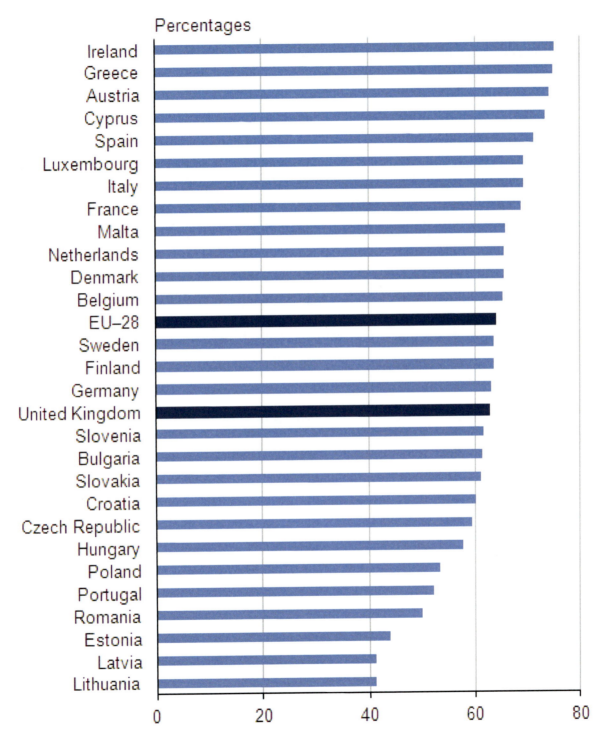

Percentages

Source: Third European Quality of Life Survey

Notes:

1. Adults aged 16 and over who rated their health as very good or good.

Download chart

XLS **XLS format**
(27 Kb)

Table 6: Comparison of National Well-being measures and European measures - Health

National Well-being measures (UK)	European comparison measures
Healthy life expectancy at birth (male/female)	Healthy life years (male/female)
Source: Office for National Statistics (2008–10)	Source: Eurostat (2012)
Reported a long-term illness and a disability	Having a long-standing illness or health problem
Source: Labour Force Survey, Office for National Statistics (January to March 2013)	Source: Eurostat (2012)
Somewhat, mostly or completely satisfied with their health	Perceived health status (very good or good)
Source: Understanding Society, the UK Household Longitudinal Study (2011/12)	Source: Third European Quality of Life Survey (2011)
Some evidence indicating probable psychological disturbance or mental ill health	No comparable or similar data
Source: Understanding Society, the UK Household Longitudinal Study (2011/12)	

Download table

XLS **XLS format**
(59.5 Kb)

Notes

1. The Relationship Between Wellbeing and Health (2013). A Compendium of Factsheets: Wellbeing Across the Lifecourse, Department of Health.

What we do

Individuals divide their time between various tasks and activities. This shapes our lifestyles, our relationships with others and our overall well-being.

There are six measures in the National Well-being 'What we do' domain. Directly comparable European data are not available from the same sources for these measures, but for all measures comparisons are made using proxy measures from different sources. For more information see Table 8 at the end of this section.

Summary

Table 7 shows that the UK was above the EU average for ' job satisfaction', 'time to do things in daily life', 'cultural participation' and 'sports participation', equal for 'voluntary work' and below the EU average 'unemployment rate'. The rest of this section will describe this in more detail and highlight the countries that ranked highest and lowest in each of the measures.

Table 7: European comparisons summary - What we do

	UK	EU average	Highest ranked country	Lowest ranked country
Unemployment rate Source: Eurostat (October to December 2013)	7.1%	10.7%	Austria (5.0%)	Greece (27.4%)
Satisfaction with present job (7 or more out of 10) Source: Third European Quality of Life Survey (2011)	75.1%	73.5%	Denmark (90.4%)	Greece (59.2%)
Seldom have time to do things really enjoyed in daily life (strongly disagree or disagree) Source: Third European Quality of Life Survey (2011)	45.8%	44.8%	Netherlands (66.3%)	Romania (27.0%)
Did voluntary work Source: Eurobarometer (2011)	26%	26%	Sweden (55%)	Portugal (6%)
Index of cultural participation (very high, high or medium)	79%	66%	Sweden (92%)	Greece (37%)

	UK	EU average	Highest ranked country	Lowest ranked country
Source: Eurobarometer (2013)				
Taking part in sports or physical exercise (every day or almost every day or at least once a week)	46.8%	39.7%	Finland (72.5%)	Bulgaria (12.0%)
Source: Third European Quality of Life Survey (2011)				

Download table

XLS XLS format
(28.5 Kb)

Unemployment rate

The unemployment rate for the UK published by Eurostat was 7.1% in quarter 4 of 2013, compared with 10.7% in the EU–28 **(Figure 4)**. The highest unemployment rates were in Greece (27.4%) and Spain (25.8%) while the lowest was in Austria (5.0%) and Germany (5.2%). The unemployment rate in the UK and EU–28 was higher than 10 years earlier, in quarter 4 of 2003 (the UK was 4.9% and the EU–28 average was 9.2%). Since then, the UK unemployment rate rose, reaching a peak of 8.3% quarter 4 of 2011, while the EU average fell between 2004 and quarter 1 of 2008 before rising to a peak of 10.9% in the first two quarters of 2013.

Figure 4: Quarterly (1) unemployment rate (2), seasonally adjusted

EU and UK

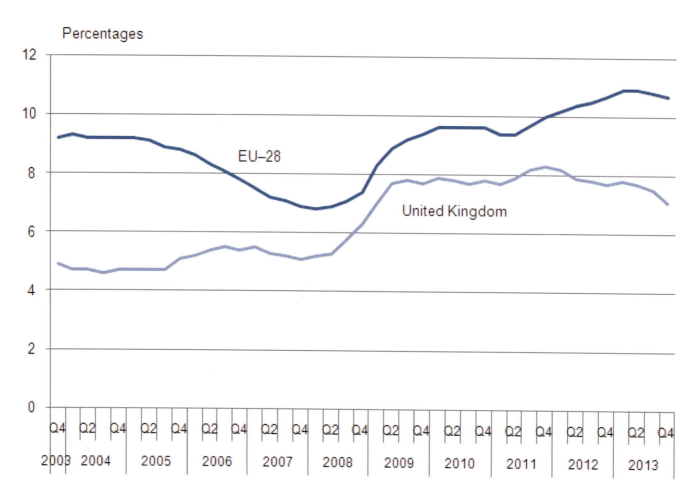

Notes:

1. Quarter 1 (Q1) is January to March, Quarter 2 (Q2) is April to June, Quarter 3 (Q3) is July to September and Quarter 4 (Q4) is October to December.
2. The unemployment rate for the UK published by Eurostat is based on the population aged 16–74 but the unemployment rate for the UK published by the Office for National Statistics is based on those aged 16 and over. There are other minor definitional differences.

Download chart

XLS XLS format
(29.5 Kb)

Satisfaction with present job

According to the European Quality of Life Survey in 2011, just over three-quarters (75.1%) of adults aged 16 and over in the UK rated their satisfaction with their present job as 7 to 10 out of 10. This was higher than the EU–28 average of 73.5%, and similar to Germany (76.0%). The highest proportion of people who rated satisfaction with their present job as 7 to 10 out of 10 was in Denmark (90.4%), while the lowest proportion was in Greece (59.2%).

Time to do things really enjoyed in daily life

Where people have disagreed or strongly disagreed when asked whether they seldom had time to do things they really enjoyed in daily life gives an idea of people's satisfaction with their amount of leisure time. in 2011, 45.8% of people aged 16 and over in the UK reported that they disagreed or strongly disagreed that seldom had time to do things they really enjoyed in daily life . This was similar to the EU–28 average of 44.8% and similar to Luxembourg (45.7%) and the same as Cyprus. The highest-ranking country where people disagreed or strongly disagreed was the Netherlands (66.3%), while the lowest-ranking country was Romania (27.0%).

Voluntary work

According to a special Eurobarometer survey run in September to November 2011, over a quarter (26%) of adults aged 15 and over in the UK were participating actively for a voluntary organisation or doing voluntary work at the time of interview[1]. This was the same proportion as the EU–27 average and the same proportion as Estonia. The highest proportion of people who did voluntary work was in Sweden(55%), while the lowest proportions were in Portugal and Greece (6% and 8% respectively).

Cultural participation

A special Eurobarometer survey run in April to May 2013 looked at cultural access and participation. Just under 8 in 10 (79%) adults aged 15 and over in the UK had a combined score of very high, high and medium cultural engagement[2]. This was higher than the EU–27 average of 66% and similar to France and Luxembourg (both 81%). The country with the highest combined score of very high, high and medium cultural engagement was Sweden (92%) while the lowest was Greece (37%).

Taking part in sports or physical exercise

According to the European Quality of Life Survey in 2011, 46.8% of people aged 16 and over in the UK took part in sports or physical exercise at least once a week **(Figure 5)**. This was higher than the EU–28 average of 39.7% and similar to Germany (47.6%). The highest proportion of people who took part in sports or physical exercise at least once a week were in Finland and Sweden (72.5% and 70.4% respectively), while the lowest proportion was in Bulgaria (12.0%).

Figure 5: Taking part in sport or physical activities at least once a week (1), 2011

EU comparison

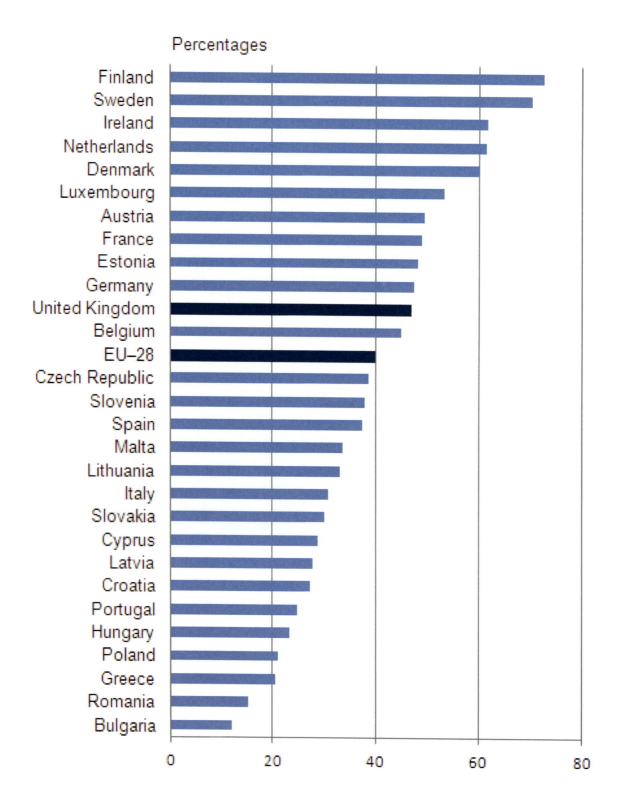

Source: Third European Quality of Life Survey

Notes:

1. Adults aged 16 and over who took part in sports or physical exercise every day or almost every day or at least once a week.

Download chart

XLS XLS format
(27 Kb)

Table 8: Comparison of National Well-being measures and European measures - What we do

National Well-being measures (UK unless otherwise stated)	European comparison measures
Unemployment rate	Unemployment rate
Source: Labour Force Survey, Office for National Statistics (October to December 2013)	Source: Eurostat (October to December, 2013)
Somewhat, mostly or completely satisfied with their job	Satisfaction with present job (7 or more out of 10)
Source: Understanding Society, the UK Household Longitudinal Study (2011/12)	Source: Third European Quality of Life Survey (2011)
Somewhat, mostly or completely satisfied with their amount of leisure time	Seldom have time to do things really enjoyed in daily life (strongly disagree or disagree)
Source: Understanding Society, the UK Household Longitudinal Study (2011/12)	Source: Third European Quality of Life Survey (2011)
Volunteered more than once in the last 12 months	Did voluntary work
Source: Understanding Society, the UK Household Longitudinal Study (2010/11)	Source: Eurobarometer (2011)
Engaged with/participated in arts or cultural activity at least 3 times in last year (England)	Index of cultural participation (very high or high)
Source: Department for Culture, Media and Sport (2012/13)	Source: Eurobarometer (2013)

National Well-being measures (UK unless otherwise stated)	European comparison measures
Adult participation in 30 minutes of moderate intensity sport, once per week (England)	Taking part in sports or physical exercise (every day or almost every day or at least once a week)
Source: Sport England (2012–13)	Source: Third European Quality of Life Survey (2011)

Download table

XLS XLS format
(54 Kb)

Notes

1. Respondents were asked 'Do you currently participate actively in or do voluntary work for one or more of the following organisations? A sports club or club for outdoor activities (recreation organisation); Education, arts, music or cultural association; A trade union; A business or professional organisation; A consumer organisation; An international organisation such as a development aid organisation or human rights organisation; An organisation for the environmental protection, animal rights, etc.; A charity organisation or social aid organisation; A leisure association for the elderly; An organisation for the defence of elderly rights; Religious or church organisation; Political party or organisation; Organisation defending the interest of patients and/or disabled; Other interest groups for specific causes such as women, people with specific sexual orientation or local issues; Other voluntary work. For more information see special Eurobarometer 378 available at Eurobarometer.

2. A simple index of cultural practice was formed to help identify levels of engagement in cultural activities among citizens from the 27 EU Member States. This is based on the frequency of participation and access to the different cultural activities included in the survey. Each respondent had been given a score based on their frequency of participation, and these scores were used to identify the different cultural index types of 'very high', 'high', 'medium' and 'low'. For more information see special Eurobarometer 399 available at Eurobarometer.

Where we live

An individual's dwelling, their local environment and the type of community in which they live may all have an effect on a person's well-being.

There are six measures in the National Well-being 'Where we live' domain. Directly comparable European data are not available from the same sources for these measures, but for three of the measures comparisons are made using proxy measures from different sources. For more information see Table 10 at the end of this section.

Summary

Table 9 shows that for the two measures that have an EU average, the UK was above the EU average for 'satisfaction with accommodation' and below the EU average for 'feeling close to people in the area where they live'. The rest of this section will describe this in more detail and highlight the countries that ranked highest and lowest in each of the measures.

Table 9: European comparisons summary - Where we live

	UK	EU average	Highest ranked country	Lowest ranked country
Feeling safe walking alone at night in the city or area where lived Source: World Gallup Poll (2012)	75.0%	..	Slovenia (85%)	Lithuania (45%)
Feel close to people in the area where I live (strongly agree or agree) Source: Third European Quality of Life Survey (2011)	58.4%	66.6%	Cyprus (80.8%)	Germany (58.3%)
Satisfaction with accommodation (7 or more out of 10) Source: Third European Quality of Life Survey (2011)	80.2%	76.9%	Finland (90.9%)	Latvia (55.2%)

Download table

Feeling safe walking alone at night in the city or area where living

According to the 2012 World Gallup Poll, three-quarters (75%) of people aged 15 and over in the UK felt safe walking alone at night in the city or area where they lived. This was similar to Finland and the Netherlands (both 77%) and Ireland (74%). People in Slovenia felt the safest (85%), while people in Lithuania and Greece felt the least safe (45% and 47% respectively).

Feeling close to people in the local area

Looking at whether people feel close to other people in the area where they live can give a sense of whether they feel a 'belonging' to their neighbourhood. According to the European Quality of Life Survey in 2011, 58.4% of people aged 16 and over in the UK reported that they felt close to other people in the area where they lived **(Figure 6)**. This was lower than the EU–28 average of 66.6% and was similar to Germany (58.3%) which was the lowest-ranking country. The highest-ranked country was Cyprus (80.8%).

Figure 6: Feeling close to people in the local area, 2011

EU comparison

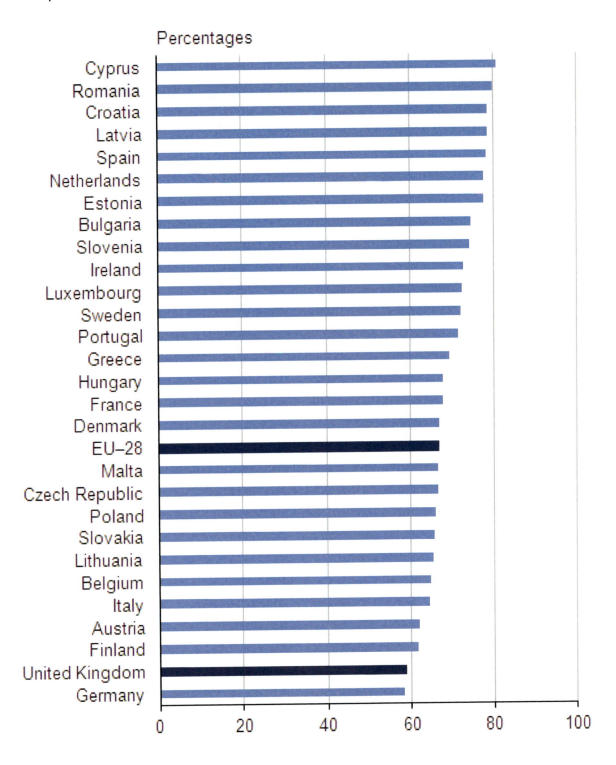

Source: Third European Quality of Life Survey

Notes:
1. Adults aged 16 and over who reported that they strongly agreed or agreed that they felt close to people in the area where they lived.

Download chart

Satisfaction with accommodation

On the European Quality of Life Survey in 2011, 80.2% of people aged 16 and over in the UK rated their satisfaction with their accommodation as 7 or more out of 10. This was higher than the EU–28 average of 76.9%, and similar to Belgium (80.7%). Finland had the highest proportion of people who rated their satisfaction with their accommodation as 7 or more out of 10 (90.9%), followed by Denmark and Malta (both 89.7%). Latvia had the lowest proportion of people rating their satisfaction with their accommodation as 7 or more out of 10 (55.2%).

Table 10: Comparison of National Well-being measures and European measures - Where we live

National Well-being measures (UK unless otherwise stated)	European comparison measures
Agreed/agreed strongly they felt they belonged to their neighbourhood	Strongly agree or agree feel close to people in the area where I live
Source: Understanding Society, the UK Household Longitudinal Study (2011/12)	Source: Third European Quality of Life Survey (2011)
Felt fairly/very safe walking alone after dark (men/women)	Feeling safe walking alone at night in the city or area where lived (all persons)
Source: Crime Survey for England and Wales, Office for National Statistics (2012/13)	Source: World Gallup Poll (2012)
Satisfaction with accommodation (England)	Satisfaction with accommodation (7 or more out of 10)
Source: Department for Communities and Local Government (2011–12)	Source: Third European Quality of Life Survey (2011)
Crimes against the person (per 1,000 adults) (England and Wales)	No comparable or similar data
Source: Crime Survey for England and Wales, Office for National Statistics (2012/13)	
Accessed natural environment at least once a week in the last 12 months (England)	No comparable or similar data

National Well-being measures (UK unless otherwise stated)	European comparison measures
Source: Natural England (2012/13)	
Households with good transport access to key services or work (2010 = 100) (England)	No comparable or similar data
Source: Department for Transport (2011)	

Download table

XLS XLS format
(62.5 Kb)

Personal finance

Personal finance can have a significant impact on people's sense of well-being and the financial situation of the population is an important aspect of National Well-being.

There are five measures in the National Well-being 'Personal finance' domain. Directly comparable European data are not available from the same sources for these measures, but for three of the measures comparisons are made using proxy measures from different sources. For more information see Table 12 at the end of this section.

Summary

Table 11 shows that for the two measures that have an EU average, the UK was above the EU average for 'median equivalised net income' and below the EU average for 'risk of poverty or social exclusion'. The rest of this section will describe this in more detail and highlight the countries that ranked highest and lowest in each of the measures.

Table 11: European comparisons summary - Personal finance

	UK	EU average	Highest ranked country	Lowest ranked country
Median equivalised net income (PPP Euros per person) Source: Eurostat (2012)	€17,636	..	Luxembourg (€26,660)	Romania (€3,601)
People at risk of poverty or social exclusion Source: Eurostat (2012)	24.1%	24.8%	Netherlands (15.0%)	Bulgaria (49.3%)
Households making ends meet with difficulty or great difficulty Source: Eurostat (2012)	20.2%	27.7%	Sweden (6.8%)	Greece (73.1%)

Table notes:

1.   Purchasing Power Parity (PPP) is used to adjust for different price levels between countries.

Download table

 XLS format
(27 Kb)

Median equivalised net income

Equivalised median income is defined as a household's total disposable income divided by its 'equivalent size', to take account of the size and composition of the household, and is attributed to each household member. In 2012 the median equivalised income (PPP adjusted[1]) of the UK was €17,636, comparable to Ireland (€16,215) and Finland (€18,202). Luxembourg had the highest median equivalised income (€26,660) while the lowest median equivalised income was in Romania (€3,601) and Bulgaria (€5,793).

At risk of poverty or social exclusion

In 2012, 24.1% of the population of the UK were in at least one of the following three conditions: at-risk-of-poverty[2], severely materially deprived[3] or living in households with very low work intensity[4]. This compared with 22.7% in 2011 and 23.2% in 2008 **(Figure 7)**. The 2012 UK figure of 24.1% was slightly lower than the EU–28 average of 24.8%[5]. The highest proportion of people at risk of poverty or social exclusion were in Bulgaria (49.3%) and Romania (41.7%), while the lowest proportion of people were in the Netherlands (15.0%) and the Czech Republic (15.4%).

Figure 7: People at risk of poverty or social exclusion (1), 2012

EU comparison

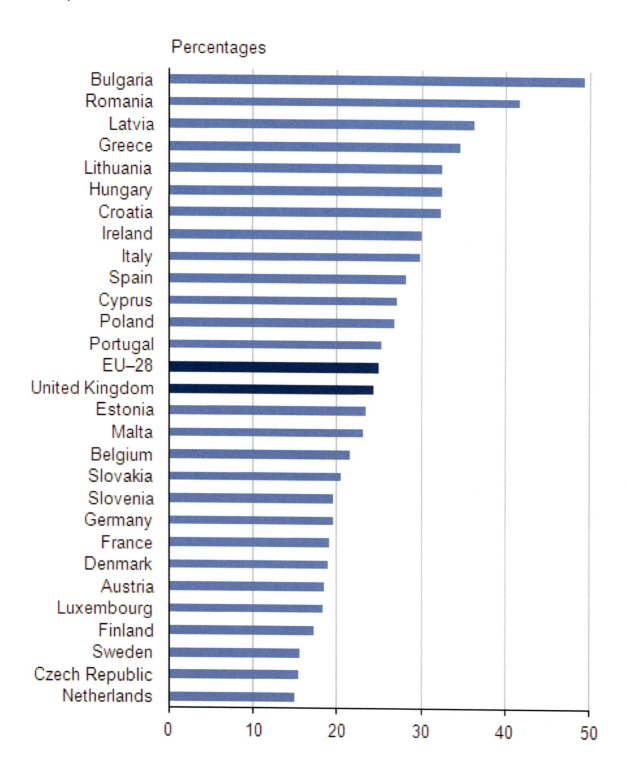

Source: Eurostat

Notes:

1. In at least one of the following three conditions: at risk of poverty, severely materially deprived or living in households with very low work intensity.

Download chart

 XLS format

(27.5 Kb)

Households making ends meet with difficulty or great difficulty

In 2012, a fifth (20.2%) of all households in the UK reported great difficulty or difficulty in making ends meet. This was lower than the estimated EU–28 average of 27.7%, and was similar to France (19.5%). The countries with the highest proportion of households reporting great difficulty or difficulty in making ends meet were Greece (73.1%) and Bulgaria (65.9%), while the lowest proportion of households were in Sweden (6.8%) and Finland (7.1%). Between 2005 and 2012 the proportion of households reporting great difficulty or difficulty in making ends meet in the UK has increased from 13.1% to 20.2%. Over the same period, the EU average has changed very little at 25.4 % (EU–27) in 2005 to 27.7% (EU–28) in 2012.

Table 12: Comparison of National Well-being measures and European measures - Personal finance

National well-being measures (UK unless otherwise stated)	European comparison measures
Individuals in households with less than 60% of median income after housing costs Source: Department for Work and Pensions (2011/12)	People at risk of poverty or social exclusion Source: Eurostat (2012)
Report finding it quite or very difficult to get by financially Source: Understanding Society, the UK Household Longitudinal Study (2011/12)	Households making ends meet with difficulty or great difficulty Source: Eurostat (2012)
Median household income Source: Office for National Statistics (2011/12)	Median equivalised net income (Euros per person) Source: Eurostat (2012)
Somewhat, mostly or completely satisfied with the income of their household Source: Understanding Society, the UK Household Longitudinal Study (2011/12)	No comparable or similar data

National well-being measures (UK unless otherwise stated)	European comparison measures
Median wealth per household, including pension wealth (Great Britain)	No comparable or similar data
Source: Wealth and Assets Survey, Office for National Statistics (2008/10)	

Download table

XLS XLS format
(62.5 Kb)

Notes

1. Purchasing Power Parity (PPP) is used to adjust for different price levels between countries.

2. Persons at-risk-of-poverty are those living in a household with an equivalised disposable income below the risk-of-poverty threshold. This is set at 60% of the national median equivalised disposable income (after social transfers). The equivalised income is calculated by dividing the total household income by its size determined after applying the following weights: 1.0 to the first adult, 0.5 to each other household members aged 14 or over, and 0.3 to each household member aged less than 14 years old.

3. Severely materially deprived persons have living conditions constrained by a lack of resources. They experience at least four out of the nine following deprivation items: cannot afford 1) to pay rent/mortgage or utility bills on time, 2) to keep home adequately warm, 3) to face unexpected expenses, 4) to eat meat, fish or a protein equivalent every second day, 5) a one week holiday away from home, 6) a car, 7) a washing machine, 8) a colour TV, or 9) a telephone (including mobile phone).

4. People living in households with very low work intensity are those aged 0-59 who live in households where, on average, the adults (aged 18-59) worked less than 20% of their total work potential during the past year. Students are excluded.

5. The total number of people at risk of poverty or social exclusion is lower than the sum of the numbers of people in each of the three forms of poverty or social exclusion as some persons are affected simultaneously by more than one of these situations.

Economy

The economy is the set of activities related to the production and distribution of goods and services. Its performance impacts on all of us financially and therefore affect our personal well-being.

There are three measures in the National Well-being 'Economy' domain. Directly comparable European data are not available from the same sources for these measures, but for all measures comparisons have been made using proxy measures from different sources. For more information see Table 14 at the end of this section.

Summary

Table 13 shows that the UK was above the EU average for all three measures (net national income per capita, inflation rate and government consolidated gross debt). The rest of this section will describe this in more detail and highlight the countries that ranked highest and lowest in each of the measures where rankings are avialable.

Table 13: European comparisons summary - Economy

	UK	EU average	Highest ranked country	Lowest ranked country
Net national income per capita (Index numbers, EU–28 = 100) Source: Eurostat (2012)	108	100	Luxembourg (171)	Bulgaria (47)
Inflation rate (Harmonised Index of Consumer Prices) Source: Eurostat (March 2014)	1.6%	0.6%	n/a	n/a
Government consolidated gross debt (% of GDP) Source: Eurostat (2013)	90.6%	87.1%	Estonia (10.0%)	Greece (175.1%)

Download table

XLS XLS format
(27.5 Kb)

Net national income per capita

When comparing net national income (NNI) per capita in 2012, the UK was 8% above the EU–28 average and similar to Ireland (9% above the EU–28 average) **(Figure 8)**. The highest rate of NNI per capita was in Luxembourg (71% above the EU–28 average), while the lowest rates were in Bulgaria (53% below the EU–28 average) and Croatia (42% below the EU–28 average).

Figure 8: Net national income per capita, 2012

EU comparison (1)

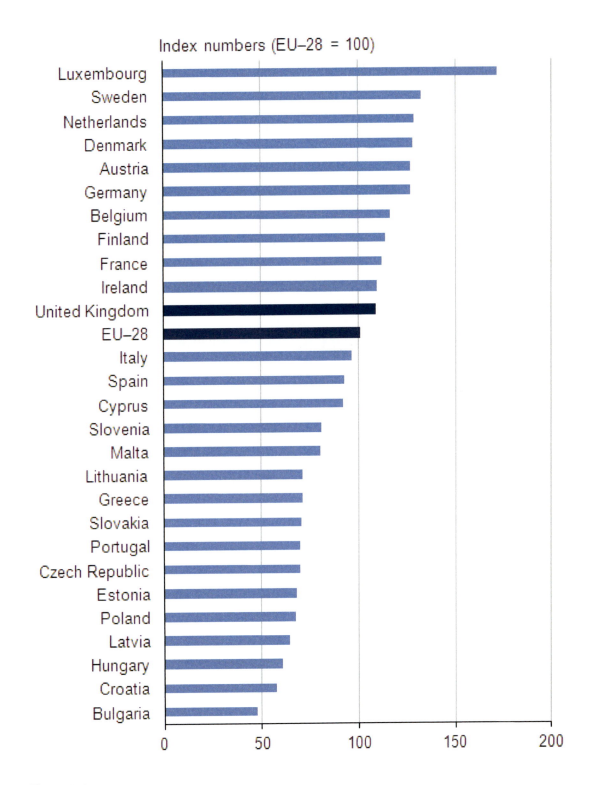

Source: Eurostat

Notes:

1. Data for Romania is unavailable.

Download chart

XLS XLS format
(26.5 Kb)

Inflation rate

A comparison of inflation rates shows that prices increased faster in the UK than in other countries in the European Union. In March 2014, the UK had the highest rate of inflation in at 1.6%, though this is below the Bank of England's official target rate of 2%. This was higher than the EU–28 average of 0.6%, and was similar to Malta and Austria (both 1.4%). Some European countries, mainly in southern and Eastern Europe, have experienced falling prices, with prices falling the fastest in Bulgaria (-2.0%), Greece (-1.5%) and Cyprus (-0.9%).

Government consolidated gross debt

The UK government consolidated gross debt was 90.6% of gross domestic product (GDP) in 2013. This was higher than the EU–28 average of 87.1%. The highest rates of government consolidated gross debt as a percentage of GDP were in Greece (175.1%) and Italy (132.6%), while the lowest rates were in Estonia (10.0%) and Bulgaria (18.9%).

Table 14: Comparison of National Well-being measures and European measures - Economy

National Well-being measures (UK)	European comparison measures
Real net national income per head	Net national income per capita (Index numbers, EU–28 = 100)
Source: Blue Book 2013, Office for National Statistics.	Source: Eurostat (2012)
Inflation rate (as measured by the Consumer Prices Index)	Inflation rate (Harmonised Index of Consumer Prices)
Source: Consumer Price Inflation, Office for National Statistics (March 2013 to March 2014)	Source: Eurostat (March 2014)
Public sector net debt as a percentage of Gross Domestic Product	Government consolidated gross debt (% of GDP)
Source: Public Sector Finances, Office for National Statistics (March 2014)	Source: Eurostat (2013)

Download table

XLS XLS format
(63 Kb)

Education and skills

A wide variety of studies have investigated the relationship between education and well-being and identified a positive relationship between the two.

There were no directly comparable or similar European data for any of the three measures within the 'Education and skills' domain. However a comparison of educational performance sourced from the Programme for International Students Assessment (PISA)[1] have been used for this article.

Summary

Table 15 shows the UK average (mean) scores in mathematics, reading and science in each subject. The rest of this section will describe this in more detail and highlight the countries that ranked highest and lowest in each of the measures.

Table 15: European comparisons summary - Education and Skills

	UK	Highest ranked country	Lowest ranked country
Mathematics, average (mean) score	494	Netherlands (523)	Bulgaria (439)
Source: Programme for International Students Assessment (PISA), 2012			
Reading, average (mean) score	499	Finland (524)	Bulgaria (436)
Source: Programme for International Students Assessment (PISA), 2012			
Science, average (mean) score	514	Finland (545)	Cyprus (438)
Source: Programme for International Students Assessment (PISA), 2012			

Download table

XLS XLS format
(27 Kb)

Performance in mathematics

The UK score in mathematics in 2012 was 494 points on average, unchanged since 2006 **(Figure 9)**. The UK's mean score in 2012 was similar to France (495). Netherlands and Estonia had the highest mean score in the EU at 523 and 521 respectively, while the lowest mean scores in the EU were in Bulgaria (439) and Cyprus (440).

Figure 9: Peformance in mathematics, 2012

EU comparison (1)

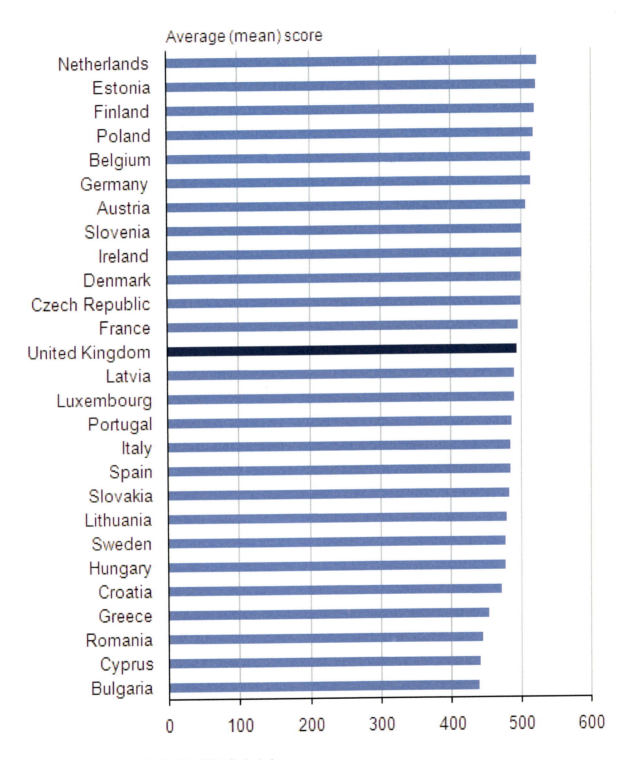

Source: OECD PISA 2012 database

Notes:

1. Data not available for Malta.

Download chart

XLS XLS format
(26.5 Kb)

Performance in reading

The UK score in reading in 2012 was 499 points in reading on average in 2012, unchanged since 2006. The UK's mean score in 2012 was similar to Denmark (496). Finland and Ireland had the highest mean score in the EU at 524 and 523 respectively, while the lowest mean scores in the EU were in Bulgaria (436) and Romania (438).

Performance in science

The UK score in science in 2012 was 514 points on average, unchanged since 2006. The UK's mean score in 2012 was the same as Slovenia. Finland and Estonia had the highest mean score in the EU at 545 and 541 respectively, while the lowest mean scores in the EU were in Cyprus (438) and Romania (439).

Notes

1. The Programme for International Student Assessment (PISA) is an ongoing triennial survey. It assesses the extent to which 15-year-olds students near the end of compulsory education have acquired key knowledge and skills that are essential for full participation in modern societies. The assessment does not just find out whether students can reproduce knowledge; it also examines how well students can take what they have learned and apply it to unfamiliar settings, both in and outside of school. More information is available at www.oecd.org/pisa/keyfindings/pisa-2012-results.htm.

Governance

A fundamental part of the work of government is to support a better life for its citizens and help build strong and resilient communities which in turn may improve the well-being of individuals. Much of the public's trust rests upon the Government being openly accountable for its decisions and actions.

There are two measures in the National Well-being 'Governance' domain. However the 'Voter turnout (at national elections)' measure is not being included in this article as some EU countries have different minimum voting ages to the UK, and therefore data might not be comparable. Directly comparable data are available for the 'Trust in National Government' measure and this will be the focus of this section.

Summary

Table 16 shows that the UK was above the EU average for the 'Trust in National Government' measure. The rest of this section will describe this in more detail and highlight the countries that ranked highest and lowest.

Table 16: European comparisons summary - Governance

	UK	EU average	Highest ranked country	Lowest ranked country
Those who have trust in National Government	24%	23%	Sweden (57%)	Spain (9%)

Source: Eurobarometer (Autumn 2013)

Download table

XLS XLS format
(18 Kb)

Trust in national Government

In the autumn of 2013, just under a quarter (24%) of people aged 15 and over in the UK reported that they tended to trust their national government. This is slightly higher than the EU–28 average of 23%. The highest proportions of trust were in Sweden (57%) and Luxembourg (51%). The lowest proportions of trust were in Spain (9%) and Greece, Italy and Slovenia (all 10%). Between 2004 and 2013, the proportion of people who trusted in government in the UK and the EU peaked in spring 2007 at 34% and 41% respectively, but the proportions have remained below these peaks since then **(Figure 10)**.

Figure 10: Trust in national Government (1)

EU (2) and UK

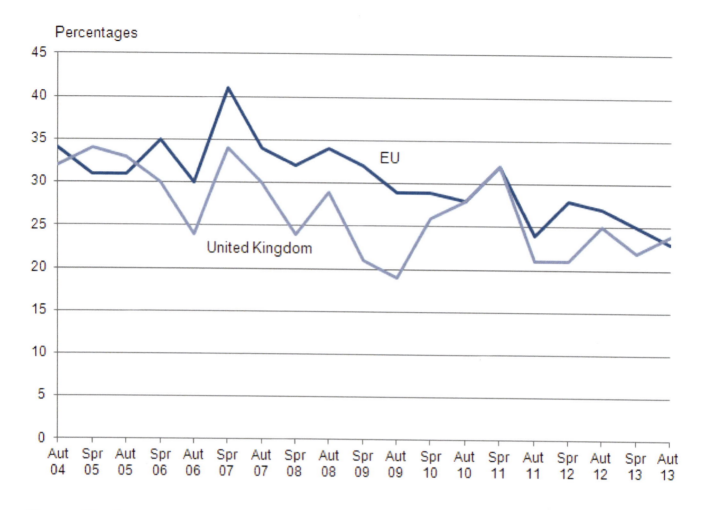

Source: Eurobarometer

Notes:

1. 'Aut' is autumn and 'Spr is spring.
2. EU total includes Bulgaria and Romania from 2007 and Croatia in 2013.

Download chart

 XLS format
(26.5 Kb)

Table 17: Comparison of National Well-being measures and European measures - Governance

National Well-being measures (UK)	European comparison measures
Those who have trust in national Government	Those who have trust in national Government
Source: Eurobarometer (Autumn 2013)	Source: Eurobarometer (Autumn 2013)
Voter turnout (at national elections)	Not included in this article
Source: International Institute for Democracy and Electoral Assistance (2010)	

Download table

XLS XLS format
(59 Kb)

Natural environment

The negative impacts of human activity and economic growth on the natural environment and ecosystem services are an important concern. Therefore, environmental problems such as pollution waste from the process of producing and using natural resources are an important consideration when looking at National Well-being.

There are four measures in the National Well-being 'Natural environment' domain. Directly comparable European data are not available from the same sources for these measures, but for three of the measures comparisons are made using similar or proxy measures from different sources. The 'Protected areas' measure is not being included in this article as the size of the area of protected areas is defined by each country's size, therefore making a comparison difficult to present. For more information see Table 19 at the end of this section.

Summary

Table 18 shows that where an EU average was available, the UK was higher than the EU average for 'recycling of municipal waste' and below the EU average for 'share of energy from renewable sources'. The rest of this section will describe this in more detail, and highlight the countries that ranked highest and lowest in each of the measures.

Table 18: European comparisons summary - Natural environment

	UK	EU average	Highest ranked country	Lowest ranked country
Greenhouse gas emissions (million tonnes of CO2 equivalent) Source: Eurostat (2011)	552.6	..	Malta (3.0)	Germany (916.5)
Share of energy from renewable sources Source: Eurostat (2012)	4.2%	14.1%	Sweden (51.0%)	Malta (1.4%)
Municipal waste that is recycled or composted Source: Eurostat (2012)	46%	42%	Germany (65%)	Romania (1%)

Download table

XLS XLS format
(19 Kb)

Greenhouse Gas Emissions

In 2011 the UK's greenhouse gas emissions[1] stood at 552.6 million tonnes (Mt) of CO2 equivalent. This figure was the second highest in the EU behind Germany (916.5 Mt of CO2 equivalent). The UK, France and Germany accounted for about 62% of the total EU net decrease between 2010 and 2011 and most EU countries had reduced greenhouse gas emissions over the period. In the UK, greenhouse gas emissions fell by 41 Mt of CO2 equivalent over the same period, the largest reduction of all EU Member States. In percentage terms, the largest reductions in emissions between 2010 and 2011 were in Finland (10%), Belgium (9%) and Denmark (8%). The largest percentage increases in emissions were in Bulgaria (10%) and Romania (6%).

Energy from renewable sources

In 2012, energy from renewable sources in the UK was estimated to have contributed 4.2% of gross final energy consumption. This was lower than the EU–28 average of 14.1% **(Figure 11)**. The highest shares of renewable energy in final energy consumption in 2012 were found in Sweden (51.0%), Latvia (35.8%) and Finland (34.3%). The lowest shares were in Malta (estimated at 1.4%), and Luxembourg (3.1%). Since 2004, the share of renewable sources in gross final consumption of energy grew in all Member States. The largest increase during this period was recorded in Sweden (from 38.7% in 2004 to 51.0% in 2012), while in the UK the share of renewable energy rose from 1.2% to 4.2% over the same period.

Figure 11: Share of energy from renewable sources, 2012

EU comparison (1)

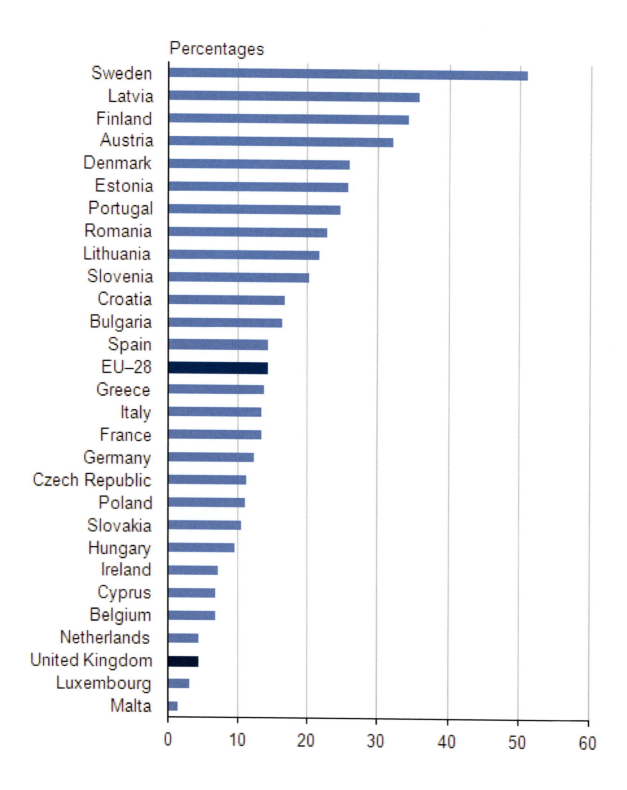

Source: Eurostat

Notes:

1. Data for Malta is estimated.

Download chart

 XLS format
(26.5 Kb)

Municipal waste that is recycled or composted

In 2012, an estimated 46% of the UK's municipal waste[2] was recycled or composted. This was above the estimated EU–28 average of 42% and was similar to Denmark and Ireland (both 45%). The country with the highest proportion of recycled or composted municipal waste was Germany (estimated at 65%). The countries with the lowest proportions were Romania (estimated at 1%), Malta and Slovakia (both 13%).

Table 19: Comparison of National Well-being measures and European measures - Natural environment

National well-being measures (UK unless otherwise stated)	European comparison measures
Energy consumed within the UK from renewable sources	Share of energy from renewable sources
Source: Department for Energy and Climate Change (2012)	Source: Eurostat (2012)
Household waste that is recycled (England)	Municipal waste that is recycled or composted
Department for Environment, Food and Rural Affairs (2012/13)	Source: Eurostat (2012)
Total green house gas emissions (million tonnes carbon dioxide equivalent)	Greenhouse Gas Emissions (million tonnes carbon dioxide equivalent)
Source: Department for Energy and Climate Change (2012)	Source: Eurostat (2011)
Protected areas in the UK (million hectares)	Not included in this article
Department for Environment, Food and Rural Affairs (2013)	

Download table

 XLS format
(61 Kb)

Notes

1. Explanation of the various totals of UK greenhouse gas emissions reported to different authorities can be found here www.gov.uk/government/publications/uk-greenhouse-gas-emissions-explanatory-notes

2. Municipal waste is mainly produced by households, though similar wastes from sources such as commerce, offices and public institutions are included.

Background notes

1. Details of the policy governing the release of new data are available by visiting www.statisticsauthority.gov.uk/assessment/code-of-practice/index.html or from the Media Relations Office email: media.relations@ons.gsi.gov.uk

Copyright

Sources related to 'European comparisons, 2014'

European Quality of Life Survey - European Quality of Life Survey (2012)

Eurostat - Eurostat

Eurobarometer - Eurobarometer

World Gallup Poll - Gallup World Poll - Gallup Worldview

Programme for International Students Assessment (PISA) - www.oecd.org/pisa/keyfindings/pisa-2012-results.htm

Member states of the EU

The European Union was created on 1 November 1993, when the Maastricht Treaty came into force. It encompasses the old European Community (EC) together with two intergovernmental 'pillars' for dealing with foreign affairs and with immigration and justice. The European Union consists of 28 member states (EU–28), where the EU–27 is referred to in this article, Croatia (which joined in 2013) is not included.

The 28 member states are as follows (year of entry in brackets):

Austria (1995)

Belgium (1952)

Bulgaria (2007)

Croatia (2013)

Cyprus (2004)

Czech Republic (2004)

Denmark (1973)

Estonia (2004)

Finland (1995)

France (1952)

Germany (1952)

Greece (1981)

Hungary (2004)

Ireland (1973)

Italy (1952)

Latvia (2004)

Lithuania (2004)

Luxembourg (1952)

Malta (2004)

Netherlands (1952)

Poland (2004)

Portugal (1986)

Romania (2007)

Slovakia (2004)

Slovenia (2004)

Spain (1986)

Sweden (1995)

United Kingdom (1973)

18 July 2014

Office for
National Statistics

Measuring Social Capital

Author Name(s): **Veronique Siegler, Office for National Statistics**

Abstract

This article on social capital is published as part as the ONS Measuring National Well-being (MNW) programme. It suggests a list of headline measures using a framework that covers four key aspects of social capital. A user consultation asks for feedback by the 26 September 2014.

Introduction

This publication proposes a **framework** of social capital, based on a report by the Organisation for Economic Co-operation and Development (OECD) in 2013 and earlier work by the ONS. The OECD report aims to provide an internationally comparable framework for measuring social capital over time. It is based around four broad aspects of social capital rather than a single definition. These are personal relationships, social network support, civic engagement and trust and cooperative norms.

Within this framework, ONS is proposing a set of **headline measures** for the UK, which cover the four aspects of social capital and supplement the existing information published by the ONS on human and natural capital. Once agreed, the measures will be used to provide an overall assessment of social capital in the UK and how it is changing over time. It will also provide further insight into the role of social capital in well-being. More detailed information will be needed for further in-depth analysis.

A suggested list of social capital measures is presented and the justification for their selection is described under the four aspects of social capital. **A set of specific questions addressed to users and experts**, regarding the social capital framework and the short-list of measures, is shown in the User Consultation section. An update of the social capital measures will be published in 2015, taking feedback from users and experts into account.

What is Social Capital and Why Measure It?

Definition of social capital

In general terms, social capital represents social connections and all the benefits they generate. The benefits for people having these social connections can occur either at an individual level (for example, through family support) or at a wider collective level (for example, through volunteering). Social capital is also associated with values such as tolerance, solidarity or trust. These are beneficial to society and are important for people to be able to cooperate.

Social capital and well-being

Social capital is important because of its positive contribution to a range of well-being aspects relevant to policy makers and researchers, such as personal well-being (Helliwell and Putnam, 2004; Helliwell, 2003), health (Veenstra, 2002 and 2000) and crime rates (Sampson, 2012; Sampson et al., 1997). These benefits occur at every level: individual, community, regional, national or even international (Halpern, 2000).

Social capital and the economy

Social capital has received such widespread attention by policy makers in recent years due to its link to the economy. Social capital has been recognised as a driver of economic growth, resulting in greater economic efficiency (Putnam, 2000 and 1993; Fukuyama, 1995). At a macro-level, it is likely that higher levels of trust and cooperative norms reduce transaction costs, thereby driving productivity (Putnam, 2000 and 1993). At an individual level, people with wider social networks are more likely to be employed (Aguilera, 2002), to progress in their career (Lin, 2001) and to be paid more (Goldthorpe et al., 1987). The importance of social capital was recently acknowledged by the Bank of England governor Mark Carney, who stated that 'prosperity requires not just investment in economic capital, but investment in social capital' (May 2014).

Social capital and sustainability

Social capital is also an important aspect of sustainability. Sustainability is seen as 'what we leave to future generations; whether we leave enough resources, of all kinds, to provide them with the opportunities at least as large as the ones we have had ourselves' (UN, 2012). The capital approach states that economic, natural, human and social capitals are all resources that matter for the present and future well-being of individuals. This was highlighted in the report by the Commission of the Measurement of Economic Performance and Social Progress (Stiglitz et al., 2009).

At an international level, the capital approach to well-being has been proposed within the OECD framework for measuring well-being in 2011. It has also been recommended by the United Nations Economic Commission for Europe (UNECE)/Eurostat/OECD Task Force for Measuring Sustainable Development (OECD, 2013). This aims to monitor whether these capital assets are sustained over time for future generations. Similarly, the Inclusive Wealth Report (IWR) presented for a United Nations Conference on Sustainable Development in 2012 highlighted the importance of the wealth of nations by capital assets to encourage international action on sustainability.

At a national level, social capital measures are part of the Sustainable Development Indicators (SDIs), which have been published by the Department for Environment, Food and Rural Affairs (DEFRA, 2013) and recently updated by the ONS (Sustainable Development Indicators, 2014).

These headline indicators, which are closely related to the National Well-being measures, will be further developed and refined within the Measuring National Well-being programme.

Approaches to Measuring Social Capital

There are two approaches to using social capital in policy evaluation and development which are:

Monetary valuation of social capital stocks

The first approach is the monetary valuation of social capital stocks, which consists of producing estimates of the value of social capital assets. Monetary value estimates for UK natural capital stocks and human capital stocks have been produced within the Measuring National Well-being programme. The value of frequent voluntary activity, which represents one aspect of social capital, has been estimated at approximately 1.5 per cent of UK GDP in 2013. World Bank efforts to estimate the 'true wealth of nations' suggest that intangible capital, made up mainly of human and social capital, represents around 60 to 80 per cent of true wealth in most developing countries (World Bank, 2006). However, social capital stocks are not presented as monetary values in this article. Although some researchers have tried to estimate the value of social capital assets as a proportion of total wealth (Hamilton and Liu, 2013), social capital differs from natural and human capital as it is a broad concept which is based largely on relationships. It is therefore difficult to value overall.

Development of a set of measures for social capital

The second approach consists of choosing relevant, independent and comparable social capital measures based on existing survey questions. This is the approach proposed in this article, with the aim to develop an agreed set of measures of social capital in the UK, if possible with international comparability. There is a lack of widely accepted measures of social capital at a national or international level, largely caused by the wide range of approaches used to define social capital.

This work on developing a set of measures builds on existing work undertaken by the ONS in 2003 (Measuring Social Capital in the United Kingdom), where a standardised set of questions on social capital was developed. These questions built upon the OECD 2001 agreed definition of social capital (OECD, 2001) and were included in the General Household Survey in Great Britain in 2004/05.

The OECD has since undertaken further development work to further define social capital for better internationally comparative measures in the future (OECD, Scrivens and Smith , 2013). The conceptual framework used in this article builds on this updated definition.

The list of suggested measures for social capital in this article was created after applying a set of criteria, as described in Annex 1.

The suggested measures aim to be comprehensive enough to capture all the relevant aspects of social capital without overlap. The social capital measures which are already part of the National

[Well-being wheel of measures (2.8 Mb Pdf)](#) are included. The suggested measures are based on the data available and gaps in measurement are also identified. Some are subjective measures whereas others are related to people's behaviours.

Framework for Measuring Social Capital

The framework adopted in this article and introduced by the OECD (OECD, Scrivens and Smith, 2013) aims to cover all the relevant dimensions of social capital. It is based on four different aspects of social capital, as described in Table 1.

Table 1: The Four Different Aspects of Social Capital

Aspect of social capital	Definition
Personal Relationships	This aspect of social capital refers to the "structure and nature of people's personal relationships" (OECD, 2013), and is concerned with who people know and what they do to establish and maintain their personal relationships.
Social Network Support	This refers to "the level of resources or support that a person can draw from their personal relationships" (OECD, 2013), but also includes what people do for other individuals on a personal basis.
Civic Engagement	This refers to "the actions and behaviours that can be seen as contributing positively to the collective life of a community or society" (OECD, 2013). It includes activities such as volunteering, political participation and other forms of community actions.
Trust and Cooperative Norms	This refers to the trust and to the cooperative norms or shared values that shape the way people behave towards each other and as members of society. Trust and values that are beneficial for society as a whole (such as for example solidarity and equity) can determine how much people in a society are willing to cooperate with one another.

Table source: Office for National Statistics

Download table

More details on each of the four aspects of social capital can be found in Annex 2.

The following sections outline proposed measures as well as possible alternatives under the four aspects of social capital.

Personal Relationships

Table 2. Personal Relationships: Suggested Measures

Suggested measures	Geography	Source
Meet socially with friends, relatives or work colleagues at least once a week	UK	European Social Survey, Core module
Have at least one close friend	UK	Understanding Society
Regularly stop and talk with people in neighbourhood	UK	Understanding Society
Belong to a social network website	UK	Understanding Society
Average rating of satisfaction with family life	UK	Eurofound, European Quality of Life survey
Average rating of satisfaction with social life	UK	Eurofound, European Quality of Life survey

Table source: Office for National Statistics

Download table

Measuring personal relationships and assessing their contribution to well-being is difficult, as an individual's range of social connections is usually complex and changes over time. The OECD has acknowledged the lack of robust, internationally comparable data for personal relationships (OECD, 2011).

The primary relationships of an individual are those maintained with family, friends, neighbours and work colleagues. 'Strong ties' (or 'bonding ties') describe the relationships of an individual with relatives and friends. Strong ties have been identified as very important for well-being in the National Debate (407.1 Kb Pdf) led by the ONS, and have shown to be strongly associated with personal well-being by data analysis ('Measuring National Well-being – What matters most to Personal Well-being?'). Connections with acquaintances such as colleagues at work or neighbours are referred to as 'weak ties' (or 'bridging ties').

People with a good range and frequency of social contact report higher levels of life satisfaction and happiness (Lelkes, 2010; Helliwell, 2008), but also better mental health (Williams et al., 1981). However, people with poorer health, particularly mental health, have been reported to have significantly smaller social networks (Halpern, 2005). Personal relationships are important for individual well-being, but can also have positive outcomes for firms and organisations, and at a community level (Halpern, 2005).

The measures aim to monitor the way people behave in terms of building and maintaining their personal relationships, particularly when these patterns are relevant for well-being.

Measure: Meet socially with friends, relatives or work colleagues at least once a week

This suggested measure indicates the proportion of people who report socialising at least once a week. Meeting socially implies meeting by choice rather than for reasons of either work or duty. The OECD (2011) has highlighted the frequency of contact with others as an important factor in people's well-being, and that this is the best indicator available to highlight differences in frequencies of contact between countries. The frequency of socialising with friends, relatives or work colleagues has been suggested as a sustainable development indicator by the UNECE/Eurostat/OECD Task Force on Measuring Sustainable Development (OECD, 2013). Having a good range and frequency of social connections brings people pleasure but can also give people access to a wider range of possible support in times of need. Socialising regularly has also been reported to enhance cognitive abilities (Ybarre et al., 2008). However, the quality of relationships an individual has with friends, family or work colleagues may be very different. Someone who socialises principally with work colleagues may not have many very close, supportive relationships; someone who socialises principally with family may not have very extensive or diverse social networks.

Measure: Have at least one close friend

This suggested measure identifies people who have at least one close friend, which is usually one trusted individual to share good moments and exchange support with in times of need. The support offered by a close friend can provide a buffer against stress, and people who are socially isolated are more likely to suffer from depression under stress and remain depressed for longer (Sherbourne et al., 1995). The lack of social connections at any age in life increases the risks of an individual to experience low personal well-being, loneliness, low self-esteem and mental health difficulties (Helliwell and Putnam, 2004). Also more socially isolated people are more at risk of risky behaviours such as smoking, drinking, physical inactivity and poor diet (Berkman and Glass, 2000).

Measure: Regularly stop and talk with people in neighbourhood

This measure shows the proportion of people who have regular contact with people in their neighbourhood. Positive personal relationships with neighbours are thought to play an important role in improving social cohesion, levels of trust and feelings of belonging (Measuring National Well-being- Our Relationships ; Bacon et al., 2011; Hothi et al., 2008; Cantle, 2005). Research by the Young Foundation suggests that personal well-being is higher amongst individuals who know and regularly talk to their neighbours (Bacon et al., 2011). Another study has shown that people's satisfaction with where they live is more affected by getting on with neighbours than by actual physical quality of housing (Halpern, 1995). It has been suggested that policies that could help with developing social interactions between neighbours could enhance well-being.

Measure: Belong to a social network website

This measure shows the proportion of people who belong to a social networking website. In recent years social media, where people interact freely, sharing and discussing information about each other and their lives, has revolutionised the way people interact with each other. Social network websites could help build social capital, allowing people to maintain contact despite being geographically separated, and to widen existing social networks. However, research has also reported a reduced personal well-being amongst young adult users of online social networks (Kross et al., 2013). Online social network usage could lead people to compare themselves negatively to others (Haferkamp and Krämer, 2011). Further research is required to investigate the exact causal pathways leading from online social network usage to reduced personal well-being.

Measures: Satisfaction with social life and satisfaction with family life

These subjective measures (satisfaction with social life and with family life) are both part of the National Well-being wheel of measures (2.8 Mb Pdf). They have been chosen as overall life satisfaction and satisfaction with relationships are related. These subjective measures can also reflect the quality of relationships an individual has with family and friends. It could be that low levels of relationships may lead an individual to be dissatisfied with their social life and family life. The satisfaction of an individual's relationships is often directly linked to the resources and support an individual has from these relationships in times of need. However, these measures are subjective and someone could be dissatisfied with their social and family lives even with strong support from family and friends, and vice versa.

Other possible measures

The measures above reflect those which best meet the criteria in Annex 1. Other measures considered, and on which views on their inclusion are welcome, are summarised:

One alternative measure is related to the **frequency of use of social networks during week days** (available from Understanding Society), but data are not available for the frequency of use during the weekend.

None of the selected headline measures relate to the size of people's networks, as it is difficult for individuals to assess the exact number of people they know. It is also difficult to measure the exact composition and diversity of individuals' personal networks, as it is likely to vary over time. Relationships can be diverse in terms of age, income, education or ethnic background. The

Community Life Survey provides a measure of the **proportion of people who have some friends of different ethnic background than own**. Contact between people of different ethnicities can decrease prejudice and increase values of cooperation (Hewstone, 2006, 2000). Data from the Community Life Survey also suggest that those who have a more diverse social network in terms of ethnicity or age are more likely to volunteer than people who have no friends outside their own ethnic groups.

Social Network Support

Table 3. Social Network Support: Suggested Measures

Suggested measures	Geography	Source
Has a spouse, family member or friend to rely on if they have a serious problem	UK	Understanding Society
Give special help to at least one sick, disabled or elderly person living or not living with them	UK	Understanding Society
Borrow things and exchange favours with their neighbours	UK	Understanding Society

Table source: Office for National Statistics

Download table

XLS XLS format
(25 Kb)

Family and friends can be vital sources of emotional, practical or financial support in times of need, and help individuals to cope with difficult times.

These measures aim to monitor whether people feel supported by their personal relationships (such as family, friends or neighbours). The measures also capture the support given to others as unpaid care, which is an important issue for policy makers. Reciprocity in support exchanges is thought to be beneficial to well-being (Li et al., 2011; Antonucci, 1990).

Measure: has a spouse, family member or friend to rely on if they have a serious problem

This indicator measures the proportion of people who think they have relatives or friends they can count on in times of need. It has been selected both as an OECD headline indicator for social connections (OECD, 2011), as part of the National Well-being wheel of measures (2.8 Mb Pdf) and is one of the UK Sustainable Development Indicators (SDIs).

Although this subjective measure does not provide details about the types of support offered, it indicates whether people feel they can get support when they need to. The support actually received in times of need is likely to be highly related to this measure.

Research has shown an age-related 'U-shaped' pattern in the proportion of people reporting having someone to count on in times of need (OECD, 2011), where the young and old are more likely to have someone to count on than those in the middle age groups. This could be because of the support given by parents to young adults (such as help with paying bills; help with decorating; childcare) and the support given by children to elderly parents (such as help with shopping; help with personal needs such as dressing).

Measure: Give special help to at least one sick, disabled or elderly person living or not living with them

This measure indicates the proportion of people who give informal care to others inside and outside the household. Informal carers have been defined in the 2011 Census as 'people who look after and support family members, friends, or neighbours in need of help because of long-term physical or mental ill health or disability or problems related to old age'.

Analysis from the 2011 Census show that approximately 5.8 million people provide unpaid care in England and Wales in 2011, representing just over one tenth of the population. The social capital of these carers is likely to be affected in terms of social and leisure activities, as well as employment opportunities.

The UK care system is currently dependent on the informal care provided by family and friends (Pickard, 2013). Research shows that demand for such care is likely to more than double over the next 30 years (Pickard, 2013; Pickard, 2008). Yet, it has been questioned whether the unpaid care is sustainable over time, because of changes in society such as children living far away from their parents or women participating more in the workforce (Pickard, 2013; Pickard, 2007). Also, it has been identified that some groups such as mid-life men living alone who have not had children and are socio-economically disadvantaged are more at risk of not being able to benefit from informal care provided by family or friends (Demey et al., 2013).

Measure: Borrow things and exchange favours with their neighbours

The suggested measure quantifies the proportion of people who are exchanging favours with their neighbours. This is one of a range of behaviours that are important indicators of neighbourhood social cohesion, such as mutual trust or willingness to pull together for the common good. Neighbourhood social cohesion has been shown to be correlated to a wide range of outcomes such as health (Fone et al., 2007; McCulloch, 2003) and crime (Fletcher and Allan, 2003; Sampson et al., 1997).

The Giving Green and White papers (Cabinet Office, 2011) seek to encourage people to give more time, skills and money to others. Several government actions, such as those described in the Giving Green and White papers, have been aiming to get people more involved in their communities. This 'community spirit' is likely to be higher in cohesive communities where people have individual relationships with their neighbours, such as regularly stopping to talk and exchanging favours with them.

Other possible measures

The suggested measures do not include any information on the percentage of people who do get regular support from their family or friends. Indeed, people might feel they have others to rely on in times of help, but they might not actively benefit from others support on a regular basis. There is a measure available from the Understanding Society survey, which captures the **proportion of people who regularly receive either practical or financial help from a parent or from a child aged 16 or over, not living with them**. However, this measure has not been included as a main headline indicator for social capital as it is only applicable for the population sub-group which has either a parent or a child.

Civic Engagement

Table 4. Civic Engagement: Suggested Measures

Suggested measures	Geography	Source
Volunteered[1] in the last 12 months	UK	Understanding Society
Have been involved in at least one social action project[2] in their local area in the previous 12 months	England	Community Life Survey
Voted in UK General Elections[3]	UK	The International Institute for Democracy and Electoral Assistance
Have been involved in at least one political action[4] in the previous 12 months	UK	Eurofound, European Quality of Life Survey
Those who are definitely, very or quite interested in politics	UK	European Social Survey

Table source: Office for National Statistics

Table notes:

1. Have given any unpaid help or worked as a volunteer for any type of local, national or international organisation or charity more than once in the last 12 months.
2. Giving unpaid help to support a community event, campaign or project: organising a community event such as street party; trying to stop something happening in local area; trying to stop closure of local service or amenity; getting involved in running local services (e.g. childcare, libraries) on a voluntary basis; setting up a new service or

amenity; taking part in decisions about how the council spends its money; getting involved in another issue affecting local area.

3. Percentage of electorate voting in General Election as a proportion of those registered to vote and those of voting age.

4. Attended a meeting of a trade union, a political party or political action group; attended a protest or demonstration; signed a petition, including an e-mail or on-line petition; contacted a politician or public official (other than routine contact arising from use of public services).

Download table

XLS XLS format
(28 Kb)

The proposed indicators aim to capture the engagement of people in the range of civic and political activities, which enable them to shape the society they live in. It has been suggested that higher levels of civic engagement encourage more efficient and less corrupt public governance institutions (Putnam, 1993) and help individuals to develop their skills and social values (such as trust in others) (Putnam, 1993) . As reported by the OECD (2011) 'civically engaged people tend to be happier (Morrow-Howell et al., 2003), report better health status (Borgonovi, 2008) and have a greater sense of purpose in life (Greenfield and Marks, 2004)'. Analysis from the Community Life Survey also suggest that those who give time or money to others are also more likely than those who do not to have high levels of interaction with neighbours, to trust people in the community and to have a diverse circle of friends.

This aspect of social capital has also been set out as a government priority by the Giving Green and White papers (Cabinet Office, 2011). In particular, policies to increase social actions in communities have been adopted (Cabinet Office, 2014).

Measure: Volunteered in the last 12 months

This measure captures the proportion of people who have volunteered more than once in the last 12 months, in activities such as running events, participation in recreational groups or help with children's schools. It has been shown that people who volunteer tend to have a better personal well-being than those who do not. Also, volunteering has an important economic value ('Household Satellite Accounts – Valuing Voluntary Activity in the UK'; OECD, 2011) and benefits the society as whole, by improving the lives of others, the community or the environment. The measure has been chosen as an important indicator of well-being by both the OECD (2011) and as part of the National Well-being wheel of measures (2.8 Mb Pdf). It is also one of the UK Sustainable Development Indicators (SDIs) and has been suggested as an SDI by the UNECE/Eurostat/OECD Task Force on Measuring Sustainable Development (OECD, 2013).

Measure: Have been involved in at least one social action project in their local area in the previous 12 months.

This measure indicates the proportion of people who have been involved in at least one social action in their community in the previous 12 months. The source of this measure is The Community Life Survey, which publishes information in relation to encouraging social action and empowering communities.

Social action, as defined by the Cabinet Office (Cabinet Office, 2013) is 'a community project, event, or activity which local people proactively get together to initiate or support on an unpaid basis. It is distinct from other forms of giving time in that it is driven and led by local people rather than through an existing group (as in formal volunteering) and tends to focus on a community need rather than the needs of an individual (as in informal volunteering). Examples could include organising a street party, preventing the closure of a local post office, helping to run a local playgroup, or improving local road safety'.

Community empowerment, which includes giving more power to local councils and neighbourhoods to take decisions and shape their local area, has been forwarded as a key element of the government Giving Green Paper (Cabinet Office, 2011).

Measure: Voted in UK General Elections

The proportion of people voting in UK General Election as a proportion of those registered to vote, and those of voting age, represents an important indicator of the vitality of a democracy and the degree of civic engagement. Voter turnout has been chosen as a headline measure both by the OECD (2011) and as part of the National Well-being wheel of measures (2.8 Mb Pdf). It has been suggested as a sustainable development indicator by the UNECE/Eurostat/OECD Task Force on Measuring Sustainable Development (OECD, 2013).

However, this measure is based on the number of people listed to vote and not the voting-age population. Therefore, it does not capture the proportion of people who lack political voice in national elections, such as non-citizens who are residents (migrants) of a country.

Measure: involvement in at least one political action in the previous 12 months (Eurofound, European Quality of Life Survey).

Another important measure of political engagement is indicating the proportion of people who have been involved in at least one political action in the previous 12 months. Examples of such political actions include attending a demonstration, contacting a public official or signing a petition.

These political actions are another way for people to express their view and needs to politicians making decisions on their behalf. This can influence public policies (Stiglitz et al., 2009), and also to make social connections and socialise with others. Participation in political activities and voter turnout are not necessarily correlated (OECD, 2011), suggesting that measures of involvement in political actions provide useful additional information to that of voting. The OECD (2011) has chosen an indicator related to political action as a secondary indicator for civic engagement.

Measure: Those who are definitely, very or quite interested in politics

The proportion of people who are very or quite interested in politics is a subjective measure, showing people's engagement with the democratic system. Lack of interest in politics is not directly correlated to political engagement (White et al., 2000), as people, in particular young adults, can be disillusioned by traditional politics but concerned by issues covering a broad political agenda. They can also be involved in political actions, such as boycotting environmentally unfriendly products. This measure could be of interest to policy makers who wish to make traditional politics more engaging to members of the general public.

Other possible measures

There is a membership measure available from Understanding Society, which captures the **proportion of people which are members of organisations, whether political, voluntary, professional or** recreational. This is an important measure of national social fabric, such as unions, faith groups, sports organisations etc. People also form social connections through being members of organisations. A European study (Special Eurobarometer 223, 2005) has shown a correlation between memberships of associations and life satisfaction, as well as levels of trust in others. However, whether active membership is more important to encourage civic attitudes than passive membership remains unclear (Putnam and Feldstein, 2003; Wollebæk and Selle, 2002). Consequently, this measure has not been included as a headline indicator for social capital.

A measure from the Understanding Society survey indicates the **proportion of people who have donated any money to charities or other organisations at least once a month in the last 12 months**. Policies have been introduced by the government to incentivise people to give more money in the Giving White Paper (Cabinet Office, 2011), as another important aspect of civic engagement. This measure has not been included as a headline measure as it relates to a positive attitude, rather than an active engagement.

Another possible measure for civic attitudes and beliefs, available from the Community Life Survey, is the **proportion of people who tend to agree or definitely agree that they can influence decisions affecting their local area**. This measure indicates how much people feel empowered to make a difference in their local area.

The Community Life Survey distinguishes between three measures of political action: civic participation, civic consultation and civic activism. Civic participation is one of the UK Sustainable Development Indicators (SDIs) and represents the **proportion of people engaged in actions designed to identify and address issues of public concern at least once a year**. Examples of civic participation include contacting an elected representative or attending a public demonstration. Civic consultation is a community measure capturing the **proportion of people taking part in consultation about local services** (such as completing questionnaires, or attending public meetings). Civic activism is another community measure indicating the **proportion of people involved in decision-making about local services or in the provision of these services** (such as being a school governor). However, these measures are available for England only, whereas the selected headline measure for political action is internationally comparable (source: Eurofound, European Quality of Life Survey) and available for the United Kingdom.

Trust and Cooperative Norms

Table 5. Trust and Cooperative Norms: Suggested Measures

Suggested measures	Geography	Source
Those who have trust in national Government	UK	Eurobarometer
Those who would say that most people can be trusted	UK	Understanding Society
Those who would say that most people in their neighbourhood can be trusted	UK	Understanding Society
Those who agree or strongly agree that people around where they live are willing to help their neighbours	UK	Understanding Society
Feel fairly safe or very safe to walk alone in their local area after dark	England and Wales	British Crime Survey

Download table

 XLS format
(17.5 Kb)

This aspect of social capital and the measures proposed encompass trust (in institutions and in others) and cooperative norms such as willingness to help each other, tolerance and respect for neighbours. It has been shown that personal well-being is higher in countries with higher levels of institutional trust (Hudson, 2006) and higher levels of trust in others (Helliwell and Putnam, 2004).

Political trust is a key element for social stability, the functioning of democracy (OECD, Morrone et al., 2009) and economic growth (Glaeser et al., 2004). Research has shown that indicators of institutional trust and measures of political participation other than voting are strongly correlated (OECD, 2011). This suggests a strong link between civic engagement and trust in institutions. Trust in institutions has been highlighted as a possible sustainable development indicator by the UNECE/Eurostat/OECD Task Force on Measuring Sustainable Development (OECD, 2013).

Trust in others, in particular strangers (also often termed 'generalised' trust or 'social' trust), is necessary for people to be able to cooperate with each other. Measures on generalised trust are not based on knowledge of the degree of honesty and integrity of others, but are subjective assessments of others. Trust in strangers is likely to be higher when values such as honesty, tolerance and solidarity are fundamental norms in the society. Trust in others and those 'shared values that underpin societal functioning and enable mutually beneficial cooperation' have been suggested as headline indicators for measuring the sustainability of well-being over time (OECD, 2013).

Measure: Those who have trust in national Government

This subjective measure, which captures the proportion of people who feel they can trust their national Government, is one of ONS's measures within the National Well-being wheel of measures (2.8 Mb Pdf). Trust in national government and Parliament was reported as key concerns during the National Debate and is essential for credible and healthy governance. Trust in national Government is likely to be positively affected by efficient and effective policies, competence, honesty and lack of corruption, accountability for its action, good communication with people, and respect for the public (Halpern, 2005).

Measure: Those who would say that most people can be trusted

The measure is based on the standard question: 'Generally speaking, would you say that most people can be trusted or that you need to be very careful in dealing with people?'. This question and variants of it are widely used in surveys across the world. It is one of the possible sustainable development indicators chosen by the UNECE/Eurostat/OECD Task Force on Measuring Sustainable Development (OECD, 2013). Several studies have shown that trust in others is associated with a wide range of positive outcomes in areas such as personal well-being (Helliwell and Wang, 2010), mental and physical health (Hamano et al., 2010; Stafford et al., 2004), crime rates and even mortality rates (Lochner et al., 2003). Also, the ability to cooperate has been ascribed to levels of trust in others.

Measure: Those who would say that most people in their neighbourhood can be trusted

The measures on trust can also be specific for particular groups of the population. This measure is specifically focusing on people in the neighbourhood and is one of the UK Sustainable Development Indicators (SDIs). Neighbourhood trust is another important indicator of social cohesion at a community level. Neighbours who trust one another are likely to work more effectively together for their collective advantage (such as helping to improve their local schools). Trust in neighbours is also correlated with higher life satisfaction (Helliwell and Wang, 2010). Research from the Community Life Survey (Cabinet Office, 2013) suggests that charitable giving is more prevalent amongst people who feel that many people in their neighbourhood can be trusted.

Measure: Those who agree or strongly agree that people around where they live are willing to help their neighbours

This subjective measure captures the proportion of people who think that people around the area where they live are willing to help each other and is an indicator of neighbourhood social cohesion. Indeed, research has shown that in areas where people tend to 'go their own way' rather than help one other, crime rates and feelings of lack of safety to walk alone after dark are much higher (Fletcher and Allen, 2003). People who are not willing to help their neighbours are likely to mistrust them, and are very unlikely to want to undertake any social action in their local communities.

Measure: Feel fairly safe or very safe to walk alone in their local area after dark

This subjective measure indicates the proportion of people who feel fairly safe or very safe to walk alone in their local area after dark, and is part of the National Well-being wheel of measures (2.8 Mb Pdf). The perception of safety is not necessarily directly correlated to crime rates. However, it has a direct causal link to the measure of trust in others: if people trust others (particularly in their neighbourhood), they are more likely to think they are safe or very safe to walk alone in their local area after dark.

Other possible measures

In some surveys (for example, the European Social Survey), trust in others and in institutions is measured on a **scale of 0 to 10**. On such scale, 0 indicates that people think that you have to be careful in dealing with people, or that they do not trust the institution at all, whereas 10 shows that they think most people can be trusted or they have complete trust in institutions. This could offer an alternative way of measuring trust in people and institutions.

Another measure from the Community Life Survey (England only) highlights the **proportion of those who trust their local council a fair amount or a lot**, as a way of assessing healthy democratic functioning at a local level.

Another possible measure is one showing the **proportion of people who agree or strongly agree that residents in their local area respect ethnic differences between people** (Understanding Society). Respect of ethnic differences is another social norm important for social cohesion.

Another measure from the British Crime Survey (England and Wales) report the **proportion of people who think there is at least one fairly big or very big problem in their local area** (within 15 minutes walk from their home). Problems can include noisy neighbours or loud parties, teenagers hanging around on the streets, rubbish or litter lying around, vandalism, graffiti and other deliberate damage to property or vehicles, people being attacked or harassed because of their skin colour, ethnic origin or religion, people using or dealing drugs, people being drunk or rowdy in public places, abandoned or burnt out cars, people being harassed or intimidated, and speeding traffic. These anti-social behaviours are likely to play an important role in limiting social cohesion and the building of social capital in local communities.

User Consultation: How to Respond

This is the first draft of proposed headline measures for social capital, which are important for the well-being of people, communities and the UK. ONS would like your input into the development of these measures, please reply to: nationalwell-being@ons.gov.uk by the 26 September 2014.

In particular, the questions we would like feedback on include:

- Is the framework a useful way of approaching measuring social capital?
- Does the list of measures cover effectively the different aspects of social capital as described in the framework?
- Are the sources of measures the best that could be used?
- How useful are the set of social capital measures for policy makers and researchers?

The ONS would like to thank in advance those who contribute to this consultation. Further publications on social capital are planned for 2014/15. An update of social capital measures will be published, taking account of feedback received. ONS will also undertake further analysis to provide insights into what the measures tell us about social capital and well-being in the UK.

Annex 1: Criteria Used for the Development of a Set of Social Capital Measures

The headline measures for social capital should be:

- Robust and meet the standard statistical requirements of accuracy, reliability and validity.
- Relevant, easy to interpret and monitor by policy makers and members of the public.
- Considered acceptable by specialists in the area and draw on existing well-recognised research work.
- Based on accessible and consistent information available over time (past and future).
- Available for the UK, whenever possible.

Other important aspects include:

- The measures should be internationally comparable, whenever possible.
- Certain questions have become well established and have been harmonised cross-nationally and cross-culturally. Where possible, these harmonised questions should be used for the measures.
- The measures should be relevant for sustainability of well-being, so that social capital will be at least maintained, or enhanced for future generations.
- The measures should be capable of disaggregation for specific groups of people and geographical areas.
- The measures should take account of the existing ONS research work that led to the development and establishment of a set of harmonised questions to measure social capital in 2003.
- The measures should be considered as very important for well-being.
- The measures should be relevant for stakeholders' endorsement.

Annex 2: More Detail About the Four Different Aspects of Social Capital

1) Personal relationships are characterised by:

- Their **sources**, which are the places and context in which people meet each other, such as through voluntary/sports activities or through social networking websites.
- Their **composition**: 'Strong ties' (or 'bonding ties') describe the relationships of an individual with their closest circle of relatives and friends. 'Weak ties' (or 'bridging ties') relate to the connections of someone with acquaintances such as colleagues at work or neighbours. 'Linking ties' are the connections of a person with others of greater status, resources and power.
- The **size** of people's networks for the various types of relationships, for example, the number of close friends.
- Their **diversity**: Examples of diversity in relationships include the proportion of friends that are of different age, sex, religion, ethnic group, level of education or income than own.
- The **type of contact**: People can have face to face, telephone, letter or email contact. Social media such as Facebook and Twitter are important new ways for people to be in contact.

- The **frequency of contact**: How often people have contact with their relatives, friends or acquaintances, etc.
- The **quality** (or strength) of people's personal relationships and people's feelings about it.

2) Social network support is characterised by the following:

- The **perceived support**, which is the support that people think they can draw from their relationships.
- The **support received**, which are the different types of resources an individual can receive from others, including emotional, practical or financial support, advice and guidance, and socialising.
- The **support provided**, including unpaid work (or informal volunteering), which is the help given by an individual to another individual on a personal basis. Examples include the help of grandparents for childcare, or care given to elderly parents.
- The **frequency of support received or provided**. Support can be available on a day-to-day basis or in times of crisis.

3) Civic engagement is characterised by:

- **Formal volunteering,** which is defined as giving time, skills or service to a club, organisation or association. Examples include participation in political parties or trade unions, professional associations, religious organisations, recreational groups such as sports activity clubs, cultural or hobby-related organisations or social clubs for the young or the retired.
- **Political engagement**, which relates to active political engagement (such as taking part to a demonstration, attending a political meeting and signing a petition or voting in elections).
- **Frequency of formal volunteering and political engagement**: how often people volunteer and are politically engaged.
- **Other civic-minded activities**: they include donating money or other goods (food or clothes) to charities or non-profit organisations; donating blood; taking part in jury duty; participation to community events such as fetes, shows etc.
- **Civic attitudes and beliefs**: Interest in national or local affairs aside from direct action, for example, through reading newspapers. This also includes people's perception of civic engagement, for example, whether people feel voting is important.

4) Trust and cooperative norms are characterised by:

- **Trust in institutions**, such as the national or local government, parliament, police force, justice system, press, etc.
- **Trust in others:** whether people think that generally speaking, most people (including strangers) can be trusted.
- **Social values of cooperation**: examples of such values include solidarity, helpfulness, honesty, generosity, politeness, equity, tolerance and non-discrimination towards people with differences based on ethnicity, language, culture, religion, nationality, sexual orientation, age or other characteristics. These are the fundamental norms that are beneficial for society as a whole, linked to fairness and inclusiveness, and which encourage people to cooperate.

References

Aguilera M (2002) 'The impact of social capital on labour force participation: evidence from the 2000 Social Capital Benchmark Survey', Social Science Quarterly 83(3), pp 853-74

Antonucci T, Fuhrer R and Jackson J (1990) 'Social Support and Reciprocity: A Cross-Ethnic and Cross-National Perspective', Journal of Social and Personal Relationships 4(7), pp 519-530

Bacon N, Brophy M, Mguni N, Mulgan G and Shandro A (2010) 'The state of happiness. Can public policy shape people's wellbeing and resilience?', The Young Foundation: London

Berkman L and Glass T (2000), 'Social integration, social networks, social support and health', in Berkman L and Kawachi I Social Epidemiology, Oxford University Press: Oxford

Borgonovi F (2008), 'Doing well by doing good: The relationship between formal volunteering and self reported health and happiness', Social Science & Medicine 66(11), pp. 2321–2334

Cabinet Office (2014) 'Promoting social action: encouraging and enabling people to play a more active part in society'

Cabinet Office (2013) 'Giving of time and money. Findings from the 2012-13 Community Life Survey'

Cabinet Office (2011) 'Giving White and Green Paper', TSO (The Stationery Office)

Cantle T (2005) 'Community Cohesion: A New Framework for Race and Diversity' Basingstoke: Palgrave Macmillan

Derney D, Berrington A, Evandrou M and Falkingham J (2013) 'Pathways into living alone in mid-life: Diversity and policy implications', Advances in Life Course Research 18 (3), pp 161-174

Department for Environment, Food and Rural Affairs (DEFRA, 2013) 'Sustainable Development Indicators (SDIs)'

Fletcher G and Allen J (2003) 'Perceptions of and concern about crime in England and Wales', in Simmons J and Dodd T Crime in England and Wales 2002/03, London: Home Office

Fone D, Dunstan F, Lloyd K, Williams G, Watkins J and Palmer S (2007) 'Does social cohesion modifies the association between area income deprivation and mental health? A multilevel analysis', International Journal of Epidemiology 36 (2), pp 338-345

Fukuyama F (1995) 'Trust: the social virtues and the creation of prosperity', Hamish Hamilton, London

Glaeser E L, La Porta R, Lopez-de-Silane F and Shleifer A (2004) 'Do Institutions Cause Growth?' NBER Working Papers 10568, National Bureau of Economic Research, Inc.

Goldthorpe J H, Llewellyn C and Payne C (1987) 'Social Mobility and Class Structure in Modern Britain', second edition, Clarendon Press: Oxford

Greenfield E A and Marks N F (2004) 'Formal Volunteering as a Protective Factor for Older Adults' Psychological Well-Being', Journal of Gerontology: Social Sciences 59B (5), pp 258-264

Haferkamp N and Kramer NC (2011) 'Social Comparison 2.0: Examining the Effects of Online Profiles on Social-Networking Sites' Cyberpsychology, Behavior and Social Networking 14, pp: 309–314

Halpern D (2005) 'Social Capital', published by Polity Press: Cambridge

Halpern D S (1995) 'Mental Health and the Built Environment: More than Bricks and Mortar?', Taylor and Francis:London

Hamilton K and Liu G (2013) 'Human Capital, Tangible Wealth, and the Intangible Capital Residual', OECD Statistics Working Paper, No. 2013/2, OECD Publishing: Paris

Helliwell J and Wang S (2010) 'Trust and Well-being', NBER Working Paper Series No. 15911

Helliwell J F (2008) 'Life Satisfaction and Quality of Development' NBER Working Papers 14507, National Bureau of Economic Research, Inc.

Helliwell J F and Putnam R (2004), 'The social context of well-being', Philosophical transactions, Royal Society of London series B Biological Sciences, pp: 1435-1446

Helliwell J F (2003) 'How's life? Combining individual and national variables to explain subjective well-being', Economic Modelling, 20 (2), pp: 331-360, Elsevier

Hewstone M, Cairns E, Voci A, Hamberger J and Niens U (2006) 'Intergroup Contact, Forgiveness, and Experience of 'The Troubles' in Northern Ireland', Journal of Social Issues 62, pp: 99-120

Hewstone M and Hamberger J (2000) 'Perceived Variability and Stereotype Change", Journal of Experimental Social Psychology 36, pp: 103-124

Hothi, M, Bacon N, Brophy M and Mulgan G (2008) 'Neighbourliness + Empowerment = Wellbeing', The Young Foundation: London

Hamano T, Fujisawa Y, Ishida Y, Subramanian S, Kawachi I and Shiwaku K (2010) 'Social Capital and Mental Health in Japan: A Multilevel Analysis', PLoS One 5.10: e13214

Hudson J (2006) 'Institutional Trust and Subjective Well-Being across the EU', Kyklos, 59:1, pp. 43–62

Kross E, Verduyn P, Demiralp E, Park J, Lee D S , Lin N, Shablack H, Jonides J, Ybarra O (2013) 'Facebook Use Predicts Declines in Subjective Well-Being in Young Adults', PLoS ONE 8(8): e69841.doi:10.1371/journal.pone.0069841

Lelkes O (2010) 'Social participation and social isolation', Eurostat Methodologies and Working Papers, EU Publications: Luxembourg

Li T, Fok H K, Fung H H (2011) 'Is reciprocity always beneficial? Age differences in the association between support balance and life satisfaction', Aging and Mental Health 15(5), pp: 541-7

Lin N (1999) 'Social Networks and Status Attainment', Annual Review of Sociology 25, pp: 467-487

Lochner K, Kawachi I, Brennan R and Luka S (2003) 'Social capital and neighbourhood mortality rates in Chicago', Social Science and Medicine (56), pp: 1797-805

McCulloch A (2003) 'An examination of social capital and social disorganisation in neighbourhoods in the British Household Panel Study', Social Science and Medicine 56, pp: 1425-38

Morrow-Howell N, Hinterlong J, Rozario P and Tang F (2003) 'Effects of Volunteering on the Well-Being of Older Adults', Journals of Gerontology: Series B: Psychological Sciences and Social Sciences 58: 3, pp: 137-145

OECD, Scrivens, K. and Smith C. (2013a) 'Four Interpretations of Social Capital: An Agenda for Measurement', OECD Statistics Working Papers, 2013/06, OECD Publishing

OECD (2013b), 'How's Life? 2013: Measuring well-being', OECD Publishing

OECD (2011) 'How's Life?: Measuring well-being', OECD Publishing

OECD, Morrone A, Tontoranelli N and Ranuzzi G (2009) 'How Good is Trust?: Measuring Trust and its Role for the Progress of Societies', OECD Statistics Working Papers, 2009/03, OECD Publishing

OECD (2001) 'The Well-being of Nations: The Role of Human and Social Capital', OECD Publishing

Office for National Statistics (July 2014) 'Sustainable Development Indicators, July 2014'

Office for National Statistics, Evans J (2011) 'Findings from the National Well-being Debate'

Office for National Statistics, Fender V (2013) 'Human Capital Estimates, 2012'

Office for National Statistics, Foster R (2013) 'Household Satellite Accounts – Valuing Voluntary Activity in the UK'

Office for National Statistics, Green H and Fletcher L (2003) 'The Development of Harmonised Questions on Social Capital'

Office for National Statistics, Harper R and Kelly M (2003) 'Measuring Social Capital in the United Kingdom'

Office for National Statistics, Oguz S, Merad S And Snape D (2013) 'Measuring National Well-being – What matters most to Personal Well-being?'

Office for National Statistics, Randall C (2012) 'Measuring National Well-being - Our Relationships, 2012'

Office for National Statistics, White C (2013), '2011 Census Analysis: Unpaid care in England and Wales, 2011 and comparison with 2001'

Pickard L (2013) 'A growing care gap? The supply of unpaid care for older people by their adult children in England to 2032'. Ageing and Society, pp. 1-28

Pickard L (2008) 'Informal Care for Older People Provided by Their Adult Children: Projections of Supply and Demand to 2041 in England', report to the Strategy Unit (Cabinet Office) and the Department of Health. PSSRU Discussion Paper 2515

Pickard L (2007) Informal Care for Younger Adults, Current Provision and Issues in Future Supply, England, 2005-2041, PSSRU Discussion Paper 2513

Putnam R D and Feldstein L M (2003) 'Better Together: Restoring the American Community', Simon and Schuster: New York

Putnam R (2000) 'Bowling Alone: The Collapse and Revival of American Community', Simon and Schuster: New York

Putnam R (1993) 'Making Democracy Work: Civic Traditions in Modern Italy', Princeton University Press: New Jersey

Sampson R (2012) 'Great American City: Chicago and the Enduring Neighbourhood Effect', The University of Chicago Press: Chicago and London

Sampson R, Raudenbush S and Earls F (1997) 'Neighbourhoods and Violent Crime: A Multilevel Study of Collective Efficacy', Science 277: 5328, pp. 978-924

Sherbourne C, Hayes R and Wells K (1995) 'Personal and psychological risk factors for physical and mental health outcomes and course depression amongst depressed patients', Journal of Consulting and Clinical Psychology 63:3, pp. 345-55

Special Eurobarometer 223 (2005) 'Social Capital', requested by the European Union Directorate General Employment and Social Affairs and coordinated by Directorate General Press and Communication

Stafford M, Bartley M, Marmot M, Boreham R, Thomas R and Wilkinson R (2004), 'Neighbourhood social cohesion and health: Investigating associations and possible mechanisms', in A. Morgan and C. Swann 'Social Capital for Health: Issues of definition, Measurement and Links to Health', Health Development Agency: London

Stiglitz J, Sen A and Fitoussi J P (2009) 'Report by the Commission on the Measurement of Economic Performance and Social Progress'

UNU-IHDP and UNEP (2012) 'Inclusive Wealth Report 2012. Measuring progress toward sustainability', Cambridge: Cambridge University Press

Veenstra G (2002) 'Social capital and health (plus wealth, income inequality and regional health governance)', Social Science and Medicine 54(6), pp: 849-68

Veenstra, G (2000) 'Social capital, SES and health: an individual level analysis', Social Science and Medicine 50:5, pp. 619-29

White C, Bruce S and Ritchie J (2000) 'Young people's politics. Political interest and engagement amongst 14-24 year olds', published for the Joseph Rowntree Foundation

Williams A W, Ware J E and Donald C A (1981) 'A model of mental health, life events, and social supports applicable to general populations'. Journal of Health and Social Behaviour, 22, pp: 324-36

Wollebaek D and Selle P (2002) 'Does participation in voluntary associations contribute to social capital? The impact of intensity, scope, and type', Non-profit and Voluntary Sector Quarterly 31(1), pp: 32-61

World Bank (2006) 'Where is the wealth of nations? Measuring Capital for the 21st Century'. World Bank publications

Ybarre O, Burnstein E, Winkielman P, Keller C, Manis M, Chan E and Rodriguez J (2008) 'Mental Exercising Through Simple Socialising: Social Interaction Promotes General Cognitive Functioning', Personality and Social Psychology Bulletin 34, pp: 248-259

Background notes

1. Details of the policy governing the release of new data are available by visiting www.statisticsauthority.gov.uk/assessment/code-of-practice/index.html or from the Media Relations Office email: media.relations@ons.gsi.gov.uk

Copyright

Measuring National Well-being: Insights across Society, the Economy and the Environment, 2014

Author Name(s): **Abbie Self, Office for National Statistics**

Abstract

This article summarises the outputs from the Measuring National Well-being (MNW) Programme since its launch in November 2010. It shows how Programme outputs have provided a better understanding of national well-being and it summarises domestic and international impacts and identifies future challenges.

Introduction

In November 2010, the Measuring National Well-being (MNW) Programme was launched to establish, "an accepted and trusted set of National Statistics, which help people to understand and monitor national well-being". The Programme took its lead from a report from the Commission on the Measurement for Economic Performance and Social Progress (the Stiglitz Sen Fitoussi report). This highlighted the need to look beyond GDP when evaluating progress of society.

The report reflected a growing international interest in this area including the European Commission's 'GDP and beyond' project and the Organisation for Economic Cooperation and Development's (OECD) global project on 'measuring the progress of societies'. Other countries with work in this area include: Measures of Australia's Progress (MAP) and the Canadian Index of Well-being. These initiatives are based on a common agreement that measures such as GDP are increasingly considered as providing an incomplete picture of the state of the nation and that other economic, environmental and social measures are needed alongside GDP to provide a complete picture of the quality of life and 'how society is doing'. In his recent speech on Inclusive Capitalism, Governor of the Bank of England, Mark Carney said that, "prosperity requires not just investment in economic capital, but investment in social capital" and emphasised the need for "a sense of society".

Three years after the first Programme report, 'Measuring National Well-being: Reflections from the National Statistician' (1.16 Mb Pdf) was published, this article summarises key outputs from the Programme and how they help to provide a better understanding of the state of the nation. Taking its lead from the Stiglitz Sen Fitoussi report, the Programme and this report are structured according to three main areas including:

- providing a fuller understanding of the economy,
- enabling a better understanding of society,
- promoting sustainable development and monitoring the environment for the well-being of future generations.

This article provides a summary of the impacts in terms of policy and international influence and the article concludes with a summary of future challenges and next steps.

Key points

- National well-being is more than the state of all individuals well-being. It is also concerned with how national level factors, for example, information about the economy, the environment or governance relate to society as a whole.
- A more rounded assessment of changes in the economy and their impact on living standards is provided by looking at measures such as GDP per capita and Real Net national Disposable Income (RNNDI) per capita alongside GDP.
- Better decisions on what affects our quality of life can be made by examining facts based information covering a range of topics, for example, our health and our finances, alongside how people think and feel about individual aspects within these areas and their lives overall.
- Focusing only on today's well-being may have an adverse effect on the environment. Understanding current stocks of human, natural, physical and social capital as well as the impact of the economy on the environment is vital for ensuring sustainability for future generations.
- Substantial progress has been made in embedding the concept of well-being in UK policy and the UK is internationally recognised for its work in this area.
- The Measuring National Well-being Programme has identified and developed a wide range of evidence in support of existing theories, for example, health being the strongest association with personal well-being; as well as new insights, for example, that expenditure is more important to our personal well-being than income. More work is needed to further develop and translate evidence into action.

What is national well-being?

There is no agreed definition of national well-being and it is often replaced with terms such as 'progress', 'quality of life' and 'sustainability'. For the Measuring National Well-being Programme, well-being, put simply is about 'how we are doing' as individuals, as communities and as a nation and how sustainable this is for the future.

Individual well-being describes how individuals are doing in terms of thoughts and feelings about their lives overall, identified through questions such as how satisfied with your life are you overall. Individual well-being also includes how we are doing and how we feel about individual aspects of our lives such as health, relationships, education and skills, what we do, where we live, our finances, the economy, governance and the environment.

Community well-being includes individual well-being but should also reflect how well individual well-being is distributed across the community, as well as local factors which may impact on well-being, for example, access to green spaces and strength of and opportunities for community involvement.

National well-being includes how individual well-being is distributed across society as well as how factors at the national level, for example, decisions about the economy, the environment or governance, which are important but contribute less directly to individual well-being, add up to determine national well-being. National well-being is also concerned with how well current levels of well-being can be sustained into the future or between generations.

National well-being is therefore more than the state of all individual well-being. It is a worthwhile aim to seek to maintain or improve current well-being by finding out what most influences our personal well-being and develop the means to address it, particularly for those with low well-being. But to fully address national well-being, a broader set of activities are needed. For example, an individual's well-being may not be directly affected by a fall in the stock of the education and skills in the labour market (human capital), but taken to the extreme, if stocks of human capital were to plummet, the future labour market would suffer from a lack of appropriate education and skills and this would have indirect consequences for individuals though the impact on the UK economy. In addition, it may be more useful from a national well-being perspective to consider linkages between different policy areas which may have indirect but nevertheless important downstream impacts on individual well-being. For example, exploring impacts of health policy alongside employment policy may lead to interventions which are beneficial to individual well-being but which were not the primary aim of the exercise.

A Framework for reporting on national well-being

In recognition of the need to look at a broad range of topics to understand national well-being, ONS created a framework consisting of 10 areas or 'domains', including areas such as Health, Education and What we do; and 41 headline measures of well-being such as the unemployment rate, satisfaction with our health, and levels of crime. To illustrate the framework, the Programme developed a Well-being Wheel of Measures, which includes all domains, measures and latest data, and is updated every six months. An interactive online version is also available which provides time series charts for each measure and links to underlying data.

The Well-being Wheel has received international praise for the way in which it concentrates a lot of complex information onto one page. Being circular, the Wheel shows that no preference is given to any one domain or measure reflecting the fact that people value things differently.

ONS are currently developing a wider conceptual framework which will include measures of national well-being as well as other relevant existing indicator sets, such as, Sustainable Development Indicators (SDIs) and those sets in development, such as, the Post 2015 Sustainable Development Goals (SDGs). The framework will help users understand how the different indicator sets fit together and can be used as a framework for reporting on these areas.

Why is measuring national well-being important?

The Stiglitz Sen Fitoussi report showed the need to measure what matters and provide statistics which lead to people being better informed when making decisions. It stated that 'those attempting to guide the economy and our societies are like pilots trying to steer a course without a reliable compass. The decisions they (and we as individual citizens) make depend on what we measure, how good our measurements are and how well our measures are understood'. The report made clear that measuring the progress of society was not about finding a replacement for GDP but to identify a range of measures to help understand the well-being of its members.

The following sections outline how the Measuring National Well-being Programme has addressed the need to better understand the economy, society and environment and how this provides a better understanding of the state of the nation's well-being.

Providing a fuller understanding of the economy

The Stiglitz Sen Fitoussi report highlights the fact that traditional measures of progress such as GDP can increase in times of war and natural disasters - both of which are detrimental to people's welfare. GDP is therefore not a reliable measure of overall progress - on its own. It also suggested that 'before going beyond GDP and tackling the more difficult task of measuring well-being, it is worth asking where existing measures of economic performance need improving'.

The report suggested:

- looking at individual and household perspectives instead of just the national economy.
- considering distributions across society of income, wealth and consumption to highlight areas less well off.
- considering wealth as well as income and to capture non-market activities - services that households provide for themselves.

Looking at the economy in this way provides a better understanding of how it impacts people at the individual and household level. This in turn can lead to more informed policy decisions focused on areas most in need.

Identifying existing measures which help describe the economy at individual and household levels

As part of a suite of measures of national well-being, the MNW Programme has included:

- Real net national income per head – to give a better understanding of material living standards and how well off individuals are compared to the state of the national economy.
- Median household income – to highlight the economic situation at the household level and take account of payments between sectors, for example, benefits received and taxes paid.
- Median wealth per household – to give a better understanding of future sustainability at the household level, for example, having a high income may lead to higher well-being in the short term through being able to satisfy one's preferences but wealth is considered a better indicator of future sustainability.
- Distributions such as households with less than 60% of median income after housing costs and UK public sector net debt – to help understand how an apparent rise in national income affects the worst and most well off.

These measures form part of the Economy and Personal Finance 'domains' of the 41 'headline' measures of national well-being, which are updated and published every six months. They are commented on in reports such as 'Life in the UK' and in more detail in the Programme's 'Economic well-being report'. The report includes several other measures such as GDP per capita and net domestic product per capita, which are due to be included in the quarterly system of National Accounts in 2014.

Figure 1 compares Gross Domestic Product (GDP) in recent years with GDP per capita. Figure 1 shows that while GDP has recovered significantly from the low point in 2009, there has been little recovery in GDP per capita as compared with 2008. However, the slow recovery in GDP since 2009 had been matched by an increase in population of roughly the same order.

The Measuring National Well-being: Economic Well-being article (April 2014), from which Figure 1 is taken, also compared GDP per capita with Real Net National Disposable Income (RNNDI) per capita. It showed that unlike the GDP per capita measure which has been broadly flat since 2009, the RNNDI per capita measure has been continuing to fall gently from £21,140 in 2009 to £20,410 at the end of 2013.

Figure 1: GDP and GDP per capita

United Kingdom

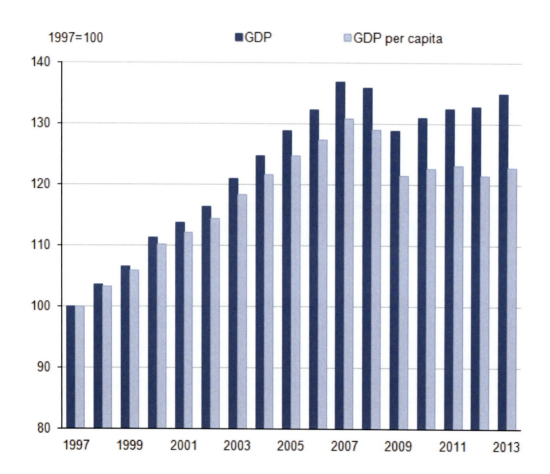

Source: Office for National Statistics

Download chart

XLS XLS format
(26 Kb)

The MNW Programme has shown that using other measures of the economy alongside GDP (such as GDP per capita and RNNDI per capita), provides a different message to looking at GDP alone. In doing so, a more rounded and complete assessment of how changes in the economy impact on living standards is provided.

Developing Household Satellite Accounts

ONS is also updating the Household Satellite Accounts (HHSA) which measure non-market household production in the UK. The HHSA provide a measure of the influence of changing patterns of unpaid work on the economy. This is divided into several principal functions providing housing, transport, nutrition, clothing, laundry services, adult care, child care and voluntary work. In 2013 and 2014, the MNW Programme has published estimates of Informal Childcare in the UK, Informal Adult Care in the UK, Valuing voluntary activity in the UK and Valuing household transport in the UK . The Programme plans to update the remaining sections of the HHSAs in the next 12 months.

Summary

Development have been made in providing measures of the economy which supplement GDP and better show issues at the individual and household levels.

Enabling a better understanding of Society

Whilst GDP may capture the overall state of the economy, it does not capture information about an individual's quality of life. The Stiglitz Sen Fitoussi report highlighted that "traffic jams may increase GDP as a result of the increased use of gasoline, but obviously not the quality of life". The importance of having 'a sense of society' was also highlighted by Bank of England Governor, Mark Carney in his recent speech on Inclusive Capitalism.

To enable a better understanding of society, the Stiglitz Sen Fitoussi report proposed the need to:

- understand what matters to people - to ensure the right things are measured and sustained into the future,
- collect objective information on things which have been collectively agreed to influence a person's well-being, for example; information about health, education, everyday activities, for example, right to decent jobs and housing, participation in the political process, the social and natural environment in which they live and the factors shaping their personal and economic security,
- capture subjective information - how people think and feel about their lives, and to report where possible across gender, age, socio-economic groups and others to highlight inequalities in quality of life.

Identifying 'what matters'

The MNW Programme has made understanding what matters to people a central focus for its activities. The Programme began by running a six month national debate in the UK, asking 'what matters?'. The debate included 175 events around the country and generated 35,000 responses. The findings (407.1 Kb Pdf) and other research were used to determine 41 measures of national well-being across 10 domains, for example, Personal Well-being, Personal Finance and the Natural Environment

Identifying measures from existing sources

The majority of measures are taken from existing data sources within and outside Government. They include objective measures, such as, crime rates; as well as subjective information, for example, fear of walking alone after dark. The original measures have been consulted upon and revised and will continue to evolve as needs change. They are updated with the latest data every six months (National Well-being Interactive Wheel) and summarised in an annual Life in the UK report.

Objective versus subjective measures

The 41 measures provide the information to determine 'how the nation is doing' in areas such as health, education and skills and the money we have in our pockets based on what citizens told us that mattered. By examining fact based information with how people think and feel, a more complete picture is provided than by looking at either type of measure alone. For example, in the 'Life in the UK 2014 report', personal crime rates per thousand fell between 2011/12 and 2012/13 while the percentage of men and women who felt fairly safe walking alone after dark fell. A similar example can be found in the Health domain. **Figure 2** shows that while healthy life expectancy has risen over time for males and females, satisfaction with health has been falling since 2008.

Figure 2: Healthy life expectancy at birth and satisfaction with health

United Kingdom

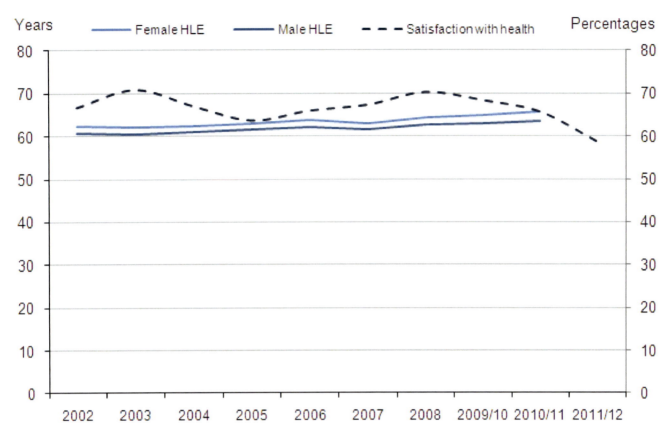

Source: Office for National Statistics, Understanding Society, the UK Household Longitudinal Study

Download chart

 XLS format
(27.5 Kb)

It is acknowledged that satisfaction with health will be determined by a variety of other factors both health related and non-health related and not simply healthy life expectancy. The measures selected here have been used to demonstrate the need to look at both facts based information as well as how people think and feel in order to more fully understand what is happening.

Using this information, policy makers can target their policies more effectively to improve quality of life. They can also identify more easily the areas where more information is needed. Individuals can also benefit from better information about how different life choices could affect their well-being.

Developing four new measures

Four of the measures were developed specifically by the MNW Programme with subject specialists to capture personal well-being. In 2011, ONS added four questions to its largest household survey, the Annual Population Survey, to capture how people in the UK think and feel about their lives. These questions capture long-term feelings of life satisfaction, the extent to which people feel the things they do in life are worthwhile, and daily experiences of positive and negative feelings such as happiness and anxiety. The data are analysed by a wide range of geographical break-downs, personal characteristics and circumstances in an annual publication, 'Personal Well-being in the UK'.

Looking at the data by age shows clear differences in personal well-being across the age groups. **Figure 3**, based on data from the Measuring National Well-being: Personal Well-being in the UK 2012/13 report shows that average levels of life satisfaction, a sense that activities were worthwhile and happiness levels were lowest for people aged 45 to 54. Also younger people gave higher average ratings than those in mid-life. Those aged 65 to 79 had significantly higher average ratings than any other age group for both worthwhile and happiness. Looking at anxiety, those in their early thirties to late fifties rated their anxiety levels highest, while younger people rated their anxiety at lower levels than those in mid-life. Those aged 80 and over did not have higher levels of anxiety on average than those aged 65 to 79.

Figure 3: Average personal well-being (1): by age group, 2012/13 (2,3)

United Kingdom

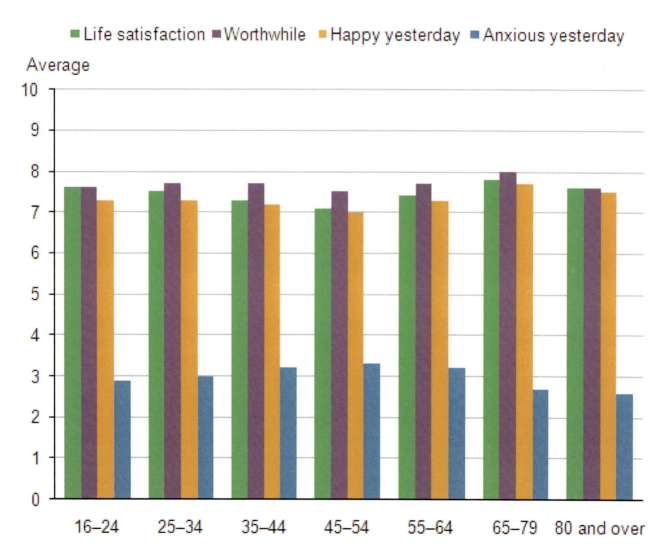

Source: Annual Population Survey (APS) - Office for National Statistics

Notes:

1. Adults aged 16 and over were asked 'Overall, how satisfied are you with your life nowadays?', 'Overall, to what extent do you feel the things you do in your life are worthwhile?', 'Overall, how happy did you feel yesterday?' and 'Overall, how anxious did you feel yesterday?' where nought is 'not at all' and 10 is 'completely'.
2. Data from April 2012 to March 2013.
3. All data weighted. Non-respondents not included.

Download chart

XLS XLS format

(27 Kb)

Having the evidence supported by other research, that personal well-being may change as we age and have different experiences, responsibilities and circumstances provides valuable information for policy makers to take into account when considering how decisions may affect personal well-being for particular sub- groups of the population.

Analysing influences on well-being

Including the four well-being questions on a large survey has allowed factors most strongly associated with our personal well-being to be analysed. This analysis has given evidence which supports the findings from the national debate that self-assessed health, employment status and relationships are most strongly associated with our personal well-being.

Further work has also looked at how well-being is associated with commuting to work; household income and expenditure; and the place where we live. The Commuting and Personal Well-being, 2014 article showed how different commuting times and modes of travel are related to personal well-being. The Income, Expenditure and Personal Well-being, 2011/12 article showed that whilst people in households with higher incomes report higher life satisfaction and happiness and lower anxiety (holding other factors fixed), an increase in the proportion of household income from cash benefits such as Housing Benefit and Job Seeker's Allowance is linked with lower reported life satisfaction, happiness and perceptions in life are worthwhile and higher anxiety. These effects are strongest for men. The same research showed that household expenditure appears to have a stronger relationship than household income with how people rate their life satisfaction, perceptions that what they do in life are worthwhile and happiness. Looking at these influences in more depth provides a powerful new understanding into what drives our well-being.

The four ONS questions are now being included on a growing number of other surveys, for example, the Crime Survey for England and Wales, the Wealth and Assets survey, Living Costs and Food survey and the English Housing Survey, which provide a further rich source information with which to analyse influences on well-being. A full list of surveys on which the four ONS questions are asked is available online within Personal Well-being: Frequently Asked questions.

Also the Programme recently used the 41 measures, alongside existing work in this area as a basis for proposing indicators which help measure the well-being of children and young people.

Summary

National well-being is now being measured regularly using a wide variety of existing measures, selected using evidence on what matters to society, as well as new nationally representative measures. This provides more extensive and robust data with which to measure the progress of the nation over and above GDP, and make decisions on those things which affect our quality of life than ever before.

Promoting sustainable development and monitoring the environment

As well as understanding the nation's current progress and quality of life, we also need to be conscious as to how they can be sustained for the future and between generations. This concerns both the sustainability of the environment as well as stocks of our human, physical, natural and social capital.

Sustainability refers to an economy's total stock of capital being maintained over time. The economy's total capital stock comprises the sum of physical capital (for example, buildings), natural capital (sub-soil assets, woodlands and ecosystems), human capital (education and skills) and social capital (personal relationships, support networks, civic engagement and trust). Capturing stocks in this way helps ensure we are conscious of their current status and their decline or sustainability for future generations.

Despite emphasis on the environment in recent years, environmental degradation is still a key concern. The Stiglitz Sen Fitoussi report makes the point that whilst important, simply focusing on today's well-being may have an adverse impact on the environment. For example, buying a car may make life for the consumer easier in the short term but may release emissions harmful to the environment when the vehicle is in use. This coupled with more immediate environmental concerns, for example global warming, mean that it is essential that sustainability and the environment are considered within the realm of national well-being.

Valuing and maintaining our stocks

The MNW Programme has developed estimates of stocks of human capital and stocks of natural capital. A discussion paper about what constitutes social capital has also been published.

Figure 4, taken from the Programme's Human Capital Estimates, 2012, illustrates the effect of the economic downturn on the UK's employed human capital stock. In the years 2004 to 2007 the value of the UK's human capital stock increased steadily, at an average of 3.1% per year. Growth in employed human capital slowed into 2008 (0.2%) before falling slightly in 2009 (-0.7%) beginning to reflect the effect of the economic downturn. With falling employment rates and falls in real earnings, 2010 and 2011 saw further falls in the value of the UK's human capital stock (of 2.0% and 2.8% respectively). Following these substantial falls in 2010 and 2011, the value of the UK's human capital stock began to stabilise in 2012. In 2012 the value of employed human capital was £17.15 trillion. This is a fall of £68 billion from £17.22 trillion in 2011. Full human capital, which also includes the unemployed, followed a similar pattern as the employed human capital. However, full human capital declined less in the recent years reflecting the impact of unemployment on the employed human capital estimates.

Figure 4: Employed and Full Human Capital (1,2,3)

United Kingdom

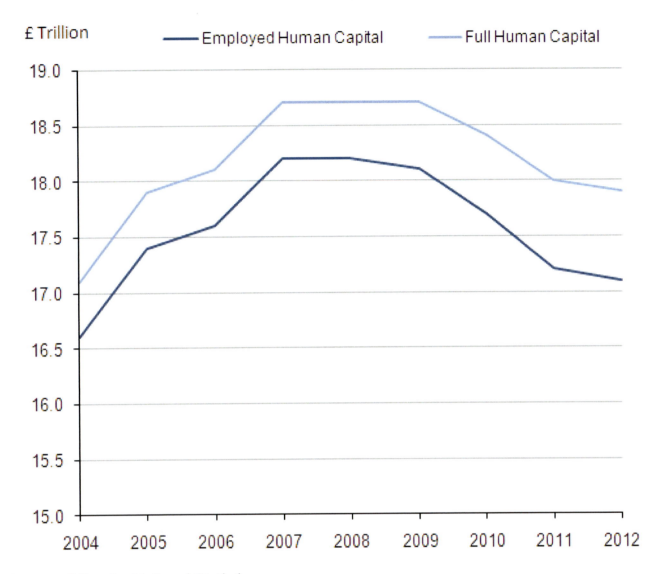

Source: Office for National Statistics

Notes:

1. Figures in 2012 prices.
2. Labour productivity growth rate = 2%.
3. Discount rate = 3.5%

Download chart

 XLS format
(26 Kb)

There is much development work still to do, but by providing such estimates of these and other stocks, the UK has a benchmark with which to determine the need for policy intervention or monitor the impact of future activities.

Measuring the impact of the economy on our environment

The Programme has published and will continue to develop a set of Environmental Accounts. With the National Accounts, Environmental Accounts help to determine the impact of the economy on the environment by looking at environmental assets (such as, oil & gas reserves, woodlands), how they are used (such as energy, material flows) and the pressure they place on the natural environment (such as, from emissions and waste). They also provide information on environment related taxes.

Figure 5 shows the decline in total energy consumption of fossil fuels since 2005. The chart shows energy consumed from fossil fuels is still dominant but in 2008 energy consumption from fossil fuels dramatically declined. From 2009 a gradual increase in energy consumption from other sources occurred, particularly in renewable and waste sources. Energy consumed within the UK from renewable sources was 1.1% in 2004 and 4.2% in 2012.

Figure 5: Energy consumption of primary fuels and equivalents: by source

United Kingdom

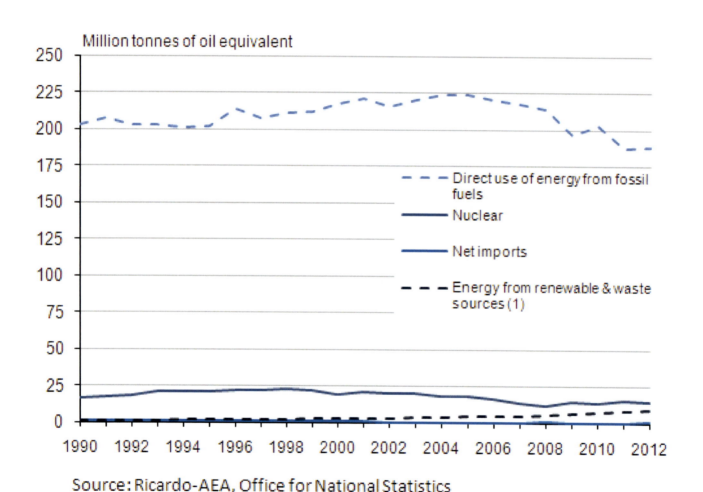

Source: Ricardo-AEA, Office for National Statistics

Notes:

1. Renewable and waste sources includes hydroelectric power, solar photovoltaic, geothermal aquifers, energy from wind, wave and tide, wood, charcoal, straw, liquid biofuels, biogas from anaerobic digestion, bioethanol and biodiesel, biomass combustion, sewage gas, landfill gas, poultry litter and municipal solid waste.

Download chart

XLS XLS format
(27 Kb)

Such information adds to the evidence, which is used to consider decisions on what actions need to be taken and in what areas to ensure a more sustainable future. Work has already led to the identification of the need for more detailed information about companies' products, investments and processes which can be considered 'low carbon'. This helps to inform policy strategies to facilitate more 'green growth'.

The MNW Programme includes a natural environment domain, which includes measures such as Green house gas emissions; protected areas; energy consumed from renewable resources and household waste recycled.

Sustainable Development Indicators

In addition, the MNW Programme is now responsible for providing annual updates to the sustainable development indicators (SDIs), which used to be the responsibility of Department for Environment, Food and Rural Affairs (Defra). ONS are also coordinating work across the Government Statistical Service (GSS) to lead the UK's statistical input to the UN Post 2015 Sustainable Development Goals (SDGs). The SDGs will replace the Millennium Development Goals and consider essential requirements of sustainable development as being: to promote poverty eradication, change unsustainable and promote sustainable patterns of consumption and production and protect and manage the natural resource base of economic and social development.

The MNW Programme is developing a framework to explain how SDIs, measures of national well-being and Post 2015 SDGs fit together.

Impacts of the Measuring National Well-being Programme

The impacts of the MNW Programme are summarised in terms of UK policy, international influence and emerging impacts outside Government.

UK policy

Measuring national well-being is a long term development programme. Information and understanding of well-being from the Programme could help to focus policy activities on what is needed, which is crucial in times of limited resource. It is too early to expect to have examples of major policy decisions which are affected by well-being research but the foundations are very much in place.

Well-being is now considered by every major Government department with activities including adding subjective well-being questions into policy surveys to further explore relationships within their policy areas. Examples of this are, the well-being of victims of crimes, housing quality, adult learning, sport culture and health.

Also, there are several examples of legislation that have been or will be introduced with a strong focus on well-being. Such legislation highlights the approach for seizing opportunities for improving existing initiatives through the consideration of well-being, as opposed to creating legislation specifically targeted at well-being. Examples include the following:

- Care Bill, where Part 1 aims to modernise and reform current social care law so that whenever a local authority makes a decision about an adult, they must promote that adult's well-being.
- Right to Request Flexible Working, which has been extended from 30th June 2014 so that all employees, not just those with children or caring responsibilities, are better able to balance their work and life.

The Queen's Speech also announced a Serious Crime Bill which will help protect the most vulnerable children by making sure that child cruelty includes emotional as well as physical harm. Also there is a Social Action, Responsibility and Heroism Bill which will remove legal barriers and disincentives to 'good deeds' to promote selfless behaviour.

More specific examples of the application of quality of life and well-being to UK policy can be considered in terms of:

- policy need
- policy appraisal
- policy evaluation

Policy need

Areas where quality of life questions can be and are starting to be considered in UK policy include, "what do we need to do, where, and for which sub groups?"

Subjective measures of well-being used with objective measures can help with identifying need and targeting of policies. For example, when we look at how scores for life satisfaction and feeling that life is worthwhile, we can see they vary by objective measures such as age (see Figure 3), employment status, health and ethnic group. These conclusions can help to target areas or sub groups of the population most in need.

In the UK, the Department for Work and Pensions (DWP) looked at the well-being of those searching for a job. The study, conducted in 2012 by NatCen Social Research on behalf of DWP found that the unemployed have the highest proportion of low well-being, most notable at the start of a claim, and that this low well-being impacts on their ability to obtain a job through low interview confidence. The study has led to questions as to whether there is a role for mental health intervention to overcome these barriers to getting a job.

Policy appraisal

Using well-being and impacts on quality of life as a means to assess whether a policy should be granted approval is another way in which quality of life considerations are starting to be used in UK policy.

In 2011, the Government published a Green Book discussion paper on how to use subjective well-being to inform cost-benefit analysis and to monetise non-market goods and services. Social cost-benefit analysis aims to show the full social costs and full social benefits of policies in monetary terms. The Green Book is the UK Government guidance on how to appraise proposals before committing funds to a policy. The Department for Culture Media and Sport (DCMS) have used the guidance to place a value on participating in sport once a week. This is equivalent to £11,000 increase in annual income, with a value on frequent volunteering of £13,500.

Also, the UK Department for Transport (DfT) now ensures wider social impacts are included in business cases for major transport schemes. This helps to find adverse impacts and mitigation options for the schemes as well as recognise social benefits that could be brought. DfT has also released an interactive tool based on the ONS well-being wheel to help policy makers appraise transport investment decisions based on how they will impact the domains of national well-being.

Policy evaluation

The impact of policies is increasingly being evaluated in subjective well-being terms allowing us to capture a better understanding of their effect on individuals.

The UK National Citizenship Service (NCS) is one of the Government's most important initiatives for building a bigger, stronger society. The programme is a voluntary eight week summer programme in which young people (aged 16 and over) come together to design and carry out a social action project in their local area. In 2011, a survey was conducted among NCS participants as well as a control group of 16-year-olds before and after the service. The survey asked the four ONS questions of subjective well-being to measure the impact of the programme. **Table 1** shows the findings.

Table 1: Well-being before and after National Citizen Service

United Kingdom (Percentages)

	Baseline NCS	Baseline control	Follow-up NCS	Follow-up control
High satisfaction with your life	64	61	79	73
High level of happiness felt yesterday	66	67	72	69
Feel things you do in life are worthwhile	65	64	79	73
Low levels of anxiety felt yesterday	45	56	49	51
Bases (numbers)	1612	1571	1625	1580

Source: NatCen et al, 2011. Evaluation of National Citizen Service: Findings from the evaluation of the 2012 summer and autumn NCS programmes

Download table

 XLS format

(27 Kb)

The table shows that well-being clearly increased among NCS participants compared with the control group. Qualitative research also highlighted feelings of pride, achievement, overcoming fears and making a difference to others among participants.

The Department for Communities and Local Government (DCLG) are also running a Troubled Families Programme which will measure the well-being of families (adults and children) to assess improvements following their participation. The research will include national measures and the final report is due in late 2015.

Other initiatives

A full summary of how well-being research is being used across the Government is available in the evidence submitted by the Cabinet Office to the Parliamentary Environmental Audit Committee (EAC) in 2013. Current examples are mostly around the impact on personal well-being of selected activities.

There is more work to do to make sure that policies reflect the full range of domains of well-being and 'what matters'. The final report from the EAC showed the need for policy makers to be more active in creating policies based on well-being. they stated that 'well-being considerations should increasingly drive policy-making, including "nudge" programmes, as the extent and understanding of well-being data is increased. The so far 'experimental' nature of the data, and current gaps in understanding of cause and effect, has prompted Government caution. The Government should begin using the already available data to "wellbeing-proof" existing policy proposals, and set out a clear plan for how and in what circumstances the data should start to be used proactively to identify new policies'.

A Commission on well-being and policy has also been established by the Legatum Institute, led by Lord Gus O' Donnell, former Head of the Civil Service. The commission aims to advance the policy debate on well-being. A recently published report, 'Well-being and policy' outlines the usefulness of well-being as a measure of progress in society and aims to give policy makers a greater understanding of how well-being data can be used to improve public policy and advance prosperity. The Government is currently considering its response to this report.

International influence

UK work on measuring national well-being, often used synonymously with terms such as 'progress' or 'GDP and beyond' is highly regarded internationally. This is shown through ONS's membership of several international working groups and their invitations to provide methodological guidance for several international handbooks. A summary of these is provided below. A more comprehensive report on the international influence of the MNW Programme will be published in the autumn.

Personal Well-being

Measuring personal well-being was a recommendation of the Stiglitz Sen Fitoussi report. The UK is recognised as an international leader in this area and is the only country to directly measure personal well-being. In recognition of advances made, ONS were key contributors to 'OECD guidelines on Measuring Subjective Well-being'.

Human Capital

The stock of our human capital provides important information to help make sure our stocks can be monitored and sustained for the future. Through the MNW Programme, ONS is involved in the OECD and United Nations Economic Commission for Europe (UNECE) international expert groups. ONS is currently drafting guidance on measurement for inclusion in the UNECE guidelines on measuring human capital.

Economic Well-being

ONS have drafted an economic well-being chapter for the OECD framework for statistics on the distribution of household income, consumption and wealth. This is helping to lead the way for an internationally agreed framework. The UK approach has also been referenced as best practice in OECD guidelines on wealth statistics.

Environmental Accounts

Working closely with the UN Statistical Development Division, ONS have been instrumental in developing the System of European Environmental Accounts (SEEA). The UK is one of the leading countries in using the SEEA Framework and developed the UK Environmental Accounts in line with it.

Natural Capital

Natural Capital Accounts within the UK Environmental Accounts are currently being developed (with Defra, Department for Energy and Climate Change (DECC) and the UK Natural Capital Committee) as part of the natural capital accounting roadmap published by ONS in December 2012. In June 2013, the MNW Programme published a number of experimental statistics on natural capital that were in line with the SEEA Central Framework.

SEEA Experimental Ecosystem Accounting (EEA) is not an international standard but is considered the best guidance to develop ecosystem accounts. The UK is one of the leading countries in developing the ecosystem accounts by implementing SEEA EEA. The ONS roadmap has a major focus on developing ecosystem accounts. In June 2013, the MNW Programme published experimental statistics on woodland ecosystem accounts (273.5 Kb Pdf) in line with the SEEA EEA guidelines. Working with the UN, six method papers for measuring natural capital have also been drafted and incorporated in the UN and World Bank libraries.

Impact outside Government

Examples where well-being is recognised outside Government are also growing. Housing developer Berkeley Homes, have recognised the importance of well-being in its drive to 'make sustainable places' and understanding what makes a place thrive and function as a community, now and in the future, as opposed to just house building. It outlines its approach as creating '…high quality, sustainable places where people choose to live, work and spend their time. These will be places that directly encourage people's well-being and quality of life and offer them a space and a base from which to lead safe and fulfilling lives'.

In addition, the British Red Cross has identified increased well-being as an intended outcome for people using refugee services. In a pilot study, the British Red Cross has used all five MNW measures from the MNW Personal Well-being domain (four ONS questions and the population and mental well-being measure which uses the Warwick and Edinburgh Mental well-being (WEMWbs) form questionnaire) to capture the well-being of refugees at the beginning and end of the support period. Through measuring change in the refugee's well-being, the British Red Cross aim to:

- better understand emotional as well as practical needs of those that it helps,
- improve the design of its services to better meet user needs, and
- be better equipped to raise awareness of well-being issues among specific vulnerable groups and respond to growing interest in well-being from its commissioners and funders.

Challenges

The MNW Programme has delivered a range of information and insights on national well-being. A full list of Programme outputs is provided at the end of this report. Ongoing challenges are summarised below.

Index of measures or single headline measure?

There is still much appeal and debate for national well-being to be summarised as one number, in the same way as GDP. But as the recent report from the Environmental Audit Committee and Natural Capital Committee stated, 'it runs the risk of not being accepted by those who do not agree the weightings given to particular components of well-being. Such a move should not be contemplated until a track-record has been built up and a general consensus and acceptance secured on the appropriate component measures of well-being'.This reflects the ONS viewpoint that whilst the ease of a single number is recognised, one number would hide too much detail, which is needed to show where interventions are needed. It would also hide changes in its makeup, for example, a positive change in one area could be offset by a negative change in another and leave the overall number the same. Without the detail of the components which make up the overall number, we cannot get a true reflection of 'how we're doing' and where intervention may be needed.

Measuring change in well-being

The MNW Programme is developing measures of change in well-being. It is recognised that in order to monitor well-being, some measure of how things are changing, at an individual as well as overall level would be helpful. At the moment, the interactive Well-being Wheel provides time series charts to give users an overall sense of change over time. The challenge is to develop a solid and consistent methodology for measuring and presenting change across 41 measures taken from over 20 different sources. Providing measurements of change remains a priority for the MNW Programme and work is currently underway across the Government Statistical Service (GSS) to address this.

Further understanding of what affects well-being and why

Much of the focus so far has been on getting a better understanding of what matters and what influences well-being. For example, regression analysis of the four ONS questions against other data collected via the Annual Population Survey showed that factors such as our self assessed health, relationships and employment status are most strongly associated with well-being. More recent analysis highlighted the differences income and expenditure have on our well-being as well as differences in these effects for men and women. The Programme has provided a lot of information on 'what' influences our well-being and will continue to add to this body of evidence. It will also provide more work on 'why' these things appear to affect our well-being more than others.

Sub group analysis

Part of the answer may lie in providing and analysing data on sub groups, whether sub UK areas or sub groups of the population such as gender, ethnic group or age. Part of the challenge in this area is data availability. The MNW Programme has already given proposed measures of well-being of children and young people and will continue to develop work in this area. It is also considering how measures of national well-being, currently defined for the UK level can be identified at the sub regional level.

Turning evidence into action

The biggest challenge is to turn the evidence on well-being into action, so that policies truly reflect our quality of life; more consideration is given to economic impacts at the individual and household level (rather than just economy wide) and future sustainability of our human and natural capital and the impact of the economy on the environment is measured. ONS will continue to work with stakeholders across Government and beyond to make this happen.

Summary

Measuring national well-being is a long term development programme. In its first three years, the Programme has:

- asked the nation, 'what matters' and started a conversation to make sure measures continue to reflect what matters, through regular open consultations;
- started to uncover, in both a quantitative and qualitative way, answers to the question 'what' affects our well-being, with more work needed to understand 'why';
- undertaken numerous development activities, for example, developing the system of environmental accounts and how to measure human capital;
- provided a wealth of analysis which has both provided evidence in support of existing theories, such as, health being the strongest association with personal well-being; as well as given new insights, for example, that expenditure is more important to our personal well-being than income;
- using largely existing sources of information, provided a large quantity of information which has the capacity to give a better understanding of the economy and it's impacts on people and households; a better understanding of the things which impact on our quality of life and a clearer picture of our capital stocks in terms of our education and skills and the environment to make sure the UK is not heading towards an unsustainable future.

Working with people across Government and beyond, we have made great progress has been made in emphasising the concept of well-being in UK policy and the UK is considered as being among the world leaders in this increasingly important area. Engagement with a broad range of users has provided a 'mandate' for measures of national well-being. They are rooted in what people have said is important to their lives, and help to link policy makers and their decisions to what really matters. If the main purpose of Government is to support the social and economic well-being of citizens then this framework is an essential aid to decision making.

There is still a need to ensure that this large amount of evidence, information and understanding of well-being which will continue to grow - is not wasted. The Programme has started to highlight the potential for using economic, environmental and social measures, alongside traditional measures of progress such as GDP, to provide a wider lens on how society is doing. The information provided has the ability to create real change in the way problems are identified and tackled. There is a need to make sure that the information is not only provided but can be and is interpreted and used by policy makers and others. It is recognised that there is still a need to translate the information and understanding in more meaningful ways.

Background notes

1. Details of the policy governing the release of new data are available by visiting www.statisticsauthority.gov.uk/assessment/code-of-practice/index.html or from the Media Relations Office email: media.relations@ons.gsi.gov.uk

Copyright

Sources, reports and surveys related to 'Insights across society, the economy and the environment, 2014'

Introduction

Commission on the Measurement of Economic Performance and Social Progress report

www.stiglitz-sen-fitoussi.fr/en/index.htm

European Commission's GDP and Beyond project

ec.europa.eu/environment/beyond_gdp/index_en.html

OECD Measuring the Progress of Societies

www.oecd.org/statistics/measuringwell-beingandprogress.htm

Measures of Australia's Progress (MAP)

www.abs.gov.au/ausstats/abs@.nsf/mf/1370.0

Canadian Index of Well-being

uwaterloo.ca/canadian-index-wellbeing/

Inclusive capitalism: creating a sense of the systemic speech given by Mark Carney, Governor of the Bank of England

www.bankofengland.co.uk/publications/Pages/speeches/2014/731.aspx

Impacts of the Measuring National Well-being Work Programme

UK policy

Queens speech 2014

www.gov.uk/government/speeches/queens-speech-2014

Green Book Discussion Paper on Valuing Social Impacts

sd.defra.gov.uk/2011/08/green-book-discussion-paper-on-valuing-social-impacts/

Environmental Audit Committee - Fifteenth Report of Session 2013–14

parliament.uk/business/committees/committees-a-z/commons-select/environmental-audit-committee/publications/

Evaluation of the National Citizenship Service

natcen.ac.uk/our-research/research/evaluation-of-national-citizen-service-pilots/

Legatum Institute: Well-being and Policy report

www.li.com/programmes/the-commission-on-wellbeing-and-policy

International Influence

OECD guidelines on measuring subjective well-being

www.oecd.org/statistics/guidelines-on-measuring-subjective-well-being.htm

OECD Framework for Statistics on the Distribution of Household Income, Consumption and Wealth

www.oecd.org/statistics/icw-framework.htm

Impact outside Government

Berkeley Homes Creating Successful Places

www.berkeleygroup.co.uk/sustainability/social-sustainability

Challenges

Environmental Audit Committee - Fifteenth Report of Session 2013–14

parliament.uk/business/committees/committees-a-z/commons-select/environmental-audit-committee/publications/

List of publications from Measuring National Well-being Programme

Outputs are listed in date order with the most recent at the top. The latest articles and reports are available at Measuring National Well-being.

2014

Sustainable Development Indicators, July 2014

Household Satellite Accounts - Valuing household transport in the UK, 2010

UK Environmental Accounts, 2014

Measuring National Well-being - European Comparisons, 2014

Measuring National Well-being - Income, Expenditure and Personal Well-being, 2011/12

Measuring National Well-being - Economic Well-being

Measuring National Well-being - Life in the UK, 2014

National Well-being Measures, March 2014

Measuring National Well-being - Children's Well-being, 2014

Measuring National Well-being, Young People's Well-being, 2014

Measuring National Well-being - Governance, 2014

Measuring National Well-being, Commuting and Personal Well-being, 2014

2013

Household Satellite Accounts - Valuing Volunteering in the UK

Human Capital Estimates, 2012

Personal well-being across the UK, 2012/13

Measuring National Well-being Domains and Measures, September 2013

Measuring National Well-being - What we do

Personal well-being in the UK, 2012/13

Household Satellite Accounts, Valuing Informal Adult care in the UK

UK Environmental Accounts, 2013

Measuring National Well-being - Health, 2013

Self-reported financial situation, 2013

What matters most to personal well-being

Measuring National Well-being Domains and Measures, May 2013

The Economy - International Comparisons

Differences in well-being by ethnicity

Measuring National Well-being - Older people and loneliness, 2013

Measuring National Well-being - Older people's leisure time and volunteering, 2013

Measuring National Well-being - Older People's Neighbourhoods, 2013

Household Satellite Accounts, Valuing Informal Childcare in the UK

Personal Well-being Survey User Guide: 2012-2013 Dataset

Towards Wealth Accounting - Natural Capital within Comprehensive Wealth

Measuring UK Woodlands Area and Timber Resources

Measuring the UK Woodlands Ecosystem

Monetary Valuation of UK Timber Resources

Land Use in the UK

Monetary valuation of UK continental shelf oil and gas reserves

Updated estimates of UK Resource Use using Raw Material Equivalents

Development of Water Statistics and Water Accounts in the UK

Review of available sources and measures for children and young people's well-being

2012

Individual responses to the consultation on accounting for the value of the nature in the UK

Roadmap on Natural Capital accounting

Measuring National Well-being - Life in the UK 2012

National Well-being wheel of measures poster version

Measuring National Well-being - The Natural Environment

Measuring National Well-being - Governance, 2012

Measuring National Well-being - Children's well-being, 2012

Measuring National Well-being - The Economy

Measuring National Well-being - Measuring young people's well-being, 2012

Measuring National Well-being - Personal finance

Measuring National Well-being - summary of proposed domains and measures

Measuring National Well-being - health

Measuring National Well-being - where we live

First Annual ONS Experimental Subjective Well-being Results - 24 July 2012

Measuring National Well-being - Education and Skills

UK Environmental Accounts, 2012

The effects of taxes and benefits on household income 2010/11

Comparisons of UK and EU at risk Poverty Rates 2005-2010

How the economy impacts on the environment, World Environment Day 2012

Measuring national well-being - Households and families, 2012

Quarterly Household Release, Q4 2011

Measuring National Well-being - what we do, 2012

Initial findings from the consultation on proposed domains and measures of national well-being

Analysis of experimental subjective well-being data from the Annual Population Survey, April - September 2011

Subjective well-being survey user guide

Measuring National Well-being - Our relationships

Is there more to life than GDP and happiness?

Measuring National Well-being - Population

Developments in Environmental Protection Expenditure Accounts

New approaches to the measurement of Quality of Life

Human Capital - Methodology paper

Human Capital consultation response

Measuring National Well-being - the Contribution of Longitudinal Studies

Subjective Well-being Survey User Guide

User guidance for ONS's subjective well-being experimental dataset released July 2012, based on Annual Population Survey information April 2011 to March 2012.

Report on the Consultation on Proposed Domains and Measures

Consultation on proposed domains and measures of national well-being: responses received

2010 and 2011

Human Capital estimates - 2010

Initial investigation into Subjective Well-being data from the ONS Opinions Survey

Measuring National Well-being - Discussion paper on domains and measures

Time-Use Surveys and the Measurement of National Well-Being

Measuring what Matters: National Statistician's Reflections on the National Debate on Measuring National Well-being

Findings from the National well-being debate

Measuring subjective well-being

Developing a framework for understanding and measuring national well-being

Measuring children's and young people's well-being

Measuring economic well-being

Comparing measures of subjective well-being and the views about the role they should play in policy.

Measuring Subjective Well-being for Public Policy

There's more to life than GDP but how can we measure it?

Personal Well-being in the UK, 2013/14

Coverage: **UK**
Date: **24 September 2014**
Geographical Areas: **Local Authority and County, Region**
Theme: **People and Places**

1. Key points

- The latest personal well-being estimates suggest year-on-year improvements in reported well-being since 2011/12, when ONS started to collect the data.

- Over this three-year period, there have been small but significant improvements in average personal well-being ratings in each UK country and across all four measures of well-being.

- The proportions of people reporting the highest levels of personal well-being have grown since 2011/12 for each of the four measures. The greatest gain has been in reduced anxiety levels. The proportion of people in the UK reporting very low anxiety grew between 2011/12 and 2013/14.

- There were also reductions in the proportions of people in the UK rating their well-being at the lowest levels for all of the measures.

- In 2013/14, people in Northern Ireland gave higher ratings for each aspect of their personal well-being on average than those in any other UK country. This has been the case in each year since ONS began collecting the data.

- In 2013/14, people in London reported lower personal well-being on average for each of the measures than the equivalent UK averages, but since 2011/12 London has had improvements across all the average measures of well-being.

- Since 2011/12, average ratings of personal well-being have improved significantly across all measures in the West Midlands. The region also had the lowest average anxiety rating of any English region in 2013/14.

2. Summary

The personal well-being estimates in this bulletin are based on data from the Annual Population Survey (APS) which includes responses from around 165,000 people. This provides a large representative sample of adults aged 16 and over living in residential households in the UK.

In 2013/14, the average ratings for each of the four measures of personal well-being were:

- 7.5 points out of 10 for life satisfaction (up 0.06 points on the previous year)
- 7.7 out of 10 for feeling that what one does in life is worthwhile (up 0.05 points on the previous year)
- 7.4 out of 10 for happiness yesterday (up 0.09 points on the previous year)
- 2.9 out of 10 for anxiety yesterday (down 0.10 points on the previous year)

The year-on-year differences are small but statistically significant in each case. These latest estimates suggest improvement in the past year in the average ratings of personal well-being in the UK across all of the measures.

The proportion of people giving the highest ratings for each aspect of personal well-being also increased significantly in 2013/14, compared to the previous year.

There were significant reductions in the proportions of people giving the lowest ratings of happiness (down 0.7 percentage points) and highest ratings of anxiety (down 0.9 percentage points).

The proportions rating their life satisfaction and the sense that what they do in life is worthwhile at the lowest levels remained stable in 2013/14, and were not significantly different to the previous year.

Also released today:

8 insights into personal well-being showing the latest UK estimates and changes since 2012/13

Interactive maps for exploring the personal well-being estimates in each UK country, the English regions and more local areas of the UK

Interactive graphs for exploring the personal well-being estimates using different thresholds, averages or distributions

Short story exploring 'has personal well-being improved for people in and out of work?'

3. Personal well-being in the UK, 2013/14

This bulletin is published as part of the Office for National Statistics (ONS) Measuring National Well-being programme. It presents annual estimates of personal well-being in different areas of the UK for April 2013 to March 2014. It also compares the latest results to previous ONS personal well-being estimates covering the same periods in 2011/12 and 2012/13 (ONS, 2012; ONS, 2013b). The latest estimates of personal well-being among people with different characteristics or circumstances are also included in the reference tables with this release and in a separate publication, National Well-being Measures, September 2014.

The personal well-being estimates in this bulletin are based on data from the Annual Population Survey (APS) which includes responses from around 165,000 people. This provides a large representative sample of adults aged 16 and over living in residential households in the UK.

Personal well-being, people's thoughts and feelings about their own quality of life, is an important aspect of national well-being. It is part of a much wider initiative in the UK and internationally to look beyond GDP to measure what really matters to people. ONS regularly monitor 41 different headline measures in areas such as the natural environment, our relationships, health, what we do, where we live, personal finances, the economy, education and skills, governance and personal well-being to measure the progress and well-being of the nation. The latest updates to these headline measures are available in National Well-being Measures, September 2014. Section 7 provides further information about how the well-being data are used.

The UK Statistics Authority has designated the ONS personal well-being statistics as National Statistics, signifying compliance with the Code of Practice for Official Statistics.

Designation can be broadly interpreted to mean that the statistics:

- meet identified user needs;
- are well explained and readily accessible;
- are produced according to sound methods; and
- are managed impartially and objectively in the public interest.

Once statistics have been designated as National Statistics it is a statutory requirement that the Code of Practice shall continue to be observed.

3.1 How personal well-being is measured

ONS began measuring personal well-being in April 2011. Since then, the APS has included four questions which are used to monitor personal well-being in the UK:

1. Overall, how satisfied are you with your life nowadays?
2. Overall, to what extent do you feel the things you do in your life are worthwhile?
3. Overall, how happy did you feel yesterday?
4. Overall, how anxious did you feel yesterday?

People are asked to give their answers on a scale of 0 to 10, where 0 is 'not at all' and 10 is 'completely'. These questions allow people to make an assessment of their life overall, as well as providing an indication of their day-to-day emotions. Although 'yesterday' may not be a typical day for an individual, the large sample means that these differences 'average out' and provide a reliable assessment of the self-reported anxiety and happiness of the adult population in the UK over the year.

It is important to remember that the findings presented are based on survey estimates and are subject to a degree of uncertainty. They should therefore be interpreted as providing a good estimate, rather than an exact measure of personal well-being in the UK. For more information about how the statistics are produced and implications for the accuracy of the estimates, please see section 8 (Methodology).

Throughout, differences in the personal well-being estimates over time are described only where they are statistically significant. That is where the change is not likely to be only due to variations in sampling, but to a real change over time. A 5% standard is used for "not likely". This means that there is no more than a 5% chance that a difference will be classified as significant when in fact there is no underlying change. The country and regional estimates for 2013/14 are compared to the equivalent estimates for the UK and discussed only where a statistically significant difference is found (see section 8 for further details).

3.2 How people in the UK rated their personal well-being in 2013/14

Figure 1 shows how people rated each aspect of their personal well-being based on the 0 to 10 scale in each of the three years.

Figure 1: Distribution of personal well-being ratings, 2011/12 - 2013/14 (1)

United Kingdom

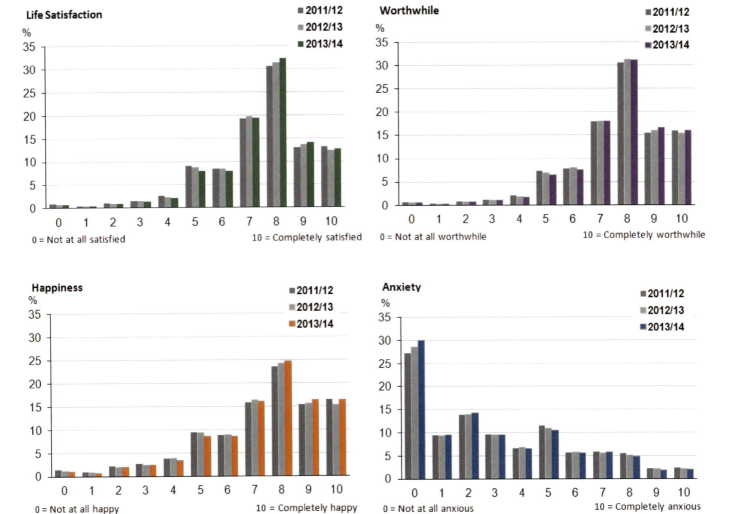

Source: Annual Population Survey (APS) - Office for National Statistics

Notes:

1. Adults aged 16 and over were asked 'Overall, how satisfied are you with your life nowadays?', 'Overall, to what extent do you feel the things you do in your life are worthwhile?', 'Overall, how happy did you feel yesterday?' and 'Overall, how anxious did you feel yesterday?' where 0 is 'not at all' and 10 is 'completely'.

Download chart

XLS XLS format
(29 Kb)

People in the UK tend to rate their life satisfaction, feeling that what they do in life is worthwhile and happiness at the high end of the scale. This suggests high personal well-being on these measures. People most commonly rated each of these questions at 8 out of 10. A higher proportion rated their life satisfaction and feelings that what they do in life are worthwhile at 8 out of 10 (just over 30% in each case) than rated their happiness levels this way (just under 25%).

The pattern for how people rate their anxiety is different to the other questions. A much higher proportion of people rate their anxiety at the lower end of the scale (as 0 or 1), but more also rate their anxiety levels in the middle of the scale (as 5 out of 10). In each year, the majority of people rated their anxiety at a low level between 0 and 3. The most common response was 0 out of 10, which indicates that they felt 'not at all anxious' on the previous day.

This pattern of personal well-being ratings in the UK has been fairly consistent for each of the three years with small (but statistically significant) variations emerging year-on-year.

Explore the data in this section using:

Personal Well-being distribution interactive chart

3.3 Average ratings of personal well-being in the UK

Average ratings of personal well-being are a simple method of drawing comparisons over time. In 2013/14, the average ratings for each of the four measures of personal well-being were:

- 7.5 points out of 10 for life satisfaction (up 0.06 points on the previous year)
- 7.7 out of 10 for feeling that what one does in life is worthwhile (up 0.05 points on the previous year)
- 7.4 out of 10 for happiness yesterday (up 0.09 points on the previous year)
- 2.9 out of 10 for anxiety yesterday (down 0.10 points on the previous year)

The year-on-year differences are small but statistically significant in each case. In summary, the latest estimates suggest improvement in the past year in the average ratings of personal well-being in the UK across all of the measures.

Comparing the latest average estimates with those from 2011/12, there have also been small but significant improvements in personal well-being across all four measures (see **Figure 2**).

Figure 2: Change in average annual UK personal well-being ratings compared to 2011/12

United Kingdom

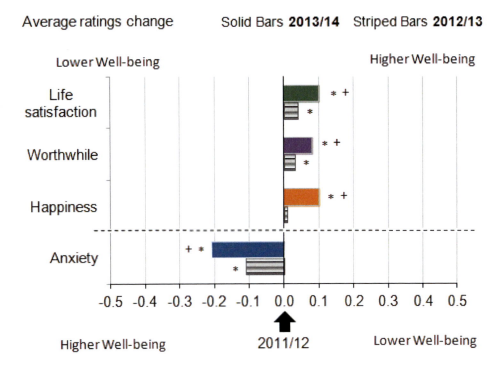

Source: Annual Population Survey (APS) - Office for National Statistics

Notes:

1. * Indicates significant from 2011/12 at the 0.05 level.
2. \+ Indicates significant from 2012/13 at the 0.05 level.

Download chart

 XLS format
(29 Kb)

3.4 Highest and lowest personal well-being in the UK

Average ratings of personal well-being provide a useful summary of overall levels of reported well-being, but they do not tell the whole story. Another key consideration is whether people assess their personal well-being in similar ways across areas and population groups and how this changes over time. Here, we look at the proportions of people in the UK who rated their well-being at the highest and lowest levels in 2013/14, compared to the previous two years.

3.4.1 Measuring 'highest' and 'lowest' personal well-being

The highest levels of personal well-being for life satisfaction, worthwhile and happiness are defined as ratings of 9 or 10. For reported anxiety, ratings of 0 or 1 are used because lower levels of anxiety suggest better personal well-being.

On the other hand, lowest levels of personal well-being are defined as ratings of 0 to 4 for life satisfaction, worthwhile and happiness. For reported anxiety, ratings of 6 to 10 are used because higher levels of anxiety suggest lower personal well-being.

3.4.2 Highest and lowest personal well-being in the UK, 2013/14

Figure 3 shows the percentages of people in the UK reporting the highest and lowest levels of well-being in 2013/14 and how this has changed since 2011/12.

For the picture of highest and lowest well-being for 2013/14:

* 26.8% rated their life satisfaction at the highest levels compared to 5.6% at the lowest;
* 32.6% rated their sense that what they do in life is worthwhile at the highest levels, compared to 4.2% at the lowest levels;
* 32.6% rated their happiness at the highest levels, while 9.7% rated their happiness at the lowest;
* 39.4% rated their anxiety at the lowest levels, while 20% rated it at the highest levels.

Figure 3: Percentages rating personal well-being at highest and lowest levels, 2011/12-2013/14

United Kingdom

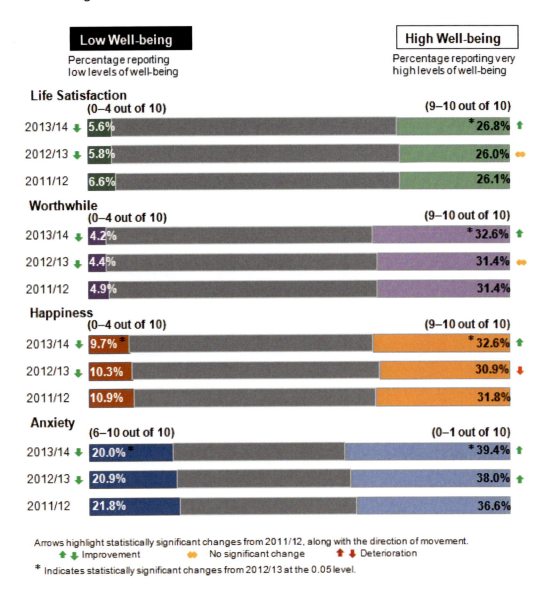

Arrows highlight statistically significant changes from 2011/12, along with the direction of movement.

⬆️ ⬇️ Improvement ⬅➡ No significant change ⬆️ ⬇️ Deterioration

* Indicates statistically significant changes from 2012/13 at the 0.05 level.

Source: Annual Population Survey (APS) - Office for National Statistics

Download chart

XLS XLS format
(29 Kb)

3.4.3 Changes over time in highest and lowest personal well-being in the UK

The proportion of people giving the highest ratings for each aspect of personal well-being increased significantly in 2013/14, compared to the previous year. This suggests that more people in the UK are feeling positive about their lives and is consistent with the higher average ratings of personal well-being noted in the previous section.

On the other hand, for those reporting lowest personal well-being, the picture is more mixed. There were significant reductions in the proportions of people giving the lowest ratings of happiness (down 0.7 percentage points) and highest ratings of anxiety (down 0.9 percentage points). The proportions rating their life satisfaction and the sense that what they do in life is worthwhile at the lowest levels remained stable in 2013/14, compared to the previous year.

Looking at how ratings have changed over the three-year period, there have been statistically significant gains in the proportions of people reporting very high personal well-being for each of the four measures. The smallest gain was in the proportion of people giving the highest ratings of life satisfaction (up 0.64 percentage points). The largest gain was in the proportion of people rating their anxiety as very low (up 2.82 percentage points).

The proportions of people rating their personal well-being at the lowest levels decreased significantly for all four measures. The reductions in very low personal well-being ratings ranged from 0.67 percentage points in the case of low ratings for 'worthwhile' to 1.76 percentage points in the case of very high ratings of anxiety.

Overall, these estimates suggest improvements in reported personal well-being since 2011/12. These are shown in both the greater proportions of people giving high ratings for each aspect of well-being and in the smaller proportions giving low ratings.

3.5 Possible reasons for the improvement in reported personal well-being in the UK

The latest picture of personal well-being is more positive across all of the measures compared to 2012/13, and even more so compared to 2011/12. This is only the third year ONS have collected the personal well-being data, so it is too early to speculate on trends over time. However, one possible reason for the small scale improvements in personal well-being may be the more positive economic outlook in the UK.

ONS recently published analysis (ONS, 2013a) looking at what matters most to personal well-being. The findings, similar to other research in this area, suggested that self-assessed health, employment status and relationship status are particularly strongly related to personal well-being. Further analysis (ONS, 2014a) also added household income and household expenditure to this list, but found they were not as strongly linked to well-being as some other aspects of life, such as health and employment.

Other academic research also suggests that, apart from individual circumstances, aspects of the wider economic environment such as unemployment and inflation are negatively related to national ratings of well-being (Blanchflower et al, 2013). Comparing the relative influence of both inflation and unemployment rates on life satisfaction ratings across countries and over time, the study concluded that: "In the Great Recession, unemployment has been a much bigger problem than inflation for ordinary people."

This suggests that as unemployment rates fall in the UK, we should expect to see life satisfaction rise.

The Economic Review (ONS, 2014b) recently summarised the improved labour market conditions in the UK for the period covered by the latest personal well-being estimates:

"The unemployment rate for those aged 16 plus, which fell just 0.4 percentage points in the year to April 2013, has fallen a further 1.2 percentage points over the last year to 6.6% in the 3 months ending in April 2014...The employment rate has risen by 1.4 percentage points over the last year reflecting an increase in employment of 780,000."

The continuing fall in UK unemployment rates over the past two years appears to be mirrored by the small but significant improvements in the personal well-being estimates over this period.

Some research evidence (Lim and Laurence, 2013) suggests that there may be both direct and indirect effects of a recession and unemployment on personal well-being. For example, people's evaluations of their lives may be affected directly by their own experiences of unemployment and its effects such as reduced financial security, loss of social contacts, daily structure, and sense of meaning and purpose.

Further to this, during a recession, people who are employed may also become fearful of losing their job (Blanchflower, 1991). Other research has also found that life satisfaction is reduced among those living with unemployed people (Lim and Laurence, 2013). Although the effects are less severe than for the unemployed person, these studies suggest that the negative impacts of unemployment on personal well-being are spread out beyond those directly affected by job loss. Also, the increased financial anxiety linked with bad economic news may have an indirect effect on how people rate their personal well-being. The opposite may be true as the media focus is on economic recovery.

Other non-official sources suggest that people in the UK are beginning to feel more positive about the economy and about their own financial security. For example, a monthly survey of 2000 UK consumers carried out by Which? found statistically significant increases between March 2013 and March 2014 in the proportions of people describing the economy as good (up 13 percentage points) and expecting their personal finances to get better (up 3 percentage points).

These findings suggest that, at the national level, people may be feeling more positive about their lives as unemployment rates fall, the economic news becomes more positive and their expectations for the future improve.

This may be the case even if they may not yet have seen much improvement in their own circumstances. For example, some estimates suggest that real wages which take inflation into account have fallen continuously since 2009 (ONS, 2014b).

The improvement in the national estimates of personal well-being may also mask important differences between people in different economic and employment circumstances. A short story also published by ONS today looks in more detail at personal well-being ratings in relation to employment status and how they have changed since 2011/12.

4. Personal well-being across UK countries

This section examines the latest findings on personal well-being across UK countries. Interactive charts and graphs are also available to explore the findings further:

Personal Well-being average interactive chart

Personal Well-being thresholds interactive chart

4.1 Average reported personal well-being in UK countries

Figure 4 shows the latest average ratings of personal well-being across the UK countries and how they compare to the UK averages.

- In 2013/14, Northern Ireland and Scotland had the highest average ratings of life satisfaction (7.7 and 7.6 out of 10, respectively). These were above the UK average (7.5).
- Northern Ireland was the only country where average ratings for worthwhile (8.0), happiness (7.7) and anxiety (2.8) were significantly different to the UK averages. Average reported happiness and sense that what one does in life is worthwhile were above the UK averages, while average reported anxiety in Northern Ireland was lower than in the UK.

Figure 4: Average personal well-being ratings compared to UK averages: by country, 2013/14

United Kingdom

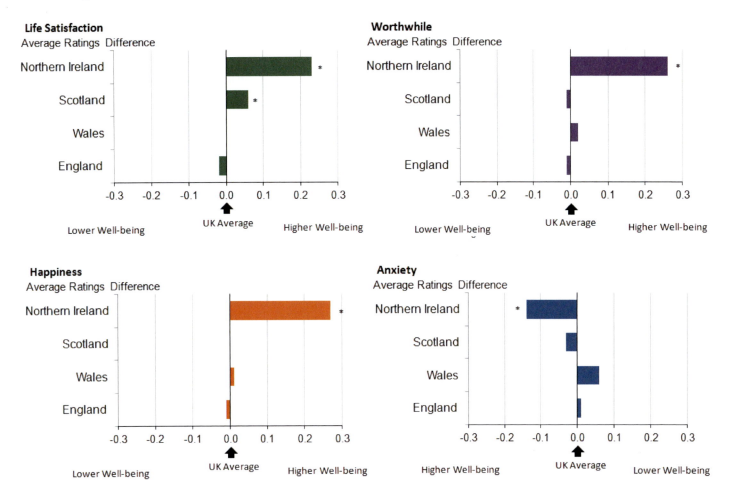

Source: Annual Population Survey (APS) - Office for National Statistics

Notes:

1.   * Indicates statistical significance determined on the basis of non-overlapping confidence intervals.

Download chart

XLS XLS format

(29.5 Kb)

4.2 Changes over time in average reported personal well-being in the UK countries

Comparing the latest average estimates for each country to the 2012/13 estimates, key points include (see **Figure 5**):

- England and Wales had significant improvements in the average estimates of life satisfaction, the sense that what we do in life is worthwhile and happiness.
- Scotland had an increase in average reported life satisfaction and happiness while Northern Ireland had an increase in average ratings that what we do in life is worthwhile.

- England, was the only country with any significant change in average anxiety ratings, with a reduction in reported anxiety levels.

Since 2011/12, when ONS first collected the personal well-being data, there have been significant improvements across all of the measures and in each of the UK countries.

Figure 5: Change in annual average UK personal well-being ratings compared to 2011/12: by country

United Kindgom

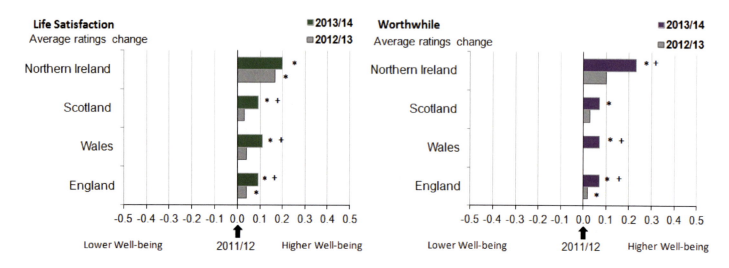

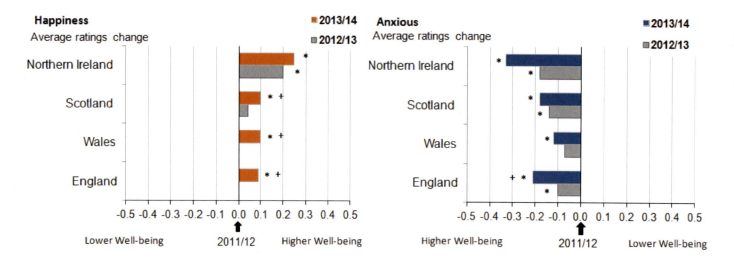

Source: Annual Population Survey (APS) - Office for National Statistics

Notes:
1. * Indicates significant from 2011/12 at the 0.05 level.
2. + Indicates significant from 2012/13 at the 0.05 level.

Download chart

 XLS format
(31.5 Kb)

4.3 Highest and lowest ratings of personal well-being across UK countries

This section provides the latest estimates of the proportions of people in each country reporting the highest and lowest levels of personal well-being.

For concentrations of highest well-being across the UK countries:

- In 2013/14, England, Scotland and Wales all had similar proportions of people reporting the highest levels of life satisfaction, sense that what they do in life is worthwhile, and happiness.
- Northern Ireland had the highest percentages of people rating life satisfaction, worthwhile and happiness as very high. It was the only country which was significantly different to the UK (36.4% rated their life satisfaction as 9 or 10 in Northern Ireland compared to 26.8% in the UK).
- In 2013/14, Scotland was the only country with a greater proportion of people reporting very low anxiety than the equivalent UK percentage (40.8% in Scotland compared to 39.4% in the UK).

For concentrations of lowest well-being across the UK countries:

- None of the countries had a greater proportion of people rating any aspect of personal well-being as very low than the equivalent proportions for the UK.

4.4 Changes over time in highest and lowest personal well-being across the UK countries

Comparing the latest estimates of highest well-being for each country to the 2012/13 estimates, key points include:

- The percentages of people giving the highest ratings for each aspect of well-being either increased or remained stable in all countries.
- England was the only country with significant increases in the percentages of people reporting the highest well-being on all four measures compared to the previous year. It was also the only country in which the proportion reporting low anxiety grew.
- Wales and Northern Ireland also had significant increases in the proportions of people rating their personal well-being as very high on two of the four measures
- Scotland remained stable on every measure over this period.

Comparing the latest estimates of lowest well-being for each country to the 2012/13 estimates, key points include:

- Only Wales and England had any significant changes in the proportions of people reporting very low well-being over this period. In Wales, there were significant reductions in the proportions of people rating their life satisfaction and happiness as very low. In England, there were reductions in the proportions of people rating happiness as very low and anxiety as very high.
- Scotland remained stable in the proportions of people rating their well-being as very low across all measures.

Since 2011/12, when ONS first collected this data, there have been changes in the lowest and highest personal well-being ratings in each UK country (see **Figure 6**).

- Northern Ireland and England have each had significant increases in the proportions of people reporting very high well-being across all four measures.
- In Scotland, the proportion reporting very low anxiety has grown. There were no significant changes in the proportions of people reporting highest well-being on any other measures.
- In Wales, the proportion of people reporting very high well-being remained stable.

The changes were more striking in relation to the proportions of people reporting lowest well-being over this period. For example:

- In all UK countries, there were significant reductions in the proportions of people reporting very low life satisfaction and happiness. Scotland and England also had significant reductions in the proportions giving very low ratings for the sense that what they do in life is worthwhile.
- There were significant reductions in the proportions rating their anxiety as very high in Northern Ireland, Scotland and England. Wales remained stable in the proportion reporting high anxiety.

Figure 6: Percentages rating personal well-being at highest and lowest levels: by country, 2013/14 and change since 2011/12

United Kingdom

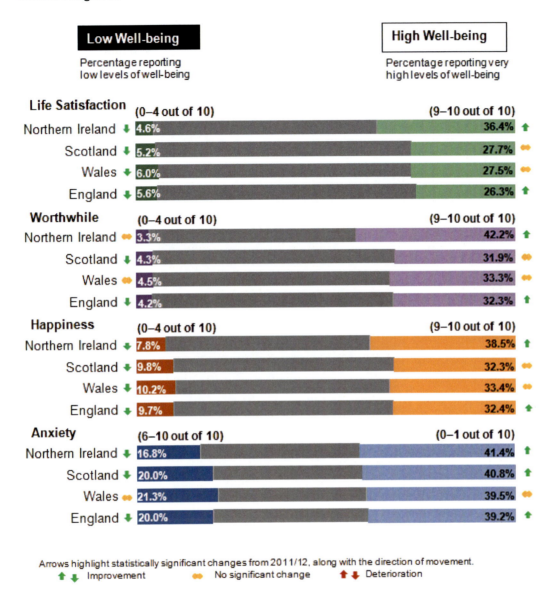

Arrows highlight statistically significant changes from 2011/12, along with the direction of movement.

⬆ ⬇ Improvement   ⬌ No significant change   ⬆ ⬇ Deterioration

Source: Annual Population Survey (APS) - Office for National Statistics

Download chart

XLS XLS format

(33 Kb)

5. Personal well-being in the English regions

This section focuses on personal well-being across the English regions in 2013/14 and changes over time. Previous analysis by ONS (ONS, 2013c) found that after taking account of a range of characteristics relating to individuals and where they live, the region where we live and whether we live in an urban or rural area are related to personal well-being. However, the effect is not as strong as other aspects of life, such as employment situation, for example.

As the differences between regions may not be statistically significant, comparisons are made between each region and the equivalent UK figure. They are commented on only where there is a statistically significant difference (Section 8, Methodology).

5.1 Average personal well-being ratings in the English regions

The average ratings across the regions for each measure of personal well-being in 2013/14 are shown in **Figure 7**, as well as how they compare to the UK averages. Regions where average ratings were significantly above the UK averages include the following:

- The South East had higher average ratings of life satisfaction, sense that what we do in life is worthwhile and happiness than the UK (average life satisfaction was 7.6 and happiness 7.5 compared to 7.5 and 7.4 respectively for the UK).
- The East of England had higher average ratings for the sense that what one does in life is worthwhile than the UK (7.8 in the East of England compared to 7.7 for the UK).
- The West Midlands was the only region with a lower average anxiety rating than the UK (2.7 compared to 2.9 for the UK).

Regions where average ratings were significantly below the UK averages include the following:

- People in London reported lower personal well-being on average for every measure than the UK. For example, life satisfaction was 7.4 compared to 7.5 for the UK, and average reported anxiety in London was 3.2 compared to 2.9 for the UK.
- The North West also had lower average ratings than the UK for life satisfaction, the sense that what we do in life is worthwhile and happiness. For example, in the North West, the average happiness rating was 7.3 compared to 7.4 in the UK. Average reported anxiety levels in the North West did not differ significantly to the UK average.
- People in the North East also had lower average happiness ratings than the UK (7.3 compared to 7.4 for the UK). Average ratings for other aspects of well-being were not significantly different to the UK averages.

Figure 7: Average personal well-being ratings compared to UK averages: by region, 2013/14

United Kingdom

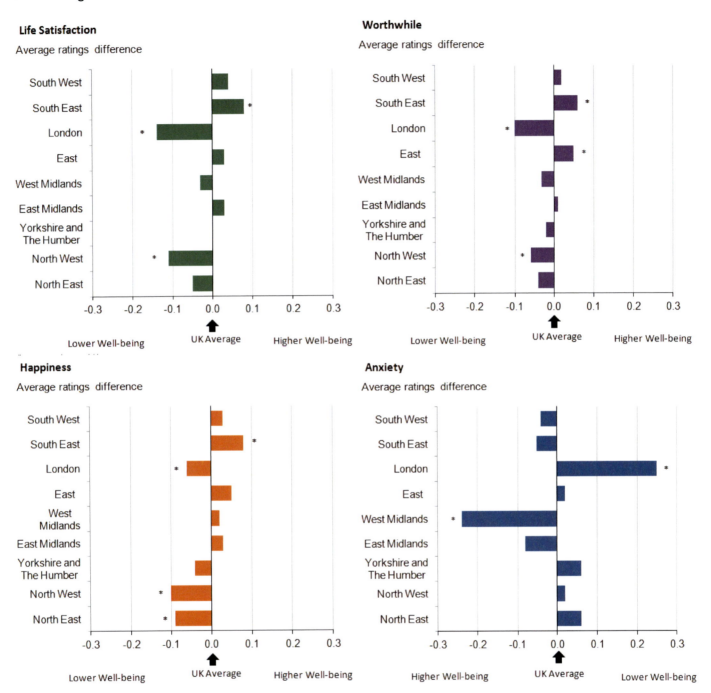

Source: Annual Population Survey (APS) - Office for National Statistics

Notes:

1.   * Indicates statistical significance determined on the basis of non-overlapping confidence intervals.

Download chart

XLS XLS format

(31 Kb)

5.2 Changes over time in average personal well-being ratings in the English regions

Comparing the latest average estimates for each region to the 2012/13 estimates, many regions had higher average ratings for the positive aspects of well-being and reductions in average reported anxiety. This suggests small but widespread improvements in personal well-being across the English regions.

Since 2011/12, when ONS first collected these data, the following summarises the changes in the regional average ratings (see **Figure 8**):

- This pattern of small improvements in average reported personal well-being has continued for two years. Average personal well-being ratings have not deteriorated significantly in any region.
- Average reported well-being improved on all measures in London, the South East, and the West Midlands.
- The East of England saw a significant improvement in average reported life satisfaction, sense that what we do in life is worthwhile and a reduction in anxiety levels.
- In some areas, average personal well-being has remained largely stable. For example, the North West has not had any significant improvement in average ratings of life satisfaction, happiness or feelings that what we do in life is worthwhile since 2011/12. There have been significant reductions in anxiety year-on-year since 2011/12.

Figure 8: Change in annual average personal well-being ratings: by region

United Kingdom

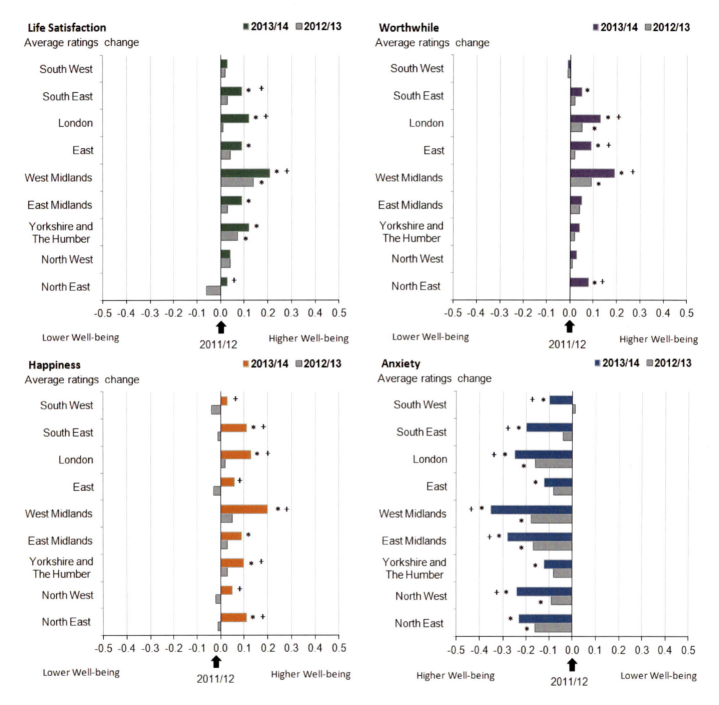

Source: Annual Population Survey (APS) - Office for National Statistics

Notes:

1. * Indicates significant from 2011/12 at the 0.05 level.
2. + Indicates significant from 2012/13 at the 0.05 level.

Download chart

 XLS format

(36 Kb)

5.3   Highest and lowest personal well-being in the English regions in 2013/14

This section considers whether the highest and lowest reported personal well-being is spread evenly across the regions or is concentrated in certain areas.

The percentages of people in each region reporting the highest well-being in 2013/14 are shown in **Map 1**, with the lowest reported well-being shown in **Map 2**. These maps also show the direction of changes in the estimates since 2011/12.

For the concentrations of highest levels of reported personal well-being across the English regions, key points are as follows:

- The percentages of people reporting the highest level of personal well-being in each region were generally not significantly different to the UK, though there were a few exceptions.
- For life satisfaction, feeling that what we do in life is worthwhile and happiness, no region had a significantly greater percentage of people reporting very high well-being than the UK. This suggests a high degree of similarity in the concentrations of people reporting highest personal well-being across the regions.
- Only the West Midlands had greater proportions of people reporting very low anxiety levels than in the UK (44.1% rated their anxiety as very low compared to 39.4% in the UK).

Map 1: Percentages rating personal well-being at highest levels: by region, 2013/14 and change since 2011/12

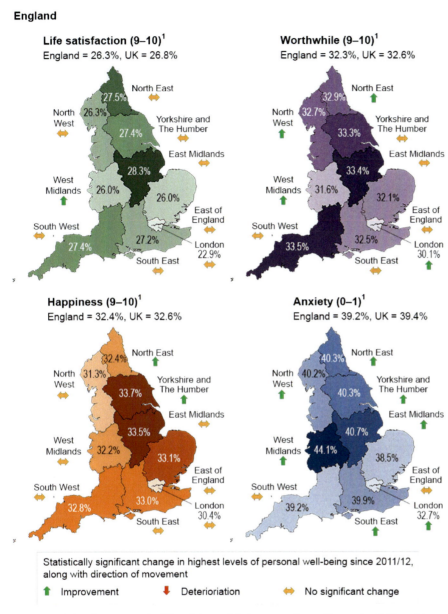

England

Life satisfaction (9–10)[1]
England = 26.3%, UK = 26.8%

Worthwhile (9–10)[1]
England = 32.3%, UK = 32.6%

Happiness (9–10)[1]
England = 32.4%, UK = 32.6%

Anxiety (0–1)[1]
England = 39.2%, UK = 39.4%

Statistically significant change in highest levels of personal well-being since 2011/12, along with direction of movement

⬆ Improvement   ⬇ Deterioriation   ⬌ No significant change

1 Adults aged 16 and over were asked 'Overall, how satisfied are you with your life nowadays?', 'Overall, to what extent do you feel the things you do in your life are worthwhile?', 'Overall, how happy did you feel yesterday?' and 'Overall, how anxious did you feel yesterday?' where 0 is 'not at all' and 10 is 'completely'.
Source: Office for National Statistics
Contains National Statistics data © Crown copyright and database right 2014
Contains Ordnance Survey data © Crown copyright and database right 2014

Source: Annual Population Survey (APS) - Office for National Statistics

Download map

PNG PNG format
(364.4 Kb)

For concentrations of the lowest levels of reported personal well-being across the English regions, key points are:

- The North East and the North West both had greater proportions of people reporting very low well-being than the UK. In each region, the proportions of people giving low ratings for life satisfaction, feeling that what they do in life is worthwhile, and happiness were significantly greater than in the UK.
- Yorkshire and The Humber also had a greater proportion of people (10.8%) rating their happiness as very low than in the UK (9.7%).

Map 2: Percentages rating personal well-being at lowest levels: by region, 2013/14 and change since 2011/12

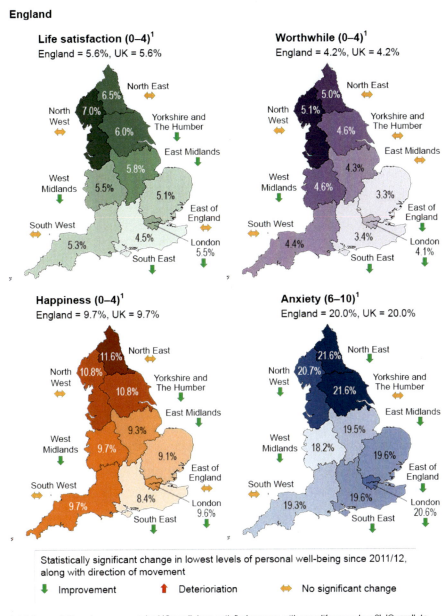

England

Life satisfaction (0–4)[1]
England = 5.6%, UK = 5.6%

North East 6.5%
North West 7.0%
Yorkshire and The Humber 6.0%
East Midlands 5.8%
West Midlands 5.5%
East of England 5.1%
South West 5.3%
South East 4.5%
London 5.5%

Worthwhile (0–4)[1]
England = 4.2%, UK = 4.2%

North East 5.0%
North West 5.1%
Yorkshire and The Humber 4.6%
East Midlands 4.3%
West Midlands 4.6%
East of England 3.3%
South West 4.4%
South East 3.4%
London 4.1%

Happiness (0–4)[1]
England = 9.7%, UK = 9.7%

North East 11.6%
North West 10.8%
Yorkshire and The Humber 10.8%
East Midlands 9.3%
West Midlands 9.7%
East of England 9.1%
South West 9.7%
South East 8.4%
London 9.6%

Anxiety (6–10)[1]
England = 20.0%, UK = 20.0%

North East 21.6%
North West 20.7%
Yorkshire and The Humber 21.6%
East Midlands 19.5%
West Midlands 18.2%
East of England 19.6%
South West 19.3%
South East 19.6%
London 20.6%

Statistically significant change in lowest levels of personal well-being since 2011/12, along with direction of movement

↓ Improvement   ↑ Deterioriation   ⇔ No significant change

1 Adults aged 16 and over were asked 'Overall, how satisfied are you with your life nowadays?', 'Overall, to what extent do you feel the things you do in your life are worthwhile?', 'Overall, how happy did you feel yesterday?' and 'Overall, how anxious did you feel yesterday?' where 0 is 'not at all' and 10 is 'completely'.
Source: Office for National Statistics
Contains National Statistics data © Crown copyright and database right 2014
Contains Ordnance Survey data © Crown copyright and database right 2014

Source: Annual Population Survey (APS) - Office for National Statistics

Download map

PNG PNG format
(356.2 Kb)

5.4 Changes over time in highest and lowest personal well-being in the regions

Comparing the concentrations of highest reported personal well-being in the regions to those of 2012/13:

- London, the West Midlands and the South East all had increases in the proportions of people reporting the highest levels of well-being on three of the four measures.
- The North East had greater proportions of people reporting the highest levels of happiness and feeling that what they do in life is worthwhile.
- The North West had a greater proportion of people reporting the lowest levels of anxiety.
- In the South West, and Yorkshire and The Humber there were no significant changes in the percentages of people reporting very high well-being on any of the measures.

Comparing the concentrations of lowest reported personal well-being to those of 2012/13, there were fewer significant changes in the proportions of people reporting very low personal well-being than very high well-being. All of the changes involved reductions in the percentages of people reporting lowest personal well-being.

- London had reduction in the percentages of people rating their life satisfaction at the lowest levels and their anxiety at the highest;
- The South East had a reduction in the proportions reporting very low happiness and very high anxiety;
- The East of England had a reduction in the proportion of people rating the sense that what they do in life is worthwhile at a very low level;
- The West Midlands had a reduction in the proportion of people rating their anxiety as very high.

Since 2011/12, when ONS first collected these data, changes in concentrations of highest reported personal well-being across the regions include (see Map 1):

- The West Midlands had an increase in the proportions reporting the highest levels of life satisfaction and sense that what they do in life is worthwhile and the lowest levels of anxiety.
- In the North East there were increases in the proportions reporting the highest levels of happiness and sense that what they do in life is worthwhile, and the lowest levels of anxiety.
- Most regions had significantly greater proportions of people reporting very low anxiety. Only the East of England and the South West remained stable on this measure.
- There were no significant reductions in any region in the proportions of people rating their well-being at the highest levels over this period (on any of the four measures).

Since 2011/12, when ONS first collected the data, changes in concentrations of lowest reported personal well-being across the regions include (see Map 2):

- The West Midlands, South East, and London all had significant reductions in the proportions of people reporting the lowest levels of personal well-being for all four measures.
- The East Midlands had a significant reduction in the proportions of people reporting the lowest levels of life satisfaction and happiness and the highest levels of anxiety
- In the North East and North West, the only significant reductions in lowest reported well-being were in the proportions of people in these regions reporting very high anxiety.

- The South West remained stable in the proportion of people reporting the lowest levels of well-being. This was the only region in which there were no significant reductions in the percentages of people reporting the lowest well-being for any of the measures.
- Across the regions, there were no significant increases in the proportions of people reporting the lowest well-being on any measure.

Explore the data in this section using:

Personal Well-being average interactive chart

Personal Well-being thresholds interactive chart

6. PWB in local areas of the UK

For more local areas of the UK, the personal well-being estimates are available as interactive maps that can be explored in a variety of ways and in the reference table (646 Kb Excel sheet) accompanying this bulletin. The personal well-being estimates have been published for the following administrative areas in England, Scotland, Wales and Northern Ireland in the reference tables:

- Unitary Authorities/ Counties in England
- Local Authority Districts in England
- Unitary Authorities in Wales
- Local Authorities in Scotland
- District Council Areas in Northern Ireland

ONS have also published further analysis looking at how personal well-being differs according to the characteristics of areas and the people living there (ONS, 2013a; ONS, 2014c).

By the end of 2014, ONS plan to release a further dataset which will combine the first 3 years of personal well-being data (April 2011 to March 2014). This should provide larger sample sizes and more robust analysis of personal well-being in local areas and among smaller population sub-groups.

We would welcome feedback on this bulletin, particularly how the data are used. Please contact us via email at: personal.well-being@ons.gsi.gov.uk or telephone Dawn Snape on 01633 45 5674.

7. Uses of the data

The personal well-being statistics are used to inform decision making among policy-makers, individuals, communities, businesses and civil society. They complement other traditional measures of progress and quality of life such as unemployment and household income. The personal well-being estimates are used by ONS as part of a wider programme to monitor and understand UK national well-being over time and in comparison to other countries.

One of the main benefits of collecting personal well-being data is that people are able to give their views about each aspect of their well-being. Without it, assumptions must be made about how objective conditions, such as people's health and income, might influence their individual well-being. On the other hand, personal well-being measures are grounded in individuals' preferences and take account of what matters most to them by allowing them to decide what is important when providing an assessment of their own quality of life.

The uses of personal well-being data are varied, but four main uses have been identified:

- Overall monitoring of national well-being
- Use in the policy making process
- International comparisons
- Public decision making

7.1 Overall monitoring of national well-being

Collected regularly, personal well-being data can provide an indication of how the well-being of a nation is changing. To get a full picture of national well-being, ONS believe it is important to use this information to supplement existing objective information. ONS have identified different aspects (or domains) of well-being that sit alongside the personal well-being domain. These include such areas as:

- health
- our relationships
- what we do
- where we live
- personal finance
- education and skills
- the economy
- the environment
- governance.

The National Well-being wheel of measures includes indicators for all these.

7.2 Use in policy making

Personal well-being data, within the framework of wider measures of national well-being, focuses on how people think and feel about their lives. This is an important addition to official statistics, helping policy makers understand how their decisions may affect pople's quality of life. Personal well-being data is increasingly being used both in the UK and internationally in the development and evaluation of policies and services.

7.2.1 Identifying need and targeting policies

The large sample size of the APS Personal Well-being dataset allows for comparisons between different groups of the population (for example, different age groups or different ethnic groups) and between different areas in the UK (for example, countries, regions and local authority districts). This can help policy-makers target policy at the groups or areas with highest need in terms of personal well-being.

Analysis can also be carried out to look at how different objective circumstances relate to personal well-being and which are most strongly associated with it. This can help to identify which policies could be most effective in improving personal well-being. In May 2013, ONS published analysis looking at 'What matters most to personal well-being?' (ONS, 2013a) and this identified health, relationship status and employment status as the factors most highly associated with personal well-being in the Annual Population Survey. Recent publications by ONS have also looked at relationships between commuting and personal well-being (ONS, 2014d), household income and expenditure (ONS, 2014a), and aspects of where we live (ONS, 2014c).

7.2.2 Policy appraisal

Another use is in cost-benefit analysis for policy appraisal. Personal well-being estimates can provide an alternative method to value the costs and benefits of different policies. This process could also help inform decisions around which forms of spending will lead to the largest increases in personal well-being (Dolan et al, 2011).

The Green Book is HM Treasury's guide for government departments on the appraisal of the costs and benefits of projects through social cost-benefit analysis. A Green Book discussion paper (Fujiwara and Campbell, 2011), produced jointly by HM Treasury and the Department for Work and Pensions, looks at the potential uses of personal well-being measures in social cost-benefit analysis. Another recent example of the use of personal well-being data in this area has been to produce a method for the monetary valuation of volunteering (Fujawara et al, 2013).

7.2.3 Examples of use of personal well-being data for policy evaluation and monitoring

Personal well-being data are increasingly being used to evaluate and monitor the effectiveness of policy interventions in the UK. A recent example is the National Citizen Service where a pilot evaluated the personal well-being of young people before and after their participation in the service. The results compared people's reported personal well-being before and after participation in the programme and found statistically significant increases. The well-being of participants' also improved compared to a control group of similar people who had not participated in the programme. As well as government interventions, other civil society and third sector interventions could be evaluated in a similar way.

Added to this, looking at policies through a 'well-being lens' and using data to inform not only the formulation of policy but also how policy could be better implemented with people's well-being in mind is also important. The Social Impacts Taskforce (SITF), comprising of senior analysts from across government, has been working to make use of personal well-being data and share approaches and findings across government. The Cabinet Office has also convened a cross-Whitehall steering group of senior policy makers to encourage the consideration of well-being in policy.

Separate initiatives to investigate well-being are being undertaken by the devolved governments. These include: the National Performance Framework, which forms part of the 'Scotland performs' initiative and the recently published 'Analysis of subjective well-being in Wales: Evidence from the Annual Population Survey'. These initiatives reflect the specific needs of the countries they represent.

Most UK government departments are actively engaged in well-being research in some way, particularly analysis of personal well-being data. This explores how people's ratings of their personal well-being are associated with particular policy areas including housing, crime, adult learning, sport, culture, volunteering and health.

Further information, including examples of how personal well-being data are being used in the policy process, is available in recent government evidence submitted by the Cabinet Office to the UK Parliament's Environmental Audit Committee as part of their inquiry on well-being

Also available is 'Well-being Policy and Analysis' , a document providing updated information about well-being work across Whitehall (including use of the ONS personal well-being questions and data in evaluations, surveys and specialised data exploration tools).

7.3 International developments to monitor well-being

The benefit of understanding where the UK is placed compared to other nations is another important reason for the collection of personal well-being data.

There are increasing calls from international organisations such as Eurostat and the Organisation for Economic Cooperation and Development to develop national personal well-being estimates and increasing recognition internationally that this should be included in official data collection.

Eurostat (the Statistical Office of the European Union) have started to collect personal well-being statistics from member states as part of the European Statistics on Income and Living Conditions (EU-SILC) in an ad-hoc well-being module in 2013. Eurostat's Quality of Life Indicators, currently being developed, will also include personal well-being information to supplement objective information already collected across Europe.

The Organisation of Economic Cooperation and Development (OECD) has also published guidance on the measurement of subjective well-being and ONS contributed to this.

8. Methodology

8.1 The APS Personal Well-being dataset

The data analysed in this bulletin are from the Annual Population Survey (APS) Personal Well-being dataset, covering the period April 2013 to March 2014. ONS will release a new annual APS Personal Well-being dataset every year, soon after the publication of the latest Personal Well-being in the UK statistical bulletin in September. The dataset includes responses to the four ONS personal well-being questions as well as a range of other variables useful for the analysis of personal well-being. Also, special weighting is included in the dataset to make the data representative of the UK population. The weighting also adjusts for the fact that each respondent must answer the questions for themselves, with no one else in the household allowed to answer on their behalf.

Since 2012, the annual version of the APS Personal Well-being dataset has been archived so that approved researchers can use the data for their own analysis. Further details of how researchers can access the data are available from our Frequently Asked Questions page or by contacting the Personal Well-being Team: personal.well-being@ons.gsi.gov.uk.

8.2 The ONS personal well-being questions and their development

The ONS personal well-being questions were developed as part of the Measuring National Well-being Programme. ONS sought advice from experts working in the field of subjective well-being (see Dolan et al, 2011) and consulted with specialists on the National Statistician's Measuring National Well-being Advisory Forum and Technical Advisory Group. Based on this, as well as extensive question testing, four questions were designed. They provide a concise and balanced approach to the measurement of subjective well-being, drawing on three main theoretical approaches (Dolan et al, 2011, ONS, 2011a). These include:

*   The 'evaluative' approach which asks people to reflect on their life and assess how it is going overall in terms of their satisfaction with life;
*   The 'eudemonic' approach which asks people to consider the extent to which they feel a sense of meaning and purpose in life;
*   The 'experience' approach which ask about people's positive and negative experiences and emotions over a short period of time to assess these aspects of personal well-being on a day-to-day basis.

ONS conducted focus groups with members of the public in 2013, and found that 'personal well-being' is clearer and simpler for people to understand than 'subjective well-being'. Since then, both the questions and estimates have been referred to as 'personal well-being'.

The following are the ONS personal well-being questions that have been included on the Annual Population Survey each year since 2011:

*   Overall, how satisfied are you with your life nowadays? (evaluative approach)
*   Overall, to what extent do you feel the things you do in your life are worthwhile? (eudemonic approach)
*   Overall, how happy did you feel yesterday? (experience approach)
*   Overall, how anxious did you feel yesterday? (experience approach)

All are answered using a 0 to 10 scale where 0 is 'not at all' and 10 is 'completely'.

Further information on the ONS approach to measuring personal well-being can be found in the paper 'Measuring Subjective Well-being' (240.8 Kb Pdf) (ONS, 2011a).

8.3 APS design and its implications for the personal well-being statistics

Early in the Measuring National Well-being Programme, ONS selected the Annual Population Survey (APS) as the key survey on which to include the personal well-being questions for the national estimates of personal well-being. The APS is one of the largest household surveys run by ONS and offers a very cost-effective means of measuring personal well-being in a representative way across the UK and for each UK country. Also, because of its very large sample size, it provides opportunities for analysis of the personal well-being estimates of smaller groups, such as minority ethnic groups, and across regional and local areas. These are important considerations in deciding how best to monitor the personal well-being of the nation.

Whenever including new questions on a survey originally designed for another purpose, there are some aspects of the design and coverage of the survey which present challenges. These are highlighted in this section wherever they are relevant.

8.3.1 How the APS is constructed

The APS is an annual version of the quarterly Labour Force Survey (LFS). It is constructed by combining data collected on the LFS (waves 1 and 5), and also includes data from LFS 'boost' samples in England, Wales and Scotland (all 4 waves). The APS is comprised of data collected over a 12 month period, and includes a panel element where a household, once selected for interview, is retained in the sample for a set period of time (known as 'waves'). The way the APS is constructed makes sure that no person appears more than once in the dataset. **Table 1** shows this, with all the shaded areas highlighting the waves contributing to the APS data between April 2013 and March 2014:

Table 1: Data structure of the APS Personal Well-being dataset, 2013/14

	APS Personal Well-being dataset: April 2013 to March 2014			
	April - June 2013	July - August 2013	Sept - Dec 2013	Jan - March 2014
LFS cohort 1 (first sampled April - June 2012)	**Wave 5**			
LFS cohort 2 (first sampled July - August 2012)	Wave 4	**Wave5**		
LFS cohort 3 (first sampled Sept - Dec 2012)	Wave 3	Wave 4	**Wave 5**	
LFS cohort 4 (First sampled Jan - March 2012)	Wave 2	Wave 3	Wave 4	**Wave 5**
LFS cohort 5 (First sampled April - June 2013)	**Wave 1**	Wave 2	Wave 3	Wave 4
LFS cohort 6 (first sampled July - August 2013)		**Wave 1**	Wave 2	Wave 3
LFS cohort 7 (first sampled Sept - Dec 2013)			**Wave 1**	Wave 2
LFS cohort 8 (First sampled Jan - March 2014)				**Wave 1**
LFS boost cohort 1 (first sampled April 2010 - March 2011)	**Wave 4**			
LFS boost cohort 2	**Wave 3**			

(first sampled
April 2011 - March
2012)

**LFS boost cohort
3**   **Wave 2**

(first sampled
April 2012 - March
2013)

**LFS boost cohort
4**   **Wave 1**

(first sampled
April 2013 - March
2014)

Table source: Office for National Statistics

Table notes:

1.   LFS households are interviewed over a 5-wave period, with 3 months between interviews.
2.   LFS boost households are interviewed over a 4-wave period, with 1 year between interviews.

Download table

XLS XLS format
(28.5 Kb)

8.3.2 Sample sizes and representativeness

In total, the APS personal well-being file includes responses from over 300,000 people per year, based in around 135,000 households. Unlike other questions on the APS, people are only asked the personal well-being questions directly and no one else in the household is allowed to respond on their behalf. For this reason the sample size for the APS Personal Well-being dataset is smaller than the normal APS dataset, at around 165,000 people per year. This still makes it the largest dataset in the UK to include the personal well-being questions.

The APS is a household survey, and after weighting, the APS Personal Well-being dataset provides a representative sample of adults (aged 16 and over) living in residential households in the UK. It is not representative of young people under the age of 16 nor people living in institutional settings such as nursing homes, care homes, prisons or hostels. It also does not include homeless people. It is important to acknowledge that the personal well-being of people living in these circumstances might differ substantially from that of adults living in household settings. As a result, the estimates of personal well-being from the APS can only be seen as representative of the adult population of the UK living in household settings and any generalisations should be made on this basis.

8.3.3 Data collection methods and their implications

The APS uses both face-to-face and telephone interviewing methods. These different data collection methods appear to affect how people respond to the personal well-being questions. On average, people rate each aspect of their well-being more positively when interviewed by telephone than when interviewed face-to-face by an interviewer. For example, in 2013/14, higher ratings were given on average for the life satisfaction, worthwhile, and happy yesterday questions during telephone interviews compared to face-to-face (see **Table 2**).

Table 2: Average personal well-being, by mode of interview, 2013/14

United Kingdom

		Average
	Telephone	**Face-to-face**
Life satisfaction	7.6	7.5
Worthwhile	7.8	7.7
Happy yesterday	7.5	7.3
Anxious yesterday	3.0	2.9

Table source: Office for National Statistics

Download table

XLS XLS format
(28.5 Kb)

The relationship between the mode of interview and average responses to the personal well-being questions has been examined using regression analysis to hold other possible influences on personal well-being constant. This shows the same pattern found in descriptive statistics: on average, people give more positive responses when interviewed by telephone than when interviewed face-to-face. These findings, first published by ONS in May 2013 (ONS, 2013a), are reproduced in **Table 3**.

Table 3: Effects of interview mode on ratings of personal well-being after controlling for individual characteristics

Great Britain

				Coefficients
	Life satisfaction	**Worthwhile**	**Happy yesterday**	**Anxious yesterday**
Reference group: Telephone Interview[1]				
Face to Face Interview	-0.171*	-0.165*	-0.132*	0.054*

Table source: Office for National Statistics

Table notes:
1. The reference group for interview mode is 'telephone interviews'.
2. * shows that the relationship is statistically significant at the 5% level.

Download table

XLS XLS format
(28 Kb)

The findings in Table 3 indicate the size and statistical significance of the mode effects, or the extent to which people rate their well-being differently by telephone or in person. The effect is smallest for the question about anxiety yesterday which people rate 0.05 points higher on average on the 0-10 scale when interviewed face-to-face compared to telephone. The effect is greatest on ratings of life satisfaction which people rate 0.17 points lower on average when interviewed face-to-face compared to telephone. These differences are statistically significant for all four questions, implying that they are likely to be due to factors other than sampling variation.

Table 4 shows proportions of people interviewed via each method in each of the three years for which the personal well-being data are available.

Table 4: Proportions of respondents: by mode of interview, 2011/12 to 2013/14

United Kingdom

Percentage

Type of Interview	2013/14	2012/13	2011/12
Telephone	44.2	41.7	42.2
Face-to-face	55.8	58.3	57.8
Total	100.0	100.0	100.0

Table source: Office for National Statistics

Table notes:
1. Data is weighted

Download table

XLS XLS format
(28.5 Kb)

8.3.4 Implications of mode effects for personal well-being estimates

It is challenging to account for mode effects when using statistics. As regression analysis has found mode of interview to be significant to all personal well-being measures, it is advisable to include mode of interview in any planned regression analysis using the APS Personal Well-being dataset.

In the ONS national estimates of personal well-being, the impact of mode is statistically significant. It has been roughly consistent over the period for which the data are available, suggesting that mode effects are unlikely to affect any substantive conclusions drawn.

There may be more of an impact of mode effects on comparisons between personal well-being for lower level geographical estimates. This is for two reasons: different groups may have different balances of telephone and face-to-face response; and the impact of mode may differ by area.

In general, most wave 1 interviews will be conducted face-to-face and subsequent wave interviews will be by telephone. This should lead to a roughly equal balance of face-to-face and telephone respondents for most geographic regions south of the Caledonian Canal. North of the Caledonian Canal all APS interviews are conducted by telephone. Care should therefore be taken when comparing geographies north of the Caledonian Canal to those which are south of the Caledonian Canal, and users may wish to disregard any differences between such areas which are only marginally statistically significant.

There is some preliminary evidence that the impact of mode may vary between areas, potentially introducing bias into geographical comparisons. However, this impact tends to be smaller than the standard error, implying that a difference which is statistically significant according to the published standard errors would be likely to remain if it were possible to account for the variation in mode effects (although it may no longer be significant). ONS plan to investigate this further and to make the results of further analysis available to users.

8.3.5 Topic coverage of the APS

As the APS is based on a labour market survey, it includes an extensive range of questions which are important for understanding labour market participation, many of which are also useful for the analysis of personal well-being. For example, it includes a wide range of social and demographic questions as well as items about housing, employment and education. For full details of the variables included in the APS Personal Well-being dataset, please see the survey user guide.

As interest in personal well-being data extends to the full spectrum of policy areas, ONS has also included the questions on other major surveys that it runs. It has worked collaboratively with other UK government departments and with the European statistical institute, Eurostat, to encourage wide use of the questions. A list of the surveys that currently include the questions, their broad topic coverage and how to get further information is available on our Frequently Asked Questions page or from the Cabinet Office website.

8.4 How to access the APS personal well-being data

There are a range of ways in which the data are made available. A regular set of key estimates from the data are available in Excel spreadsheets published alongside the Personal Well-being in the UK statistical bulletin:

Reference Table 1: Personal Well-being estimates geographical breakdown, 2013/14 (646 Kb Excel sheet)

Reference Table 2: Personal Well-being estimates change over time, 2011/12 to 2013/14 (134 Kb Excel sheet)

Reference Table 3: Personal Well-being estimates personal characteristics, 2013/14 (143 Kb Excel sheet)

There are also plans to make the same estimates available in CSV format in future as part of the wider ONS open data roll out.

The APS Personal Well-being data are deposited with the UK Data Service (UKDS) about six weeks after the publication of the Personal Well-being in the UK statistical bulletin. It is available from UKDS in two formats:

- End User License (a fully anonymised non-disclosive set of data containing basic demographic information, available to UK and overseas academics),
- Special License versions (a more disclosive set of data, containing more detailed variables such as Unitary Authority / Local Authority, however Unitary Authority / Local Authority level data is only available for Great Britain but not for Northern Ireland. Access to this data requires Approved Researcher accreditation, and is only available to UK-based researchers).

Further information about these options and how to access the data is available from the UK Data Service

Data can also be accessed through the ONS Virtual Microdata Laboratory (VML) or through the Secure Data Service of UKDS. This is usually the way to access more detailed data with smaller sample sizes or lower levels of geography, which require access through a more secure route. Users accessing data in this format will require Approved Researcher accreditation. Overseas academics interested in this can also apply through this route but they must travel to the UK to use these facilities. Please contact either UKDS or socialsurveys@ons.gov.uk for further details.

ONS also provide the data directly to UK Civil Service statisticians and government researchers. Government analysts interested in this option should please contact ONS at: socialsurveys@ons.gov.uk.

8.5 Interpreting the personal well-being estimates

8.5.1 Using average ratings versus grouped ratings

When comparing differences between average ratings of groups or areas, remember that this does not account for variability within the groups. Just because the average of sample respondents has a certain rating of personal well-being does not necessarily mean that all people with that characteristic will have that particular outcome. For example, even though women on average have higher life satisfaction than men, it is important not to infer that all women are more satisfied with their lives than men. Recent research suggests that women may tend to rate their life satisfaction as either very high or very low. This pattern of responses may be masked when using averages alone.

Looking at the percentage who rate their well-being at different levels can add further insight into patterns of well-being and this is why both methods are used in this bulletin. It also helps to make clear that what is true for part of the sample with a certain characteristic is unlikely to be true for all people with that characteristic.

8.5.2 Association versus causation

The APS personal well-being data have been analysed by different personal characteristics and circumstances in the online reference tables accompanying this bulletin, but any relationships observed should not necessarily be taken to imply causation. It can only be asserted that a specific characteristic or circumstance is associated with higher or lower well-being, not that it has caused this outcome. Although some groups are more likely to give higher life satisfaction ratings on average, it may not be the particular characteristic that is causing them to rate their well-being at a higher level. There are other factors that could also influence their ratings which would need to be controlled for in a regression model, and even then causation is often difficult to infer. For example, although married people on average rate their happiness at higher levels, it is difficult to say with certainty whether marriage increases reported happiness or whether happier people are more likely to marry. Longitudinal data which tracks people's characteristics, experiences and views over time is needed to establish whether the well-being or the circumstance came first.

8.5.3 The meaning of small differences

The size of differences between ratings of personal well-being between groups of people with certain characteristics or in specific areas of the UK can appear fairly small. This is also the case for the size of year-on-year changes in the national personal well-being estimates. The personal well-being estimates in this bulletin are generally presented to one decimal place, but the estimates relating to change over time are presented to two decimal places. This is to present more clearly the direction of change over time for these estimates.

A key challenge is to determine the relevance of these changes. One theory suggests that people may have a personal set-point for well-being to which they naturally return after a positive or negative life event. This would suggest that levels of well-being may only vary within a fairly small range over time, particularly in the aggregate (Cummins,1998; Allin and Hand, 2014, p.13).

Other research suggests that there may be some shocks from which people do not necessarily regain their previous set-point such as the death of a spouse (Dolan, Peasgood and White, 2008; Lucas et al, 2004) or that policy initiatives can affect levels of personal well-being in a sustained way (Helliwell, Layard, Sachs, 2012).

Although the size of the changes reported in this bulletin may appear small in the aggregate, they may mask larger changes in the well-being of particular groups within society or within particular areas of the UK. This is why ONS look not only at changes in average levels of personal well-being, but also in the proportions of people who rate their personal well-being as very high or very low and how this changes over time and between groups. Both are required to get a rounded picture of personal well-being in the UK and regular monitoring will help to uncover any important patterns.

8.5.4 Approaches to statistical significance

In this bulletin, when describing changes over time the term 'significant' refers to statistical significance (at the 95% level). Unless otherwise stated, the changes over time mentioned in the text have been found to be statistically significant at the 95% confidence level. Standard errors have been calculated and used in tests of statistical significance and are available in the reference tables published alongside this bulletin.

The statistical significance of differences in the estimates for a specific area of the UK and the equivalent UK estimate are approximate, and determined on the basis of non-overlapping confidence intervals. This method provides a conservative estimate of statistical significance but may result in estimates which are statistically significantly different to one another being assessed as not. The result is that some estimates which may be significantly different to the UK estimates may not be identified as such. This would tend to underestimate the differences observed in personal well-being between a country or English region, and the equivalent UK estimates.

As the personal well-being data have only been collected for three years, it is not yet possible to know how volatile the data will be over time. This makes it difficult to put the seemingly small changes reported here into a wider context which would help to shed light on how important they are. This is also a key reason why ONS do not plan to change the questions in the near future as building up a consistent time series will help interpretations.

8.6 Personal well-being question testing

A number of other methodological issues have been/ are being tested as part of a programme of work looking at how the questions perform in different circumstances (see ONS, 2011b). This involves both quantitative testing of question variations using the Opinions and Lifestyle (OPN) Survey, and qualitative testing methods in which people are asked to explain more about the way they answered the questions and why. It is important to note that, although ONS continue to test the questions they have not been changed on the APS since they were first introduced in 2011. This is to make sure a consistent time series is developed.

The Personal Well-being Team are also in contact with researchers who have used the questions in a range of different settings. Their feedback provides valuable information for ONS and other prospective users. If you have used the questions or have done analysis which could benefit others, please let us know by contacting the Personal Well-being Team at personal.well-being@ons.gsi.gov.uk. One way we intend to share the results of our question testing is via the Measuring National Well-being group of StatsUserNet. We would encourage other researchers to share their findings there as well.

The following section summarises some of the key issues looked at by ONS in the question testing to date.

8.6.1 Contextual effects

The respondent's mood and the immediate context of the interview can affect responses to evaluative questions. In a household survey context, responses to the personal well-being questions could be affected by other household members being present during face-to-face interviews. ONS have explored this issue in cognitive testing conducted in 2013 among OPN respondents. The results suggested that people may give both more positive and more negative responses to the questions depending on which other member of the household is present. In order to test this more fully, a 'flag' has been added to the OPN survey to indicate if someone else is present when a respondent is interviewed. This work is ongoing and results are expected later in the year.

Another effect of context that appears to influence responses is the day of the week on which the respondent is interviewed. Interviewing on the APS is conducted every day of the week throughout the year, but many fewer interviews are conducted on Sundays and certain public holidays. As two of the questions refer to 'yesterday', there are inevitably fewer responses relating to Saturdays, when personal well-being ratings may be different to other days of the week.

The process for identifying the day of the week on which a respondent has been interviewed is complicated. ONS are currently working on a simpler means of identifying day of the week when the interview took place so this can be added to the dataset.

The month of the year in which a respondent is interviewed may also affect responses. Preliminary evidence suggests that there may be a seasonal effect, but with only three years of data available, it is too early to be sure. This is something that ONS will continue to monitor as the time series builds.

8.6.2 Question order

Responses to personal well-being questions have been shown to be affected by earlier questions in the survey (for example, questions about health or labour market status). Prior to the introduction of the questions on the APS in April 2011, ONS carried out cognitive testing of the placement of the personal well-being questions (see: Measuring Subjective Well-being (240.8 Kb Pdf)). This suggested that the questions should be asked early in the interview, immediately after the questions on household and individual demographics. This allows time for rapport to be built up between the interviewer and respondent but does not allow questions on other topics, such as health or employment, to influence responses to the personal well-being questions. ONS advise researchers to follow this approach whenever the questions are included on surveys in order to avoid potential bias from earlier questions.

Quantitative question testing found that the order in which the personal well-being questions are asked does not significantly affect responses (Summary of results from testing of experimental subjective well-being questions). Qualitative testing showed that respondents preferred the positive questions first as they were easier to answer. ONS always include the four questions in the same order on every survey to be sure that the findings are as consistent and comparable as possible. The recommended order is:

- life satisfaction
- worthwhile
- happy yesterday
- anxious yesterday.

8.6.3 Response scales

For all APS personal well-being questions, an 11 point scale is used. This ranges from 0–10 where 0 is 'not at all' and 10 is 'completely'. This means that the scales are consistent between the questions, which helps respondents to answer the questions more easily and also aids subsequent analysis. Additionally, 11 point scales are commonly used across other similar surveys, particularly internationally. The use of this type of scale will also aid comparisons with other survey findings.

Cognitive testing has suggested that people may misinterpret the scale for the anxiety question as this is the only question where a higher score suggests worse well-being. The use of show cards (which provide a visual aid of response options for respondents) has been tested on the OPN survey to see whether this helps to remind people of how the scale works for each question. The results of this work showed that while higher scores were given for the life satisfaction, happiness and anxiety questions when show cards were used, the differences were only significant for the life satisfaction and happiness questions. These results were not as expected but the sample used for this test was small. Further details are available in the paper: Summary of results from testing of experimental subjective well-being questions .

Show cards are not used on the APS and it is not feasible to use them due to interviews being conducted both face-to-face and by telephone. For this reason, we have not done any further testing of the effects of show cards on responses.

8.6.4 Question wording

ONS have used both cognitive testing techniques and split trial testing of data collected on the Opinions Survey to look at whether asking the questions in different ways may affect responses to the questions. For example, cognitive testing has suggested that the word 'anxious' may be interpreted by some people as representing severe mental distress, while 'stress' or 'worry' are more commonly used to describe daily emotions. These differences are also being tested using the OPN to see how people respond to each way of asking the question.

9. The Measuring National Well-being programme

NWB logo 2

This bulletin is published as part of the ONS Measuring National Well-being programme.

The programme aims to produce accepted and trusted measures of the well-being of the nation - how the UK as a whole is doing. It is about looking at 'GDP and beyond' and includes:

- Greater analysis of the national economic accounts, especially to understand household income, expenditure and wealth.
- Further accounts linked to the national accounts, including the UK Environmental Accounts and valuing household production and 'human capital'.
- Quality of life measures, looking at different areas of national well-being such as health, relationships, job satisfaction, economic security, education environmental conditions.
- Working with others to include the measurement of the well-being of children and young people as part of national well-being.
- Measures of 'personal well-being' - individuals' assessment of their own well-being.
- Headline indicators to summarise national well-being and the progress we are making as a society.

The programme is underpinned by a communication and engagement workstream, providing links with Cabinet Office and policy departments, international developments, the public and other stakeholders. The programme is working closely with Defra on the measurement of 'sustainable development' to provide a complete picture of national well-being, progress and sustainable development.

ONS published the second 'Life in the UK' report in March 2014, giving the latest snapshot of the nation's well-being. The most recent update of the National Well-being Measures data is released today. A summary of all the work completed during the first three years of the Measuring National Well-being Programme is available here. A full list of outputs from the Measuring National Well-being programme is available here.

Find out more on the Measuring National Well-being website pages.

10. Further Information

Further information and guidance can be found in the various downloads available on the Personal Well-being survey user guide page. Additionally, the Personal Well-being Frequently Asked Questions page provides answers to common questions about the ONS personal well-being questions and data.

11. References

Allin P. and Hand D.J. (2014) "The Wellbeing of Nations: Meaning, Motive and Measurement", John Wiley & Sons Ltd, Chichester.

Blanchflower D.G, Bell D.N.F, Montagnoli A and Moro M. (2013) "The effects of macroeconomic shocks on well-being".

Blanchflower, D.G. (1991), 'Fear, unemployment and pay flexibility', Economic Journal, March, pp. 483-496.

Cabinet Office (2013), Evidence to the Environmental Audit Committee.

Cummins, R.A. (1998). The second approximation to an international standard of live satisfaction. Social Indicators Research, 43, 307-334.

Dolan P, Layard R and Metcalfe R, Office for National Statistics (2011). Measuring Subjective Well-being for Public Policy (99.8 Kb Pdf).

Dolan P, Peasgood T and White M (2008). Do we really know what makes us happy? A review of the economic literature on the factors associated with subjective well-being. Journal of Economic Psychology; 29:94-122.

European Quality of Life Survey (2012).

Eurostat (2013), Quality of Life Indicators.

Fujiwara, D, Oroyemi, P & McKinnon, E. Cabinet Office and Department for Work and Pensions (2013), Well-being and Civil Society; Estimating the value of volunteering using subjective wellbeing data.

Fujiwara D and Campbell R, HM Treasury and Department for Work and Pensions (2011). Valuation Techniques for Social Cost-Benefit Analysis: Stated Preference, Revealed Preference and Subjective Well-Being Approaches.

Helliwell, J., Layard, R., Sachs, J. (2012) World Happiness Report, The Earth Institute, Columbia University, New York, USA.

Lim C and Laurence J. (2013) "Economic Hard Times and Life Satisfaction in the U.K. and the U.S".

Lucas, R.E., Clark, A.E., Georgellis, Y., Diener, E. (2004), 'Unemployment alters the set point for life satisfaction', Psychological Science, 15 (1), pp. 8-13.

OECD (2013), Guidelines on measuring subjective well-being.

Office for National Statistics (2014a), Income, Expenditure and Personal Well-being, 2011/12.

Office for National Statistics (2014b), The Economic Review July 2014.

Office for National Statistics (2014c), Exploring Personal Well-being and place in the UK.

Office for National Statistics (2014d), Commuting and Personal Well-being.

Office for National Statistics (2013a), Measuring National Well-being – What matters most to Personal Well-being?

Office for National Statistics (2013b), Measuring National Well-being – Personal well-being in the UK, 2012/13

Office for National Statistics (2013c), Personal Well-being across the UK, 2012/13.

Office for National Statistics (2012), First Annual ONS Experimental Subjective Well-being Results

Office for National Statistics (2011a), Measuring Subjective Well-being (240.8 Kb Pdf).

Office for National Statistics (2011b), Initial investigation into Subjective Well-being data from the ONS Opinions Survey.

Which? Quarterly Consumer Report, (June 2014), "Growing Optimism: How economic improvement is affecting consumer sentiment and behaviour".

Background notes

1. If you have comments on the ONS approach to measuring personal well-being and/ or the presentation of the personal well-being data, please email us at personal.wellbeing@ons.gsi.gov.uk.

2. The data analysed in this report was collected from the Annual Population Survey (APS) which is the largest constituent survey of the Integrated Household Survey. The sample size of the 12 month APS dataset is approximately 165,000 adults aged 16 and over and living in residential accommodation in the UK (England, Scotland, Wales and Northern Ireland). Data used are

weighted to be representative of the population and to take account of the fact that responses made on behalf of other household members are not accepted.

3. The UK Statistics Authority has designated these statistics as National Statistics, in accordance with the Statistics and Registration Service Act 2007 and signifying compliance with the Code of Practice for Official Statistics.

    Designation can be broadly interpreted to mean that the statistics:

    *   meet identified user needs;
    *   are well explained and readily accessible;
    *   are produced according to sound methods; and
    *   are managed impartially and objectively in the public interest.

    Once statistics have been designated as National Statistics it is a statutory requirement that the Code of Practice shall continue to be observed.

4. © Crown copyright 2014

    You may use or re-use this information (not including logos) free of charge in any format or medium, under the terms of the Open Government Licence, write to the Information Policy Team, The National Archives, Kew, London TW9 4DU, or email: psi@nationalarchives.gsi.gov.uk.

5. Details of the policy governing the release of new data are available by visiting www.statisticsauthority.gov.uk/assessment/code-of-practice/index.html or from the Media Relations Office email: media.relations@ons.gsi.gov.uk

    These National Statistics are produced to high professional standards and released according to the arrangements approved by the UK Statistics Authority.

Copyright

Statistical contacts

Name	Phone	Department	Email
Dawn Snape	+44 (0)1633 455674	Measuring National Well-being	personal.well-being@ons.gsi.gov.uk
Lucy Tinkler	+44 (0)1633 455713	Measuring National Well-being	personal.well-being@ons.gsi.gov.uk

Issuing Body:
Office for National Statistics

Media Contact Details:
Telephone: 0845 604 1858
(8.30am-5.30pm Weekdays)

Emergency out of hours (limited service): 07867 906553

Email:
media.relations@ons.gsi.gov.uk

Office for
National Statistics

National Well-being Measures, September 2014

Author Name(s): **Chris Randall, Office for National Statistics**

Abstract

Updated national well-being measures data are published in Spring and Autumn each year. This article provides the Autumn 2014 update. The ONS Measuring National Well-being programme aims to produce accepted and trusted measures of the well-being of the nation - how the UK as a whole is doing.

Summary of changes to measures

This section summarises the changes made to national well-being measures since the last publication in March 2014. Details are provided in subsequent sections. No measures have been added or deleted.

- The thresholds for the four personal well-being measures have changed.
- The classification for 'Percentage who reported a long term illness and disability' has changed.
- 'Real net national income per head' has changed to 'Real net national disposable income'.
- 'Median household income' has changed to 'Real median household income'.
- The title for 'Some evidence indicating probable psychological disturbance or mental ill health' has been changed to 'Some evidence indicating depression or anxiety'.

Explanation of changes to measures

This section explains the changes made to national well-being measures since the last publication in March 2014.

1. The thresholds for the four personal well-being measures have changed and are shown in **Table 1**. The change was made because policy-makers are particularly interested in people reporting the highest or lowest levels of personal well-being. Looking at the ratings in this way helps to shed more light on these groups and is consistent with thresholds used in the separate Personal well-being release.

Table 1: Changes to Personal Well-being thresholds (1) used as a headline measure

	Threshold used in March 2014	Threshold used in September 2014
Rating of life satisfaction	7 to 10 out of 10	9 to 10 out of 10
Rating of how worthwhile the things they do are	7 to 10 out of 10	9 to 10 out of 10
Rating of happiness yesterday	7 to 10 out of 10	9 to 10 out of 10
Rating of anxious yesterday	0 to 3 out of 10	0 to 1 out of 10

Table notes:

1. On a scale of 0 to 10 where 0 was not at all and 10 was completely.

Download table

XLS XLS format
(58.5 Kb)

2. The classification for 'Percentage who reported a long term illness and disability' has changed. In April 2013 the health questions on the LFS changed to the ONS harmonised standards used on other social surveys. This was to bring these questions in line with the Equality Act Legislation.

3. 'Real net national income per head' has changed to 'Real net national disposable income' as it is a better measure of the total income available to residents of a country. It includes net current transfers (for example, current international co-operation or remittances between households) from and to other countries.

4. The measure 'Median household income' has changed to 'Real median household income'. This measure is now adjusted for price changes, allowing analysis over time on a consistent basis.

5. The title for 'Some evidence indicating probable psychological disturbance or mental ill health' has been changed to a more accurate description. It is now ' Some evidence indicating depression or anxiety'.

Details of which measures data has been updated since the March 2014 publication can be found in the National Well-being Measures Excel spreadsheet (856 Kb Excel sheet).

Where to find national Well-being measures data

There are 41 measures of national well-being split across 10 domains. Information and data for the latest release of domains and measures is available in various formats:

- National Well-being Measures Excel spreadsheet (856 Kb Excel sheet)containing the latest and time series data plus links to data sources. This spreadsheet has also been revised to include age, sex and regional breakdowns to some of the headline measures. Additionally, confidence intervals for the latest headline measures have been included where possible.

- <u>Interactive wheel of measures</u> which includes data for the latest and previous periods plus time series charts.
- <u>Wheel of measures (2.8 Mb Pdf)</u> PDF 'print and keep' version showing the latest data.
- <u>Interactive charts</u> showing the latest data for selected measures by region and country.

Background notes

1. Details of the policy governing the release of new data are available by visiting <u>www.statisticsauthority.gov.uk/assessment/code-of-practice/index.html</u> or from the Media Relations Office email: <u>media.relations@ons.gsi.gov.uk</u>

Copyright

Office for
National Statistics

Measuring National Well-being - Exploring the Well-being of Children in the UK, 2014

Coverage: **UK**
Date: **08 October 2014**
Geographical Area: **Country**
Theme: **People and Places**
Theme: **Children, Education and Skills**

Introduction

Children's well-being is an important part of the nation's well-being. In 2013, there were an estimated 12 million children aged 0 to 15, nearly a fifth of the UK population. Research from The Children's Society has shown that a significant minority of UK children suffer from low well-being, which impacts on their childhood and life chances, and their families and communities (The Children's Society, 2014).

Children's well-being needs to be measured in a different way to adults. The framework for measuring national well-being puts indicators into 10 domains. Three domains (Governance, Natural Environment and Economy) are contextual and do not specifically relate to children's well-being. The remaining 7 domains are consistent at all ages. To measure children's well-being, the 7 domains have been adopted as a framework but have been populated with measures that reflect the aspects of children's lives that are important to them, and have the greatest effect on their well-being.

ONS has developed a provisional set of 31 headline measures of children's well-being across the 7 domains. These include both objective and subjective measures in the domains of:

- Personal well-being
- Our relationships
- Health
- What we do
- Where we live
- Personal finance
- Education and skills

In March 2014, ONS published a consultation on the first version of these measures. The consultation response was published in July 2014 and an updated set of measures will be published in 2015. This report presents estimates for 22 of the 31 measures of children's well-being[1]. These estimates can be thought of as a baseline for children's well-being. The report also considers how selected measures have changed over time or differ by gender, where this information is available.

Notes

1. Other measures are still in development and need further consideration in response to the consultation. They will be included in the updated set of measures in spring 2015.

Key Points

- Around three-quarters of children aged 10 to 15 in Great Britain rated their life satisfaction, the things that they do as worthwhile, and their happiness yesterday as moderate to high in 2013.
- In 2011–12 in the UK, 8 out of 10 boys (79%) reported being relatively happy with their appearance. Fewer than 7 out of 10 girls (68%) reported the same.
- Around 6 in 10 UK children aged 11 to 15 (61%) talked to their mother about things that matter more than once a week in 2011-12, compared with half (51%) in 2002. Similarly, 37% talked to their father frequently in 2011-12, compared with 31% in 2002.
- Around 1 in 8 children (12%) aged 10 to 15 in the UK reported being frequently bullied physically, in other ways, or both in 2011–12.
- The proportion of children in England aged 2 to 15 who were overweight, including obese, was 28% in 2012. Children aged 11 to 15 years had a higher prevalence of being overweight, including obese (35%) in 2012 compared with those aged 2 to 10 (23%).
- Nearly all children (98%) aged 10 to 15 in the UK used a computer at home during 2011–12. Girls were more likely to use it to complete their homework, while boys were more likely to play computer games.
- Around 12% of children aged 10 to 15 in the UK reported being a victim of crime in 2013/14, half of whom were victims of violent crime.
- The proportion of UK children living in households with less than 60% median income was 17% in 2011/12, down from 26% in 1998/99.

Personal Well-being

Personal well-being measures are subjective indicators of a person's quality of life. They are based on how individuals report the different aspects of their lives including their lives overall, sense of purpose and how happy they are. Including personal well-being measures for children allows us to incorporate children's views, providing a fuller picture of UK children's well-being.

The Children's Society's household survey has included three of the four ONS personal well-being questions since 2012. It asks children to rate their happiness yesterday, their satisfaction with life overall, and whether they consider the things they do are worthwhile. The rating is on a scale of 0 to 10, where '0' is not at all and '10' is completely. The ONS measure of 'anxiety yesterday' is not included for children, due to ethical considerations. The proportion of children with a moderate to high level of well-being, which is defined as a score of 7 or more is used as the 'headline' measure.

In 2013, just over three-quarters (77%) of children aged 10 to 15 in Great Britain rated their life satisfaction as moderate to high (Figure 1). Similarly, three-quarters (75%) reported that they felt the things they did in their lives were worthwhile as moderate to high. Just under three-quarters (74%) reported a moderate to high level of happiness yesterday.

Figure 1: Proportion of children scoring their personal well-being as moderate to high, 2013

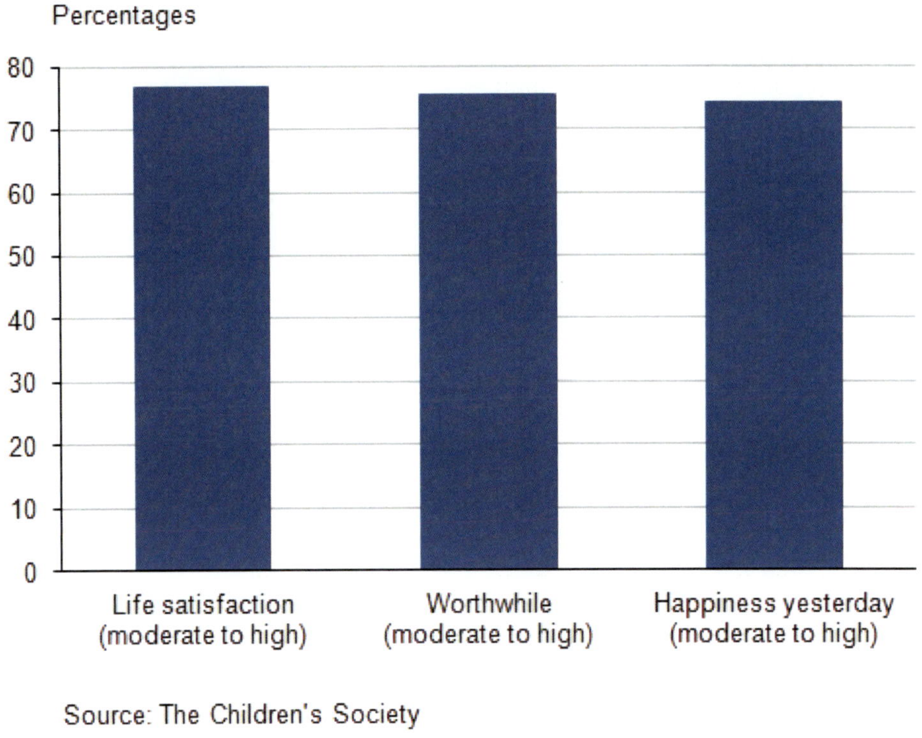

Percentages

Source: The Children's Society

Notes:

1. Respondents were asked: 'Overall, how satisfied are you with life nowadays?', 'Overall to what extent do you feel the things you do in your life are worthwhile?', and 'Overall, how happy did you feel yesterday?'.

2. 'Moderate to high' is a score of 7 or more on a scale of 0 to 10.

Download chart

XLS XLS format
(25.5 Kb)

Appearance

A key aspect of children's overall well-being is their satisfaction with their appearance. Cusumano and Thompson (2001) suggest that lower levels of satisfaction with appearance could be linked to the high importance of image in the current culture, or the greater public scrutiny occurring from the increasing use of various media such as social networking websites. It has been suggested that strong feelings of unhappiness about personal appearance (or dysmorphia) could be related to mental health problems, such as depression, social isolation or intense self-consciousness.

In 2011–12, nearly three-quarters (74%) of children aged 10 to 15 were relatively happy with their appearance. Around 1 in 8 (12%) were relatively unhappy with the way they look. This is according to data from the UK Household Longitudinal Study (also referred to as Understanding Society survey)[1].

In 2011–12, girls aged 10 to 15 were more than twice as likely to be relatively unhappy about their appearance as boys of the same age at 17% and 8% respectively (Figure 2). In the same year, 8 out of 10 boys (79%) reported being relatively happy with their appearance. Fewer than 7 out of 10 girls (68%) reported the same.

Figure 2: Happiness with appearance, 2011-12

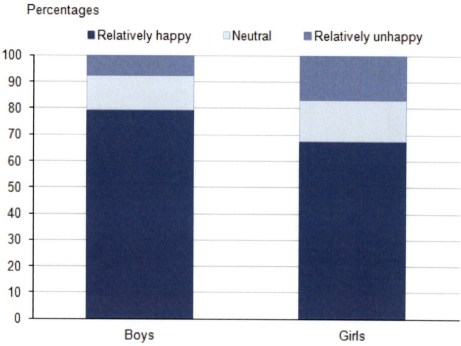

Source: Understanding Society, the UK Household Longitudinal Survey

Notes:

1. Respondents were asked: "where '1' is completely happy and '7' is not at all happy, please tick the box which comes closest to expressing how you feel about each of the following things... your appearance". Relatively happy is a score of 1 to 3, relatively unhappy is a score of 5 to 7, neutral is a score of 4.
2. Boys and girls aged 10 to 15

Download chart

 XLS format
(26 Kb)

UK Household Longitudinal Study estimates can be compared with those from the British Household Panel Survey (BHPS) for children aged between 11 and 15. The proportion of children aged 11 to 15 who reported that they were relatively happy with their appearance has decreased from 77% in 2002 to 71% in 2011–12. The proportion of 11 to 15-year-olds reporting they were relatively unhappy with their appearance has increased from 10% in 2002 to 14% in 2011–12.

Notes

1. The UK Household Longitudinal Survey asks UK children aged 10 to 15 to rate their happiness with their appearance on a scale of 1 to 7 (1 being completely happy and 7 being completely unhappy).

Our Relationships

In The Good Childhood Report 2013, The Children's Society highlighted the importance of family relationships to children's subjective well-being. It found that a measure of family harmony was substantially more indicative of children's well-being than family structure. Also, it found that 'the quality of family relationships is one of the three most significant aspects of life which contribute to children's overall sense of well-being' (The Good Childhood Report, 2013).

'Predicting well-being' published in 2013 by NatCen analysed data from the Millennium Cohort Study 2008. It found that 'children tend to have higher levels of wellbeing when they have good social relationships with family and friends...'. It also analysed changes in subjective well-being among 10 to 15-year-olds using two waves of data from the UK Household Longitudinal Survey. This showed that 'social relations – both in the home and in school – continue to stand out as important predictors of well-being among young people'.

Family

In 2011–12, around 28% of children aged 10 to 15 years reported quarrelling with their mother more than once a week, according to UK Household Longitudinal Survey data. This compares with 20% of children reporting quarrelling with their father more than once a week; most children reported hardly ever quarrelling with their father (60%). It should be noted that more children live with their mothers than with their fathers, which may explain some of the variation. Nearly all children who reported hardly ever quarrelling with their mother reported the same with their father (91%). However, among those children reporting quarrelling frequently with their mother, around half (51%) reported the same with their father.

Figure 3: Children's frequency of quarrelling with and talking to parents, 2011-12

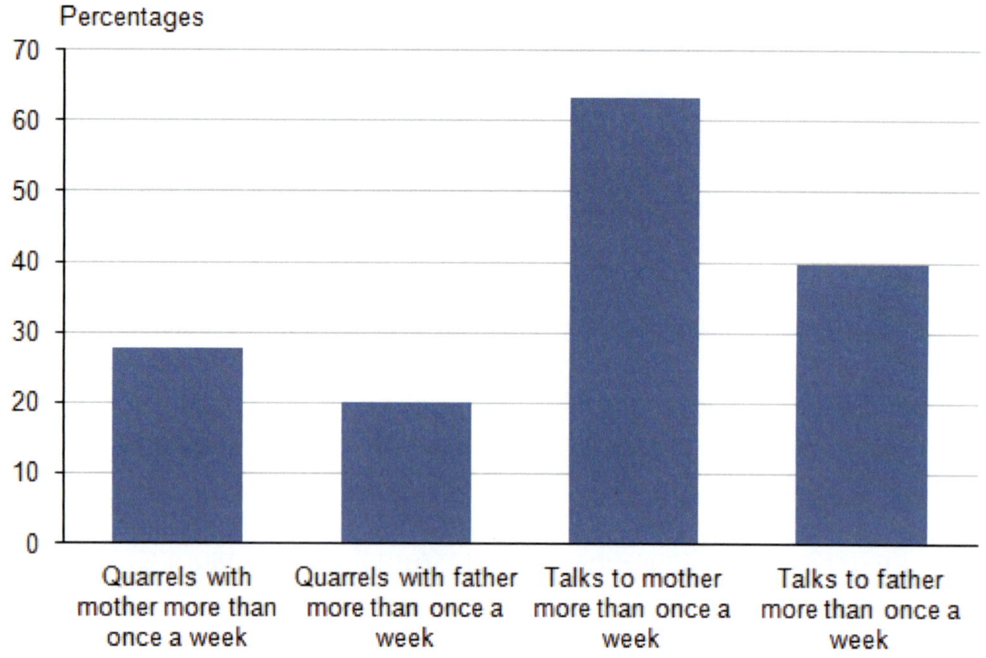

Percentages

[Bar chart showing four vertical bars on a y-axis scale from 0 to 70:
- Quarrels with mother more than once a week: approximately 28
- Quarrels with father more than once a week: approximately 20
- Talks to mother more than once a week: approximately 63
- Talks to father more than once a week: approximately 40]

Source: Understanding Society, the UK Household Longitudninal Survey

Notes:

1. Respondents were asked: 'How often do you quarrel with your mother/father?' 'How often do you talk to your mother/father about things that matter?'. Response options were: most days, more than once a week, less than once a week, hardly ever, don't have mother/father.

Download chart

 XLS format

(26 Kb)

Children were more likely to report talking frequently to their mother than to their father about things that matter. In 2011–12, nearly two-thirds (63%) of children aged 10 to 15 years talked to their mother more than once a week about things that matter. This compares with nearly two-fifths (40%) who reported talking to their father.

The proportions of children aged 11 to 15 talking to either parent have increased since 2002. Around half of children aged 11 to 15 (51%) talked to their mother more than once a week about things that matter in 2002, compared with 61% in 2011–12. Similarly, 31% talked to their father more than once a week in 2002, compared with 37% in 2011–12.

Among children aged 10 to 15 who reported talking with their mother more than once a week about things that matter, 58% also reported talking frequently with their father about things that matter. Around 3 in 20 (15%) children in this age group reported hardly ever talking to either parent about things that matter in 2011–12.

Figure 4 illustrates that children who reported relatively high satisfaction with life overall also reported better communication patterns with their parents[1]. In 2011–12, nearly 70% of children aged 10 to 15 who reported being relatively satisfied with their life overall quarrelled less than once a week with both parents. This compares with just over 40% of children who reported being relatively unsatisfied quarrelling more than once a week with both parents. Children who were relatively unsatisfied with life overall were almost twice as likely to quarrel with both parents more than once a week as children who were relatively satisfied with life overall (24% compared with 13% respectively). Also, children who reported being relatively satisfied with life overall were around 2.5 times more likely to talk to both of their parents about things that matter more than once a week than children who reported being relatively unsatisfied with life overall.

Figure 4: Children's quarrelling with and talking to parents by satisfaction with life overall, 2011-12

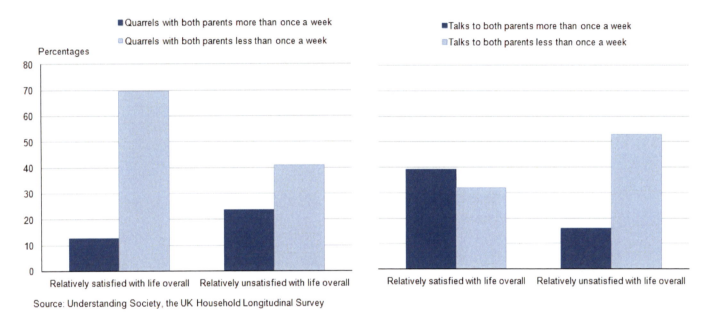

Source: Understanding Society, the UK Household Longitudinal Survey

Notes:
1. Excludes children who reported quarrelling with/talking to one parent more than the other.
2. Respondents were asked: 'How often do you quarrel with your mother/father?' 'How often do you talk to your mother/father about things that matter?'. Response options were: most days, more than once a week, less than once a week, hardly ever, don't have mother/father.
3. Respondents were asked: "where '1' is completely happy and '7' is not at all happy, which best describes how you feel about your life as a whole?". Relatively happy is a score of 1 to 3, relatively unhappy is a score of 5 to 7, neutral is a score of 4.

Download chart

 XLS format
(27.5 Kb)

Figures from The Children's Society schools survey show that nearly 60% of children aged 8 to 15 in the UK rated their happiness with their family as high[2] in 2010. Interestingly, boys were more likely than girls to rate their happiness with their family as high, at 62% and 56% respectively.

Being bullied

Being bullied in school can affect a child's sense of self-worth, disrupt their education and potentially lead to mental ill-health. The Good Childhood Report 2013 found that children with low well-being were almost five times as likely to have been recently bullied. Similarly, the NatCen report found that children in the Millennium Cohort Study 2008 who were never bullied at school were more likely to report being happy all of the time.

According to the UK Household Longitudinal Study, around 1 in 8 children (12%) aged 10 to 15 in the UK reported being frequently bullied at school (either physically, in other ways, or both), in the six months prior to interview during 2011–12. Nearly two-thirds (64%) of children reported never having been bullied at school in the six months prior to interview. Boys are slightly more likely to be bullied physically, with 6% reporting frequent physical bullying, compared with 4% of girls.

Over two-thirds (68%) of the children who reported relatively high life satisfaction in 2011–12 reported that they had never been bullied (Figure 5). This compares with less than one-third (28%) of those reporting relatively low life satisfaction who reported that they had never been bullied. Over a fifth (21%) of those reporting relatively low life satisfaction stated they had been bullied a lot (either physically, in other ways, or both).

Figure 5: Frequency of being bullied by life satisfaction, 2011-12

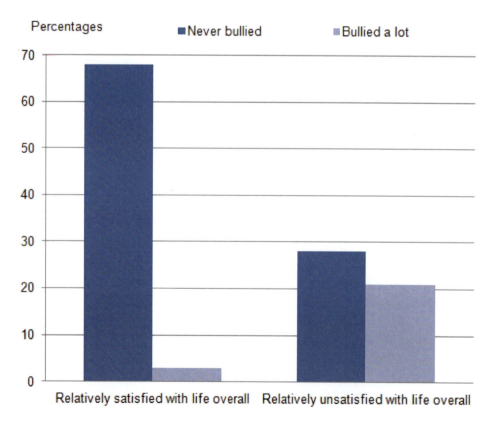

Source: Understanding Society, the UK Household Longitudinal Survey

Notes:

1. Excludes children who reported being bullied a little or quite often.

2. Respondents were asked: 'How often do you get physically bullied at school, for example getting hit, pushed around or threatened, or having belongings stolen?' and 'How often do you get bullied in other ways at school such as getting called names, getting left out of games, or having nasty stories spread about you on purpose?'. Responses options were: never, not too much (1-3 times in the last 6 months), quite a lot (more than 4 times in the last 6 months), a lot (a few times every week).

3. Respondents were asked: "where '1' is completely happy and '7' is not at all happy, which best describes how you feel about your life as a whole?". Relatively happy is a score of 1 to 3, relatively unhappy is a score of 5 to 7, neutral is a score of 4.

Download chart

 XLS format
(26.5 Kb)

According to data from The Children's Society's schools survey in 2010, just under two-thirds (63%) of children aged 8 to 15 rated their happiness with their friends as high. Around 6% of children rated their happiness with their friends as very low. There was no difference between boys and girls.

Notes

1. The UK Household Longitudinal Study survey asks children aged 10 to 15 to rate their satisfaction with life overall on a scale of 1 to 7 (with 1 being completely happy and 7 being completely unhappy). These responses have been used to analyse how aspects of well-being compare according to different personal well-being scores.

2. The Children's Society survey asks children to rate how happy they are with various aspects of their lives on a scale of 0 to 10. This scale has been categorised using the definitions from the ONS personal well-being publication.

Health

A healthy life cycle from before birth to teenage years is highly important for children's well-being as well as the future prospect of the child as an adult. The independent report 'Fair Society, Healthy Lives' (Marmot Review, 2010) states that policy objectives to reduce health inequality in the UK are required to 'give every child the best start in life' and to create a 'healthy standard of living for all'.

Low birth weight

The 'life course perspective' as explained in the independent report 'Fair Society Healthy Lives' (Marmot Review, 2010) shows that early disadvantage is closely associated with poor outcomes in adulthood. This shows in various domains such as health, educational achievement and socio-economic status. A healthy transition from foetal development through to young adulthood enhances different aspects of human capital, and benefits society as a whole.

Low birthweight[1] is often linked to pre-term birth, foetal growth restriction and multiple births. Low birthweight is closely associated with disability, morbidity and mortality in infants and children, and has long-term consequences for health and social outcomes in adulthood. It is directly linked to the physical and emotional health and health behaviours of the mother before and during pregnancy. Mothers smoking during pregnancy, who are underweight because of poor nutrition, who have a long-standing illness such as hypertension or heart disease, or who suffer from alcohol abuse or drug addiction have higher risks of having a baby with low-birth weight (Bradshaw, 2011; Bakeo and Clarke, 2006; Chomitz et al., 1995).

For babies born with low birthweight in 2011 in England and Wales, around 61% were pre-term, and around 37% were born at term or post-term (ONS, 2011). Of babies born at term or post-term, just under 3% were born with low birthweight. This proportion has remained stable since 2009. In Scotland, around 2% of babies born at term were born with low birthweight.

Obesity

Obesity in children has become a public health issue in the turn of the 21st century. Research has suggested that being overweight or obese in childhood is linked to immediate and long-term physical and mental health risks. Mental health risks can come from body dissatisfaction, social discrimination, low self-esteem and low quality of life (Griffiths et al., 2010; Xavier and Mandal, 2005). Obese children rate their personal well-being as low, because of problems such as bullying at school, fatigue and difficulties in doing physical activities (Schwimmer et al., 2003).

In 2012, 14% of children aged 2 to 15 living in England were classified as overweight and 14% as obese, according to the Health Survey for England. The prevalence of being overweight including obesity among children in England has fallen since 2004 when the proportion was 34%.

In 2012, children aged 11 to 15 had a higher prevalence of being overweight including obese compared with those aged 2 to 10 (35% and 23% respectively). Prevalence was the same for boys and girls in all age groups.

Figure 6: Proportion of children who are overweight, including obese; by age group, 2003 to 2012

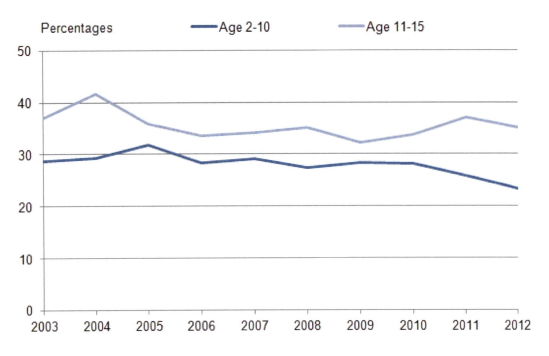

Source: Health Survey for England

Notes:

1. Children with a valid height and weight measurement
2. In 2008, the definitions for children who were overweight or obese were revised from those used in previous years. This was to correct an error which meant that small numbers of children that should have been classified as either 'overweight' or 'obese' were omitted from these categories because of rounding of age and BMI thresholds. In no cases were results significantly different from those presented previously. This chart uses the new definitions for all years

Download chart

 XLS format
(28 Kb)

Data from the Welsh Health Survey suggest that 34% of children aged 2 to 15 living in Wales were overweight or obese in 2012. Data from the Scottish Health Survey show that 31% of children aged 2 to 15 living in Scotland were overweight or obese in 2012. In Northern Ireland, 21% of children aged 2 to 15 were overweight or obese in 2012/13, according to the Health Survey for Northern Ireland.

Self-assessed health

According to the UK Household Longitudinal Study, 93% of children aged 10 to 15 perceived their health as excellent, very good or good in 2010–11. This is an indication of good physical health for a large majority of children. Various surveys include questions on self-assessed health for children[2] and all indicate that the majority of children in the UK are happy with their health. The Health Survey for England shows that between 2003 and 2011 over 9 out of 10 (94% to 95%) children aged 15 and under (or their parents, in the case of young children) consistently rated their health as good or very good. Similarly the Welsh Health Survey shows that 95% of children under 16 years were reported to have very good or good health in 2013. There has been little change since 2007. In Scotland, 95% of children under 16 reported very good or good health in 2011, while in Northern Ireland, 92% were reported as having very good or good health in 2012/13. Children are less likely to suffer chronic health problems than adults. Some of children's unhealthy behaviours (such as lack of exercise or smoking) have medium to long-term effects on health, rather than an immediate effect.

According to The Children's Society's 2010 schools survey, just over half (53%) of children aged 8 to 15 in the UK rated their happiness with their health as high. In contrast, nearly 1 in 10 (9%) rated their happiness with their health as very low.

Notes

1. Under 2,500g

2. For example: The Children Society survey; The British Household Panel Survey; The Health Behaviour of School-aged Children survey

What We Do

Leisure time is spent doing non-compulsory activities such as participating in sports and engaging in culture and arts, according to preferences and lifestyles and can form part of a child's identity. 'The amount and quality of leisure time is important for people's well-being for the direct satisfaction it brings. Additionally leisure, taken in certain ways, is important for physical and mental health'. (OECD, 2009).

Leisure activities

According to the Taking Part survey run by the Department of Culture, Media and Sports, 9 out of 10 (90%) children in England aged 11 to 15 reported taking part in sport during the last week in 2013/14. Nearly three-quarters (71%) of children aged 5 to 10 had participated in sports in the last week[1].

In 2013/14, 90% of children aged 5 to 15 years had participated in sports in the four weeks prior to interview, a figure comparable with 2008/09 (Figure 7). Older children aged 11 to 15 years had a higher rate of sports participation in the four weeks prior to interview compared with those aged 5 to 10 (97% and 84% respectively).

Boys were more likely than girls to participate in sport in 2013/14. Among 5 to 10 year olds, for whom sport in school is not included, 88% of boys aged 5 to 10 took part in sport in the four weeks prior to interview compared to 80% of girls. Among 11 to 15 year olds, 99% of boys participated in sport in the four weeks prior to interview, compared with 95% of girls.

Figure 7: Leisure activities undertaken by children aged 5 to 15 years

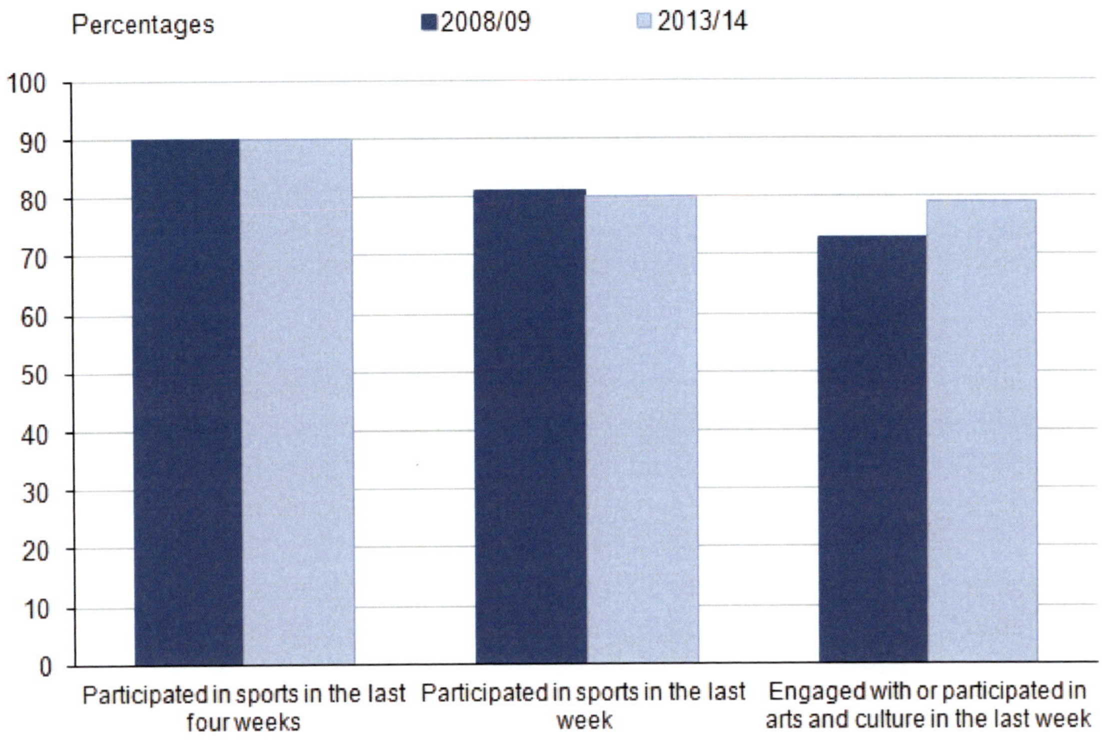

Percentages ■2008/09 ▢ 2013/14

(Bar chart showing three categories. "Participated in sports in the last four weeks": 2008/09 ≈ 90%, 2013/14 ≈ 90%. "Participated in sports in the last week": 2008/09 ≈ 82%, 2013/14 ≈ 81%. "Engaged with or participated in arts and culture in the last week": 2008/09 ≈ 74%, 2013/14 ≈ 80%.)

Source: Department for Culture, Media and Sport; Taking Part Survey

Notes:

1. Arts or cultural activity includes dance activities, music activities, theatre and drama activities, art and craft activities, street arts, circus, festival or carnival events, film or video activities, and engagement with libraries, museums or galleries, or heritage sites.

Download chart

 XLS format
(26 Kb)

'Swimming, diving or lifesaving' was the most common sport in which children aged 5 to 10 participated in during the four weeks prior to interview at 51%. For children aged 11 to 15 the most common sport was 'football' at 50%.

According to the Welsh Health Survey, 51% of children aged under 16 were reported to have undertaken physical activity for at least an hour on five or more days of the previous week in 2012. The Scottish Health Survey 2012 reported that children's participation in sport and exercise had decreased from 73% in 2009 to 66% in 2012. The 'Experience of sport and physical activity by young people in Northern Ireland' report published by the Department of Culture, Arts and Leisure states that 96% of 11 to 17 year olds were involved in sport or physical activity within the week prior to interview in 2013.

The Taking Part survey also showed that in 2013/14, 98% of children aged 5 to 15 in England had taken part in an art or cultural activity (excluding reading) at least three times in the previous year[2]. The proportion of children aged 5 to 15 participating in at least one arts or cultural activity in the week prior to interview increased from 73% in 2008/09 to 79% in 2013/14. The 2011 Children and Young People's Wellbeing Monitor for Wales reported that during 2009 nearly three-quarters (74%) of children and young people aged 7 to 18 attended an arts event at least once a year, and 83% took part in an arts activity at least once a year. In Northern Ireland, 76% of those aged 11 to 17 had participated in arts activities in 2013, and 88% had attended an arts event.

Screen time

Concerns about the amount of time children spend in front of a screen, such as a TV or computer, and how it could be detrimental to physical and mental health have become widespread in recent years. A 2013 report by Public Health England found that higher levels of screen time, including watching TV and playing computer games, have a negative effect on self-esteem and self-reported happiness. However, using data from the UK Household Longitudinal Survey, Booker et al. found that moderate amounts of screen time (1 to 3 hours a day) were associated with better well-being than excessive screen time (4 hours or more a day) or none at all. This finding was reaffirmed in the latest Good Childhood report by The Children's Society.

According to the UK Household Longitudinal Study, nearly all children (98%) aged 10 to 15 have used a computer at home in 2011–12. Children were more likely to use the computer at least once a week to connect to the internet than for schoolwork or coursework (88% compared with 70%). In addition, 85% belonged to a social network site, 96% had a games console and 75% spent more than an hour on a school night watching TV or DVDs.

Figure 8 shows that computer use has increased among children aged 11 to 15 between 2002 and 2011–12. It has increased particularly for browsing the internet, from 48% to 90%. The proportion of children using the computer for homework at least once a week also increased steadily between 2002 and 2007. Since 2008, the proportion has remained fairly stable and was 75% in 2011–12. In contrast, between 2009–10 and 2011–12, the proportion using the computer to connect to the internet at least once a week has decreased from 93% to 90%. This may be indicative of an increase in smartphone and tablet use by children to connect to the internet or for completing homework.

Figure 8: Proportion of children age 11 to 15 using the home computer at least once a week; 2002 to 2011-12

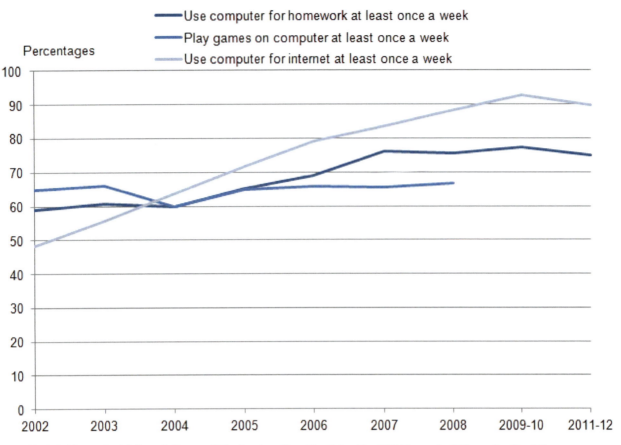

Source: British Household Panel Survey/ Understanding Society, the UK Household Longitudinal Survey

Notes:

1. Respondents were asked: 'How often do you use a computer at home for doing schoolwork or course work?' 'How often do you use the computer at home for connecting to the Internet, including for playing games?' 'How often do you use the computer at home for playing games?' Responses options were: every day, at least once a week, at least once a month, less often than once a month, never.

2. 'Play games on the computer at least once a week' is only available from the BHPS. UKHLS asks children how many hours they spend playing computer games on a typical school night.

Download chart

 XLS format

(27.5 Kb)

A similar proportion of boys and girls aged 10 to 15 used the computer to connect to the internet in 2011–12. However, there was a difference between the proportions of boys and girls using home computers for other purposes. Nearly three-quarters of girls (73%) used the home computer for completing homework at least once a week, compared with around two-thirds of boys (67%). Conversely, nearly three-quarters of boys (73%) spent up to three hours playing games on the home computer on a typical school night, compared with two-thirds of girls (67%). Boys were almost twice as likely as girls to spend over four hours playing games on the home computer (9% and 5% respectively).

The Children's Society 2010 schools survey shows that around 54% of children aged 8 to 15 rated their happiness with their time use as high, while 7% rated it as very low. Happiness with time use can be used as a proxy measure of how much control and independence children have in their lives.

Notes

1. It should be noted that the difference in sports participation could be due to 5-10 year olds only being asked (via a parental proxy) about sports participation outside of school, while 11-15 year olds are asked about sport in and outside school.

2. Arts or cultural activity includes: dance activities, music activities, theatre and drama activities, art and craft activities, street arts, circus, festival or carnival events, film or video activities, and engagement with libraries, museums or galleries, or heritage sites.

Where We Live

A child's perception of the area they live in is important as it affects participation in local activities. Children who live in an area they consider safe will be confident to go outside and play. If they consider the neighbourhood to be friendly they may make friends with other local children.

Crime

If a child has been a victim of crime, their perception of where they live can be affected. Being a victim of crime can be a traumatic experience, and can present itself emotionally or through changes in behaviour, such as taking precautions to avoid becoming a victim again.

Around 12% of children aged 10 to 15 reported being a victim of crime at least once between April 2013 and March 2014, in England and Wales. This is a decrease of one percentage point from the previous year[1]. This compares with 17% of adults reporting that they were a victim of crime between April 2013 and March 2014. The most common type of crime children aged 10 to 15 were victims of was violent crime; around 7% of children experienced violent crime, with 5% victims of violent crime that resulted in injury.

Fear of crime can also affect how a child perceives their local area, and may restrict what they do and the activities they participate in. When asked about how safe they feel walking alone in their area after dark, 56% of children aged 10 to 15 felt very or fairly safe, according to the UK Household Longitudinal Survey. However, boys were more likely to feel very or fairly safe at 63%, compared with 49% of girls (Figure 9). Children who reported feeling very or fairly safe walking alone in their area after dark were also more likely to be satisfied with their lives overall (91%), compared with those who said they felt very or a bit unsafe walking alone after dark (85%).

Figure 9: Feeling safe walking alone in their neighbourhood after dark, 2011-12

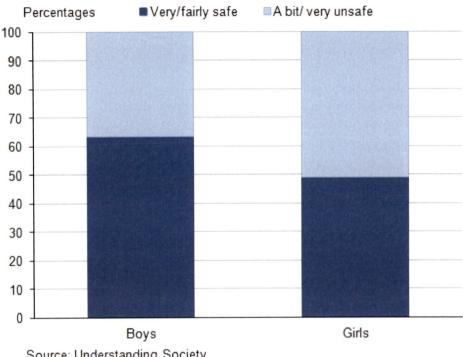

Source: Understanding Society

Notes:

1. Boys and girls aged 10 to 15.
2. Respondents were asked: 'How safe would you feel walking alone in this area after dark?'. Responses options were: very safe, fairly safe, a bit unsafe, very unsafe.

Download chart

XLS XLS format
(25 Kb)

Like their neighbourhood

In 2011–12, 88% of those aged 10 to 15 liked the neighbourhood they lived in, according to the UK Household Longitudinal Study. The data also showed an association between liking the local area and being satisfied with life overall. Of those who like their neighbourhood 90% were satisfied with their lives overall compared with 75% of those who did not like their neighbourhood.

Around two-thirds (64%) of children aged 8 to 15 who responded to The Children's Society's 2010 survey rated their happiness with their accommodation as high. The proportion rating their happiness with their accommodation as very low was 7%.

Notes

1. The Crime Survey for England and Wales (previously known as the British Crime Survey) asks respondents about their experiences of crime in the 12 months prior to the interview.

Personal Finance

Personal finance can have a significant impact on people's sense of well-being, and the population's financial situation is an important aspect of National Well-being. It is also important for the well-being of children. A lack of finances can affect a person's health, their access to community resources and their contribution to the community. Being unable to do the things you would like to due to lack of money can reduce your level of life satisfaction, make life seem less worthwhile and affect how happy you may be.

Households with less than 60% of median income

The Department of Work and Pensions (DWP) estimates that in 2012/13, there were 2.3 million children[1] (17% of all children) living in relative low-income households before housing costs (below 60 per cent median net disposable income in that survey year, before housing costs) in the UK[2]. The proportion of children living in relative low-income households has remained relatively stable since 2010/11, but has decreased by 9 percentage points compared with 1998/99 (Figure 10).

Figure 10: Proportion of children living in households with less than 60% of median income; 1998/99 to 2011/12

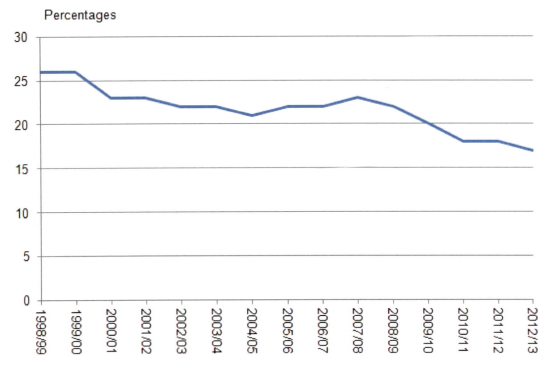

Source: Department for Work and Pensions, Family Resources Survey

Download chart

XLS XLS format
(26 Kb)

Workless households

A recent ONS analysis looked at the childhood factors that matter the most to the transmission of poverty and disadvantage between generations of people in the UK. It found that those who lived in a workless household at age 14 were around 1.5 times more likely to be in poverty, compared with those where one adult was working.

The Labour Force Survey shows that in 2013, the proportion of children aged 0 to 15 in the UK living in workless households[3] was 14%. This compares with 1 in 5 children (20%) in 1996. The proportion of children in workless households steadily decreased between 1996 and 2008. However, following the onset of the economic downturn in 2008, it increased from around 15% in that year to just under 17% in 2009. Since 2009, the proportion has decreased at a faster rate than between 1996 and 2009[4].

Material deprivation

DWP figures also show that the proportion of children in combined low income and material deprivation households[5] has remained around 13% since 2010/11. Numbers from 2010/11 onwards cannot be compared with those from previous years, as the list of items which compromise the material deprivation index was updated to make it more representative of families' needs today.

Data from The Children's Society's 2010 schools survey shows around 63% of children aged 8 to 15 rated their happiness with their possessions (including money) as high. A higher proportion of boys rated their happiness with their possessions as high (66%) than girls (61%).

Notes

1. A child is defined here as an individual under 16 years of age, or an unmarried or non-cohabiting 16 to 19-year-old in full-time non-advanced education. Unmarried or non-cohabiting 19-year-olds in full-time non-advanced education have been included in this definition since April 2006.

2. Caution needs to be taken when interpreting changes in the proportion of households below 60% of median income. Median income can fluctuate changing the proportion below 60% without making people better off, as explained by Seddon: 'The reduction in the percentage below the poverty rate between 2009/10 and 2010/11 is in part attributable to the fall in median income rather than any substantial improvement of the financial situation of the people at the bottom of the distribution.'

3. Workless households are households that include at least one person aged 16 to 64 where no-one aged 16 or over is in employment.

4. These figures will be updated at the end of October 2014, and will include re-weighted LFS figures.

5. Material deprivation is an additional way of measuring living standards and refers to the self-reported inability of individuals or households to afford particular goods and activities that are typical in society at a given point in time, irrespective of whether they would choose to have these items, even if they could afford them. A suite of questions designed to capture the material deprivation experienced by families with children has been included in the FRS since 2004/05 and by pensioners since 2008/09. A child is considered to be in low income and material deprivation if they live in a family that has a final material deprivation score of 25 or more out of a possible 100 and an equivalised household income below 70 per cent of median income BHC.

Education and Skills

Children's education and development of skills are important for their well-being and for that of the nation as a whole. Learning ensures that children develop the knowledge and understanding, skills, capabilities and attributes that they need for mental, emotional, social and physical well-being now and in the future (ONS, 2012).

Educational attainment

In line with national well-being measures, pupils' academic performance, as measured by achievement in their last year of compulsory education is included. In 2011/12, 59% of pupils in England, Wales and Northern Ireland achieved at least five or more GCSEs at grade A* to C including English and mathematics. This increased from 53% in 2009/10. In Scotland, the percentage of pupils in their last year of compulsory education achieving five or more qualifications at SCQF level 5 or better was 37% in 2011/12.

Happiness with school

It is not just children's achievements but also experience within school that is important to their overall well-being. A study of the Avon Longitudinal Study of Parents and Children looked at pupil and school effects during primary school. It found that different children have different experiences even at the same school, and that for well-being, 'child-school' fit is as important as attending a 'good' school (Gutman and Feinstein, 2008).

Data from the UK Household Longitudinal Survey shows that when asked how happy (on a scale of 1 to 7) they were with their school, nearly 83% of children aged 10 to 15 were relatively happy in 2011–12. It also shows that children who reported being relatively satisfied with life overall were over 1.5 times more likely to be relatively happy with school than those who were relatively unsatisfied with their life overall (86% and 54% respectively) (Figure 11). Children who reported being unsatisfied with life overall were over six times more likely to be relatively unhappy with school than those who were relatively satisfied with life overall (36% and 6% respectively).

Figure 11: Children's happiness with school; by life satisfaction, 2011-12

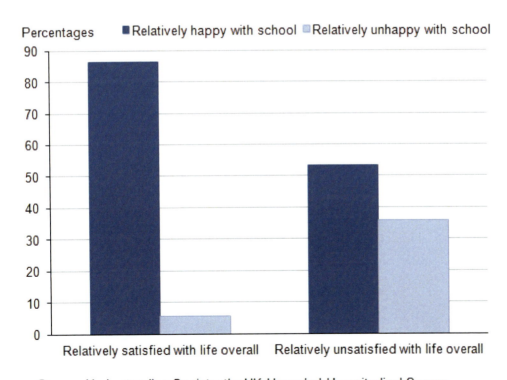

Source: Understanding Society, the UK Household Longitudinal Survey

Notes:

1. Excludes children who reported being neither happy or unhappy with the school that they go to.

2. Respondents were asked: 'where '1' is completely happy and '7' is not at all happy, please tick the box which comes closest to expressing how you feel about each of the following things... the school you go to.' Relatively happy is a score of 1 to 3, relatively unhappy is a score of 5 to 7, a neutral score is 4.

3. Respondents were asked: 'where '1' is completely happy and '7' is not at all happy, which best describes how you feel about your life as a whole?' Relatively happy is a score of 1 to 3, relatively unhappy is a score of 5 to 7, a neutral score is 4.

Download chart

XLS XLS format
(27 Kb)

Aspirations

Having aspirations and an idea of where your life is heading is important for well-being. The UK Household Longitudinal Study asks children what they would like to do at age 16, for example, carrying on with education or getting a job. The categories, however, are too vague to capture definite aspirations and goals, for example, 'I want to train as a plumber and start my own business'. As such, the best measure available only captures academic aspirations.

In 2011–12, over three-quarters (76%) of 10 to 15 year olds stated that they would like to go to university. However, a higher proportion of girls aspire to university than boys (83% and 69% respectively) (Figure 12).

Figure 12: Proportion of children who would like to go to university or college; boys and girls, 2011-12

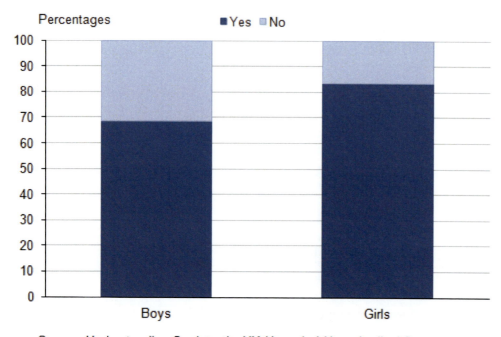

Source: Understanding Society, the UK Household Longitudinal Survey

Notes:

1. Boys and girls aged 10 to 15.
2. Respondents were asked: 'What would you most like to do when you have completed your final GCSE/Standard Grade year at around age 16?', 'Would you like to go on to do further full-time education at a college or University after you finish school?' Responses options were: get a full time job; stay at school or college to do A levels/ highers; get an apprenticeship; do some other form of training; do something else.

Download chart

XLS XLS format
(25.5 Kb)

Background notes

1. The UK Longitudinal Household Survey (UKHLS) also referred to as Understanding Society is a unique and valuable academic study that captures important information every year about the social and economic circumstances and attitudes of people living in 40,000 UK households. It also collects additional health information from around 20,000 of the people who take part. Information from the longitudinal survey is primarily used by academics, researchers and policymakers in their work, but the findings are of interest to a much wider group of people. These include those working in the third sector, health practitioners, business, the media and the general public. The data in this analysis is from the youth self-completion questionnaire module of Waves 1-3 of the Survey and has been weighted using the combined cross-sectional youth interview weight. More information about the UKHLS.

2. The British Household Panel Survey (BHPS) was the precursor to the UKHLS. From Wave 2 of the UKHLS, around 6,700 respondents from the BHPS were added into the UKHLS panel. As the BHPS sample only included children aged 11 to 15, any comparisons with UKHLS data (2009 onwards) are for this age group only. More information about the BHPS.

3. The Children's Society has conducted a regular online well-being survey since July 2010 with a sample of 2,000 children and their parents. This uses a household panel that is run by the research agency Research Now. The survey was run every quarter until 2013 and then every six months since January 2013. Each wave has so far covered a representative sample of approximately 2,000 children, initially in UK, but in Great Britain since Wave 3. The survey includes quota sampling for age, gender and family socio-economic status (i.e. occupation of the main income earner, information provided by parent). Waves 1 to 9 included children aged 8 to 15, while Wave 10 included children aged 10 to 17. Each wave of the survey has included a standard set of questions that make up 'The Good Childhood Index' together with questions covering additional topics which have varied for each wave. The three ONS questions were added as additional questions for the first time in Wave 7 and repeated them in Waves 8, 9 and 10. More information about The Children's Society surveys

4. The Children's Society's 2010 schools survey was administered for The Children's Society by the National Foundation for Educational Research (NFER). The sample covered a stratified sample of primary, middle and secondary schools in England. Schools were divided into five strata on the basis of the proportion of children attending the school who were entitled to free school meals. Schools were selected randomly within each stratum. The survey was administered in schools as an online self-completion questionnaire to children in Years 4 and 6 in primary schools and Years 8 and 10 in secondary schools. Data collection took place from October 2010 to January 2011. There were two alternative versions of the questionnaire for children in Years 6, 8 and 10 with mostly shared content but some variation to increase the topic coverage. These two versions were assigned randomly to different children in each school. There was a separate shorter version of the questionnaire for Year 4 children.

5. Where UK data are not available other sources from Wales, Scotland and Northern Ireland have been included where available. Caution must be taken when comparing across countries due to differences in sources and methods.

6. Throughout the bulletin, only statistically significant findings are commented on.

7. Authors: Rachel Beardsmore and Veronique Siegler

8. Details of the policy governing the release of new data are available by visiting www.statisticsauthority.gov.uk/assessment/code-of-practice/index.html or from the Media Relations Office email: media.relations@ons.gsi.gov.uk

Copyright

References

Bakeo and Clarke., (2006) Risks factors for low birth weight based on birth registration and census information, England and Wales, 1981-2000. Health Stat Q (30): 15-21.

Beardsmore, R., (2014) Measuring National Well-being: Measures of Well-being for Children and Young People Consultation Response, Office for National Statistics .

Booker, C .L., Skew, A.J., Kelly, Y.J., Sacker, A., (2014). Media Use, Sports Participation, and Well-Being in Adolescence: Cross-Sectional Findings From the UK Household Longitudinal Study. American Journal of Public Health.

Bradshaw J (2011)., Child poverty and deprivation, in J. Bradshaw (ed.) The Well-being of Children in the UK, 3rd ed, The Policy Press, Bristol, pp.27-52.

Chanfreau, J., Lloyd, C., Byron, C., Roberts, C., Craig, R., De Feo, D., McManus, S., (2013) Predicting well-being, research report, NatCen Social Research, London.

Chomitz V.R., Cheung L.W.Y., Lieberman E., (1995) The Future of Children. Vol. 5, No. 1, Low Birth Weight, pp. 121-138.

Corp, A., (2013) Measuring National Well-being - Domains and Measures - September 2013, Office for National Statistics

Cusumano, D. L., and Thompson, J. K., (2001), "Media influence and body image in 8–11-year-old boys and girls: A preliminary report on the multidimensional media influence scale." International Journal of Eating Disorders, 29: 37–44

Griffiths L.J., Parsons T.J., Hill A.J., (2010) Self-esteem and quality of life in obese children and adolescents: a systematic review. International Journal of Pediatric Obesity 5: 282–304

Gutman and Feinstein., (2008) Children's Well-Being in Primary School: Pupil and School Effects. Wider Benefits of Learning Research Report No.25. Centre for Research on the Wider Benefits of Learning.

OECD, (2009) Special Focus: Measuring Leisure in OECD Countries. http://www.oecd.org/berlin/42675407.pdf

Pooley, J., (2013) Gestation-specific Infant Mortality in England and Wales, 2011, Office for National Statistics.

Public Health England, (2013) How healthy behaviour supports children's wellbeing.

Rees, G., et. Al., (2013) The Good Childhood Report, London, The Children's Society.

Schwimmer J.B., Burwinkle T.M., Varni J.W., (2003) Health-related quality of life of severely obese children and adolescents. Journal of American Medical Association. Vol. 289 Nb 14.

Seddon, C., (2012) Measuring National Well-being - Personal Finance, 2012, Office for National Statistics.

Serafina, P. and Tonkin, R., (2014) Intergenerational transmission of disadvantage in the UK & EU, 2014, Office for National Statistics.

The Children's Society (2014), The Good childhood Report 2014, London: The Children's Society.

The Marmot Review, (2010) Fair Society, Healthy Lives. http://www.instituteofhealthequity.org/projects/fair-society-healthy-lives-the-marmot-review

Xavier, S., Mandal, S., The psychosocial impacts of obesity in children and young people: A future health perspective. Public Health Medicine 2005;6(1):23-27.

Office for
National Statistics

Measuring National Well-being - Exploring the Well-being of Young People in the UK, 2014

Coverage: **International**
Date: **03 December 2014**
Geographical Area: **Country**
Theme: **People and Places**
Theme: **Children, Education and Skills**

Foreword

There were around 7.5 million young people aged 16 to 24 in the UK in 2012, according to the Office for National Statistics (ONS) mid-year population estimates. This is an important age of transition from childhood to adulthood, and the ways in which this transition is negotiated may affect current and future well-being. Arnett (2004) coined the phrase 'emerging adulthood' to describe this stage of life. As many have yet to make 'the transitions historically associated with adult status', such as marriage and parenthood, the aspects of life affecting a young person's well-being will differ from those of the rest of the adult population, and those that are the same may differ in their impact.

The framework for measuring national well-being indicators is grouped into ten domains. These domains of well-being are consistent at all ages. Most of the national well-being measures for the adult population also apply to 16 to 24 year olds. However, there are some measures which are particularly relevant for young people, such as not being in education, employment and training. Three domains – governance, natural environment and economy – are more contextual, so are not included in the young people's measurement framework.

ONS has developed a provisional set of headline measures of young people's well-being across seven domains, alongside a set of measures for children up to the age of 15. In March 2014, ONS published a consultation on the first iteration of these measures. The consultation response was published in July 2014 and an updated set of measures will be published in 2015. This report presents a baseline for 27 of the 28 measures[1] young people's well-being. It considers how selected measures compare across age groups, change over time or differ by gender[2] for young people aged 16 to 24. A similar analysis of the children's measures was published in October 2014.

Notes:

1. The measure 'proportion of young people who are fairly/very satisfied with their accommodation' needs further consideration.

2. The differences between young men and women for selected measures have been explored previously.

Key points

- In 2013/14 in the UK, around 8 out of 10 young people aged 16 to 24 reported high or very high life satisfaction.
- Around 1 in 5 young people aged 16 to 24 in the UK reported some symptoms of anxiety or depression in 2011-12.
- 1 in 3 young people aged 16 to 24 in England were overweight including obese in 2012 compared with 3 in 5 adults aged 16 and over.
- The proportion of young people in England engaging with or participating in arts or cultural activities at least three times a year has increased from 78% in 2008-09 to 85% in 2013-14.
- 1 in 4 young people aged 16 to 24 in England and Wales were victims of crime in 2013-14, down from 1 in 3 in 2006-07.
- 1 in 10 young people aged 16 to 24 in the UK were finding their financial situation difficult or very difficult in 2011-12.

Personal Well-being

Young people's personal well-being

Since April 2011, the Annual Population Survey has included four questions which are used to monitor personal well-being in the UK:

1. Overall, how satisfied are you with your life nowadays?
2. Overall, to what extent do you feel the things you do in your life are worthwhile?
3. Overall, how happy did you feel yesterday?
4. Overall, how anxious did you feel yesterday?

Responses are on a scale of 0 to 10 where 0 is 'not at all' and 10 is 'completely'. High or very high levels of personal well-being for life satisfaction, worthwhile and happiness are defined as 7 or more out of 10. However, for anxiety 3 or less out of 10 is used because lower levels of anxiety indicate better personal well-being.

A higher proportion of young people reported having low or very low levels (0-3) of anxiety than all adults. Nearly 66% of 16 to 24 year olds reported low or very low anxiety in 2013/14, compared with around 63% of all adults aged 16 and over. Young people are also more likely to report higher levels of satisfaction with their life compared with all adults.

In 2013/14, just over 81% of 16 to 24 year olds reported high or very high levels of life satisfaction (7-10), compared with nearly 79% of all adults. This may relate to the increase in freedom, independence and self-focus associated with the 'emerging adulthood' life stage. A similar proportion of young people reported high or very high levels of happiness yesterday (7-10), compared with all adults in this period.

Despite larger proportions of young people reporting higher levels of life satisfaction and happiness and lower levels of anxiety, young people are less likely than all adults to consider the things they do in their life are worthwhile. In 2013/14, around 79% of 16 to 24 year olds considered the things they do in life to be worthwhile as high or very high (7-10), compared with nearly 82% of all adults. This measure fluctuates across age groups.

Figure 1: Personal Well-being measures by age group, 2013/14

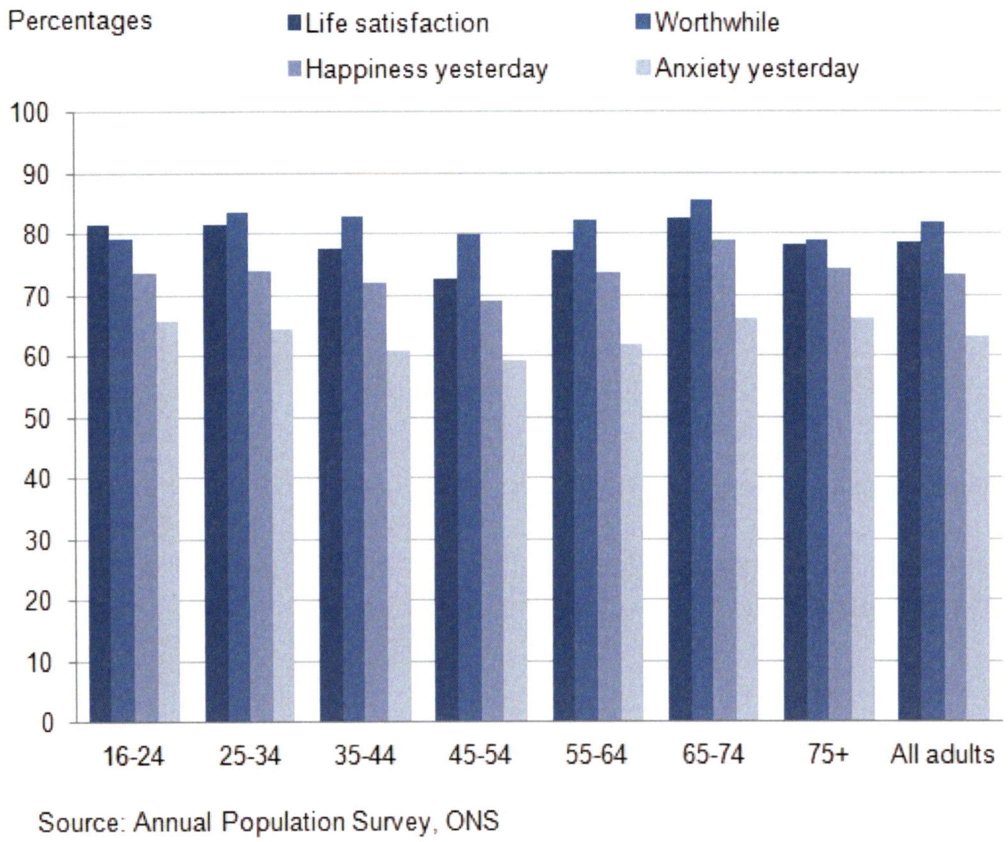

Source: Annual Population Survey, ONS

Source: Annual Population Survey (APS) - Office for National Statistics

Notes:
1. The data presented are derived from a customised weighted 12 month APS micro dataset. This dataset is not part of the regularly produced APS datasets and was produced specifically for the analysis of subjective well-being data.
2. Life satisfaction, Worthwhile and Happiness percentages relate to those who responded 7 to 10 on a scale of 0 to 10 where 0 was not at all and 10 was completely.
3. Anxiety percentage relates to those who responded 0 to 3 on a scale of 0 to 10 where 0 was not at all and 10 was completely.

Download chart

XLS XLS format
(28 Kb)

There has been little change in how young people rate their personal well-being over the three years 2011/12 to 2013/14. The proportion of 16 to 24 year olds reporting high or very high life satisfaction and that the things they do in life are worthwhile have remained stable. There has however been an increase in the proportion reporting high or very high happiness, from 71% in 2011/12 to just less than 74% in 2013/14, and low or very low anxiety, from 63% in 2011/12 to 66% in 2013/14. This compares with significantly increased proportions of all adults reporting improved well-being across all four personal well-being measures. Measuring national well-being, personal well-being in the UK, 2013/14, provides an in-depth analysis of personal well-being over the last three years.

Mental well-being

The mental well-being measure is the shortened version of the Warwick-Edinburgh Mental Well-being Scale (SWEMWBS). This was developed to measure the mental well-being of populations and groups over time. The SWEMWBS provides a mean score (out of 35) of mental well-being for the population. Changes over time can be assessed by examining differences in the mean score.

However, it cannot be used to categorise good, average or poor mental well-being[1].

The mean score of mental well-being for 16 to 24 year olds in 2009-10 was 25.0, which is very similar to the mean score of 25.2 for all adults.

Notes

1. As well as not being designed to identify people who have, or probably have a mental illness, WEMWBS does not a have a 'cut off' level to divide the population into those who have 'good' and those who have 'poor' mental well-being, in the way that scores on other mental health measures do, for example the GHQ 12.

Our Relationships

A person's relationships with family and friends can affect their well-being in a number of ways. Good communication is important to healthy relationships: 'People who have close friends and confidants, friendly neighbours and supportive co-workers are less likely to experience sadness, loneliness, low self-esteem and problems with eating and sleeping...Subjective well-being is best predicted by the breadth and depth of one's social connections' (Helliwell and Putnam, 2004). An analysis of experimental data from the Annual Population Survey found that overall life satisfaction and personal relationships are related; those who reported a higher level of life satisfaction were more likely to report higher satisfaction with their personal relationships than those with lower levels of life satisfaction.

Family

The young adults' module in the UK Household Longitudinal Survey (also referred to as Understanding Society) asked all 16 to 21 year olds about their relationship with their parents, whether or not they still lived in the family home. This data shows that young people aged 16 to 21 were more likely to quarrel with their mother than their father. Around 25% quarrelled with their mother more than once a week in 2011-12, whereas only 16% quarrelled with their father more than once a week. This compares with nearly 28% of 10 to15 year olds quarrelling with their mother more than once a week and 20% quarrelling with their father more than once a week. The smaller proportion of 16 to 21 year olds quarrelling with either parent, compared with children aged 10 to 15, is indicative of the increased independence young people experience.

As well as being more likely to quarrel with their mothers than with their fathers, young people were also more likely to talk to their mother about things that matter. Around 58% of 16 to 21 year olds talked to their mother more than once a week, compared with nearly 36% who talked to their father about things that matter more than once a week. This compares with around 63% of 10 to15 year olds talking to their mother about things that matter and nearly 40% talking to their father. Amongst 16 to 21 year olds, women were far more likely to talk to their mother about things that matter, at 67%, than men, at 50%.

Young people who reported being relatively dissatisfied with life overall were 1.5 times more likely to quarrel with both parents more than once a week than those who were relatively satisfied with life overall. Furthermore, they were also less likely to talk to both parents about things that matter very often.

Figure 2: Young people's quarrelling with and talking to parents by satisfaction with life overall, 2011-12

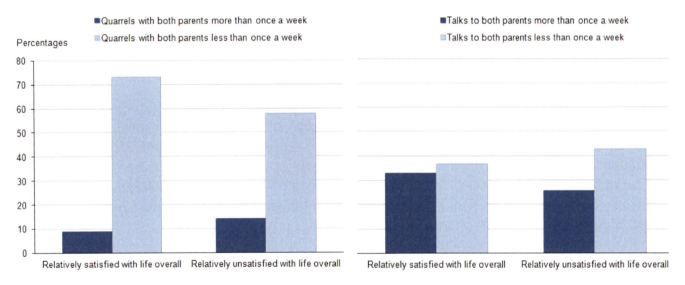

Source: UK Household Longitudinal Survey

Notes:

1. Young people age 16 to 24.
2. Respondents were asked 'How often do you quarrel with your mother?'; 'How often do you quarrel with your father?'; 'How often do you talk to your mother about things that matter?' and 'How often do you talk to your father about things that matter?'
3. Excludes respondents who reported quarrelling with/talking to one parent more than the other.
4. Respondents were asked: "where '1' is completely happy and '7' is not at all happy, which best describes how you feel about your life as a whole?". Relatively happy is a score of 1 to 3, relatively unhappy is a score of 5 to 7, neutral is a score of 4.

Download chart

Click on the image to view an enlarged version

Data from the UK Household Longitudinal Survey shows that in 2010-11 82% of 16 to 24 year olds had someone to rely on a lot. This is less than the proportion of all adults, where over 87% had someone to rely on a lot. The difference may be accounted for by the higher levels of marriage and partnerships in older age groups, compared with 16 to 24 year olds. Young women are more likely than young men to have someone they can rely on a lot (86% compared with 78%).

Health

Analysis of the Annual Population Survey showed that amongst adults in the UK, self-reported health was the most important factor associated with subjective well-being. According to the World Health Organisation a person's health is affected by the social and economic environment, the physical environment and personal characteristics and behaviours. People with very bad health reported lower levels of life satisfaction and higher levels of anxiety than people in good health. In addition, further analysis identified that young people were more likely to report satisfaction with their health than any other age group.

Satisfaction with health

Data from the British Household Panel Survey (BHPS) and the UK Household Longitudinal Survey show that until recently, the majority of young people reported being relatively satisfied with their health. In 2010-11 three-quarters (75%) of young people reported being relatively satisfied with their health, a similar proportion to that in 2002 (75%). However, in 2011-12 only two-thirds (66%) of 16 to 24 year olds reported the same. This recent decrease is reflected in the whole adult population: in 2010-11, two out of three (67%) adults reported being relatively satisfied with their health, whereas in 2011-12 fewer than three out of five (59%) were. Health problems develop with age, as can be seen in the proportions of adults with long-term illnesses or disabilities, so it is reasonable to expect young people to be more satisfied with their health than older people.

In 2011-12, young people who were relatively satisfied with their health were more likely to report being satisfied with life overall (87%) compared with those who were relatively dissatisfied with their health (48%).

Mental health

The General Health Questionnaire (GHQ) scores from the UK Household Longitudinal Survey show that 21% of young people reported some symptoms of depression or anxiety in 2011-12. This is a similar proportion to all adults (18%). Measuring national well-being – health has an illustration of how GHQ scores differ by age group.

Figure 3: Young people's satisfaction with life overall by symptoms of depression or anxiety, 2011-12

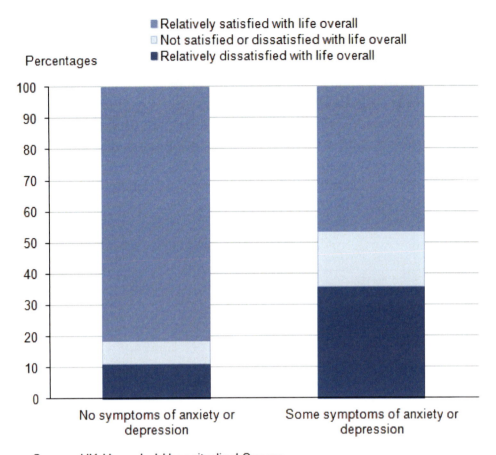

Source: UK Household Longitudinal Survey

Notes:
1. Young people age 16 to 24.
2. GHQ12 assessment of psychosocial health.

Download chart

XLS XLS format
(26.5 Kb)

Of those young people reporting some symptoms of mental ill-health in 2011-12, around 46% were relatively satisfied with life overall, compared with 82% of those not reporting symptoms. Furthermore, this group was around three times as likely to be relatively dissatisfied with life overall than those not reporting symptoms.

Disability and long-term illness

Data from the Labour Force Survey shows that around 12% of 16 to 24 year olds reported a long-term illness or disability in April to June in 2014. This compares with 19% of 16 to 64 year olds reporting long term illness or disability in the same period[1].

Obesity

Obesity can increase the risk of developing serious diseases, damage a person's quality of life and may trigger depression. The Health Survey for England uses objective measurements of height and weight to calculate Body Mass Index. It shows that the proportion of young people age 16 to 24 that are overweight including obese increased in 2012 compared with 2003.

In 2003, 31% of 16 to 24 year olds were overweight, including obese. In 2009 the prevalence for this age group reached 37%. There was a slight decrease between 2009 and 2011, before the rate increased to 36% in 2012. There was no significant difference in the rate of overweight including obese between 16 to 24 year old men and women in 2012. The 16-24 year old age group has significantly lower rates of overweight including obese when compared to the older age groups.

Table 1a: Proportion of adults overweight, including obese, by survey year and age group (1, 2, 3)

England, 2003-2007

Percentages

	2003	**2004**	**2005**[4]	**2006**	**2007**
16-24	31.2	33.5	31.8	32.7	32.9
25-34	52.8	53.6	53.4	54.9	49.3
35-44	63.9	65.1	63.9	63.6	64.8
45-54	67.5	70.5	69.2	69.3	68.4
55-64	71.9	73.2	70.3	72.6	73.5
65-74	74.4	72.3	73.3	76.2	73.0
75 and over	68.2	69.3	65.2	68.9	69.0
All aged 16 and over	60.5	61.8	60.5	61.6	60.8

Table source: Information Centre for Health and Social Care

Table notes:
1. Adults aged 16 and over with a valid height and weight measurement 2003-2012
2. Overweight = BMI 25 to less than 30.
3. Obese = BMI 30 or more (includes morbidly obese).
4. All adults from core and boost samples in 2005 were included in analysis of 65-74 and 75+ age groups but only the core sample was included in the overall total.

Download table

XLS XLS format
(29 Kb)

Table 1b: Proportion of adults overweight, including obese, by survey year and age group (1, 2, 3)

England, 2008-2012

Percentages

	2008	2009	2010	2011	2012
16-24	33.5	37.0	33.4	32.4	36.3
25-34	51.9	48.0	53.1	51.0	51.3
35-44	64.5	62.1	66.3	64.6	63.8
45-54	69.2	71.0	71.1	71.5	72.2
55-64	73.4	74.6	75.5	71.9	73.0
65-74	77.1	78.3	77.5	74.4	73.0
75 and over	68.4	65.9	69.6	72.4	70.0
All aged 16 and over	61.4	61.3	62.8	61.7	61.9

Table source: Information Centre for Health and Social Care

Table notes:
1. Adults aged 16 and over with a valid height and weight measurement 2003-2012
2. Overweight = BMI 25 to less than 30.
3. Obese = BMI 30 or more (includes morbidly obese).
4. All adults from core and boost samples in 2005 were included in analysis of 65-74 and 75+ age groups but only the core sample was included in the overall total.

Download table

XLS XLS format
(20 Kb)

Notes

1. Background note regarding comparisons of disability data over time has more information.

What We Do

Unemployment Rate

People may be economically inactive for a number of reasons; they are full-time carers, sick or disabled, or in full-time education, for example. Due to the economic downturn resulting in pressures in the job market (44 Kb Excel sheet) young people may decide to continue in full-time education. A lack of money due to unemployment may increase feelings of social isolation in young people as they cannot afford to socialise or go out and meet other people as often as they may like to. The

Prince's Trust Macquarie Youth Index 2014 claims that, 'the longer people are out of work, the more likely they are to feel a lapse in confidence. Those who are long-term unemployed are significantly more likely to feel this way than those out of work for less than six months'.

Data from the Labour Force Survey shows that the unemployment rate[1] for young people has increased over the last decade from 12% in April-June 2004 to around 21% in the same quarter of 2013, before decreasing to just less than 17% in April-June 2014. During the last decade, unemployment in the 16 to 24 age group increased in most years with the largest increase of 5 percentage points between April-June 2008 and April-June 2009. This corresponds with the onset of the 2008 economic downturn. The unemployment rate in the 16 to 24 year old age group was higher for men than for women in every year from April-June 2004 to April-June 2014. Young people may be unemployed due to a lack of experience, education, qualifications, training or available jobs.

Figure 4: Unemployment rate and unemployment proportion for 16 to 24 year olds, 2004-14

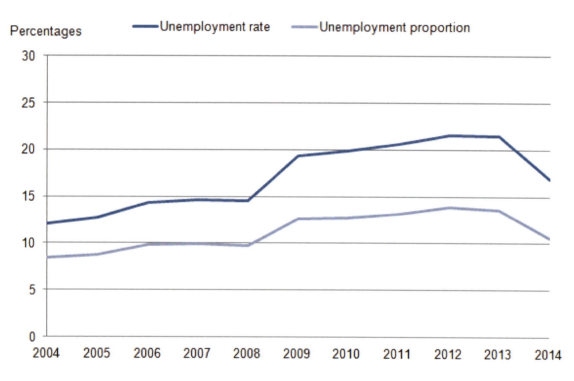

Source: Labour Force Survey, Office for National Statistics

Notes:

1. April – June quarter
2. The unemployment rate is the proportion of economically active people who are not currently working but who have been looking for work in the last four weeks and are available to start within the next two weeks.
3. The unemployment proportion is the proportion of the total population of 16 to 24 year olds who are unemployed.

Download chart

XLS XLS format
(26.5 Kb)

While there has been an increase in unemployment amongst 16 to 24 year olds between April-June 2004 and April-June 2014, there has also been an increase in the proportion of young people remaining in full-time education beyond the age of 18. As a result, the number of economically active young people has reduced, thereby over-inflating the unemployment rate. Another measure of unemployment for young people is the unemployment proportion; the proportion of the total population of 16 to 24 year olds who are unemployed.

Over the last ten years the unemployment proportion followed a similar pattern to the unemployment rate. Amongst 16 to 24 year olds in April-June 2004 the unemployment proportion was around 8%. It then increased to around 13% in April-June 2013, before decreasing to just under 11% for the same period in 2014. Analysis by ONS disaggregated the unemployment proportion further to identify young people who were not in full-time education and were unemployed. It found that around 9% of 16 to 24 year had this status at the end of 2013, compared with 12% in 1993. This may be explained by the fact that more young people are remaining in full-time education.

Leisure time

The UK Household Longitudinal Survey asks respondents to state how satisfied they are with the amount of leisure time they have. As a subjective measure, this is important to understand how people's time-use can affect their well-being. 'The amount and quality of leisure time is important for people's well-being for the direct satisfaction it brings. Additionally leisure, taken in certain ways, is important for physical and mental health.' (OECD, 2009)

About two thirds of 16 to 24 year olds reported being satisfied with their amount of leisure time in 2011-12, little changed since 2002. Just over two thirds of men (67%) were satisfied with their leisure time compared with 57% of women in the 16 to 24 age group.

Around 40% of young people who were relatively dissatisfied with their leisure time reported being dissatisfied with life overall. This compares with around 6% of young people who were relatively satisfied with their leisure time being dissatisfied with their life overall. Furthermore, young people satisfied with their leisure time were almost twice as likely to be relatively happy with life overall than those who were relatively dissatisfied with their leisure time (89% compared with 46%).

Figure 5: Young people's satisfaction with life overall, by satisfaction with leisure, 2011-12

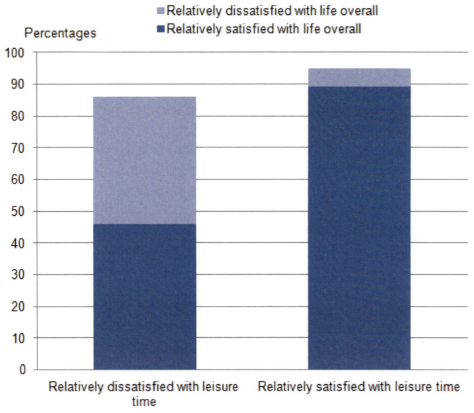

Source: UK Household Longitudinal Survey

Notes:

1. Young people age 16 to 24.
2. Excludes young people who reported being neither satisfied nor dissatisfied with their leisure time.
3. Responses to "How dissatisfied or satisfied are you with.........The amount of leisure time you have" on a 7 point scale varying from completely (or very) satisfied to completely (or very) dissatisfied.
4. Respondents were asked: "where '1' is completely happy and '7' is not at all happy, which best describes how you feel about your life as a whole?" Relatively happy is a score of 1 to 3, relatively unhappy is a score of 5 to 7, neutral is a score of 4.

Download chart

XLS XLS format
(27.5 Kb)

Volunteering

'We define volunteering as any activity that involves spending time, unpaid, doing something that aims to benefit the environment or someone (individuals or groups) other than, or in addition to, close relatives. Central to this definition is the fact that volunteering must be a choice freely made by each individual. This can include formal activity undertaken through public, private and voluntary organisations as well as informal community participation' (Volunteering England).

In 2010-11 the UK Household Longitudinal Survey asked respondents if they had volunteered in the last twelve months. There was little difference in volunteering amongst the 16 to 24 year old age group compared with all those aged 16 and over, at around 17%. However, this comparison masks differences between the age groups. Young people and those of retirement age are more likely to volunteer than any other age group, as illustrated in figure 6.

Figure 6: Proportion of adults volunteering by age group, 2010-11

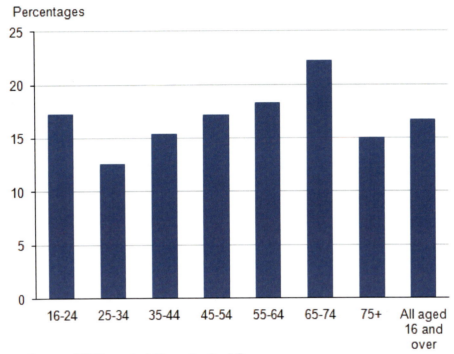

Source: UK Household Longitudinal Survey

Notes:

1. Respondents were asked: In the last 12 months, have you given any unpaid help or worked as a volunteer for any type of local, national or international organisation or charity?; Including any time spent at home or elsewhere, about how often over the last 12 months have you generally done something to help any of these organisations?
2. Excludes responses 'One-off activity' and 'helped or worked on a seasonal basis'.

Download chart

XLS XLS format
(27 Kb)

Participation in at least one session of moderate activity a week

Participation in physical activity and sport has been shown to be effective for reducing depression, anxiety, psychological distress and emotional disturbance. A review of research on this topic found that low-to-moderate physical exercise, even in a single session, can reduce anxiety. Another year-long study concluded that increases in aerobic fitness have both short and long-term beneficial effects on psychological health. Research also shows taking part in and spectating sport can have a positive impact on the well-being and happiness of individuals (Sport England).

Results from the Active People Survey show that in the 12 months April 2013 to March 2014, just over half (55%) of young people aged 16 to 25 in England participated in at least one session of moderate activity a week. This is a decrease compared with the 12 months October 2005 to Sept 2006 (56%) and compares with around a third (32%) of adults aged 26 and over.

In all age groups in 2012-13 more men than women played sport at least once a week at 41% and 30% respectively. 'At a younger age, men are much more likely than women to play sport. But this difference declines sharply with age' (Sport England).

Engagement or participation in an arts or cultural activity

'Creative activity has long been known to have tangible effects on health and quality of life. The arts, creativity and the imagination are agents of wellness: they help keep the individual resilient, aid recovery and foster a flourishing society' (A Charter for Arts, Health and Well-being; National Alliance for Arts Health and Wellbeing).

According to the Taking Part Survey, in 2008-09, around 78% of 16 to 24 year olds engaged or participated in an arts or cultural activity at least 3 times in the 12 months prior to the survey. This increased to just over 85% in 2013-14. There was little difference between the 16 to 24 year old age group and all those aged 16 and over in 2013-14.

Figure 7: Young people engaging with or participating in arts or cultural activities at least 3 times a year, 2008/09 to 2013/14

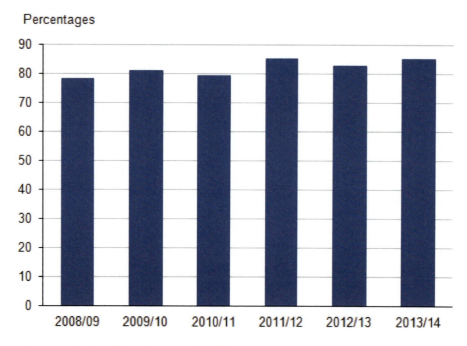

Source: Taking Part Survey, DCMS

Notes:
1. Young people age 16 to 24.
2. Art and cultural activities include: heritage, museums, galleries, libraries and arts (includes attending e.g. theatre, and participating, e.g. painting).

Download chart

XLS XLS format
(27 Kb)

Notes

1. The unemployment rate is the proportion of economically active people who are not currently working but who have been looking for work in the last four weeks and are available to start within the next two weeks.

Where We Live

Victims of crime

A person's well-being can be affected in many ways if they have been a victim of crime. There can be short or long term effects of crime and some people cope well with horrific crimes while others can be distressed by a minor incident (Victim Support).

According to the 2013-14 Crime Survey for England and Wales, 1 in 4 (25%) young people aged 16 to 24 were victims of crime[1], down from more than one in three (37%) in 2006-07. The proportions for men and women in this age group were similar in 2013-14 (24% and 26% respectively). Furthermore, over 1 in 10 young people aged 16 to 24 had been victims of personal crimes, which include violence, robbery, theft from the person, and other theft of personal property. The proportion of young people aged 16 to 24 in England and Wales who had been victims of crime in 2013-14 was 8 percentage points higher than for all respondents aged 16 and over.

Feeling safe walking alone in their local area after dark

According to the 2013-14 Crime Survey England and Wales, 70% of young people aged 16 to 24 felt very or fairly safe walking alone in their local area after dark. This is very similar to the percentage of all adults aged 16 and over (71%). In the 16 to 24 age group a considerably higher proportion of men (85%) felt very or fairly safe walking alone after dark than women (54%). However, it should be noted that this may reflect 'social desirability bias': the CSEW is conducted face-to-face and young men may be reluctant to admit feeling unsafe in their local area.

Figure 8: Young people feeling safe walking alone in their local area after dark, by sex, 2013-14

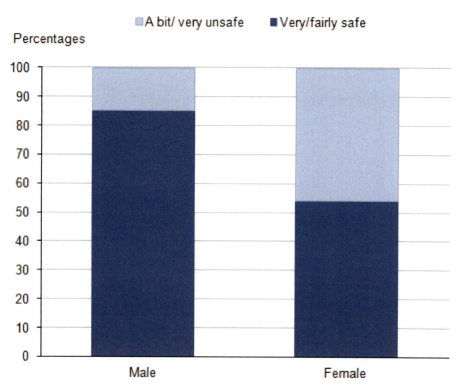

Source: Crime Survey for England and Wales, Office for National Statistics

Notes:

1. Young people age 16 to 24.
2. Although this question is asked in the Crime Survey of England and Wales, it does not ask specifically about safety in relation to crime.
3. There is also possible social desirability bias; in the context of a survey conducted face-to-face, young males may be reluctant to admit that they feel unsafe.

Download chart

 XLS format
(27 Kb)

Belonging to the neighbourhood

Data from the UK Household Longitudinal Survey shows that in 2011-12, around half (49%) of 16 to 24 year olds reported that they felt they belonged to their neighbourhood. This compares with nearly two-thirds (63%) of all adults aged 16 and over. Even so, nearly 90% of young people reported that they liked their neighbourhood, which is similar to the proportion of all adults (94%).

Belonging to the neighbourhood leads to a greater sense of community and feelings of security. Of those young people who agreed or agreed strongly that they belonged to their neighbourhood in 2011-12, around 4 out of 5 reported being relatively satisfied with their life overall. This compares with 3 out of 5 young people who disagreed or disagreed strongly that they belonged to their neighbourhood being relatively satisfied with their life overall.

Accessing the natural environment

In a meta-analysis of twenty-five studies, Bowler et al, found that natural environments may have direct and positive impacts on well-being. They explain that a natural environment setting may encourage physical activity, which can improve physical and possibly mental health. Furthermore, the natural environment may have 'intrinsic qualities' that may enhance well-being.

The Monitor of Engagement with the Natural Environment, published by Natural England, presents data about visits taken to the natural environment and related behaviours and attitudes. In the year ending February 2013, around 62% of 16 to 24 year olds in England visited the natural environment[2] at least once a week. This compares with around 55% of all adults during the same period. Around 6% of young people had never accessed the natural environment in this period. The proportion of young people accessing the natural environment at least once a week has remained stable since the year ending February 2010 (58%).

Notes

1. All CSEW crime

2. The natural environment is defined as the green open spaces in and around towns and cities, as well as the wider countryside and coastline. It excludes private gardens.

Personal Finance

Respondents to the National Debate on 'what matters to you?' identified the importance of having adequate income or wealth to cover basic needs, such as somewhere to live and food on the table. A lack of finances can affect a person's health, their access to community resources and their own contribution to that community. Analysis by ONS explored the relationship between personal well-being and income. Using data from the Annual Population Survey, it found that the lowest two income groups had the lowest scores in life satisfaction, worthwhile and happiness yesterday, and the highest anxious scores.

Household income

In 2011, around one fifth (20%) of 16 to 24 year olds lived in households with less than 60% of median income[1]. In 2005 just under a quarter (23%) of young people were in households with less than 60% of median income. Part of the change in the proportion living with this level of income could be attributed to the variation in median income. Using data from the Living Costs and Food survey, the Office for National Statistics identified that between 2007/08 and 20011/12 the median household income had decreased for non-retired households, but had increased for retired households.

The analysis of personal finance illustrates the changes to median household income before and after housing costs since 1994/95. It explains that the fall in median income between 2009/10 and 2010/11 was mainly due to earnings increasing by less than the relatively high inflation rate over the period. The recent decrease in the proportion of individuals living in households with less than 60% of median income is not necessarily due not to incomes increasing, but is a result of the fluctuations in the median income threshold. Median household income fell nearly 4% between 2007/08 and 2011/12.

Subjective measures

As would be expected, with average earnings falling in real terms since 2009, the proportion of young people who report being satisfied with their household income has decreased. Data from the UK Household Longitudinal Survey indicates that the proportion of young people who were relatively satisfied with their household income has decreased from around 56% in 2002, to 52% in 2011-12.

This decline in satisfaction with household income is mirrored by an increase in the proportion of 16 to 24 year olds who found their financial situation difficult or very difficult. The BHPS data show that in 2002, 10% of young people reported that their financial situation was difficult or very difficult. This compares with 11% in 2011-12, according to the UK Household Longitudinal Survey. The economic downturn, which began in 2008, could be one reason affecting the financial situation of young people.

Figure 9: Young people's satisfaction with life overall, by financial situation, 2011-12

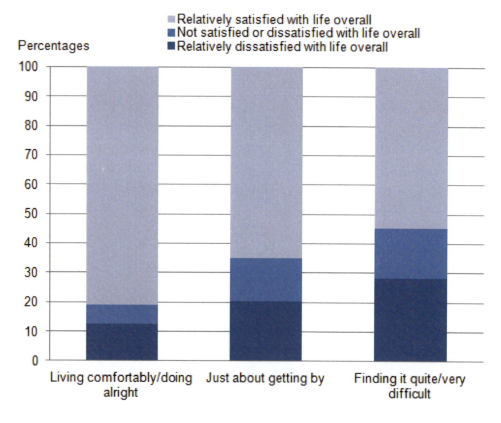

Source: UK Household Longitudinal Survey

Notes:

1. Young people age 16 to 24.
2. Responses to "How well would you say you yourself are managing financially these days? Would you say you are.... ?".
3. Respondents were asked: "where '1' is completely happy and '7' is not at all happy, which best describes how you feel about your life as a whole?" Relatively happy is a score of 1 to 3, relatively unhappy is a score of 5 to 7, neutral is a score of 4.

Download chart

 XLS format

(27 Kb)

Data from the UK Household Longitudinal Survey illustrate the association between finances and well-being. In 2011-12, around 9 out of 10 (91%) young people who were relatively satisfied with their household income reported being relatively satisfied with life overall. This compares with around 5 out of 10 (49%) young people who were relatively dissatisfied with their household income. Similarly, nearly 13% of young people who were finding it difficult or very difficult to manage financially in 2011-12 reported being relatively dissatisfied with life overall, compared with around 28% who were 'doing alright' or 'living comfortably'.

Notes

1. This threshold is used as a proxy measure of poverty as it is considered an indicator of the income below which households are likely to be at risk of suffering hardship. Median household income is the middle point of the range of household income in the UK. Half of UK households have less than the median and half have more. Household income is equivalised to take account of the different sizes and composition of households.

Education and Skills

Education and skills were highlighted in the National Debate as being important to well-being. Having a good education and a strong skills-set equips you for the future. It is associated with a higher income, greater emotional resilience, and better physical health (Sabates, R and Hammond, C, 2008), all of which may have an impact upon personal well-being.

There is contradictory evidence about the effects of education on personal well-being, with some studies suggesting that middle-level education is related to the highest levels of well-being. Although there is a positive association between education and life satisfaction, Sabates and Hammond suggest that 'Maybe education has negative as well as positive impacts, for example through raising expectations that are not met and by leading to occupations that carry high levels of stress.'

Qualifications

Statistics from the Department for Education show that the proportion of young people achieving the equivalent of five GCSEs graded A*-C (National Qualifications Framework Level 2) by age 19 has increased every year since 2004. Around 86% of young people had attained a level 2 qualification[1] by age 19 in 2013, compared with just under 67% in 2004, an increase of 19 percentage points. Similarly, the proportion achieving the equivalent of 2 or more A-levels by age 19 has increased by 17 percentage points since 2004. Around 59% of young people had attained a level 3 qualification by age 19 in 2013, compared with just over 42% in 2004.

Not in Education, Employment or Training

The Princes Trust Macquarie Youth Index 2014 found that young people categorised as NEET ranked lowest in terms of happiness and confidence. ONS estimates that around 13% of 16 to 24 year olds were not in education, employment or training (NEET) in the quarter April – June 2014, a similar proportion to the same period in 2003. There has consistently been a higher proportion of young women than young men categorised as NEET. In 2014, around 14% of young women were not in education, employment or training, compared with just over 12% of young men.

Figure 10: Proportion of young people not in education, employment or training, by sex, 2004-14

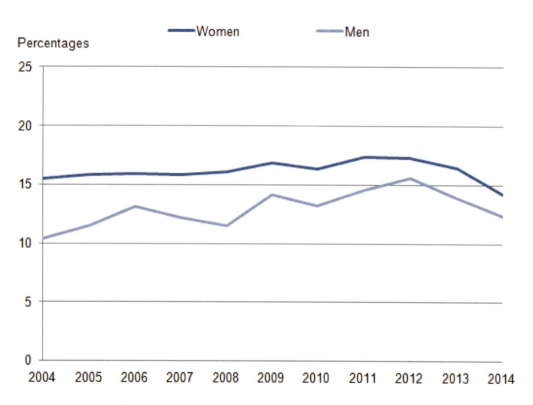

Source: Labour Force Survey, ONS

Notes:
1. Young people age 16 to 24.
2. April – June quarter.

Download chart

XLS XLS format
(26.5 Kb)

Notes

1. Attainment of Level 2 equates to achievement of 5 or more GCSEs at grades A*-C or equivalent qualifications, and Level 3 equates to achievement of 2 or more A-levels or equivalent qualifications

References

1. Arnett, JJ, (2004), Emerging Adulthood; The Winding Road from Late Teens through the Twenties, Oxford University Press
2. ONS, 2011 - Findings from the National Well-being Debate

Background notes

1. The UK Longitudinal Household Survey (UKHLS) also referred to as Understanding Society is a unique and valuable academic study that captures important information every year about the social and economic circumstances and attitudes of people living in 40,000 UK households. It also collects additional health information from around 20,000 of the people who take part. Information from the longitudinal survey is primarily used by academics, researchers and policymakers in their work, but the findings are of interest to a much wider group of people. These include those working in the third sector, health practitioners, business, the media and the general public. More information about the UKHLS.

2. The British Household Panel Survey (BHPS) was the precursor to the UKHLS. From Wave 2 of the UKHLS, around 6,700 respondents from the BHPS were added into the UKHLS panel. More information about the BHPS.

3. The four main estimates of personal well-being are based on data from the Annual Population Survey (APS) which includes responses from around 165,000 people. This provides a large representative sample of adults aged 16 and over who live in residential households in the UK. These questions allow people to make an assessment of their life overall, as well as providing an indication of their day-to-day emotions. Although 'yesterday' may not be a typical day for any one individual, the large sample means that these differences 'average out' and provide a reliable assessment of the anxiety and happiness of the adult population in the UK over the year.

4. The estimates of people with disabilities are derived from statistics on the economic activity of disabled people obtained from the Labour Force Survey (LFS). The disability questions on the LFS have undergone several changes since 2010 and this has meant that comparisons over time have become difficult to interpret. There are two sets of changes in particular that have resulted in discontinuities in time series: 1. in January 2010, a rewording of the introduction to the section of the survey covering disabilities; and 2. in April 2013, changes to the wording of the disability questions in order to bring the LFS more into line with the definitions and questions used in other household surveys in the UK (see Table 1, below).

Consequently the estimates from 2010 onwards are not directly comparable with those for previous years. Also, the estimates from April 2013 are not comparable with those for either the 2010-2012 or the pre-2010 periods. In addition, from 2010 onwards it has been possible to produce estimates for women aged 16-64. Prior to 2010, estimates for women were only available for those aged 16-59.

The discontinuity in 2010 resulted from some differences in the reporting behaviour of respondents as a result of a change in the wording of the questionnaire. It resulted in higher estimates of the number of people either with a disability or long-term health problem. The most prominent effect was an increase, or step change, in the number of economically active people with a disability between Q4 2009 and Q1 2010 of around 300,000, or 8 per cent. At the same time there was a commensurate decrease in the number of people who were not long-term disabled.   The discontinuity in April 2013 resulted from a further change in the reporting behaviour of survey respondents following changes to the wording of the questionnaire. These changes brought the LFS into line with the Government Statistical Service (GSS) Harmonised Standards for questions on disability and also enabled the LFS estimates to be consistent with the definitions used in 2010 Equality Act. The 2010 Equality Act superseded the Disability Discrimination Act (DDA) 1995 which was the basis of the previously published LFS estimates.

The GSS Harmonised Standards focus on a 'core' definition of people whose condition currently limits their activity. In summary the core definition covers people who report:

- (current) physical or mental health condition(s) or illnesses lasting or expected to last 12 months or more; and
- the condition(s) or illness(es) reduce their ability to carry out day-to-day activities.

This differs from the DDA-based definition of disability previously used in the LFS in that it excludes the following groups which are "non-core" under the new Act:

- people with a progressive condition (specified in the Equality Act as HIV/AIDS, cancer or multiple sclerosis) that does not currently reduce their ability to carry out day-to-day activities.
- people whose activities would be restricted only without medication or treatment.

As with all new questions, they are subject to ONS monitoring of responses for several quarters, and should therefore be interpreted with caution, especially when comparing with estimates for previous periods.

5. Art and cultural activities include: heritage, museums, galleries, libraries and arts (includes attending eg theatre, and participating, eg painting).

6. Throughout the bulletin, only statistically significant findings are commented on.

7. Details of the policy governing the release of new data are available by visiting www.statisticsauthority.gov.uk/assessment/code-of-practice/index.html or from the Media Relations Office email: media.relations@ons.gsi.gov.uk

Copyright

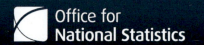

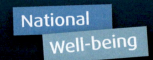

September 2014 release

Measuring what matters:
Understanding the nation's well-being

More data and interactive version
available at: **www.ons.gov.uk/well-being**

Data are the latest available
at August 2014